World of Our Making

World of our Making is a major contribution to contemporary social science. Now reissued in this volume, Onuf's seminal text is key reading for anyone who wishes to study modern international relations.

Onuf understands all of international relations to be a matter of rules and rule in foreign behaviour. The author draws together the rules of international relations, explains their source, and elaborates on their implications through a vast array of interdisciplinary thinkers such as Kenneth Arrow, J.L. Austin, Max Black, Michael Foucault, Anthony Giddens, Jurgen Habermas, Lawrence Kohlberg, Harold Lasswell, Talcott Parsons, Jean Piaget, J.G.A. Pocock, John Roemer, John Scarle and Sheldon Wolin .

Nicholas Greenwood Onuf is Professor Emeritus, Department of Politics and International Relations, Florida International University, Miami, and Professor Associado, Instituto de Relações Internacionais, Pontifica Universidade Católica do Rio de Janeiro.

The New International Relations
Edited by Richard Little, *University of Bristol*, Iver B. Neumann, *Norwegian Institute of International Affairs (NUPI), Norway* and Jutta Weldes, *University of Bristol*.

The field of international relations has changed dramatically in recent years. This new series will cover the major issues that have emerged and reflect the latest academic thinking in this particular dynamic area.

International Law, Rights and Politics
Developments in Eastern Europe and the CIS
Rein Mullerson

The Logic of Internationalism
Coercion and accommodation
Kjell Goldmann

Russia and the Idea of Europe
A study in identity and international relations
Iver B. Neumann

The Future of International Relations
Masters in the making?
Edited by Iver B. Neumann and Ole Wæver

Constructing the World Polity
Essays on international institutionalization
John Gerard Ruggie

Realism in International Relations and International Political Economy
The continuing story of a death foretold
Stefano Guzzini

International Relations, Political Theory and the Problem of Order
Beyond international relations theory?
N.J. Rengger

War, Peace and World Orders in European History
Edited by Anja V. Hartmann and Beatrice Heuser

European Integration and National Identity
The challenge of the Nordic states
Edited by Lene Hansen and Ole Wæver

Shadow Globalization, Ethnic Conflicts and New Wars
A political economy of intra-state war
Dietrich Jung

Contemporary Security Analysis and Copenhagen Peace Research
Edited by Stefano Guzzini and Dietrich Jung

Observing International Relations
Niklas Luhmann and world politics
Edited by Mathias Albert and Lena Hilkermeier

Does China Matter?
A Reassessment
Essays in memory of Gerald Segal
Edited by Barry Buzan and Rosemary Foot

European Approaches to International Relations Theory
A house with many mansions
Jörg Friedrichs

World of Our Making

Rules and rule in social theory
and international relations

Nicholas Greenwood Onuf

LONDON AND NEW YORK

First published in 1989
by University of South Carolina Press in Columbia, South Carolina, USA.

Reissued in 2013
by Routledge
2 Park Square, Milton Park, Abingdon, Oxon, OX14 4RN

Simultaneously reissued in the USA and Canada
by Routledge
711 Third Avenue, New York, NY 10017

Routledge is an imprint of the Taylor & Francis Group, an informa business

© 2013 Nicholas Greenwood Onuf

British Library Cataloguing in Publication Data
A catalogue record for this book is available from the British Library

Library of Congress Cataloging-in-Publication Data
A catalog record has been requested for this book

ISBN: 978-0-415-63039-9 (pbk)

Typeset in Times New Roman
by RefineCatch Limited, Bungay, Suffolk

CONTENTS

Contents

PREFACE

In this world of our making, scholarship is social construction, and any piece of scholarship has many authors. Most of the authors of this book I cannot name because I do not remember who they are and how they helped. The influence of others I acknowledge by reference to their written work as the book proceeds. A few people have made contributions I cannot forget and deeply appreciate.

Among them were my teachers. As I worked on this book, I repeatedly encountered the names of Frederic Lane, Maurice Mandelbaum, and Hillis Miller. These scholars were teachers of mine respectively in History, Philosophy and Literature during my first year at Johns Hopkins University. They and their like provided me with a matchless introduction to the world of scholarship. Later, other teachers made more specific contributions to this work. Robert Tucker introduced me to International Relations as a field of study and then taught me how to read closely. George Liska imparted both a love of theory and a view of international relations that finds it clearest expression in the last pages of chapter 6. Harold Lasswell's and Myres McDougal's shared concern for categories and classificatory schemes pervades this book. Karl Deutsch's advice to distinguish between constitution and regulation for the purposes of a paper I was writing for him proved to be a bomb with a very long fuse. It goes off in chapter 1. A paper I wrote for Robert Osgood saw the first, tentative articulation of one of chapter 8's major themes.

Louis Henkin's invitation to address a seminar at Columbia Uni-

versity early in 1982 prompted my first sketch of what was to become the book's conceptual structure. Work subsequently undertaken
with Spike Peterson decisively advanced this structure, with chapter
4 one consequence. At her urging, I also engaged postpositivist social
theory seriously and found myself rethinking most of my scholarly
convictions. Chapter 1 is only the most tangible result. Friedrich
Kratochwil and I discussed issues raised in chapter 2 on many occasions, always to my benefit. His support and critical assistance
also made a mark on chapters 5 and 6. Theodore Couloumbis played
a similar role in the development of chapter 7, as did Frank Klink
in the instance of chapter 8. Robert Keohane's careful reading of
what was to become chapter 5 significantly affected the final version. A remark of his about the project overall, and a similar remark
of Peter Cowhey's, both made at a critical juncture, clarified for me
choices I had yet to make about the book's form and thrust. Neither
of them will find me having chosen as they recommended.

I am grateful to Fouad Ajami and my brother Peter Onuf for their
encouragement over the course of my labors. Both read the full text,
and Peter most of its pieces before their assembly. My wife Sandra
Keowen and Jason Wittenberg also read the full text, and in so doing
provided me with indispensable editorial assistance. Timothy Buch,
Kurt Burch, William Olson and, as readers for the University of
South Carolina Press, Fritz Kratochwil (again), Donald Puchala,
and R. B. J. Walker all made useful suggestions for the final revision.
I must also acknowledge the innumerable ways in which my gradu-
ate students at American University shaped my thoughts on so many
of this book's concerns.

Much of the material in these pages first took an independent
form. At Raymond Duvall's invitation, I presented a version of the
introduction at the American Political Science Association's 1987
Convention under the title, "After International Relations: The Constitution of Disciplines and Their Worlds." Substantial parts of chapter 2 first appeared in 1985 under the title, "Do Rules Say What They
Do? From Ordinary Language to International Law," *Harvard International Law Journal* 26: 385–410. They are copied with permission.
Copyright © 1988 by the President and Fellows of Harvard College.
Chapter 3 incorporates material first appearing in 1987 in *Human
Development* 30: 257–267, under the title, "Rules in Moral Development." Reprinting is with the permission of S. Karger A. G., Basel.

A small grant from the College of Public and International Affairs, American University, expedited the development of chapter 3.

Chapter 5 grew out of my comments on papers presented by Hayward Alker and Richard Ashley at the Griffith Lecture Series, School of International Service, American University in 1986. Another version will appear in a volume entitled *After Anarchy,* with Alker and Ashley its editors. Chapter 6 first took the form of a paper Frank Klink and I presented to the International Studies Association's 1986 Convention. Much of it is appearing this year in the *International Studies Quarterly* under the title "Anarchy, Authority, Rule." Anonymous reviewers and Rick Ashley, as one of the journal's editors, deserve credit for many improvements in the published versions of this material. Chapter 7 began as a presentation before a postgraduate seminar in the Law School of the Aristotelian University of Thessaloniki, Greece. Another version was to have appeared in the *Hellenic Review of International Relations,* which has regrettably ceased publication. Excerpts from *Goethe's Faust, Part 1,* translated by Randall Jarrell, are reprinted by permission of Farrar, Straus and Giroux, Inc. Copyright 1959, 1961, 1965, 1973 by Mary von Schrader Jarrell.

I thank Charles Kegley and Don Puchala for their invitation early in 1984 to undertake a book for the Series in International Relations which they edit for the University of South Carolina Press. Ted Couloumbis and Dimitri Constantopoulos provided me with superb working circumstances in Thessaloniki in the fall of 1984, and Amal Jayawardane and Stanley Wijesundera did the same in Colombo, Sri Lanka, during the first six months of 1987. Wherever I have worked on this book, my wife Sandi made the circumstances ideal.

INTRODUCTION

The point of this book is to reconstruct a self-consciously organized field of study, or discipline, called International Relations. To do so necessarily involves reconsideration of international relations as something to study.[1] I use the term "reconstruct" deliberately, both because my goal is ambitious and because I am committed to a philosophical position, detailed in chapter 1, which I call "constructivism." In my view, people always construct, or constitute, social reality, even as their being, which can only be social, is constructed for them.[2]

In order to show how, why, and in what degree I part company with other scholars, I begin this introduction with a brief construction of their endeavors. This I do first by defining the terms "politics" and "international relations" and then by showing that their routine sense constitutes Political Science and International Relations as disciplines. By presenting an informal history of International Relations and then, more abstractly, the properties of disciplines, I situate myself in respect to my own discipline and its constitutive premises.

---

1. For convenience, disciplines and fields of study will always be designated in the Upper Case, their subjects of concern in the lower case.
2. Hereafter I will use the terms "construct" and "constitute" interchangeably. This is the usual practice of scholars taking a position like mine.

Finally I state my difficulties with the discipline as constituted and announce an alternative. The rest of the book is given over to this alternative.

THE QUEST

The term "international relations" is generally understood to be lacking in precise definition. Nevertheless, it would seem to have a core meaning both in ordinary language and current scholarship. "International relations" refers to an ensemble of activities that is recognizably political despite its sweep and diffuseness. Activities are political when members of a social unit construe those activities to be the most important ones engaging their attention. When those activities extend beyond the immediate, established locale within which members of a social unit ordinarily act on their urgent concerns, international relations result.

I am not aware that any one scholar has proposed just this definition of politics. On the contrary, I find myself chastized for its vagueness and context dependence; it cannot be made operational (compare Connolly 1974: 15–17). The same can be said of many other definitions of the term. Take Vernon Van Dyke's:

> Activity is political when it relates to a public issue, and it relates to a public issue when two conditions are met. In the first place, it must relate to the decision making of a group, i.e., it must concern group policy, group organization, or group leadership, or it must concern the regulation of intergroup relations. In the second place, it must come within the realm of the controversial (1960: 133).

Surely everyone agrees that politics are a social activity. Thus for Van Dyke, politics "must relate to the decision making of a group. . . ." He went on to say that politics reside in "the realm of the controversial." Not all controversies yield to decision. To say, as is often said, that not deciding is indeed a way of deciding is to rob the term "decision" of any content. Rather, we quite often speak as if failure to decide identifies what is controversial for any group. Further-

more, politics may well concern "the regulation of intergroup relationships," but, in Van Dyke's terms, decision is a group, and not
an intergroup, activity.

Problems raised by Van Dyke's attempt to specify conditions necessary for politics disappear if one resorts instead to importance as
a criterion of political activity. We know that any given group takes
matters to be important when controversy attends them. We know
that matters are important when groups establish sites and methods
for deciding them. While controversy and established venues for decision are undoubtedly the two most reliable clues that politics are
present in people's affairs, we can hardly suppose that they exhaust
the possible manifestations of politics. Notice also that words and
phrases like "controversy" and "established venues for decision"
foster the illusion of concreteness without being any less vague or
context dependent than the term "importance" (compare Van Dyke
1970: 135 on the term "institution").

Does Van Dyke's more general definition of politics as activity
relating to public issues do better? The term "issue" would seem to
substitute for "controversy" as well as for matters available for group
decision without any great change in specificity. The term "public"
adds nothing if it does no more than describe a group. I suspect that
Van Dyke had something more in mind. Nevertheless, what one can
mean by "public"—beyond that connoted by reference to matters
subject to decision, controversy, that which is at issue or matters of
importance to members of a social unit—I cannot begin to say.

I know of two alternative definitions of "politics" that avoid the
problem of vagueness. One finds any social unit's politics confined
to formally and specifically designated sites and methods for deciding important matters—government and law in the usual sense. The
other finds politics in everything social. In the first instance, precision is achieved by excluding activities as sweeping and diffuse as
those covered by the term "international relations." In the second,
precision is offset by the mass and diversity of those activities that
are included. Locating politics between these poles is both necessary
and contentious.

Disagreement over the term "politics" suggests the relativity of its
subject. My recourse to the criterion of importance suggests the
same. Yet acknowledgment that politics are relative need not be
taken as capitulation to the position that everything social is politi-

cal. On this I concur with William E. Connolly (1974: 13–15) and Fred M. Frohock (1979: 860–862). Politics is a "cluster concept."[3] As such it has a limited number of "structural features" identified by "core terms" (Frohock 1979: 865). Frohock found two such terms, "directiveness" and "aggregation" (pp. 865–867).

Obviously my definition includes the second of these terms. Only in aggregates can people practice politics. I am also persuaded by the first term, "directiveness," which for Frohock "denotes agents acting on one another, 'directing' one another's behavior" (1979: 865), but not by his explication of it.[4] Frohock held that directiveness

> is suggested by traditional concerns for power, authority, in the history of political thought, but also describes more modern transactions like bargaining, gaming (action in conditions of no-authority), providing rational incentives . . . , control of agendas and general social conditions. 'Directiveness' also concerns human behavior originating in both *decisions* and *non-decisions,* where the latter can accommodate tradition, habit, unconscious behavior in general (maps can give 'directions,' for example), as well as that species of politics emphasized of late . . . where people act upon one another by *not* making decisions which could transform some state of affairs (p. 865, two citations deleted, his emphases).

The difficulty with Frohock's attempt at specificity is inclusiveness. Everything is thrown in, from *"general* social conditions" to "un-

---

3. Both Connolly and Frohock discussed the concept of "cluster concept" in the context of W. B. Gallie's influential idea that some concepts, including many that are political (his examples are democracy and justice), are "essentially contested" (1962). Gallie argued that one of the conditions defining such concepts is that they derive "from an original exemplar whose authority is acknowledged by all the contestant users of the concept" (p. 131). While this condition effectively delimits contested concepts, it does so too narrowly. The clustering of invocations and applications to which a given concept may be subjected can have other bases.
4. Although I am persuaded by Frohock's criterion of directiveness, I will abstain after the discussion at hand from using the word "directive" or any of its cognates as he did. This is to avoid confusion with the terms "directive speech act" and "directive-rule," which I introduce in chapter 2 and use extensively thereafter.

conscious behavior in *general*" (my emphases). Lost is any conceivable gain from the kind of terms that Van Dyke and I have used.

The term "directiveness" can help, however, if it is taken to exclude much of what Frohock included. Members of an aggregation tell, or somehow make it known, what others in that aggregation should do. They can do the telling directly, as the authority of "the history of political thought" directs us to believe, or indirectly, through controlling agendas, deciding what maps should say, and so on. If directing is at the core of politics, it is because some or all members of a social unit treat some matter as important enough to expend resources to affect the disposition of that matter. Direction results when some member or members prevail. What they say serves as a direction to others, with consequences that we think of as mapping the direction in which a matter goes.

The nexus of directing and direction, giving and taking, suggests that politics has to do with contests of wills or, as Van Dyke emphasized, struggle — "struggle among actors pursuing conflicting desires on public issues" (1960: 131; see also p. 134). It suggests that contestants use resources to prevail. In popular understanding and most treatments of international relations, power and struggle are inextricable elements of politics. (Consider the title of Hans J. Morgenthau's legendary textbook: *Politics among Nations, The Struggle for Power and Peace,* 1948.) Finally, the directiveness of politics suggests that contests and consequences are asymmetrical. Some members of a social unit prevail more often than others do, and they benefit more from having done so.

This last conclusion is difficult to resist insofar as politics is understood mainly by reference to specific institutions like the state. It is resisted when such institutions are not in evidence, international relations being a case in point. Since these activities escape the confinement of established venues, collisions of wills and endless contests make for uncertainty among the diverse people affected by them and foster an unwillingness by at least some of those affected to accept the consequences. As most people see it, the result is plenty of struggle but little of the stable asymmetry implied by politics' directiveness. Depending on one's perspective, international relations are politics at the limit, perhaps the limiting case of politics, perhaps beyond.

The ambiguous way in which politics and international relations

come together is not just a matter of sloppy usage or popular mis-
understanding. Scholars reproduce this ambiguity when they refer
to international relations in terms of decentralization, self-help, and
especially of late, anarchy.[5] These terms are nearly synonymous, conveying as they do the same two notions. First, international relations
form a bounded and distinctive social reality. Second, what makes
this particular set of social relations distinctive is that they are manifestly political even though directiveness in its fullest sense is not to
be found. As Political Scientists are wont to say, the element of
authority is lacking.

Political Science is a discipline marked by its preoccupation with
relations of authority—stable and accepted asymmetries in capacities and outcomes. One need only recall David Easton's extraordi-
narily influential decree that "political science be described as the
study of the authoritative allocation of values for a society" (1953:
129; see also later in this chapter). Most scholars who devote their
attention to international relations are trained in Political Science.
Yet they profess to work in a discipline of their own, one which is
only a few decades old. The insecurities of youth are compounded
by ambiguous relations with neighboring disciplines. Stanley Hoffmann has suggested that the need to be free from History and Law
while maintaining proprietary interests in diplomatic history and international law inspired early disciplinary claims (1977: 44). I would
add to this the need to be free of Political Science while professing
that international relations, as a bounded and distinctive social reality, is nevertheless manifestly political.

At least in the United States, most scholars identifying themselves
with International Relations hold appointments in departments of
Political Science. Many more of these scholars are active members
of the American Political Science Association than of the American
Historical Association or the American Society of International Law.
They are more frequently members of editorial boards of scholarly
journals in Political Science than in History or Law. In these circumstances, we could reasonably expect that in recent decades scholars

---

5. Illustratively: "International systems are decentralized and anarchic" (Waltz 1979:
88). "Self-help is necessarily the principle of action in an anarchic order" (p. 111).

of international relations have been more mindful of their uncomfortably initimate relation to Political Science than of their distant, occasional, even opportunistic association with other disciplines, including Anthropology, Psychology, and Sociology.

The situation is less clear outside the United States. In Britain, for example, History and Law have always appealed to scholars with interests in international relations. Nevertheless, as Hoffmann (1977) so forcefully demonstrated, International Relations is substantially an American discipline. As such, its initiatives and achievements, detours and disappointments are the work of a small band of scholars. They share many assumptions, not least about politics and Political Science. They find in each other support and solace, and they follow each other like zigzagging shoals of minnows.

To a degree unmatched in the proliferation of disciplines in the modern university, International Relations was shaped from the beginning by the exhortations and example of one scholar—the same Hans Morgenthau whose textbook I remarked on a page or two back. Morgenthau's lasting gifts to the discipline were two. One was his preoccupation with clashes of power and interest (see further in chapters 7 and 8), which wrested a piece of politics for the new discipline. The second was his commitment to "scientific inquiry . . ." (1948: 4; see also Hoffmann 1977: 44).

The first edition of *Politics among Nations* fails to mention theory specifically. Morgenthau nevertheless saw theory as the centerpiece of scientific inquiry. "Science is theoretical, or it is nothing" (1959): 16). Thus the opening words of a later edition of *Politics among Nations:* "This book purports to present a theory of international politics" (1967: 3).

Morgenthau held that "a scientific theory is a system of empirically verifiable, general truths, sought for their own sake" (1959: 16). He believed in objective "laws of politics" and "in the possibility of developing a rational theory that reflects, however imperfectly and onesidedly, these objective laws" (p. 4). This is, as Hoffmann observed in 1960, "theory as a set of answers" (p. 30). Morgenthau presented no such theory. Instead his "peremptory pronouncements . . . incited readers to react and by reacting, criticizing, correcting, refuting, to hold onto other designs. He was both a goad and a foil" (Hoffmann 1977: 45). Theory as a set of questions invited alternative assumptions, more rigorous formulations, the kind of science that Morgenthau did not himself pursue. Only then could a better, clearer set of answers eventuate and the promise of a discipline be fulfilled (Hoffmann 1960: 40).

Hoffmann later called this complex response to Morgenthau "the quest for certainty" (1977: 57). For Hoffmann, this quest is specifically an American concern. Peoples with longer histories and a less self-conscious will to change the world are less likely to take up the quest. For James N. Rosenau, "the restless quest" (although, properly speaking, scholars are restless, not the quest) is shared by all those who engage in science, whatever their specific disciplinary concerns (1976: 1). Restlessness defines the enterprise. For Yale H. Ferguson and Richard W. Mansbach, the vicissitudes of international relations are responsible for "the elusive quest," as their book is entitled (1988). Although it is the goal of theory, not the "quest for theory" (p. 3), that eludes us, their point is clear: The comforts of theory as a set of answers, and with it a tidy discipline, seem farther away now, forty years later, than they ever did (see, for example, pp. 23–24).

Not every scholar holding forth on the subject speaks of quest. To me the metaphor hints that theory is a holy grail. Once found, it will give us some kind of transcendental knowledge that I for one do not believe is possible (see chapter 1). Yet I share with almost everyone committed to the discipline a sense of disarray and loss of well being, to paraphrase K. J. Holsti (1985: 1–2). How have we gotten here?

Even to ask this question is to invite the charge of historicism, the presumption that history is going somewhere in particular (Mandelbaum 1971: 41–138). I risk this charge to follow the convenient historicist practice of breaking up history into epochs. For this purpose, I start, as Hoffmann has (1977: 43–47), with the Second World War and the response in the United States to its end. The discipline's formative period, dominated by the redoubtable figure of Morgenthau, continued for about a decade. (See also Liska 1966: 5; Olson 1971 used a different periodization, retained by Olson and Onuf 1986, noting two prior phases in "an emerging discipline," p. 6) The next period, 1955–1965, George Liska aptly called "the heroic decade" (1966). If the "first decade was one of discovery," then the second "was one of heroic effort at conquest . . ." (p. 5). The conquerors were few in number and mostly younger scholars. Each proposed a highly generalized account of the way that international relations work. Each account was unrelated to the others. Yet each was held to get at the core of international relations.

This was a time of high hopes. Liska, himself one of the decade's heroes and writing at its end, eloquently captured both the hopes and soon to be realized fears of the time.

> Here was an effort to break through to a really new mode, level, and scope of theoretical investigation which would make conventional styles of analysis and generalization obsolete and would lift international relations to the self-same exact and social sciences by which new approaches were largely inspired. The problem from the outset was how to connect refined and rigorous abstract formulations with the crude and contingent data of international relations, to produce new insights and explanations rather than elaborately overlaid restatements and tautologies, and to do so with reference to questions and data which were at once amenable to the new techniques of inquiry and intrinsically significant (p. 6).

The decade from 1965 to 1975 saw proliferating efforts to cope with the problem Liska foresaw. Inevitably attention turned from theory to methods. Coincidentally substantial funding and powerful computing machinery became available in the United States to support empirically directed research into international relations. Such theory as we find is carefully bounded. For example, Dina Zinnes (1976) elaborated formal models of arms races. Robert Jervis (1976) ransacked social psychology for hypotheses on misperception. In each instance, formal rigor or empirical credibility was achieved by locating theory at the edge of what Morgenthau had held to be the discipline's core concerns. Under the influence of Thomas S. Kuhn's depiction of "normal science" (1970a), many scholars saw themselves engaged in "puzzle solving" and identified "the cumulation of knowledge" as their primary concern (Rosenau 1976a: 145–215).

The next decade, 1975–1985, is one in which funding for large research projects evaporated and interest in problems of method diminished. There was also a modest revival of theory. The intrusion of doubt in the United States about Morgenthau's view of the world, long ensconced in public policy, played a part in this change (Ferguson and Mansbach 1987: 104–106). The American discipline of International Relations opened up to a larger, previously uncongenial world of ideas on how international relations take place and what activities they properly encompass. Terms like "dependency," "world-system," "interdependence," and "transnational relations" were much discussed.

The late 1970s amplified the incoherence of competing theoretical orientations left over from the heroic decade. Perhaps in response to this incoherence, and certainly in response to widely held anxieties about the changing position of the United States in the world (Ferguson and Mansbach 1988: 106–107), many scholars returned to Morgenthau's vision of politics not beholden to authority as the core of international relations. That core was enlarged by recognition that matters of economy are indubitably political and stiffened by a renewed commitment to rigor. This new-old theoretical orientation secured important, though hardly similar, expositions from Kenneth Waltz and Robert Gilpin (1979 and 1981 respectively). By the end of this period, we find a younger scholar (Snidal 1985a) making claims on behalf of theory worthy of the young heroes of an earlier time (for example, Kaplan 1961).

While International Relations experienced a revival of theory between 1975 and 1985, many other branches of intellectual and scholarly life experienced their own, more spectacular, changes. The common point of departure was a repudiation of the positivist model of science as a canonical characterization of theory and its relation to methods of inquiry. This model had, of course, dominated all the social sciences from the time of their emergence as disciplines, or soon thereafter, until the mid-1970s. To read outside of International Relations in recent years is to drink from the swirling waters of postpositivism. This is a heady experience, disorienting in its critical assaults against established ways of systematic thinking and refreshing in its challenge to think differently.

Since 1985, most scholars in International Relations seem to have been intent on consolidating the gains of the preceding decade. This entails substantiating available theoretical propositions. The problem is to do so without the cost and distraction of returning to the methodological concerns of an earlier time. For many of these scholars, the solution is to undertake case studies and submit them to informal comparison. They guide their students into doing the same. While there is an attractive modesty to this kind of activity, its effect is to deny the discipline any direction at all. Sensing stasis, a few scholars have begun to test the critical currents washing through the rest of the social sciences.

Conspicuous among them is Richard K. Ashley, who has emerged as champion of a "critical social theory of international politics" that is poststructuralist in inspiration (1987, 1988). Poststructuralism centers on the deliberately provocative work of two French writers, Michel Foucault and Jacques Derrida, and has become especially prominent in literary criticism in the United States. Poststructuralist critics use "language against itself," a practice Derrida called "deconstruction" (see Norris 1982 for a useful introduction, quoting here from a chapter title, p. 18). As will become clearer in the next chapter, poststructuralism repudiates the deepest assumptions of Western rationalism and all that is built upon them. Given that all is built on words and with words, deconstruction is the method of choice in pursuing this extraordinary reversal.

One of the crowning achievements of the West over the past several centuries is the edifice of theory: theory as an idea and objective, theory as an enterprise, theory as an economic statement of what we think we know about the world and ourselves, theory as the grounds for judgment. Much, most of what poststructuralists and indeed most postpositivists have to say against this edifice is well taken. I subscribe to it without drawing the conclusion that the quest for some kind of theory must be abandoned. Thus I take to heart Foucault's injunction to "dispense with 'things'" (see the quotation introducing part I), not just as a critical strategy, but as a guideline for constituting a social theory of international politics.

This is where Ashley and I differ. For all his talk of theory, Ashley cannot do theory without doing what is incorrigibly implicated in the Western project he would cast off. The best he can achieve is "a view from afar, from up high" (1987: 408). I think it would help to quote at length the passage in which these words appear.

> Eschewing any claim to secure grounds, the appropriate pos-
> ture would aspire to an overview of international history in the
> making, a view from afar, a view up high. The appropriate
> posture is disposed to a view very much like that of Michel
> Foucault's *genealogical* attitude: "a form of history which ac-
> counts for the constitution of knowledge, discourses, domains

of knowledge, etc. without having to refer to a subject, whether it be transcendental in relation to the field of events or whether it chases its empty identity throughout history."

From a distant genealogical standpoint, what catches the eye is motion, discontinuities, clashes, and the ceaseless play of plural forces and plural interpretations on the surface of human experience. Nothing is finally stable. There are no constants, no fixed meanings, no secure grounds, no profound secrets, no final structures or limits of history. Seen from afar, there is only interpretation, and interpretation itself is comprehended as a practice of domination occurring on the surface of history. History itself is grasped as a series of interpretations imposed on interpretations — none primary, all arbitrary (pp. 408–409, Ashley's emphasis, two parenthetical references to Foucault deleted).

Evidently method, including interpretation as the only method admissible to most postpositivists, must be discarded along with theory in favor of the view from afar. What does this leave for dealing with the close at hand? Poststructuralists variously suggest politics as rhetorical subversion and play as rhetorical exercise. Lacking any direction, denying theory, parodying method (Megill 1985: 227–231, 284), these activities will not satisfy everyone. Nor will they turn around a discipline like International Relations, which is predicated on premises quite different from Literature. For the latter, criticism and not politics is its primary vocation, and the notion that one reads for pleasure its deepest claim.

PARADIGMS

Claims that international relations are matters of politics falling outside the purview of Political Science constitute that set of relations as a bounded and distinctive social reality. At the same time, they constitute International Relations as a discipline. There is nothing unusual about this. That all disciplines are constituted by claims of distinctiveness makes them conspicuous examples of the general, and more generally diffused, phenomenon of social constitution.

Claims constituting a discipline do more than this, however. They serve a paradigmatic function. The term "paradigm," now so widely if carelessly appropriated from Kuhn (1970a), suggests a "construction project." In Kuhn's famous account of natural science paradigms, such a project offers an exclusive community of scholars a "paradigm theory" (pp. 26, 27) demarcating the limits of their interests and a series of puzzles—empirical questions unanswered by the theory as initially proposed—waiting to be solved.[6] Most solutions that come along clarify and strengthen the theory orienting this kind of activity. This is normal science. Those not doing so cumulatively threaten the theory's integrity, and conditions are met for the consolidation of dissonant puzzle solutions under the terms of a new, more powerful paradigm theory. The process then repeats itself.

In the natural sciences, theories that plausibly represent reality and allow for puzzle-solving orient science; in the social sciences, claims about reality—constitutive claims, as argued above—orient puzzle-solving as science duly leading to theory.[7] At best the social sciences possess proto-theories, which assemble constitutive claims

---

6. Gary Gutting (1980: 2, 12–13) has called the contents of a Kuhnian paradigm a "super-theory" inasmuch as "a diverse assemblage of law, method and metaphysics" is included (p. 2). While I think Gutting has aptly characterized the contents of a paradigm, Kuhn meant to separate out laws and their explanation when he referred to theory.

7. Richard Bernstein (1978: 243–246) has contended that Kuhn never wanted theories to be central to his scheme. When pressed to clarify what he had meant by the term "paradigm," Kuhn identified just two mutually reinforcing elements: "community structure" as shared commitments and "exemplars" or shared examples of problem solving. He was careful to say that exemplars are not theories or theory statements (laws and rules), but rather "physical situations" to which theories relate in an especially revealing way (1970a: 191). Unhappily this attempt at precision weakens Kuhn's model of the growth of science, because growth comes not from challenges to exemplars, but from exemplars that challenge theory and thereby bring on a revolution, necessarily in theory. In keeping with this model, Kuhn elsewhere remarked that "the proto-sciences, like the arts and philosophy, lack some element which, in the mature sciences, permit some of the more obvious forms of progress. . . . These conditions are, of course, tantamount to the description of a good scientific theory" (1970b: 244–246). For a position similar to the one taken here, see Pocock (1971: 13–14).

in a reasonably coherent doctrine. Yet social science proto-theories look enough like the theories of natural scientists to persuade people that the communities of scholars espousing them are warranted in their disciplinary claims and projects. They also provide scholars with a stock of puzzles.

These same scholars are keenly aware that their proto-theories fail to provide much help in recognizing either puzzle solutions as such or their role in supporting or challenging those proto-theories. The response to these limitations is a quest, the same quest animating scholarship in International Relations. Each discipline's scholarly community seeks a proper paradigm theory. Those theories that are proposed are either too narrow or too vague to satisfy. Thereupon follow ceaseless self-criticism and finally dejection.

In the instance of International Relations, the puzzles in question are the presence of or need for order, equilibrium, or cooperation in the face of unconfined political activities. Why does not anarchy always give way to chaos? In short, constitutive claims about international relations supply puzzles. A prospective paradigm theory must generalize puzzle solutions to explain what is only now stipulated for constitutive purposes—explain, that is, how the social reality of international relations works as a decentralized order, self-help system, or anarchy.

I do not believe a paradigm theory for International Relations is forthcoming. I do not believe it is even possible. This is because I have grave doubts about the claim that anarchy is the central and defining feature of international relations. I would not deny the incidence of anarchical events, but these events always take place under conditions that must be characterized otherwise.

Later I propose and defend a different set of claims responsive to those conditions. In so doing, I question whether, or to what extent, international relations constitute a "paradigm of an operative kind," to borrow Sheldon Wolin's provocative extension of the Kuhnian idea of paradigm (1980). Operative paradigms are those ensembles of human practices seen by those engaging in or observing them to have a coherence setting them apart from other practices. Those that are seen as coherent in furthest degree are taken as having a natural objective reality.

Kuhn's model presupposes that while natural science disciplines constitute themselves, they do not constitute what I have here called the operative paradigms to which they respond. Physicists believe that physics is a discernibly independent part of "nature," the coherence of which stems from features exclusive to it; so does almost everyone else. That this is how people treat the matter makes it true for operative purposes. Even when Physics as a discipline undergoes paradigmatic changes, it is seen as having a continuous identity corresponding to the operative paradigm of physics, itself subject to incremental redefinition in the face of disciplinary changes.

For Kuhn's purposes, it does not matter whether operative paradigms are naturally real or socially constructed.[8] Either way, claims constituting natural science disciplines only marginally affect their operative paradigms. Those claims do not generate paradigmatic activity. Theories do that. The latter's generative power, at least in Kuhn's model, stems from the fact that they are never entirely adequate representations of what is taken to be a substantially independent reality. Fully the opposite situation holds for a discipline like Literature. If natural reality in the form of operative paradigms is safely construed as separate from corresponding disciplinary paradigms, literature is indistinguishable from paradigmatic assertions that particular texts are, or are not, Literature. In other words, literature is not an operative paradigm; no set of human practices can be identified as such in the absence of disciplinary cues.

The social sciences fall somewhere in the middle of this continuum. Far more evidently than with the operative paradigms attributed to nature, social reality, and thus its operative paradigms, can only be constituted by human practices. Constitutive claims on behalf of social science disciplines, and the projects they engender, are among these practices. Clearly they affect the ensemble. So do an indeterminately large number of other practices, not to mention material conditions. In degree an economy is what Economists instruct us to think it is; in degree it operates as an economy whatever Economists

---

8. There is currently a furious debate among philosophers of science, prompted in part by Kuhn's work, over whether science discloses a reality independent of human construction. I touch on it in chapter 1.

say about it. Nevertheless, because Economics was constituted long ago, any operative paradigm inspiring its development has itself been transformed by the discipline created in its name.

The situation is somewhat different for international relations. The discipline of International Relations constituted itself on the belief that it corresponds to an operative paradigm. This is exactly the meaning of claims that international relations make up a bounded and distinctive social reality. Such claims have some plausibility, if they are taken to refer to the ensemble of activities engaged in by a bounded and slowly changing set of entities conveniently denominated by the term "states." Historical concreteness, as conveyed by the term "Western state system," reinforces the propensity to see international relations in operative terms. Indeed, these claims are persuasive to a great number of people who have no stake in constituting a discipline on them. Were International Relations not to exist, international relations would still be seen rather much as they are now—and always have been.

All this said, I must reassert my doubt that international relations constitute an operative paradigm in nearly the degree presupposed by the constitution of International Relations as a discipline. As much is revealed by the ambiguity in International Relations' constitutive claims and early development. While it was claimed that anarchy is the distinctive condition to which the discipline responds, it is by no means clear that the Western state system is the only concrete instance of international relations available for study. Yet from the 1950s on, this is the overwhelming if largely unarticulated judgment of scholars in the discipline (for details see Onuf 1982a). Nor, as intimated above, do I find the Western state system to be a particularly good example of an operative anarchy, even if the incidence of important but uncoordinated activities is high and, on occasion, the conditions of anarchy achieved. (Chapter 5 treats this matter more systematically.) What's worse, recent scholarship has stridently insisted that international relations are overwhelmingly anarchical in character, with the result that those within the discipline are dissuaded from an examination of the operative paradigm as it is— heterogeneous, amorphous, elusive.

The way to proceed should now be clear. It is to look for a substantial ensemble of practices, the coherence of which is not reflected in, much less produced by, the constitutive claims of established social science disciplines. In other words, we must stop thinking that each disciplinary paradigm corresponds to its own distinctive operative paradigm. If viewed skeptically, claims constituting these disciplines, especially claims made by more than one of them, can lead us to operative paradigms cutting across the current map of social science disciplines. Three such paradigms are discernible.

Surprisingly the first possibility is suggested by what may be taken as the strongest, most plausible disciplinary paradigm in the social sciences. Microeconomics, as the central part of liberal Economics, is covered by a theory of high formal specificity and enormous explanatory power—properties achieved by postulating that autonomous individuals act rationally, that is, use whatever means at their disposal to maximize benefits to themselves. (On rationality so conceived, see further chapter 8). To keep matters simple, microeconomic theory confines this postulate to a particular slice of social reality known conventionally as the market.

A market is any large set of exchanges (paired choices) among autonomous entities, in which exchanges are expedited through a medium of exchange, allowing a rate of exchange, or price, to be calculated, but which are otherwise uncoordinated. By specifying its range of application, microeconomic theory constitutes Microeconomics as a distinctive disciplinary endeavor. That market exchanges are not coordinated, on the presumption that no single one of them is important enough to warrant intervention, demarcates the discipline from its neighbors like Sociology, Anthropology, and Social Psychology, which do not preclude the presence of politics, and even more, Political Science and International Relations, in which politics in one form or another prevails.

After World War II, scholars versed in microeconomic theory sought to extend its range of application, in the first instance to cover a new slice of social reality brought into being by public welfare policies. In so doing, these scholars poached on the disciplinary domain of Political Science most successfully—they produced elegant and satisfying solutions to a number of puzzles that had either defied Political Scientists or had eluded their attention. This move beyond the market came at no cost to microeconomic theory's formal specificity and explanatory power. Indeed microeconomic theory was seen as a special, highly developed case of a more general, and rapidly developing, theory of social choice. (For an accessible introduction to social choice theory, see Bonner 1986, and, for a formal presentation, Schwartz 1986). Adherents argue that all relations of authority should be considered in its light. This of course is a claim to constitute a new, far-reaching discipline, now dubbed Political Economy, for which the theory of social choice is said to be a proper paradigm theory.[9]

Social choice theorists recognized the applicability of their theory whenever a discipline assigned paradigmatic significance to terms like "rational actor" or "interest," whether the context was marketing, voting, or fighting. The range of relevant practices stretched across several, perhaps all, of the social science disciplines. As soon as we abandon disciplinary preconceptions, we see a coherence so readily identified that it has a longstanding label: the operative paradigm to which Political Economy is a latter-day response is liberalism.[10] That Microeconomics, as the source of Political Economy's paradigm theory of social choice, is the core of Liberal Economics comes as no surprise under the circumstances. Nor does the fact that liberalism posed a series of paradoxes for Political Science that could only be solved with help from the theory of social choice. Finally there is no surprise to renewed assertions, influenced by the theory of social choice, that international relations are purely anarchic (Young 1978, Oye 1985a), for anarchy is liberalism carried to its logical ex-

---

9. Proponents of Political Economy as a new discipline have settled on this label at least in part because they claim to recover the original, wider scope of Economics when it emerged and when it was appropriately called Political Economy. Of course Marxists never accepted the subsequent division of labor between Liberal Economists and Political Scientists, with scraps going to Sociology, and held on to the term "Political Economy" for themselves. The result is considerable confusion, with two rival camps of Political Economy making incompatible constitutive claims and conducting unrelated disciplinary projects.

10. By liberalism I mean the view of human beings as individually autonomous, "related to each other as proprietors of their own capacities and of what they have acquired by their exercise" (Mcpherson 1962: 3.) This account of liberalism's premises by no means exhausts the content of liberalism as an operative paradigm. Thus the liberal presumption of equal opportunity is implicit here, as it is in the theory of social choice (Frohock 1987: 45–72). More generally, liberal concern for the condition of society as a whole yields Political Science its many puzzles and the theory of social choice its particular relevance (see further Frohock 1987).

treme: The only limits on rational conduct are those imposed by material conditions.

If international relations are purely anarchic, then Political Economy is their perfected description. If anarchy is the general condition of international relations, then Political Economists can puzzle over exceptional instances of international cooperation undertaken in response to market failures (Keohane 1982: 332–337, 1984: 80–83). If, as I have insisted, international relations are not primarily anarchic, then they stand largely outside the operative paradigm of liberalism. International Relations constituted itself on the assumption that international relations constitute a coherent operative paradigm. Behind this assumption is another one—that the practices identified with international relations come as close to unalloyed liberalism as human practices are ever likely to. Insofar as international relations resist encapsulation and incorporation in the operative paradigm of liberalism, International Relations is a liberal illusion.

Marxism offers a second operative paradigm crossing existing disciplinary lines. Relations of production parallel liberalism's relations of exchange, and they are no less abstractly conceived than is the market. After criticizing liberals for taking the operative centrality of the market for granted, Marxists situate historical manifestations of their alternative in a materially grounded, logically necessary succession of modes of production. Liberals are deeply suspicious of this feature of Marxism for a variety of reasons. They find its determinism philosophically alien, its dialectical logic unduly simplified, its formulation in the universalizing language of nineteenth-century evolutionism outmoded, and its conception of material grounding muddled.

While most of these suspicions have some merit, they do not add up to a decisive rejection of relations of production as an operative paradigm. Nor is that the intent of liberal criticism. After all, liberals acknowledge that feudalism and capitalism are significant and connected historical experiences exhibiting distinctive modes of production, just as Marxists say. Rather, liberal criticism targets the ideological and programmatic implications that Marxists draw from their construction of an undeniable operative paradigm. Many scholars today are more interested in clarifying the operative paradigm than in saving a particular construction of it for partisan reasons. The result is a burgeoning of a disciplinary paradigm long established under the name "Political Economy." As noted, there are thus two disciplines called Political Economy, one Liberal, one Marxist. On the face of it, relations of production are important to a social unit; they are political. The operative paradigm of Marxism is indisputably centered on political economy. Yet this is not so clearly the case with the Marxist disciplinary paradigm.

Karl Marx oriented his systematic work on capitalism with a theory of considerable elegance and power — the labor theory of value (see Weeks 1981 for an exposition). It is the closest thing to a paradigm theory that Marxist Political Economy has today. This theory gains its power by excluding from its terms most of the activities that members of capitalist societies take as important enough to be called political. Instead politics is confined to the direct connection between the valuation of products and the appropriation of surplus value.

The labor theory of value gives an economic account of what happens to appropriated surplus — it comes to a market — but not a political account, except in the vaguest sense — some of that surplus may be used to support relations of authority, pay for international relations and so on. Secondary, ad hoc theories abound, such as V. I. Lenin's theory of imperialism, but disciplinary coherence is lost. Evidently Marxist Political Economy, like its Liberal counterpart, is not a discipline with a paradigm theory suited to the whole of political economy. Thus the discipline cannot replace its rivals — Liberal Political Economy, Political Science, and International Relations — whatever their limitations and defects.

There is a third possibility for an operative paradigm reaching across disciplines. This one overlaps the operative paradigms of liberalism and Marxism, though its coherence depends on neither. As an operative paradigm, it is matched historically to a long tradition of political and social theory which, though relevant to Liberal and Marxist paradigms, is coterminous with neither. Wolin had it in mind when he proposed that

> we conceive of political society as itself a paradigm of an operative kind. From this viewpoint society would be envisaged as a coherent whole in the sense of its customary political practices, institutions, laws, structure of authority and citizenship, and operative beliefs being organized and interrelated. A po-

litically organized society contains definite social arrangements, certain widely shared understandings regarding the location and use of political power, certain expectations about how authority ought to treat members of society and about the claims that society can rightfully make upon its members. . . . This *ensemble* of practices and beliefs can be said to form a paradigm in the sense that society tries to carry on its political life in accordance with them (1980: 183–184).

Wolin's sense of the social reality at stake is inclusive but still bounded. His formulation is wanting to the degree that it depends on both tautology and organic imagery for bounding (political society is a paradigm insofar as it tries to carry on political life). To his credit, however, he used the term "authority" (twice) without giving it pride of place, much less claiming that relations of authority delimit the paradigm. Were Wolin to have used authority to bound the ensemble of practices constituting the operative paradigm of political society, then he could have aligned it neatly with Easton's paradigmatic claim that Political Science describes "the authoritative allocation of values for a society" (1953: 129). The next step, which Easton himself did not take, but Harry Eckstein did in refining Easton's claim, would have been to exclude international relations from the operative paradigm (Easton 1953: 138–139, Easton 1965: 387, Eckstein 1973: 1157–1158).

Wolin refused a narrow view of what politics is about, such as the term "authority" connotes when it is used by paradigm guardians like Easton and Eckstein. This left Wolin without a better idea of what the operative paradigm is than can be provided by a checklist of evidently political practices, including those associated with international relations. Wolin's checklist is even less helpful in guiding us toward a disciplinary paradigm corresponding to the operative paradigm of political society.

What is required first is an effort, however preliminary, to identify the common denominator in Wolin's or any comparable checklist. In other words, we must characterize the operative paradigm in terms sufficiently general that they fit any set of practices we would want to include in the paradigm. I believe there are two such general properties pertaining to political society in all its manifestations. One is the pervasive presence of rules which, in guiding, but not determining, human conduct, gives it social meaning. Whenever rules have the effect of distributing advantages unequally, the result is rule, which is the second general property of political society. The prevalence of rule reflects the importance that people attach to the advantages rule—through rules—helps them secure and maintain. Of course people also use resources to their advantage, but never without rules being implicated. The paradigm of political society is aptly named because it links irrevocably the sine qua non of society— the availability, no, the unavoidability of rules—and of politics—the persistence of asymmetric social relations, known otherwise as the condition of rule.

I dwell on these properties and their implications later in this book. I assert them now as a plausible construction of the properties of the operative paradigm of political society and note that, as such, they should also constitute essential elements in any disciplinary paradigm corresponding to this operative reality. Accepting this, however, does not mean that an equally plausible theory centered on the general properties of political society and orienting any such disciplinary paradigm is just around the corner.

Wolin understood that "great theories" of the Western political tradition are responses to the operative reality of political society (1980: 182; see further 1969: 1078–1080 on "epic theorists"). Yet none of them suffice as a paradigm theory. That they were put to selective use in the constitution of Political Science and International Relations and thus contributed to their respective proto-theories suggests the same procedure could help in the construction of a new disciplinary paradigm. Although it is immodest to say so, I see my work here as a tentative first step toward that paradigm. Taking a cue from Wolin, I support this step by having recourse to the great theories of the past, but not just those of the Western political tradition. If the emphasis is on political society, then comparable theories of society are equally pertinent.

Use of these materials is necessarily selective. Once selected, I subject them to the most careful scrutiny I can manage. The close reading of texts is a favorite method of Philosophy. My endeavors here should be construed not as Philosophy but as a philosophically informed foray into the social sciences. One might ask, to quote Jeffrey C. Alexander, "why engage in readings rather than embark on a more straightforward and contemporary discussion of telling empirical problems, . . . ?" (1982: 1). My answer is Alexander's. I do close reading "because, in certain critical respects, it is by interpreting and reinterpreting 'classical' works that fundamental argument is conducted in the social sciences" (p. 1). In other words, I think this method pays off with a supply of materials for a disciplinary construction project.

In this work I propose to take a second step as well. My close reading is intended to render the operative paradigm of political society in an overarching set of categories. More precisely I believe I have identified three categories of rules — categories understood in the traditional sense of the term as "abstract containers, with things inside or outside the category" (Lakoff 1987: 6). These categories derive from a consideration of language as enabling people to perform social acts and achieve ends by making statements of assertion, direction, and commitment.

Once aware of these categories, I encountered various formulations of them in many of the texts, classic and contemporary, to engage my attention. They are discernible in great theories from which International Relations scholars have adduced the centrality of anarchy for international relations, and they are conspicuous in discussions of the conditions of rule. Because these categories apply equally to rules and rule, I see them significantly supporting the rules-rule coupling as decisive for political society. Because they bear on the full range of human practices for which political society is the operative term, they are indispensable for sorting out the materials that close reading provides for the disciplinary construction project.

Again there is nothing original or surprising in my method — It goes back to Aristotle. To establish categories presupposes that within the operative paradigm are nodes of practice. These we may see as response to the puzzles that humanity repeatedly confronts in its social existence. Puzzle solutions are passed on, diffused, or reinvented with such consistency that they lend themselves to observers' typification, which then contributes to their social constitution. They are Max Weber's ideal types (Shils and Finch 1949: 90–110). This is a misleading label, however, because it is so widely taken to mean that the act of typification takes place only in the observer's mind.

As we saw with the term "paradigm," tendencies in practice and

observers' portrayals are separately constituted but mutually reinforcing. This is just Weber's position.[11] Weber understood the interaction of practices and portrayals to operate in large ensembles of practices not seen from within as having any coherence, liberalism being
an example (Shils and Finch 1949: 97). He also identified it in smaller contained and recurrent ensembles of practices, the coherence of
which is evident even to those engaging in them. The former are
what I have already called operative paradigms. The latter are typified puzzle solutions, typed in the first instance by those whose solutions they are. Inasmuch as typified puzzle solutions share with
paradigms a constitutive function in relating practices and portrayals, there is a point in calling them paradigms and, more particularly, puzzle paradigms.

The close reading of texts discloses observers' renditions of puzzle
paradigms. These too are recurrent. Often they are highly abstract,
the observer presenting them as "pure" types. To claim that there are
only three pure types of rule in political society, as did Weber (1968:
215; see chapter 6 for elaboration), is to hold that humanity has devised only three durable solutions to the problem of using rule to
advantage. I also claim that there are only three durable solutions
to the problem of rule. They are not identical to Weber's. I believe
my three categories of rule, and not his types, are pure.

Types cannot be pure, because they are swarms of things, including ensembles of practice, having no firm boundaries. Instead of
pure types, we are likely to have proto-types, stereotypes (Lakoff

---

11. Weber used the term "ideal" because ideal types are "mental constructs" (*Gedan-
    kenbild,* also rendered by his translators as "constructions," "analytical con-
    structs" and "conceptual constructions"; Shils and Finch 1949: 88–93), but not
    just an observer's. Weber noted that

    > there are certain relationships between the "idea" in the sense of a ten-
    > dency of practical or theoretical thought and the "idea" in the sense of
    > the ideal *typical* portrayal of an epoch constructed as a heuristic device.
    > An ideal type of certain situations, which can be abstracted from certain
    > characteristic social phenomena of an epoch, might—and this is quite
    > often the case—have also been present in the minds of the persons living
    > in that epoch as an ideal to be striven for in practical life or as a maxim
    > for the regulation of certain social relationships (p. 95, emphasis in original).

1987), and exemplars (compare note 7). Categories can be pure, however; "a container form might be called a 'pure form'" (Lakoff 1987: 354). Boundaries must be definite and candidates for membership determinately in or out, not in and out or in between. In turn, an observer must independently formulate criteria for bounding categories and judging candidates for inclusion. (Hereinafter I use the term "category" only for pure categories.)[12] No category stands alone. At minimum, categories come in pairs, because all candidates excluded from one category must be a member of a second category defined by what is bounded out of the first. In other words, categorizing puzzle paradigms, as with anything else, requires a classificatory scheme.

Unlike Weber, I attempt to relate puzzle paradigms of rule to each other as categories. Each category of rule corresponds to one of three categories of rules, which are themselves solutions to problems raised by the social character of language. Maker-users of such puzzle paradigms need not relate these paradigms to each other or the operative paradigms within which they arise. Yet they often, perhaps always, do so.[13] Scholars have no choice but to do so if they wish to have their typifications in categories, their categories

------

12. I should emphasize that most categories are not pure. The longstanding presumption is that concepts are containers for kinds of things, metaphorically extended to all predicates. (On container metaphors, see Johnson and Lakoff 1980: 29–30). Recent research, masterfully synthesized by George Lakoff (1987), decisively challenges this view. One might better describe impure categories as families, understood by reference to "family resemblance" among members (p. 16; see also chapter 1, footnote 10), or species and genera (Lakoff 1987: 31–38, 185–193).
13. Claude Levi-Strauss has argued that categorizing and classifying, so conspicuous in preliterate social experiences, are a universal consequence of a cognitive constant: The human mind, like a computer, performs binary operations, which it then nests and compounds in systems of transformations (1966; see Gardner 1981: 133–144 for a useful summary). This Structuralist view strikes me as a congenial one for social choice theory, which also presupposes the primacy of binary operations — making choices — but fails to consider how such operations can yield the categories within which choices are made. I do not deny the importance of binary operations. Even this book is organized on them, as will be seen presently. Nevertheless, I doubt that they and correlative operations exhaust the cognitive competence of human beings — a matter I return to in chapter 3.

pure. And without categories they cannot propose theories and construct disciplines.

Classificatory schemes systematically relating categories are also
paradigms constructed by operative practices and observers' portrayals. Following the lead of Robert K. Merton and Talcott C. Parsons,
I would call them codificatory paradigms.[14] They stand between puzzle paradigms on the one hand and disciplinary and operative paradigms on the other. C. Wright Mills derisively called Parsons' construction "grand theory" (1959b: 25–49), thus anticipating the fall
of all such efforts from disciplinary favor. Recently, however, interest
in "grand theories" has revived (Skinner 1985). Foucault's work is
held as an example, despite evidence that he wished only to expose,
or possibly invent (Megill 1985: 234–236), unacknowledged operative paradigms. Anthony Giddens and Jürgen Habermas afford other
examples of consequence for the work at hand.

Grandly conceived, these undertakings are not theories — certainly
not paradigm theories orienting disciplines, for they stand athwart
the current array of social science disciplines. While some of them
resemble the "great theories" of a predisciplinary era, they tend to
be codificatory paradigms. They are devised for operative paradigms
more encompassing than those of contemporary social science disciplines. Consequently they undercut existing disciplines and their
proto-theories. Grand theories so-called do not reject the possibility

---

14. Merton (1968: 64–72) and through him Parsons (1978: 352–353) used "paradigm"
    from the mid-1950s in reference to codifying Sociological scholarship. "As con-
    strued here, codification is the orderly and compact arrangement of fruitful pro-
    cedures of inquiry and the substantive findings that result from their use" (p. 69).
    Note that Merton was not concerned with Sociology's proto-theory. Instead
    "theory" is shorthand for the what and how of puzzle solutions. In practice
    Merton and Parsons both tended to codify related sets of puzzle solutions in a
    taxonomic scheme, which then became the paradigm. Perhaps the best illustra-
    tion is Parsons' fourfold "paradigm" of functional requirements for any social
    system: "any social system may be analyzed in terms of four logically indepen-
    dent functional requirements, which we formulate as *adaptation, goal-attainment,
    integration,* and *latent pattern maintenance*" (1967: 260). The first clearly relates
    to economy, the second to polity, the third to personality and the fourth to cul-
    ture (pp. 259–263). How they may be said to be "logically independent" is not
    so clear.

of a disciplinary reorientation; indeed this is one reason for their recent appearance and enthusiastic reception. Much at odds with the
ethos of normal science, the arrival of grand theories speaks to the
growing malaise within existing disciplines.

Grand theories are codificatory paradigms that cannot be ignored.
I have rummaged through a number of them, not just for scraps of
support, but with a larger ambition. I would have my codificatory
paradigm join the others in what, for lack of anything better, we call
"social theory." As social theory gains coherence, it will substitute
for discredited disciplinary paradigms. If disciplines are to endure,
they will depend on paradigmatic claims that lesser operative paradigms can be distinguished without overriding theoretical significance attaching to their distinctiveness.

The reconstruction of International Relations requires that the
discipline be stripped of its current pretensions. If this is taken as
abandonment of International Relations (the discipline as it is) and
the possibility of international theory (theory peculiar to International Relations), then I agree. I do not agree that it means giving up on international relations as well. Rather it honors their importance and thus their place in the operative paradigm of political
society. More than other matters of politics, international relations
are the subject of this book only because I have thought more about
them. Such is the legacy of my discipline.

PLAN OF THE BOOK

Most books, even when they are as relentlessly abstract as this one,
tell a story, more or less coherently, in accord with a plan which the
author may or may not divulge. There are exceptions, perhaps, such
as Ludwig Wittgenstein's *Philosophical Investigations* (1968), to
which chapter 1 attends, or works in the currently fashionable deconstructive mode of criticism. Modernist fiction is either deliberately unplanned or, I think more often, guilefully planned to dis-
orient the reader. This book is merely modern (I define the terms
"modern" and "modernist" on p. 234). It stands resolutely in the tradition of reasoned persuasion that has dominated Western thought
for several centuries. The plan is to take the reader through a series
of steps, each of which leads ineluctably—or so I try to persuade

the reader—to the next. In the end, and if I have succeeded, the reader will accept my argument rather than retreat along the many steps so arduously taken.

I do this twice. To come to the same conclusion twice is doubtless more persuasive than one time through the steps, but probably less than twice as persuasive. Not only do declining marginal returns prompt an end after two forced marches. Esthetic considerations come into play. This book has a binary format. Its two parts face each other in complementary opposition. The symmetry of parts is repeated in the arrangement of chapters. In the familiar language of Structuralism (recall footnote 13), each of the four chapters in Part Two is a transformation of one of the four chapters in Part One, the parts themselves being transformations of each other.[15] Because the first chapter in Part two is a transformation of the last chapter in Part One, they together constitute a hinge connecting the two parts of the book and allowing them to be turned back on, or toward, each other. The first and last chapters are also transformations of each other, together constituting a clasp. The book closes by coming around on itself, ending where it began. Chapters 2 and 6 and chapters 3 and 7 are also transformations of each other. Their arrangement propels the text forward rather than tying it together.

If all this seems artful or contrived (it does as I write about it), then I can only reply that all books which tell a story use such ploys, but they do so generally unself-consciously. My own strongly inter-disciplinary interests foster awareness of these matters. More to the point, I suppose, they have robbed me of the illusion that books are anything other than artful constructions. Art that follows a careful plan can only do a better job of persuasion, or so I believe.

Part One is entitled "Rules," Part Two "Rule." Part One tells what

---

15.   Indeed, all known structures—from mathematical groups to kinship systems—are, without exception, systems of transformation. But transformation need not be a temporal process: $1 + 1$ "make" 2; 3 "follows hard on" 2; clearly, the "making" and "following" here meant are not temporal processes. On the other hand, transformation can be a temporal process: getting married "takes time." Were it not for the idea of transformation, structures would lose all explanatory import, since they would collapse into static forms (Piaget 1970: 11–12).

rules are and what they do, which is to enable or effectuate rule. Part Two tells what rule is and how it works, which is through the medium of rules. Because rules transform into rule, and rule into rules, it follows that chapters in each part be made transformations of each other. One might suppose that the opposition of rules and rule repeats the recurrent opposition in social science scholarship between micro- and macrolevel phenomena. The power and importance of this opposition can hardly be denied. Nevertheless, Parts One and Two are not organized around the micro-macro opposition and its many transformations, because the constructivist position I defend in chapter 1 emphasizes the continuous co-constitution of micro- and macrolevel phenomena. Neither has causal or temporal primacy. My construction of rules and rule constantly shuttles between macro- and micro-level considerations, always in hopes of fixing attention on what would be a mere point of transformation if I stayed first on one side of the opposition and then on the other.

After I make my constructivist case in chapter 1, I develop a microlevel understanding of what rules are in chapter 2, but go to the macrolevel by considering what they do. Chapter 3 asks how individual people know how to use rules, but concludes by asking how competence with rules constitutes culture, which is certainly a macrolevel concern. Chapter 4 assays "the problem of order," which is macrolevel on the face of it, but does so from the long established perspective of individuals and their discretionary response to rules.

Much the same can be said of Part Two. Chapter 5 deals with "the presumption of anarchy," which is a transformation of the problem of order, but not a shift from the macro- to the microlevel. Again, however, microlevel concerns come to the fore as I describe the decline of a normatively rich conception of anarchy in Western political thought and its replacement with an emphasis on utilitarian ideas and finally social choice theory. Chapter 6 is devoted centrally to rule, but always in the context of rules. Chapter 7 turns to rule in world politics, but always from the point of view of skillful individuals. The final chapter connects individuals' choices, through interests, to resources and their exploitation. The point is not to substitute a new opposition—individual and nature—for the opposition of individual and society. Rather it is to correct any impression, such as chapter 1 may have created and subsequent chapters strengthened, that social construction proceeds without reference to material conditions and consequences. Thus is chapter 8 brought back to chapter 1, after many peregrinations between rules and rule, individual and society, in the name of social construction.

The opposition of rules and rule lends itself to a different interpretation. A significant proportion of the literature devoted to rules reflects the centrist affinities of its authors. Because liberalism is at the center of the Western experience over the last three hundred years, centrism means moderately conservative or ameliorative predilections to be served by rules, within a world constituted on liberal assumptions. By contrast, a significant proportion of the literature devoted to rule reflects ideological and temperamental extremism on the part of its authors. Both the Marxist paradigm and the paradigm of rule stand at the margins of the Western experience, because the center belongs to liberalism. Those who recognize the operative significance of either of these paradigms must also stand at the margins, whether in anger or resignation.

I possess (a word I choose for its ironic effect) a background, training, and privileged position in liberal society. The concern with rules makes sense to me. I must also confess an attraction to a Nietzschean view of rule (and thus of rules: read the quotation from Foucault introducing Part Two) and to the Left's position on exploitation (chapter 8). Again, my constructivist position allows me to negotiate between temperamental and ideological polarities without having to declare a lasting allegiance. The cost is a certain detachment, as manifest in a logocentric stance (elaborated in chapter 1) and a tendency toward irony (defined in chapter 4, footnote 21). Identifying the pervasiveness of asymmetric and exploitive social relations is not to condone this situation. It does not preclude a personal, liberal commitment to making one's immediate circumstances less this way, nor an attitude of world weariness so much favored by advantaged, alienated intellectuals. Constructivism tolerates all this and more.

Someone glancing through the book's table of contents might discern an entirely different opposition. Part One is a general treatment of social relations; Part Two narrows the focus to international relations. There is some merit to this conclusion. Chapter 1 barely mentions international relations as such. Chapter 2 does examine international legal theory as particularly revealing the limits of prevailing legal theory, if only to set the stage for a view of rules not at all dependent on legal theory. The alternative view starts with language, which is, needless to say, a general social phenomenon. Chapter 3 is also developed in the most general terms, beginning as it does with cognition and ending with broad generalizations about cultural differences. International relations command an important place in chapter 4, although this chapter begins and ends in general terms.

Part Two is more attentive to the specifics of international relations, but not exclusively so. Chapter 5 considers anarchy in Western political thought without supposing that international relations represent the only or even an appropriate instance of anarchy. Chapter 6 attempts to show the presence of rule in all social relations, including international relations as a usually exempted case. Rule in contemporary international relations is the subject of chapter 7. Nevertheless, the discussion undercuts any firm distinction between relations among states, as international relations are conventionally understood, and other activities undertaken in the circumstances of modernity. Finally, chapter 8 relates the choice of means and ends to the material conditions of human existence, with international relations an apposite illustration.

In examining oppositions not central to the book's symmetry, I provide brief descriptions (twice actually) of each chapter. Any further description is unlikely to help the reader much unless it is more detailed, in which case it will repeat the exposition undertaken in each chapter. I do begin each chapter with a sketch of themes to come. Again, to avoid repetition, I offer no conclusion, either to the chapters, or to the book as a whole. Instead, I append a Synoptic Table to record the three categories of rules and rule I allude to, and all the correspondences to them I discuss in the course of the book.

PART 1: RULES

What, in short, we wish to do is dispense with 'things'. To 'depresentify' them. . . . To substitute for the enigmatic treasure of 'things' anterior to discourse, the regular formation of objects that emerge only in discourse. To define these *objects* without reference to the *ground,* the *foundation of things,* but by relating them to the body of rules that enable them to form as objects of a discourse and thus constitute the conditions of their historical appearance.

Michel Foucault
The Archeology of Knowledge
(1972: 47–48,
emphasis in original)

1

CONSTRUCTIVISM

> Language—I want to say—
> is a refinement, *im Anfang war die Tat*
> ('in the beginning was the deed').
>
> *Ludwig Wittgenstein*
> *(1976: 420; compare 1972; par. 402)*

One must begin somewhere. Perhaps there is no beginning, and the search will lead in circles. Most International Relations scholars have not begun far enough back or, switching metaphors, gone deep enough to say. Instead they share in the common judgment of social scientists that one begins on the ground, with data (Glaser and Strauss 1967: 1). Already dug into the ground are foundations, "'foundations of knowledge'—truths that are certain because of their causes rather than because of the arguments given for them . . ." (Rorty 1979: 157; see generally pp. 155–164; Connolly 1986: 116–126). These foundations are ancient and durable. They were laid in Classical Greece, and they are used today to erect conceptual frameworks and construct theories.

If this is the language of construction, constructivism it is not; constructivism goes further. The ground itself is but the rubble of construction. Truths as we take them to be are inextricable from the arguments offered for them. One may begin with facts, "things" as they are, thereby taking for granted the argument for their facticity. One may begin with words, ideas, arguments, taking for granted the facts to which they refer. Constructivism begins with deeds. Deeds done, acts taken, words spoken—These are all that facts are.

Social scientists freely assume that they build on firm ground and strong foundations because these are deeded to them by their disciplines. Social theory, which I take to be that loose array of codificatory paradigms sprouting in the debris of failed proto-theories and decrepit disciplines, necessarily challenges these assumptions. Consequently social theorists cannot avoid the question of where one begins. I see my own effort to reconstruct International Relations as a contribution to social theory. As such it too must attend to the subject of beginnings, which is a philosophical question.

If I begin this chapter with a philosophical question, moving on to social theory has its pitfalls, as my recourse to Wittgenstein's work on rules will show. I conclude the chapter by associating myself with a codificatory paradigm called structuration theory. Rules are central to this scheme, but less has been said about them than is needed for a social theory that begins where I begin.

IN THE BEGINNING

I begin with Goethe's aphorism, which for Wittgenstein seemed to express a philosophical position: In the beginning was the deed.[1] I call this position constructivism. In simplest terms, people *and* societies construct, or constitute, each other. Inasmuch as I take the terms "construct" and "constitute" to be synonymous, I could just as well call the position their use reflects constitutivism but for the evident awkwardness of the term.[2]

---

1. And not just for Wittgenstein. "Marx, Nietzsche, Wittgenstein and Heidegger: they are the heirs of Faust. . . . Each of them in his own way takes as his starting point Faust's first principle, 'Im Anfang war die Tat,' but each interprets and develops it differently" (Redner 1982: 52; see further pp. 41–77).
2. "Constructivism," as I use the term here, bears only a distant affinity to constructivism as an important movement in Soviet art after the October Revolution. Soviet constructivists saw art as necessarily social and their approach as "the communist expression of material structures." They inveighed against "the speculative aesthetic activity of art," and they directed their attention to technical processes and working materials (Lodder 1973, quoting Aleksei Gan, "theoretician of the First Working Group of Constructivists" pp. 237–238).

As a philosophical position, constructivism is by no means mine alone. It has a considerable following in contemporary philosophy and social theory, and it comes in variations and degrees. Among philosophers Nelson Goodman is a constructivist perhaps to the furthest degree. In Jerome Bruner's apt summary of Goodman's position, "no one 'world' is more real than others. None is ontologically privileged as the unique real world" (1986: 96). Goodman's concern is not merely the world as social reality.

> The many stuffs — matter, energy, waves, phenomena — that worlds are made of are made along with the worlds. But made from what? Not from nothing, after all, but *from other worlds.* Worldmaking as we know it always starts from worlds already on hand; the making is the remaking (1978: 6, emphasis in original).

Goodman's position is nominalist; he has called himself a constructive nominalist (1984): 50–53). Long unfashionable, nominalism holds that things exist only insofar as they are named as such. The world is what we take it to be. Long ascendant is the antithesis to this position, realism (Goodman has also called himself an "irrealist"), which holds that the world exists independent of ourselves and the things within it await our naming. The rise of science licensed realism but, from G. W. Leibniz, did not prevent realists from contemplating the existence of "possible worlds" — worlds that do not, as far as we know, really exist, but which would if anything in this world happens other than it does. David Lewis has recently (1986) pointed out how many philosophical problems are made more tractable simply by granting the "plurality of worlds." Lewis' position does not grant existential standing to plural worlds. My position, and Goodman's, as I understand it, does.

Goodman's constructive nominalism is perhaps not quite as radical as some passages from his work (such as the one I quoted) might suggest. He has never denied the existence of some independent phenomenal world. He has asserted that we can never know all the features of that world independent of discourse about it. Even if some features of the real world are independent, we cannot, in our discourse dependency, know which ones they are (Goodman 1984: 41). We construct worlds we know in a world we do not.[3]

Nor is Goodman's position wanting of antecedents. Not Leibniz, but René Descartes and Immanuel Kant are his philosophical progenitors. While constructivism accepts the Cartesian duality of mind and matter, the distinctive feature of this position is its Kantian pedigree: It "began when Kant exchanged the structure of the world for the structure of the mind, ..." (Goodman 1978: x, compare Putnam 1981: 60–64). Yet it claims too much to say, with Bruner, that Kant "fully developed" constructivism (1986: 96). Indeed, Kant's most famous use of the term "constitutive" refers to logically necessitated relations of givens, expressed in quantities, and not the construction of worlds through "analogies of experience." "The general principle of the analogies is: All appearances are, as regards their existence, subject a priori to rules determining their relation to one another in one time" (Kant 1933: 208). Kant's term for those rules is "regulative."[4] More justly, John Rawls (1980) found Kant's moral theory to be constructivist, though in a weaker sense.[5]

Nevertheless, Kant's influence on later versions of constructivism is considerable. More than anyone else Kant propelled Philosophy toward its "epistemological turn," which, in codifying the Cartesian dualism of mind and world, gave philosophers primary responsibility for the former and left the latter to social theorists. The "linguistic turn" of twentieth-century Philosophy effectuated a *rapprochement* of sorts between Philosophy and social theory.[6] This was manifested

---

3. Some realists are not far from this position. I have in mind Hilary Putnam's "internal" realism (1981: 49–74) and George Lakoff's "experiential" realism (1987: 260–268). Note Putnam's remark that "Nelson Goodman and I have detected a convergence in our views, . . ." (1981: xii).

4. "It stands quite otherwise with those principles which seek to bring the *existence* of appearances under rules a priori. For since existence cannot be constructed, the principles can apply only to the relations of existence and can yield only *regulative* principles" (1933: 210, emphasis in original).

5. "Kantian constructivism holds that moral objectivity is to be understood in terms of a suitably construed social point of view that all can construct" (Rawls, 1980: 519).

6. Jerrold L. Aronson (1984: 260) gave credit for the term "epistemological turn" to Robert Paul Wolff (1963). Richard Rorty (1967) used "linguistic turn" in collecting a wide range of valuable material appearing in the preceding thirty-five years.

in an unending burst of interest in cognition, "the architecture of the human mind-brain" (Goldman 1986: 1), but the result was a kind of epistemological imperialism. Through the medium of language, mind subordinated world. The triumph of epistemology resonates with the Greco-Christian presentiment so powerfully expressed in the New Testament of the Bible: In the beginning was the word.

My dictionary says that "logos," the word, is "the rational principle that governs and develops the universe," and "the divine word or reason incarnate in Jesus Christ" (Random House 1967: 843). The triumph of epistemology finds the "rational principle" a permanent home in the mind, and in so doing satisfies several presumptions, namely, that humans as language users are uniquely affiliated with the divine, that cognitive activity is pulled toward reason, that the mind finds, or makes, the order in the world. Given Western culture's penchant for word-world dualism and, under Kantian auspices, grant of priority to the former, Goodman's constructivism breaches commonsense realism — the belief that there is one real world "out there" — with a perverse plausibility.

Constructivism also challenges empiricist and realist assumptions of working science.[7] Constructivist philosophers of science like Bas C. van Fraasen (1981) are given to argue, in Richard N. Boyd's words (1984: 52), that "the world that scientists study, in some robust sense, must be defined or constituted or 'constructed' from the theoretical tradition in which the scientific community in question works." This sounds as radical as some of Goodman's rhetoric. Yet we can take it to mean that the world science knows is *in degree* a social construction. Although methods are "theory-dependent," and theory is mind-made, neither theories, methods, nor data are simply made up in, or by, the mind. This brand of constructivism does not deny the existence of phenomena (van Fraasen would save them — "phenomena are saved when they are exhibited as fragments of a larger unity"). Instead it acknowledges "the limits of observation, which are not incapacitating but also are not negligible" (van Fraasen 1984: 256).

We should not be surprised that Thomas S. Kuhn is seen as a con-

---

7. Empiricists and realists are themselves divided over the status of nonobservable entities as terms in scientific theories. I found Richard N. Boyd (1984) of particular help in clarifying empiricist, realist, and constructivist positions currently debated by philosophers of science.

structivist of this genre. The discussion of paradigms to be found in the introduction to this book, which aspires to honor the sense of Kuhn's work while extending it, points to a socially made content to all knowledge, including scientific knowledge, without repudiating the material reality to which knowledge relates. Thus the proportion of social and material content to knowledge varies in different domains of knowledge. The different proportions and the different ways their interaction plays out are the very basis for the proliferation of paradigms across the realm of human knowledge and their succession through time.

The constructivism I prefer follows along these lines. It does not draw a sharp distinction between material and social realities — the material and the social contaminate each other, but variably — and it does not grant sovereignty to either the material or the social by defining the other out of existence. It does find socially made content dominant in and for the individual without denying the independent, "natural" reality of individuals as materially situated biological beings. To say that people and societies construct each other is not to imply that this is done wholly out of mind, as Goodman would seem to have suggested.

Constructivism marks a place to begin, however provisionally. Poststructuralism offers a more radical position. All grounds are groundless, all foundations specious. For Jacques Derrida, no position is radical enough because it is a position. "Every stance that Derrida articulates has its 'pro' and 'anti' aspects; every position that he adopts is immediately rendered nugatory" (Megill 1985: 266). Under the circumstance, never begin, always withhold or subvert, and say, as Derrida has said, that what one does say is always prefatory to what cannot be said (pp. 271–272).

Derrida cannot begin without adopting a logocentric stance, a position from which to begin. Just this stance hobbles Western philosophy from its Greek origins (Derrida 1976: 10–18, 30–44). In Derrida's use, the term "logocentrism" is difficult to specify straightforwardly, for any such specification would be an enactment of logocentrism. Nevertheless, I quote Richard K. Ashley's interpretation both for being faithful to Derrida's meaning (as if one could say this without seriously breaching Derrida's intent, whatever that might be) and for relevance to International Relations. The "logocentric disposition" is the expectation that all practice must secure recognition and power by appeal to some identical consciousness, principle of interpretation, or necessary subjectivity—some central and originary premise necessary to the making and interpretation of history—which is itself regarded as unproblematic, extra-historical and, hence, in need of no critical accounting. This true and central subject of historical narrative of course has no one necessary form. It might be identified with the posses-sive individual, the rational state, the national community, the scientific man, the consciousness of the proletariat, the fall of the family, the feminine voice, the general will, immanent im-peratives of mankind, the West, structuralism's Kantian "con-sciousness without a knowing subject," the universal pragmatics of Habermas's "ideal speech situation," God, king, phallus, or womb. What matters is that this subject, this viewpoint, this principle of interpretation and practice is conceived as existing in itself, as a foundation or origin of history's making, not as a contingent effect of political practice within history (1988: 93–94).

I believe that poststructuralists are substantially correct in empha-sizing the logocentric content of the many dualities long dominating Western thought. On the one side are mind, subject, consciousness, rationality, standing outside history or having the word. On the other are matter, object, not knowing or understanding, being caught in history or having fallen from grace. I would either abandon most of these dual constructions or render them so differently as to ex-pose, or even nullify, the deference demanded by difference. (Here I play with a well-known theme of Derrida's, helpfully presented by Norris 1982: 24–32, 46–48.)

Furthermore, I believe that the constructivism I offer in these pages successfully overcomes these dualities by treating people and society as each the product of the other's construction. Readers may find this reminiscent of the Hegelian solution to the duality of thesis and antithesis in the dialectical movement called synthesis. Post-structuralists are no more content with "the 'ternary rhythm' of Hegelian philosophy" than they are with the characteristic dualities of Western thought (Megill 1985: 273, quoting from an as yet un-translated text of Derrida's). Instead, "slouching onto the scene comes the Derridean four," as Allan Megill has rather colorfully put it, "a disreputable upsetting four, one that absolutely refuses to behave. The possibility of a fourth movement of the dialectic destroys the whole dialectic machine. . . . The fourth movement is the deconstructive movement" (pp. 273–274; see also Nelson 1983: 183–184 on the "Sophistic counter-tradition of four-thinking").

Throughout this book I locate instances of a recurring threefold division of whatever social construction I am alluding to at that moment. Either I have invented this pattern in an obsessive but hardly original act of logocentrism, or it results from some general property of social construction. Obviously I prefer to think I have stumbled on the latter; poststructuralists (and who else?) will think this is a transparent rationalization of a logocentric drive. Whatever the case, my penchant for threes places me as far from the countertradition of "four-thinking" as it does from the West's dominant tradition of binary thinking.

I do not wish to imply that people do not construct and then depend on dualities. Our dominant tradition is the best possible evidence of the extent to which they do. Obviously I do too, and I do so expressly in this work. Nor do I wish to imply that poststructuralists have nothing apposite to say to a constructivist. On the contrary, I find Michel Foucault's genealogical inquiries telling reconstructions of what I would call regimes of rule, Foucault himself "the endlessly repeated play of dominations." (1977: 150; for an especially concise and effective discussion, see Connolly 1983: 231–238).

What cannot be reconciled with constructivism is deconstruction, at least when that practice is carried very far. If it may be said that "Foucault deconstructs the modern subject," it is no different to say: "He constructs genealogies of modern formations which engender the subject, . ." (Connolly 1983: 234). Compare this with Derrida: "The very concept of constitution itself must be deconstructed" (Derrida quoted in Translator's Preface, 1976: li). My goal is reconstruction. With that goal comes logocentrism.

The logocentrism I concede is this: The act of construction, the co-constitution of people and society, makes history. As such, it is "the theme and central subject of historical narrative. . ." (repeating Ashley's words, 1988: 93). Even though I conceive of this "viewpoint" as "the foundation or origin of history's making," social construction is nevertheless "a contingent effect of political practices within history" (pp. 93–94). I can have it both ways because I do not accept Ashley's totalizing duality — that we are either outside history or within it. We are always within our constructions, even as we choose to stand apart from them, condemn them, reconstruct them.

Deconstruction privileges words in a war on words. It is logocentric in its own narrow way. The importance then of Goethe's aphorism, In the beginning was the deed, is that it denies priority to either the word or the world (compare Redner 1982: 56–58, 67–75). A "deed" is intelligible only as jointly a social construction and natural event, produced by mind yet phenomenal in its own right. What is revolutionary about such a position is that it turns philosophy back to ontology, thereby enabling a *rapprochement* of philosophy and social theory that privileges neither at the expense of the other (compare Aronson 1984). At least in the English-speaking world, I feel safe in saying, this "ontological turn" (my term) is more Wittgenstein's doing than anyone else's.

WITTGENSTEIN'S PLACE

Wittgenstein has had an enormous influence on Philosophy and social theory, precisely because he is seen at the juncture of the two. It would be difficult to find any recent writer whose prestige is so high, especially in relation to (perhaps because of) a body of work so slender, unsystematic, and gnomic in character. This may even be the secret of Wittgenstein's success. His texts, more than most, demand that the reader do the work of supplying meaning to the words she sees. My reading of Wittgenstein departs from that of many social theorists, though less from that of some philosophers.

Everyone agrees that early in his career Wittgenstein authored the most rigorous exposition of language as a vehicle for representing reality ever put forward (1961). This was the culmination of a centuries-long philosophical program in support of the logocentric worldview: Language affords us sufficient distance from the world that we can represent the world as it is, including our place in it, through language. Wittgenstein repudiated that program in his later work, which can be seen as a guerrilla campaign against his earlier work. That Wittgenstein did not attack his own system systematically follows from his recognition that systematic exposition — a coherent representation of an allegedly coherent reality—is the problem. Yet Wittgenstein's campaign was not merely one of random assaults. If a particular conception of language supported the prevailing worldview, then an alternative view—for Wittgenstein, what language is, is a matter of how people use it—would provide the key to discrediting that worldview.

As a whole, social theorists see the later Wittgenstein as a self-conscious constructivist who dethroned words for deeds. I do not. I see him as someone whose turn from epistemology to ontology registered in his life-long preoccupation with language. By dislodging a particular conception of language on philosophical grounds, Wittgenstein made constructivism a plausible project for social theory. Doing so did not make Wittgenstein a social theorist himself.

To the extent that Wittgenstein revealed an interest in social theory, it would seem to have been confined to the familiar thesis that humanity gives rise to custom and institutions. These in turn form the backdrop against which human activity transpires. Such a view permitted Wittgenstein to investigate what individuals do with language in socially given circumstances. In Wittgenstein's words "the *speaking* of language is part of an activity, or of a form of life" (1968: par. 23; similarly, "to imagine a language means to imagine a form of life" par. 19).

Forms of life are produced by many speakers in agreement. The conventions and institutions giving "form" to "life" more specifically make life social. Children learn language and are socially formed at the same time. In Wittgenstein's words, they "are brought up to perform *these* actions, to use *these* words as they do so, and to react in *this* way to the words of others" (1968: par. 6, his emphasis). From the individual's point of view, forms are firm enough to orient her cognitive activity, or "language games," which are countless in number and variety (1968: par. 23). Wittgenstein's point of view is consistently the individual's point of view.

On this reading, Wittgenstein's social theory is a rather naive conventionalism, to which David Hume had long before given classic expression (more on this in chapter 5). There is an alternative interpretation, however, associated with Stanley Cavell (1979: 86–111) and Hanna Fenichel Pitkin (1972: 132–139).[8] I quote Cavell:

---

8. Though not published until 1979, Cavell's work appeared in 1961 as his doctoral dissertation, in which form Pitkin used it extensively.

Here the array of "conventions" are not patterns of life which differentiate human beings from one another, but those exigencies of conduct and feeling which all humans share. Wittgenstein's discovery, or rediscovery, is of the depth of convention in human life; a discovery which insists not only on the conventionality of human society but, we could say, on the conventionality of human nature itself (1979: 111).

What is most striking about this interpretation is the rhetorical skill with which it endeavors to affirm that Wittgenstein was a brilliantly original thinker while acknowledging that his social ideas are quite ordinary. First there is his discovery, then, as an aside, rediscovery and again, finally, a discovery. What was this "discovery"? —that in the beginning, before society, are some fundamental traits common to all who are human. In the beginning was nature, "human nature." Wittgenstein's often-quoted allusions to "the natural history of human beings" (1968: 415; compare par. 25) would seem to support this interpretation, as would Wittgenstein's interest in the relation of what is normal to what is natural (Cavell 1979: 111–125).

That there is such a thing as human nature is among the most conventional of ideas about the human condition, at least in my cultural tradition, logocentric as it is. It has had its vogue in recent decades in the form of Jean Piaget's invariant stages of cognitive and moral development in children (see further chapter 3), Claude Levi-Strauss's universals of opposition and transformation in human thought and culture, Noam Chomsky's ideas about innate syntactical competence. In greater or lesser degree the inspiration for this movement, broadly described as structuralism, is the insistence that cognition has its own logical structure, independent of societies and their conventions, *and* exemplified by language, once the latter is stripped of its social content. (See Gardner 1981 for an accessible and sensible introduction to the structuralist movement.) While structuralism is one pronounced twist in this century's linguistic turn, its premises are anything but constructivist. Instead, poststructuralist repudiation of structuralism's absorption with what may be innate in the human mind has taken a constructivist line, almost as a dialectical necessity, and thus to a radical degree. If nothing is innate, then everything is precarious (Fish 1980: 215–216). The term "deconstruction" says as much.[9]

How has Wittgenstein figured in this sequence? Not at all. Whether his social theory is conventionalist or naturalist, it is in any event exiguous and pedestrian. More to the point, it is *not* constructivist. At best, Wittgenstein's insistence on "the multiplicity of language games" (his list of examples is perhaps the single most quoted passage from his work; 1968: par. 23) helps to offset the logocentric desire to find cognitive universals in recurrent cultural tendencies—a propensity which Wittgenstein as read by Cavell does nothing to dispel.

I want to make a last point on this subject. The structuralists may be right in that the beginning must be some version of the word, some innate property of mind which orients cognition and relates to culture through language competence and use. I return to this possibility in chapter 3 and there hold to an agnostic view of the subject. To do so is to accept that constructivism limits what one can profess to know about such matters. My own psychocultural penchant for logocentrism, rationalized as detachment and mediated by irony, induces an unrealizable wish to begin with a philosophical grounding for constructivism, as a matter of social theory, which is prior to, or outside of, the constitution of history and society.

Wittgenstein is no help here—no one can help. So I offer a constructivism with a false beginning: In the beginning was the deed. The quest for philosophic grounding can lead to a logocentric detachment from the ground of social experience and, in any event, finds only limits. Perhaps I should call the position I take here bounded, not grounded, constructivism. Nevertheless it *is* constructivist. Human beings, with whatever equipment nature and/or society provides, construct society, and society is indispensable to the actualization of whatever human beings may "naturally" be; society constructs human beings out of the raw materials of nature, whether inner nature or, less problematically, the outer nature of their material circumstances.

---

9. Phenomenology also emphasizes that social constitution is always, and only, a product of intersubjective accommodation, which is inevitably subject to disruption and failure. Harold Garfinckel's famous experiments in "breaching" provide vivid demonstration of the fragility of social meaning. For a sensitive introduction to Schutz's and Garfinckel's work along these lines, see Heritage (1984).

What then is Wittgenstein's contribution to constructivism as social theory, beyond an aphoristic and, as I put it, false beginning? Judging from the vast literature invoking the later Wittgenstein, it must be his concern for language in use, so explicitly revising his earlier paradigmatic formulation of language as representation. In switching from the "picture theory" of language to "language games," Wittgenstein discovered, no, rediscovered (*pace* Cavell) the place of rules in language and, if language be a matter of use (use is a social matter, after all), in society. If I may say, Wittgenstein insisted on the intimacy of *logos* and *nomos* without establishing all the connections. At best he pointed to a vague "family resemblance" between them in his use of the term "rule."[10]

In keeping with his position on language as a matter of use, Wittgenstein sought to convey the sense of the term "rule" by examining its use. His illustrations are characteristically rules used to play games (hence "language games"; see 1968: par. 53–54), although it is never quite clear what a game might be. There are two possibilities. One, a game is a system of logically related symbols — a language having no social meaning in itself. Whether people play the game, or use its language, is incidental. Two, a game must have a language or, to say the same thing, a logic, but it is not a game until people play it. In both instances, rules tell us how to play a game. In the first instance, they "govern" the game. Not to use any of these rules alters the game and contributes to the multiplicity of games. In the second instance, rules guide play. Not to use a rule sacrifices guidance but neither the fact of play nor the game itself.

Philosophers tend, I think, to see Wittgenstein's rules as governing games of language and logic. Such games do not depend on their play; play depends on them. "When I obey a rule, I do not choose. I obey the rule *blindly*"[11] (1968: par. 219, emphasis in original). On this view, however, games, and thus their rules, are necessarily public. Wittgenstein is clear that there can be no such thing as a private

---

10. The term "family resemblance" is Wittgenstein's (1968: par. 67). It is one of his most famous, and useful, formulations (Recall introduction, footnote 12).
11. Wittgenstein accepted the possibility of free play, for example, "playing aimlessly with a ball . . ." (1968: par. 83). The rule here is that rules associated with any known game to be played with a ball are suspended. Any player doing as she wishes would still be following that rule and doing so blindly. Free play depends on a game with that one rule.

language. That rules are public does not make them directly social, any more than does their existence depend on "regular use" or "custom"[12] (Wittgenstein 1968: par. 198). Rules govern language which people then use for social purposes.

Those of Wittgenstein's interpreters who want to find a social

---

12. Wittgenstein's argument about the impossibility of private language has prompted a hot debate among philosophers. On one side, Saul Kripke (1982) has argued that Wittgenstein pointed to the radically skeptical view that words or symbols in a ruled relation can have no stable meaning, even to oneself, unless supplied by community agreement. Kripke held this to be akin to Hume's "skeptical problem" about the impossibility of inferring cause. Hume's "skeptical solution" to this problem was convention — we substitute convention for cause to make reality coherent (pp. 67-69, 92-101). I am not sure that Hume's conventionalism is his solution to the problem of cause except incidentally, but rather it was his solution to the problem of how people, already constituted as such, construct societies in which regularity and predictability are achieved. In other words, I think Kripke has confused Hume the philosopher with Hume the social theorist.

Turning to the other side of the debate, Kripke's critics have rejected, I think decisively, the contention that Wittgenstein had proposed a skeptical problem akin to Hume's. They go on to conclude that Wittgenstein could not have intended Kripke's skeptical solution. This is not so clear. While Hume may not have devised his view of convention to cope with the problem of cause, Wittgenstein was an unreliable consumer of Hume's social theory and could well have presupposed it for his position on the matter of following rules and the impossibility of private language. Consider the alternative:

> Hence following a rule is an activity, a *Praxis*. It is a misinterpretation to take '*Praxis*' here to signify a social practice. . . . The point is *not* to establish that language necessarily involves a community . . . , but that 'words are deeds.' . . . Nothing in this discussion involves any commitment to a multiplicity of *agents*. All the emphasis is on the regularity, the multiple *occasions,* of action . . . (Baker and Hacker, 1984: 20; their emphasis).

> The most glaring feature of [Wittgenstein 1968: para. 198-202] is that the words 'custom,' 'practice' and 'use' are never qualified with 'social' or 'community' — and 'social custom/practice' is not *pleonastic.* Surely Wittgenstein would have inserted these qualifying adjectives if he really meant to maintain a social conception of rule-following, ...Wittgenstein does use 'custom' and 'practice' to suggest the idea of multiplicity, but it is a multiplicity of *instances* of rule-following not of *persons* who follow the rules (McGinn 1984: 78; his emphasis).

If these critics are right, then rules for Wittgenstein can have no social meaning at all. This strikes me as a perversely narrow construction of what Wittgenstein must have meant. But if Kripke's "community view" is right, then Wittgenstein had a taken-for-granted social theory that provided rules with a taken-for-granted social context.

theory in his work disregard the distinction between public rules governing language and social rules guiding use as a matter of course. Instead they want to move from the proposition that language is rule-governed (which it is whether representing reality or being "a part of an activity") to the proposition that everything human beings do, everything *social,* is rule-governed. Peter Winch methodically spelled out the latter position in *The Idea of a Social Science and Its Relation to Philosophy* (1958). Because Winch provided so much more to work with than Wittgenstein, this work has been the subject of a number of careful critiques (for example: Flathman 1972: 17–33, Bernstein 1978: 63–84, Bhaskar 1979: 169–195, Bloor 1983: 168–181). I suspect that some of these critiques are motivated by a protective concern for Wittgenstein's reputation. Others have found Winch a useful stand-in for the elusive master.

In any case, Winch's bold statement "that all behaviour which is meaningful (therefore all specifically human behaviour) is ipso facto rule-governed" (1958: 52) commands attention. Winch's project was to demonstrate a decisive difference between the realms of natural cause and thus natural science, and human intention and thus social science. Yet Roy Bhaskar has argued that "the rule-following paradigm *presupposes* the category of causality" (1979: 186, emphasis in original). I think this is correct. It is difficult to sustain the claim that causality and intention are primary, mutually exclusive sources of reality, no less than the inference drawn therefrom that natural and human sciences are inviolably distinct spheres.

Winch may have meant that rules govern, not just meaning, but behavior directly; rules are causes. On this construction, however, Winch has succeeded in keeping cause and intention separate by making people automatons. Whatever they intend, they cause nothing, not even the rules they intend to work causally on their behalf. And if rules alone can cause behavior, it is redundant to speak of rule-governed behavior. No behavior can be otherwise. Without clarifying anything further about rules, Winch cannot have said anything about behavior, whether linguistic or social.

Winch remarked that "Wittgenstein's account of what it is to follow a rule is, for obvious reasons, given principally with an eye to elucidating the nature of language" (1958: 45). Winch needed to extend that account to all intentional activity in order to defeat Michael Oakeshott's position (as Winch saw it, 1958: 57, his emphasis) "that most human behaviour can be adequately described in terms of the notion of *habit* or *custom* and that neither the notion of rule nor that of reflectiveness is essential to it." Winch substituted "rule" for "habit" to make his point here and, by doing so, supported the proposition that the social realm of intentionality stood apart from natural cause, to which "mindless" habit and custom could easily be assimilated. Winch accomplished the limited objective of exposing Oakeshott for overreaching with habit as explanation for everything, but at the cost of overreaching with his alternative, which is rule.

Furthermore, Winch failed to see that for Wittgenstein custom is central to the natural history of humanity. Others have noted a number of conservative influences and tendencies in Wittgenstein's work (Bloor 1983: 160–181, Flathman 1986: 159, 169; but see Pitkin 1972: 328–340, for a contrary view). We can hardly be surprised to find Wittgenstein adopting a view comparable to Oakeshott's well-known conservatism. In the circumstance, and somewhat ironically, Winch's rebuttal of Oakeshott exposes Wittgenstein's ingenuous social theory as well. Inasmuch as Oakeshott elsewhere developed an important social theory dedicated to showing how human practices, which include rules and habits, sort themselves into two fundamental types of human association (1975), Oakeshott is less a victim of Winch's demonstration than Wittgenstein (Bloor 1983: 169–171) and, because of his reliance on Wittgenstein, Winch himself.

What Winch lacked was any way to ask specific questions about rules that are not just rules governing language. Take Bhaskar's list of questions Winch never considered: "(a) What explains the rules themselves?; (b) what explains the agent's rule-following on any particular occasion?; and (c) what explains the acquisition of rules by the social individual in the first place?" (1979: 185). Each of these questions can be asked differently: (a) Who makes the rules and how do the makers benefit from doing so? (b) Why do people follow rules without considering who makes them and how they and others are affected by doing so? (c) How is a rule orientation ("the acquisition of rule") related to reflection, habit, cognitive development? Much of Part One is addressed to these questions. For the moment though, I reformulate them to take Bhaskar's important argument a step further.

Bhaskar accused Winch of not distinguishing between constitutive rules and regulative rules. This time-honored distinction goes back to Kant, as we saw above, and has flourished in recent decades. In

Bhaskar's version, "a rule normally tells us what forms of action are possible (if it is *constitutive*) or permissible (if it is *regulative*) . . ." (1979: 184, his emphasis). Following Wittgenstein, Winch took rules to be constitutive and then had them do service in contexts where rules must be regulative. Bhaskar was undoubtedly right in his conclusion, given the distinction upon which it rests.

Yet the distinction between constitutive rules and regulative rules is itself untenable, at least from the point of view I am proposing here. In the social reality that people construct (and constructs people), what people take to be possible and what society makes permissible depend on vantage point, one's relation to practice, and not practice itself. As categories, the possible and the permissible find no support in Kant. His concern was to discriminate between strictly logical relations, which as a category are ruled by constitutive principles, and existential relations ruled by regulative principles.

The rest of the sentence I just quoted from Bhaskar reads: "it [referring to 'a rule'] does not normally tell us how to carry on." This is exactly wrong. Rules do indeed tell us how to carry on, and they go about it in three distinct ways, to be elaborated in the next chapter. They do not tell us everything we would like to know as we carry on. No human creation could do that. In other words, rules cannot provide closure for the purposes of carrying on because rules are not the sufficient agency whereby intentions become equivalent to causes. If Winch tended to suppose otherwise in order to give the realms of intention and cause separate but equal standing, thus to advance his project of keeping the natural and social sciences apart, we are not obliged to do the same. We can easily enough construe rules as an important, perhaps even constitutively decisive agency for the realization of human intentions and thereby an indispensable part of what human beings need to take into account to be able to "carry on" in a socially constructed world.

Contemporary discussion of the Kantian distinction between constitution and regulation stems from an important essay of Rawls' (1955), which nonetheless does not use the terms "constitution" and "regulation." Instead Rawls identified two concepts of rules, one a "summary view" of rules and the other a view in which "rules are pictured as defining a practice" (1955: 24). The former refers to general rules or scientific laws which, existentially speaking, can never be more than "generalizations from experience" (p. 24). The latter, practice rules, are both constitutive and regulative (pp. 25, 30). I think that Rawls was clarifying the way we use the word "rule" to refer to both cause and intention. We have separate concepts of rule for each realm. Inasmuch as we can stand back from the web of intentional activity constituting the social and see causal patterns, we use both concepts for a socially constructed world. This, however, does not change the fact that all rules in a socially constructed reality are related to *practice*.

Not just Bhaskar, but others distinguishing between constitution and regulation (for example, Searle 1969: 33–42, Flathman 1972: 77–81) have muddied these waters considerably by insisting on the distinction as one of types.[13] I repeat: Rules are both constitutive and regulative. Rawls' association of practice and a concept of rules having to do with intentions is very much to the point. Practices are the content of carrying on. When human beings take rules into account in order to carry on, they often do so at the level of self-conscious reflection. They always do so at the level of "practical consciousness", as Anthony Giddens would have it (1979: 53–59; 1982: 30–32; 1984: 41–45). "The knowledgeability involved in practical consciousness conforms generally to the Wittgenstein notion of 'knowing a rule' or 'knowing how to go on'" (1982: 31).

STRUCTURATION

That philosophers are, at best, adventitious social theorists would seem to limit their help in constructing a constructivist position for

---

13. Rawls himself may have slipped here: "Some rules will fit one conception, some rules the other, . . ." (1955: 29). Such a position is defensible only insofar as rules are marked for functional specialization. Thus legal philosopher H. L. A. Hart (1961: 77–96) typed all rules either as primary or secondary, the former being regulative and the latter constitutive as a matter of functional specialization. In earlier work (1974: 22–35), I drew a distinction between "interactive rules" and "institutive rules," the former regulative in function and the latter constitutive. That rules are necessarily constitutive and regulative, at least on the constructivist view, does not preclude discrimination among rules by reference to their intended functional specialization. Institutions are of course the conceptual marker for such instances of specialization. Consequently it is perfectly legitimate to identify secondary or institutive rules as a conceptually established nexus of rules without requiring that they be rules of a distinctive category. For more on the relation of institution to constitution, and their relation to categories of rule, see chapters 2 and 4.

the purpose of social theory. Yet most social theorists are no help either. Even if they have constructivist inclinations, they do not develop their position systematically — they do not begin early enough. I make this generalization for the world of English language scholarship, but even here there are some exceptions.

One is the phenomenological concern with the constitution of everyday life. This concern substantially originated with Edmund Husserl and his difficult notion of "*Lebenswelt,* life-world."

> The knowledge of the objective-scientific world is "grounded" in the self-evidence of the life-world. The latter is pregiven to the scientific worker, or the working community, as ground; yet as they build upon this, what is built is something different. If we cease being immersed in our scientific thinking, we become aware that we scientists are, after all, human beings and as such among the components of the life-world which always exists for us, ever pregiven; and thus all of science is pulled, along with us, into the merely "subjective-relative" life-world (1970: 130–131, quoted in Bernstein 1978: 129; see generally Bernstein's excellent discussion, pp. 126–135).

Husserl's impact on English language social theory has been limited both by the legendary obscurity of his writing (compare 1970: xxi–xxii on the translator's problems) and because of the seeming paradox of his conjoined interest in subjectivity and transcendental philosophy. In Husserl's philosophy, the term "transcendental" refers not to Kant's a priori categories of experience (chapter 3, footnotes 3, 14) but to "*I-myself*" (1970: 98). "The whole transcendental set of problems circles around the relation of *this* [I-myself], my "I" . . . and my conscious life to the *world* of which I am conscious" (p. 98, emphasis in translation). The relation itself comes from "*direct experience* of the long-felt but constantly concealed dimensions of the 'transcender'" (p. 100, his emphasis). Whatever direct experience may be, social it is not.

The phenomenological appreciation of everyday life gained its access to the English-speaking world through Alfred Schutz. Richard J. Bernstein suggested two reasons for this (1978: 135–136). Schutz's interests centered less on subjective states and intentions than on the construction of an intersubjective world or society. In developing his interests, Schutz, who had emigrated from Germany to the United

States in the 1930s, drew on pragmatist themes in American Philosophy to support his phenomenology. I would add what Bernstein made clear, but not in the context of phenomenology's reception: Schutz downplayed Husserl's transcendental claims and subjectivist preoccupations (p. 141, but see pp. 158–159 on Schutz's "ambivalent attitude toward Husserl's project of a definitive transcendental philosophy and phenomenology").

On inspection, Schutz's phenomenology, for which Bernstein's characterization suffices better than any I might provide (1978: 135–156; see also Giddens 1976: 27–33, Shapiro 1981: 100–107), shows some cracks in its foundation (this is Bernstein's metaphor; see pp. 156–167). They are but versions of one problem. Constitution carries phenomenological freight on two tracks: the constitution of subjective meaning and the constitution of society. A constructivist approach presumably treats meaning and society as co-constituted. Here I quote Bernstein because I agree with him so completely:

> Still there are crucial ambiguities. Is our primary concern the a priori modes in which any transcendental ego constitutes a meaningful world? Are we dealing with the modes of constitution by which any wide-awake individual in the everyday world gives meaning to this world? Are we concerned with the ways whereby the group or class within which an individual functions influences the specific schemes of interpretation, forms of typification, and systems of relevance of his biologically determined situation? (1978: 160–161)

Bernstein went on to say that "an adequate phenomenology must deal with *all* these questions" (1978: 161, his emphasis). Indeed, I try to deal with them, one way or another, throughout this book. Schutz and his successors have not. Either they have performed detailed investigations of the co-constitution of meaning and society while steadfastly refusing to acknowledge Bernstein's evidently important questions. Here I have Harold Garfinckel's ethnomethodology in mind (1967, Heritage 1984). Or the co-constitution of meaning and society is collapsed into the nevertheless useful phrase, "the social construction of reality" (I use it on occasion in these pages), which Peter L. Berger and Thomas Luckmann popularized in their 1967 book of that title.

While Berger and Luckmann broached some of Bernstein's questions, "at best they made some important preliminary distinctions, rather than developing an adequate conceptual scheme" (Bernstein 1978: 255 n. 49). Because any unqualified reference to "reality" papers over the tension between the constitution of meaning and of society, it tolerates a bias in favor of one over the other. If only by their omissions, Berger and Luckmann favored the constitution of meaning. Yet Berger and Luckmann's sketchy presentation can hardly be blamed for the extent to which a useful phrase has become a cliché, an overworked excuse to say nothing further.

Giddens is another exception to the general proposition that social theorists with constructivist inclinations have failed to defend this position methodically. No less exceptional is the sophistication of Giddens' social theory and the care with which he has placed it in the context of social theory's major traditions. Two such traditions are fundamental for Giddens. One is positivist, the other interpretive; the first represented by structuralism and functionalism, the second by hermeneutics, "the art of textual interpretation" (Dallmayr and McCarthy 1977: 285; see pp. 285–365 for a useful introduction), and phenomenology. The second also includes followers of Wittgenstein (Giddens 1982: 31–32, 1984: 21–23).

In Giddens' map of social theory, these two traditions are diametrically opposed in crucial respects. The first takes a "naturalistic standpoint" and is "inclined toward objectivism" (1984: 1). Consequently, it finds no fundamental difference between natural and social science. As the very terms "functionalism" and "structuralism" suggest, this tradition emphasizes "the pre-eminence of the social whole over its individual parts (i.e., its constituent actors, human subjects)" (p. 1). By contrast, the second tradition fixes on the human subject.

> Subjectivity is the preconstituted centre of the experience of culture and history and as such provides the basic foundations of the social or human sciences. Outside the realm of subjective experience, and alien to it, lies the material world, governed by impersonal relations of cause and effect. . . . If interpretative sociologies are founded, as it were, upon an imperialism of the subject, functionalism and structuralism propose an imperialism of the social object (pp. 1–2).

Giddens' construction of the situation in social theory bears little resemblance to the situation typically presented in discussions of theory in International Relations and, for that matter, Political Science. Theory in International Relations would seem to be dominated by a different polarity (compare Singer 1961, Wendt 1987a: 340–349). One position takes an objectivist stance but emphasizes the preeminence of the individual. It does so by attributing to the individual an ability to objectivize her circumstances as a series of choices to which she responds rationally. She always chooses the alternative that, to the best of her (generally deeply flawed) knowledge, will secure the outcome she prefers.[14] The other position also takes an objectivist stance but places the social whole over individuals. It is indeed Giddens' first tradition, represented by structuralism and functionalism. International Relations simply has no name for, or experience with, Giddens' second tradition.

It would seem that Giddens has collapsed two sets of polarities, one epistemological and the other ontological. The objectivist-subjectivist polarity is epistemological, the individualist-collectivist polarity ontological. Quite properly Giddens felt that the usual practice is to identify only the first polarity (1984: 2). But in identifying the second as well, he failed to keep it separate from the first. Each is an independent ground for serious disagreement among social theorists. To acknowledge this allows the construction of a four-cell matrix of general possibilities for social theory.

Giddens' work shows ample awareness of poststructuralist and social choice orientations. He has been willing to draw from both without acknowledging either as having the foundational properties of hermeneutics and phenomenology or functionalism and structuralism. This is a mistake. All those social theorists who turn to

---

14. This position is occupied by scholars who are otherwise opposed on most substantive and methodological issues. On one side are those drawing from the largely axiomatized theory of social choice, in which rational actors act to secure preferred outcomes under externally fixed constraints. On the other side are those drawing from an experimental tradition that identifies distortions in perception, limits to knowledge, and internal impediments to action, and attributes them to the complexities of the human mind. The first takes individual rationality as a given and proceeds deductively; the second starts with behavior more or less approximating the requirements of rationality and proceeds inductively. Respective disciplinary allegiances are obvious (see also Hogarth and Reder 1987).

FIGURE 1-1

SOCIAL THEORIES: GENERAL POSSIBILITIES

EPISTEMOLOGICAL

ONTOLOGICAL	Subjectivist	Objectivist
Individual	hermeneutics, phenomenology	social choice
Collective	poststructuralism	functionalism structuralism

cognitive Psychology or liberal Economics for the model of theory to apply to society at large are effectively dismissed. In the case of International Relations, this means chiefly those who are concerned with decision-making.

Poststructuralism presents a more difficult situation. Insofar as deconstruction prevails, all foundations are repudiated. Insofar as genealogy prevails, histories result — at Foucault's instance, histories of madness, medical care, incarceration, sexuality. One might call them histories of collectively manifest subjective experience. Such histories as these do not exist as yet for international relations, although work undertaken by Karl W. Deutsch and associates on the history of national identity and state formation in the North Atlantic area (1957) comes closest. Curiously, Giddens' work on the history of violence in the making of the national states of Europe (1985) is more conventionally functionalist, despite Foucault's influence on substantive matters.

Giddens unduly simplified the situation in social theory by presenting it as two grand traditions in opposition. He did so to "put an end to each of these empire-building endeavours" (1984: 2). I would heartily endorse this position. If I am right though to replace Giddens' single polarity with two independent polarities, one epistemological and the other ontological, in order to produce four "imperial" possibilities, I should also note that the job of ending competition among them is all the harder.

Giddens has proposed his own theory to bridge subjectivist individualism and objectivist collectivism, as I would call his polar positions. In my reconstruction of the situation, Giddens' theory must operate on two axes — epistemological and ontological — in order to bridge four positions. To put the matter somewhat differently, Giddens has refused to position himself in an existing theory tradition. Instead he would operate exclusively in the domain of the relations of positions. To the extent that specifying a theory means to occupy a position, then he placed his theory above any of those upon whose relations it depends so that he could draw from them as he saw fit.

Giddens has named his theory "the theory of structuration" (1979: 69–73; 1981: 26–29; 1982: 7–11; 1984: 1–40).

> The basic domain of study of the social sciences, according to the theory of structuration, is neither the experience of the individual actor, nor the existence of any form of social totality, but social practices ordered across space and time. Human social activities, like some reproducing items in nature, are recursive. That is to say, they are not brought into being by social actors but continually recreated by them via the very means whereby they express themselves *as* actors. In and through their activities agents reproduce the conditions that make these activities possible (1984: 2).

So described, Giddens' project is to develop what I would call constructivist social theory. "In the theory of structuration, I argue that neither subject (human agent) nor object ('society' or social institutions) should be regarded as having primacy. *Each is constituted in and through recurrent practices*"[15] (1982: 8; his emphasis).

Does this theory build a four-way bridge across existing traditions of social theory? The question is more easily asked than answered, because Giddens required of himself only a two-way bridge between

---

15. The term "structuration" is itself a problematic choice for Giddens. It would seem to suggest that the emphasis is on processes relating to structures as fixed points of reference and thus a tilt toward the objectivist pole. Yet Giddens ended the passage just quoted by claiming for himself a "hermeneutic starting point . . ." (1984: 3). Giddens' treatment of structure, as difficult as it is distinctive, is intended to prevent such a tilt. "Structures exist paradigmatically, as any abstract

human agent and social object. Nonetheless, an inventory of some of his central propositions supports an affirmative answer. To start with the upper-left cell of the matrix presented in figure 1-1, Giddens has accepted a proposition dear to many who are interpretively oriented (but not all; see I. Cohen 1987: 293–295). Rules make social life intelligible to those participating in it. To paraphrase Giddens (1984: 1–2), human beings cannot survive on genetically coded programs. They need cognitive skills. Rules permit them the requisite knowledgeability for survival, which simultaneously provides their lives with subjective meaning. Social reality is the result.

Turning to the upper-right cell, Giddens has insisted that human beings are competent agents. They know what they are doing when they follow rules — they choose to follow a rule or not depending on their assessment of the consequences of either choice.

> Practical consciousness consists of knowing the rules and the tactics whereby daily social life is constituted and reconstituted across time and space. Social actors can be wrong some of the time about what these rules and tactics might be. . . . But if there is any continuity to social life at all, most actors must be right most of the time; that is to say, they know what they are doing, and they successfully communicate their knowledge (1984: 90).

Social choice theorists would accept Giddens' demonstration that most such knowledge is not articulated as such by agents (pp. 41–92); Giddens would agree with social choice theorists that an observer can specify systematically the rules and conditions of action such that any agent may be said to have acted "rationally."

The lower-left cell in figure 1-1 provides a home for a proposition conspicuously associated with Foucault. It is to be found throughout Giddens' recent work (1979: 88–101, 1981: 49–63, 1984: 14–16,

---

set of differences, temporally present only in their instantiation, in the constituting moment of social systems" (1979: 65); structures themselves can have only a "virtual existence" (p. 63). It follows then that structure cannot occupy fixed points of reference and have consequences. I detect a retreat in Giddens' most recent work from a conception of structure as a "virtual order of differences" (p. 64), with its debt to Derrida's preoccupation with *différance* (pp. 33–38), in favor of a concretized rendition, to be examined below. This gain in intelligibility necessarily risks objectivizing "structure" and thus "structuration."

256–262, 1985a: 7–17). Human agents author rules and deploy resources in accordance with those rules so as to secure and ensconce advantages over other agents. Their differential success produces asymmetries in the ability of agents to control the actions of other agents in time and space as well as the possibility that disadvantaged but competent agents can subvert or reverse such asymmetries.

For all his reservations about functionalism and structuralism, Giddens has also affirmed the proposition, belonging in the lower-right cell, that social life exhibits coherence. Not only do human agents produce social life, characteristically rule-oriented, rational behavior reproduces it with such consistency that it takes on objective properties. Social systems, and the asymmetries they entail, are accepted as real (1984: 331–332). The actions of particular agents are generally unlikely to affect decisively the continuing production of a coherent social reality. Agents know this. They live in social reality, which exists for them in its facticity.

One further proposition is necessary to secure Giddens' bridgework. Material conditions matter. The relation of rules to resources presupposes at least some control over material conditions; practical consciousness takes into account material conditions as well as socially constructed rules. The former limits or enables control through the latter depending on circumstances made intelligible by taking rules and resources into consideration.

None of the four traditions to be bridged requires or proscribes the proposition that material conditions matter. It does leak into their most influential formulations when rules, agents, power or structures are granted content or achieve historicity. It is little acknowledged in hermeneutics and phenomenology, with their tendency toward solipsism. It is relegated to a background condition in most poststructuralist and functionalist histories, and it falls before the contentless formulations of some structuralists. The proposition that material conditions matter intrudes on social choice theory hardly at all.

For Giddens, however, the proposition that material conditions matter is imperative. It anchors his four-way bridge in nature and history, not just as Wittgenstein's taken-for-granted backround reality, but as circumstances—immediate, intelligible, but not of our own choosing—in which human agents make history. Here of course I have paraphrased Karl Marx's "celebrated and oft-quoted phrase" (quoting Giddens 1984: xxi) from *The Eighteenth Brumaire of Louis Bonaparte* (1954b: 10) to the effect that people make history but not "under circumstances chosen by themselves, . . ." Giddens went so far as to describe his major statement of his position (1984: xxi) as "an extended reflection" on this remark of Marx's. Indeed, Giddens has committed much of his attention to the reformulation of historical materialism (1981, 1985a) to keep the theory of structuration from floating off its moorings.

Clearly the theory of structuration is notable in its propositional scope. But does the theory lock its diverse concerns together sufficiently that Giddens can make higher order statements not restricted to one or another propositional domains represented by the separate traditions of social theory? Can Giddens' propositional structure bear the weight of his claims for it? Giddens' own approach to this sort of question starts by replacing dualities necessary to the standing divisions of social theory—subject, object; agent, structure—with what he has called a duality of structure, but which he has explicated as a duality of structures and of systems.

The duality of structures takes "rules and resources" to be "organized as properties of social systems." The duality of systems takes "reproduced relations between actors or collectivities" to be "organized as regular social practices" (1984: 25). Structures lack subject and are "out of time and place . . . ." Systems depend on "the situated activities of human agents" but have no place, in their own terms, for rules and resources. The problem is connecting the transformation of relations effectuated through rules and resources with the reproduction of relations as regular social practices. The solution is structuration, defined as the "[c]onditions governing the continuity or transmutation of structures, and therefore the reproduction of social systems" (p. 25).

Everything hinges on those governing conditions. What are they? Giddens could have been more forthcoming on this point. I think, however, the answer lies in the proposition that "the structural properties of social systems are both medium and outcome of the practices they recursively organize" (p. 25). This is his definition of the "duality of structure," which is actually a double-duality, for it spans the duality of structures, understood by reference to the transformation of relations, and of systems, understood by reference to reproduced relations.

What unites these two dualities is recursion, the propensity of knowledgeable agents to refer to their own or others' past and anticipated actions in deciding how to act: They engage in "reflexive self-regulation" (Giddens 1979: 78; see generally pp. 73–81). Giddens used the term "organized" as a hinge for both the dualities of structures and of systems. In characterizing what I have called the double-duality upon which structuration depends, Giddens took this hinge and added to it the property of being recursive. Organization presupposes recursion and therefore cannot be its medium. Only rules can.

Giddens defined rules "as techniques or generalizable procedures applied to the enactment/reproduction of social practices" (1984: 21). Furthermore, "all rules are inherently transformational" (p. 17). Rules are fundamental both to structures and to systems and, by virtue of their "generalizable" character, lend recursion to the dualities of structures and of systems. It would follow from his treatment that rules must always be constitutive (that is, transformative) and regulative (that is, reproductive). Giddens has quite explicitly, and correctly, said just this (1979: 66). In short, rules enable Giddens to traverse each of his dualities. He should have deleted all reference to organization in this context, however, because that term presupposes rules, structures, and systems already in place. If recursion is the key conceptually, then rules are the key operationally.

Whether Giddens' propositional structure can carry the load he has assigned to it evidently depends on the answer to a further question. Has Giddens a sufficiently well-developed conception of rule to carry the theory of structuration? I think not. His inclination is to return to the very distinction which his and any constructivist social theory must repudiate — the distinction between constitutive and regulative types of rules. Consider Giddens' response to the charge (Callinicos 1985) of being "strongly influenced by Wittgenstein's *Philosophical Investigations* in my 'fondness' for the notion of 'rule,' which is true" (1985b: 169).

> I do not regard social practices as "rule-governed," or as "grounded in rules"; neither do I hold that courses of action can be "determined by rules." In speaking about structure as rules (forget-

ting for the moment about resources) I mean to get at two elements recursively involved in all social practices: codes of meaning or signification and normative sanctions (1985b: 169; see also 1984: 19–20).

Giddens put distance between his theory and Winch's interpretation of Wittgenstein by reverting to the conventional view that rules function recursively in either of two ways: by constituting meaning or imposing costs on conduct contrary to what their content indicates. Giddens was undoubtedly right to distance himself from Winch. While I do not find his reading of Wittgenstein to be persuasive — Wittgenstein saw rules as "aspects of *praxis*" (1984: 21), the last term having a specifically social meaning — I do agree that this position, even if it is not Wittgenstein's, is the necessary starting point for a constructivist social theory. The problem comes from the duality of signification and sanction, which slips too easily into an unwarranted discrimination between constitution and regulation.

Giddens forgot about resources "for the moment." Yet his discussion of resources points to something he never achieved in addressing rules as such. This is the possibility of identifying categories of rules. In Giddens' system of definitions, rules make structures, and resources make them "structures of domination" (1984: 258). Giddens has consistently divided resources into two types — allocative and authoritative (1979: 100–101, 1981: 47, 1984; 258–262, 1985a: 7–8, 13–14). These terms are all too familiar, inasmuch as they conventionally distinguish market and directed economies, and regrettably, to the extent they resonate with the duality of constitutive and regulative rules.[16] On examination, his list of allocative resources — material features of the environment, means of material production, and artifacts of production — identifies the types of material conditions implicated in the social construction of reality. His parallel list of authoritative resources — organization of social space-time, or-

---

16. All resources must be subject to allocation if they are to fit the meaning of the term. Allocation may appear to be lacking authorship, as in a market, but this ignores the authority of rules constituting and regulating the market such that the allocation of resources is neither uniform nor random. Chapters 2, 6, and 8 consider the related illusions of authorless rules and unruled allocation.

ganization of human beings in mutual association, and organization of life chances—actually describes categories of rules.[17]

Because rules are necessary for material conditions to be identified as such for social purposes, and rules cannot organize human endeavor unless they are somehow related to material conditions, both lists have to do with rules *and* resources. Yet analytically their discrimination is useful. Rules are the social component, resources the material component in all human endeavor. Giddens argued that resources are not fixed; "they form the media and the expandable character of power . . . " (1984: 258). This is not put well. Resources are nothing until mobilized through rules, rules are nothing until matched to resources to effectuate rule.[18]

Giddens has provided us with a scheme for categorizing rules that is the more persuasive because it is related to discriminant material conditions, even if those conditions are constituted as different categories through the application of rules. In the next chapter, I present a scheme for sorting rules which also has three categories. I believe my categories, for which a different rationale is provided, correspond to Giddens' resource/rules categories. I would describe Giddens' three categories as follows: (1) The category of existence and the constitution/regulation of its meaning in coordination of space and time. (2) The category of material control and the constitution/regulation of modalities of control. (3) The category of discretionary endeavor, agreement, and exchange, coupled to the constitution/regulation of agency and opportunity.

If rules are needed to allocate resources, and rules constitute a resource themselves because of the "authoritative" way they constitute and regulate other resources, the theory of structuration maintains its constructivist premises and still honors the proposition that material conditions matter. Criticism to the effect that Giddens cannot have it both ways (Callinicos 1985) misses the mark. Giddens never professed to be the usual sort of historical materialist. It is true that "his is a remarkably economic conception of practice" (p. 140),

---

17. These lists of resources are abridged from somewhat longer definitions presented in tabular form by Giddens (1984: 258) but use only his words.

18. Giddens appears not to have used the term "rule," as opposed to "rules," until quite recently. Domination is a condition of control; rule is a stable form of control (1985a: 9). See chapter 6 below for an extended discussion of rule and related terms.

if by that is meant that rules and resources substitute for nature and history. Giddens' project is precisely to show that nature and history are not some objective reality upon which human beings act. At best these are misleading labels for the rules and resources human beings constitute by their actions, even as they are constituted, and their actions regulated, by rules and resources.

I offer a rather different criticism of Giddens' theory in these pages. Giddens could strengthen his constructivism by clarifying the relation of resources to rules in the three categories of human activity he has identified exclusively (and wrongly) in terms of resources. To do so Giddens would have to pay a great deal more attention to rules than he has so far. Or, to put the matter somewhat differently, Giddens would have to leave the congenial domain marked out by Wittgenstein in order to give rules the content they need for constructivist purposes. To identify categories of rules is to find their content, not in any specific sense, rule by rule, but in the characteristic ways in which human beings, in constituting themselves as such, relate material conditions to the conditions of rule that mark all societies.

2

LAW AND LANGUAGE

In presenting the case for a constructivist view of reality as necessarily, but not exclusively, social, I tried to bring out the importance of rules for any such view. When I turned to social theory compatible with constructivism, Anthony Giddens' work being exemplary, I tried again to show the central position of rules. I determined, however, that neither Philosophers following Ludwig Wittgenstein nor Giddens as a social theorist have said enough about rules as such for us to grasp fully the ways in which rules make reality social.

One must look elsewhere. Two possibilities come to mind. One is law, which is a discipline constituted on the premise that certain rules — rules of law — systematically link individual human conduct and society. People make rules, rules make society, society's rules make people conduct themselves in specified ways. On examination, however, I find that legal theory is limited by a narrow conception of what rules are and do, and recent efforts to escape this straightjacket have been confused.

Philosophers working with language, though not in Wittgenstein's terms, are a second possibility. A very few of them have had an interest in rules and their properties. Inasmuch as they tend to avoid theory and take society as given, their contribution, though it goes beyond legal theory's, is also limited. I make an exception for speech act theory, which yields an inclusive set of categories into which all rules can be sorted. These categories identify three, and only three, distinct ways in which rules are jointly constitutive and regulative.

POSITIVISM

An objectivist epistemology underlies science and almost everything else associated with modernity. Positivism is its name. Disciplinary paradigms aspiring to science are positivist; this is as true for legal science as the social sciences. Indeed the prevailing paradigm constituting Law as a discipline is generally known as positivism. To minimize confusion I will call this paradigm "Legal Positivism," its proto-theory "legal positivism" or "positivist legal theory," and the philosophical stance behind them both "positivism."

H. L. A. Hart is widely acknowledged as Legal Positivism's ablest contemporary exponent. His reconstruction of positivist legal theory, no less than earlier versions, depends on "the simple contention that it is in no sense a necessary truth that laws reproduce or satisfy certain demands of morality" (1961: 181-182; see generally pp. 181-189). This one contention encodes the constitutive history of Legal Positivism, which emerged two centuries ago as an answer to the then prevailing paradigm of Natural Law.

For naturalists, rules obtained in social relations derive from circumstances which are necessary, inalterable — given in or by nature — and available to us through reflection, revelation or moral awareness, as privileged knowledge. Thus there can be no difference between what rules should say and what they do say, just as there is no difference between what we should do and must do. Rules are laws or not rules at all. As with any paradigm, this one supplies puzzles: Why do reasonable, moral people disagree on what nature decrees? Who decides? Must we follow rules we think are unreasonable or immoral? What is nature's remedy for disregard of its rules?

Naturalists solved their puzzles with ever more ingenuity, but less and less credibility, as positivism and the scientific attitude overtook Western thought. Legal Positivism stipulated a different set of connections for nature, morality, and rules relating to human conduct. Nature exists as a matter of fact. Rules exist only because people make them up and then accord them facticity. There is no law but "positive law." Although the distinction between nature and convention goes back to the Sophists and the alignment of justice with nature to Plato (Manley 1980: 25-28), positivism draws the line differently. It assigns morality to the realm of convention and not of nature. Rules reflect moral considerations (for Sophists, opinions) that human beings will often enough construe as moral imperatives and cast as law.

Evidently Legal Positivism depends on a momentous shift in moral philosophy. Immanuel Kant was its herald. In the English-speaking world it triumphed with utilitarianism. Jeremy Bentham, a pioneer Legal Positivist and utilitarian, recommended a particular moral principle—his "utility principle" (quoted below, p. 194)—on grounds of its favorable consequences instead of its being privileged knowledge. Alternative principles are similarly framed; arguments are over consequences. Utilitarianism permits a plurality of moral possibilities—a moral relativism its critics equate with the denial of morality.

To think that moral considerations and social rules can never be more than the facts they are suggests an ontological shift as much as a shift in epistemology and ethics. Nature has its laws, like gravity and the inevitability of death, but their effect—the fact that they bind us—presents itself to us as a matter of fact. A falling object, a death: Each is a fact. Every fact, to qualify as such, must be a discrete, identifiable item, a positivity. If the things human beings do, like the things that happen to them, are facts, then these too must be positivities. To call them "things" says no less.[1]

The proposition that reality, natural and social, is populated with positivities is positivism's ontological correlate and science's methodological imperative. Insofar as it must be imposed on reality, the procedure for doing so is to break down that reality into discrete and distinguishable entities, each the same as some, but not all, of the others. Implicit in positivist ideas of concept formation and perfected by David Hume, this conventionalizing procedure disguises its constitutive character by alleging to discover reality's natural, positive constituents. Both natural and social reality appear to be natural by having been socially constructed the same way.

I return to the Humean procedure of conventionalizing reality in chapter 5. It is an ambiguous legacy for law and the social sciences, where objectivist epistemology and its moral implications are taken

---

1. "The first and most fundamental rule is: *Consider social facts as things.*" So said Emile Durkheim in his pioneering positivist rendition of *The Rules of Sociological Method* (1964: 14, his emphasis).

for granted in the name of science, yet individualist ontology (recalling Giddens' categories, as developed in the preceding chapter) is the subject of much contention. Along with the rest of the social sciences, Law as constituted by Legal Positivism has never settled between individualist and collectivist ontological positions. In this they show their common affiliation to liberalism

Individual human beings are (conventionalized as) agents — independent, goal-oriented, and resourceful. At the same time they are moral agents. They decide what they shall do, and they reflect on what they should do. Each operation as a positivity bears on the others in the same way natural positivities are related. Yet the result makes some kind of collective sense — it works as a whole. Positivist legal theory has those same agents ask, what laws do we want? Legal practice lets them decide what laws they shall have. Again the result is an operative whole. I would call it an especially cogent operative paradigm; generally it is called a legal order.

Beginning with Bentham, Legal Positivists have taken rules as having a consistent and immediately identifiable linguistic form, that of a command or imperative statement (Bentham 1948: 330–336). In their paradigm, then, rules always say what they do. They require behavior indicated in the content of imperative statements. Such rules transparently convey the wishes of those who issue them.

Note, however, that not all imperative statements are rules. "Bring me a glass of milk" is an imperative statement which I honor "as a rule," but I do so, in good utilitarian fashion, on a case-by-case basis. John Austin identified several species of command and restricted attention to those having general applicability.[2] They are the ones for which the important question is raised, do I have a standing obligation, independent of my utilitarian calculations in each instance, to honor them? The general position of Legal Positivists is that I do indeed have an obligation to honor at least some such rules. To the extent that obligation is positive (not metaphysical), those rules are *legal*.

Now we have a clear view of what positivist legal theory hopes

---

2. He improperly concluded that all such commands issue from a determinate lawgiver or sovereign (J. Austin 1954: 18–24, 133–135). See also Hart's reconstruction of Austin's position (1961: 18–76).

to explain: the basis for a specifically legal obligation. The theory takes us beyond the rule, and what it says, to the legal order. The existence of the legal order explains both the obligation attaching to that rule and the propensity for utilitarian calculators to follow it. The order has two defining properties. One is the competence to issue legal rules, and the other is the capacity to secure compliance with them. Inasmuch as I may well have the capacity to ensure that you will bring me a glass of milk if I demand it, the distinctive property of a legal order must be the first one.

Here positivist legal theory encounters a puzzle. If an order is legal, it must be so because the rules constituting it are legal. Yet such rules can only be legal if a prior legal order produces them. The result must be an infinite regress, which can be stopped only by introducing a primary agreement or learning process in a notional state of nature (social contract or Hume's conventions). The alternative is to argue that ultimately the legal character of the rule comes from the fact that it is complied with. Said otherwise, compliance precedes obligation, the former thereby giving rise to the latter.[3] Any such solution would seem to substitute circularity for regress: That rules work makes them law, that laws are legal makes them work.

Legal Positivism's proto-theory explains nothing. By stipulating that legal rules must be properly authorized and generally complied with—valid and effective (or efficacious), in Hans Kelsen's words (1945: 39–42, 1952: 412–415)—the proto-theory constitutes Law as a scholarly enterprise. It also tells those whose vocation is the positive law what rules count as such. Consider Austin's declaration that

[e]very positive law, or every law simply and strictly so called, is set by a sovereign person, or a sovereign body of persons, to a member or members of the independent political society wherein that person or body is sovereign or supreme. Or (chang-

---

3. The clearest example is Hans Kelsen's postulate of the "basic norm of international law"—"The states ought to behave as they customarily have behaved" (1952: 417–418)—the basis for which is that people do in fact behave this way. All other legal rules derive their obligatory character from this one because, Kelsen argued, the international legal order validates all other legal orders. Kelsen, who wrote extensively in German and English, was Legal Positivism's leading voice in the first half of this century.

ing the expression) it is set by a monarch, or sovereign number, to a person or persons in a state of subjection to its author (1954: 132).

One need merely inspect the set of social relations to which given rules pertain. Whenever relations of sovereign and subject are present, then these rules are legal and the set of relations a legal order. Austin's formula orients the stipulated relation between obligation and compliance to the needs of practice, but only on the assumption that detecting the locus of sovereignty or the evidence of subjection is never problematic.

For practitioners of legal craft and scholars alike, the coherence of their endeavors comes from a narrow construction of what is properly legal. Counted out are rules that seem to be law because an evidently legally authorized voice says so but are routinely disregarded. So are rules that cannot be traced to any such author but are routinely honored. A simple procedure for determining the positive law is an advantage, not a problem, for those who use it, and a tight and tidy conception of Law no less an advantage for scholars, so long as they all stick to the hard core of law. Ambiguous instances, in which legal pedigrees are irregular or compliance episodic, need be considered only if practitioners want something to argue with and scholars to puzzle over.

As a Legal Positivist strays farther from the hard core of law, more serious problems arise. In a social environment like that of international relations or the relations of a preliterate people, it is difficult to know what, if any, relations of authority are present. Ambiguity fosters an alarming uncertainty as to what is legal and, as we shall see, even raises the possibility that legality is a relative condition. The challenge offered by a puzzling class of rules — for example, are the rules pertaining to international relations legal or not? — has prompted numerous unconvincing accommodations in positivist legal theory. The possibility that legality is not what it seems to be poses a far greater challenge to legal theory. It calls into question the ontological presumption that rules at least in the hard core of law are positivities of a kind and thus the paradigmatic claim that law is a distinctive phenomenon — an operative paradigm — worthy of its own discipline.

THE LIMITS OF LEGAL THEORY

Legal Positivism, like so many of the paradigms constituting social science disciplines, has come to an impasse. Its proto-theory cannot explain anything about law and at the same time refers only to certain stipulated properties of law. The solution must be a revamping of legal theory so that it achieves explanatory capacity without sacrificing law's distinctiveness. If such a revamping is possible, the discipline would undergo reconstruction and a proper paradigm theory could eventuate.

None of this is new. As important movements earlier in this century, sociological jurisprudence and legal realism were both predicated on this line of thought. Orthodox Legal Positivists restricted efforts to broaden the theoretical domain of law. They clearly saw that saving legal positivism from regress or circularity raised the possibility that nothing distinctively legal would be left. If legal positivists were obstinate, then their challengers were ingenuous in thinking that they could propose a better theory of law and still have it be about law. Perhaps what they wanted cannot be constructed.

In the quest for bigger, better theory, sociological jurisprudence and legal realism turned to the positivism holding sway in the social sciences. Anthropologists and Sociologists reciprocated with an abiding interest in all those positivities to which law is conceivably relevant. These developments could not help but influence international legal theory, itself a longstanding but problematic branch of positivist legal theory. Given the conventional view of international relations and the assumptions of legal positivism, the very term "international law" is a virtual oxymoron. In the last thirty years scholars disproportionately from the United States have drawn freely from the social sciences to rid themselves of their most intractable and embarrassing problem: The subject of their concern and the theory purporting to account for its existence bear no plausible relation to each other. If the solution is a theory about law yet not of law — a theory rejecting Law's narrow construction of law — so be it. They would be social scientists.

At the extreme, those international legal scholars identifying with the social sciences were content to establish regularities in international conduct and explain their occurrence by reference to "psychological pressures" (Kratochwil 1984: 350). Obligation disappeared as an inconvenient concept or was transmuted into "shared expectations" and community policies.[4] A less extreme view found rules performing different functions for their users and, in a logical leap, for the "system" as a surviving, ordered entity.[5] Within this general position, diversity reigned. Inasmuch as all rules were seen as taking the same general form, independent of their function, recourse to particular rules told nothing about their particular functions. It seemed in other words that rules did not say what they did. Only the observer could say, and observers had no agreed method for sorting out the functional or systemic meaning of what they saw.

All too understandably functionalists were inclined to retain the legal positivist notion of law as a manifestation of the relation of sovereign and subject by seeing coercion and control as one functional category of law. This left all other functional possibilities to be grouped into a single, loosely defined category called the communications function (Coplin 1965). Thus the standard, though not invariable, functional arrangement was a dichotomy. Rules either control behavior or communicate intentions and perceptions. Rules in the latter category are at the edge of law, but what is determinative for legal standing is their function.

In either functional category, working rules are necessary to the system's survival, whether they appear to work, or are apparent at all, to system participants. Those rules which do not seem to be imperative to participants, but which are nonetheless a system imperative, appear indeterminate as to their individual obligation. Such indeterminacy may even spill over into the hard core of rules that are imperative for participants. This is because, practically speaking, the system does not fall when any given participant ignores a command and coercive instrumentalities are not available to assure compliance. Indeed enforcement is often an illusion, though perhaps a necessary one.

---

4. These are concepts favored by the New Haven school of configurative jurisprudence. For a representative sample of work to be found in this tradition, see McDougal and Reisman (1981). On the New Haven school's claims to science, see Young (1972).
5. See preeminently Richard A. Falk (1971). Falk took his position as intermediate between Kelsenian positivism and the New Haven school.

The high point for functionalism in international legal theory came, I believe, in 1974, when Gidon Gottlieb took the two categories of functional possibilities and restored the first to its historic position as a sufficient characterization, or model, of law — and constructed the second into an alternative model of law (1974: 363–364). The acceptance model, as he called the latter, is not then just a characterization of the functions of some rules (especially those of doubtful legality). It is a characterization of the function of all legal rules, which is to secure acceptance of their content.

In developing the acceptance model, Gottlieb started with policies. These are general statements of wish or intent, the content of which others are encouraged to accept. Sometimes acceptance is achieved by suggesting the likelihood of coercion. Nevertheless, "willingness to limit one's discretion," which acceptance connotes, implies a principled content (1974: 373). Legal rules are necessarily those policies that are both principled enough to secure willing acceptance and specific enough to provide guidance. In this view, rules do not have to say what they do, for this (again) is always the same. Their specific, principled content communicates plausible expectations that they will be followed.

Like its alternatives, the acceptance model purports to explain how legal rules work. The explanation for compliance is not legal obligation, however; it is a behavioral propensity, namely, "the resolve to make principled and consistent decisions wherever possible . . ." (1968: 369; see also pp. 373–374). Despite appearances, Gottlieb was not making an empirical assertion about human conduct. Regularities are not the point. Instead he inferred the propensity to follow rules from "reasoning procedures" and the "logic of choice"[6] (pp. 374–376). Legal reasoning is only possible when rules provide "a 'marked degree' of firmness of guidance," in turn requiring "specificity in language . . ." (1974: 371). How specific? Gottlieb had no way to say. Indeed he made a virtue of not being able to do so. "Here again there looms a vast undemarcated terrain between the legal and the political — but the more specific the guidance in a system becomes, the more specific the norms, the pol-

---

6. The latter phrase is actually the title of Gottlieb's book (1968) in which his argument and philosophical rationale are systematically presented.

icy goals and their application, the more 'legal' this system becomes"
(1974: 371–372).

Gottlieb's much-cited essay made functional categories intelligible in the language of law. His effort to replace an authority model with an acceptance model also gave a theoretical warrant to the notion that rules on the soft margins of law are law, even if these rules cannot be shown to have become legal through a specific validating or "legalizing" process. In the functionalist view, legal indeterminacy is a system trait, and it suffuses down, so to speak, to the particulars of situations where rules are always relevant but rarely determinative. In Gottlieb's reformulation, legal indeterminacy follows from the relation of rules to reasoning and the use of language.

Given the extraordinary growth of international actors, agreements and practices of certain legal standing, especially in international economic relations, positivist practitioners of legal craft happily embraced the notion of soft law. Accounts of such law are everywhere (for example: Carreau and others 1977, Seidl-Hohenveldern 1979). Theorists committed to legal positivism have responded with sharp hostility by proving that legal indeterminacy could not be reconciled with their theory of obligation (Bothe 1980, Weil 1983). Needless to say, Gottlieb had intended this very conclusion. Thus was achieved a stalemate. Legal positivists insisted in theory on a narrow construction of law and how it works but fell into a broader one in the practice of legal craft. For his part, Gottlieb insisted in theory on a broader view of the rules that matter, but failed to explain why some rules matter more than others.

Whatever the accomplishments of scientifically inclined international legal scholarship, its vogue has clearly passed in the last few years. Throughout the social sciences, the positivist project has faltered as paradigmatic limits are reached. Meanwhile, doubts about the ontological premises of functionalism and, more recently, those of positivist epistemology have come to the fore. In a curiously parallel development, the reemergence of naturalist ideas in the form of rights thinking has had a greater impact on positivism than the scientific disposition ever did.

Consider the stormy response (for example, M. Cohen 1984) to Ronald Dworkin (1977) when he attacked legal positivism by contending that certain rules — he called them legal principles — are incontrovertibly weightier than others. Yet legal principles are integral to the hard core of law and indispensable to legal order. Dworkin saw in legal positivism a defect of such proportions that only a paradigm-challenging solution would do. Indicatively his solution was a naturalist one.[7] The positivist moment, in all its realizations, may well be passing.

Even a cursory search of the current literature leaves the impression that international legal theory is directionless. Nevertheless, postpositivist currents in Philosophy and the social sciences have prompted at least two scholars to challenge positivist premises, as I do here. They are David Kennedy and Friedrich Kratochwil, whose otherwise very different efforts (1980, 1983) focus on discourse instead of rules. Such a focus allows them to concentrate on the uses to which law is put without having to settle the question, which rules are legal?

For Kennedy, law is used to expedite conflict resolution in settings given over to adversarial discourse. (1980: 386) If the process is successful, it results in "principled decision-making," and outcomes tend to have probative value in subsequent iterations of the process in similar settings. These outcomes are legal rules. Clearly Kennedy's implicit model for the use of law is a court or tribunal. Yet the principled decision-making and the invocation of earlier principled decisions in reaching new ones are activities which take place in a wide variety of settings. Some of them, like public assemblies and bureaux, are intentionally not adversarial. Are principled decisions taken in such settings legal rules? Kennedy cannot have said, even if the question had occurred to him.

For Kratochwil, the common element in the use of law is persuasion in circumstances "in which no logically compelling solution is possible" (1983: 43). Rules are persuasive to the extent they provide instrumental guidance and reflect moral considerations. We can infer from this that rules are legal when they are both specific and principled, as Gottlieb insisted, but not just because these properties are

---

7. "Taking rights seriously" (the title of his 1977 book) propelled Dworkin in a naturalist direction. His current conception of "law as integrity" initiates a solution constituting a third way between Natural Law and Legal Positivism (1986: 176–275), though more closely allied with the former than the latter (p. 263). This combined with Dworkin's current emphasis on interpretation suggests an affinity with constructivism (pp. 45–80).

present. Legality is a property bestowed on rules through rhetoric, or practical reasoning, by people who are professionally trained in putting specific, principled rules to persuasive use. Drawing analogies, invoking precedents, justifying claims, and weighing alternatives are among the familiar ways they do so. That persuasion works is what we mean when we say the law works.

Kratochwil noted that rhetoric depends on the audience. Although the model audience is that charged with hearing the pleas of adversaries, he identified the existence of another and intimated a third. Identified as an audience are those charged with the evaluation of persuasion at the "technical level" (his quotation marks), meaning bureaucrats (Kratochwil 1983: 43). He tended to minimize their relevance to law (contrary to what his strictures on specificity imply) but not their importance for a stable order. Only intimated to exist as an audience is the aware public which hears the rhetoric of persuasion on matters of high principle. While Kratochwil's attachment to specificity would seem to deny legal quality to rules invoked in this arena, he was content to discount them because, as rhetoric, they inhibit accommodation, which from a principled point of view is the only justification for persuasion.

Like Kennedy, Kratochwil settled too easily on adversarial arenas as paradigmatic for the use of legal rules. Then he equated the style of persuasion particular to this arena — at once specific and principled — with defining conditions for the legality of rules. Other arenas, with their modalities of reasoning with rules, are eliminated from consideration, and rules used in those arenas disqualified as legal. Nevertheless, Kratochwil's shift in emphasis to discourse and his explication of practical reasoning in public settings and for public purposes as the distinctive feature of law make a notable extension of Gottlieb's groundbreaking reconstruction of 1974.

Kratochwil also extended the flaws in Gottlieb's initiatives. Principles and rules of high specificity are treated as analytically separable, then conflated in order to create a uniformly operative model of law. Such a model ignores the diverse characteristics of rules ranging from principles to procedures that work and look like law, even though convention holds that they are not. At least Gottlieb acknowledged them. Kratochwil's very effort to improve on Gottlieb required that he not. Nor did Kennedy for similar reasons.

Kennedy and Kratochwil put rules in the context of their use in discourse. In doing so, they lifted the self-imposed limits of legal positivist theory. Nevertheless, they wrongly and unnecessarily discounted discourse about principles and procedures—they failed to see such discourse as truly legal. On the basis of these independent efforts, coming to the same unwarranted conclusion, I am convinced that systematic treatment of rules and their properties is indispensable to any legal theory seeking to overcome positivist limits, including postpositivist theories centered on discourse.[8]

PERFORMATIVE LANGUAGE

Ever since Austin, positivist legal theory defines "rule" as a special case of command. In Hart's reformulation, rules are "standing orders" (1961: 73). However defined, their existence is stipulated. Scholars influenced by the social sciences ignore rules for their effects, which are the regularities of conduct they sometimes mistake for rules. As I just demonstrated, Kennedy and Kratochwil lose sight of rules in pursuit of their uses. There is a common thread. Taken for granted is what must be investigated: that rules themselves are a matter of language.

The situation is quite the opposite in contemporary Philosophy. Take Max Black's influential analysis of rules (1962: 95–139).

> There seems to be a particularly intimate connection between a rule and the set of words by which the rule is stated. The relation between the word and its statement in words is not something external and contingent, as is the case in the relation between anything and its verbal designation: the rule is, in some way, constituted by its formulation. The same can be said, however, about a verdict, a promise, a command. . . .
>
> It does not follow, however, that a promise *must* be formu-

---

8. Nor would Kratochwil disagree. He has long evinced an interest in rules (1978: 45–66) and his current unpublished work (forthcoming) elaborates a conception of rules complementary to his position on rhetoric. Inasmuch as I choose to start with rules, my own discussion of rhetoric is deferred until chapter 4.

lated in words. We can and do talk about implied promises and promises that nobody has made or even thought about. So it is prima facie not absurd to inquire into the possibility of implicit rules (rules that nobody has formulated) — or rules that perhaps never will be stated (p. 100, Black's emphasis).

Rules are statements, or at least they must be capable of statement. Given the controversy over "private language" discussed in chapter 1 (footnote 12), prudence suggests adding the requirement that rules not stated must lend themselves to public statement. Black then identified two aspects of any "rule-formulation": (i) a description of a class of actions, possibly restricted to actions performed by a designated class of persons; and (ii) an indication whether that class of actions is required, forbidden, or allowed" (1962: 108).

In the way rules are stated they assist their users — those whose actions are described — in drawing inferences as to how they should act. For Black, rules are an "indication." In the same vein, Wittgenstein called rules "sign posts," Gilbert Ryle "inference-tickets," and Gottlieb "inference warrants" (Gottlieb 1968: 33–34; see generally Gottlieb's useful discussion, pp. 33–42). As we see in Black's list of indicated instructions, the emphasis on guidance broadens the Austinian imperative to include that which is permitted as well as that which is required or forbidden — a point not lost on Hart in refurbishing legal positivism (1961: 26–43).

The kinds of inferences one might draw — I must, must not; may, need not; should, should not — broadly suggest senses in which the word "rule" is used. Black identified three such "senses" (his term) to be found in ordinary language (1962: 109–115). These are rules in the sense of regulations, by which he meant imperative rules or standing orders, rules in the sense of instructions or directions, and rules in the sense of precepts. The difference between rules like these and a fourth sense of rule — rules in the sense of principles, like rules of logic, laws of nature and statistical regularities — is that in the latter case "the use of imperative language or 'modal' words ('shall,' 'must,' 'may,' and the like) is clearly unfitting" (p. 113). Only rules in the first three senses are social rules. As such they must be capable of performance. They "must be about a kind of thing that *human beings* can do" (p. 107, his emphasis).

Improperly, I think, Black held that rules offering instruction—

rules indicating how to achieve an end—"have neither authors nor histories" (1962: 110). Certainly this is true of rules in the fourth sense. Statements always have authors, and any rule, in whatever sense, must be stated or statable. But instructions are social, even if they state conditions not subject to human control. This is because people still have discretion as to whether, under such conditions, some end is worth achieving. Take one of Black's examples: "Do not plant tomatoes until after the first frost" (p. 110). People decide on the action indicated, or not, and bear the consequences. The rule registers a long history of such decisions and thus has innumerable authors. People never decide when the first frost will be, even if they formulate a statistical regularity and predict a likely occurrence.

Although social rules necessarily have authors and histories, neither need to be known for rules to work as such. In the example just given, one would normally call the rule "customary," thereby acknowledging a long history, but denying any knowledge of it. In the Austinian view, the author's wish or will (typically a single author— whoever or whatever is sovereign) is contained in what the rule states and conveyed in the imperative form of its statement, so that nothing further need be said about the author. In Black's broadened view of rules, which accepts a wider range of inferences, authors' intentions are still contained and conveyed in the way rules are stated.[9]

In both instances we know, or can surmise, all we need to know— what the rule is about and what our relation to it is—from the rule alone. This is straightforward enough in the Austinian instance, because a rule can have only one function, which is to convey an imperative. But what of the broader view, which suggests, at least to me, that rules perform different but related functions? The problem is knowing when a rule commands a particular response to its content or merely commends it.

Modal auxiliaries do not tell enough. They are notoriously variable even within languages. Recourse to the context of a given rule's use helps resolve these ambiguities, but introduces others. Context

---

9. Reliance on "conduit" metaphors—words for containing and conveying—pervades conceptual language about language (Lakoff and Johnson 1980: 10–13). Inevitably such metaphors also dominate conceptual language about rules.

tends to invade the rule's content even as it aids in clarifying the rule's function, and the rule begins to lose its distinctive position in offering guidance. Carried very far in the search for what a rule "really" says, recourse to context tends to support either a radically objectivist position that rules are nothing more than regularities of conduct, unrelated to authors' intentions, or an equally radical subjectivist position that there are only authors' intentions and thus rules of unique content for everything that happens. Both positions have the effect of denying rules a social character.

To solve the problem of knowing a rule's function, one must take a step that Black was unwilling to. He felt that the several senses of rule are points on a "continuum of cases" (1962: 123). The needed step is to consider these senses as discrete because they are independent functional categories. One knows a rule's function by identifying its sense. Conversely one knows a rule's sense by identifying its function.

Here again the trick is to avoid regress or circularity. Obviously the function of rules in an "instruction sense" is to instruct—sense and function are strictly co-constitutive. So we must look for additional grounds for constituting Black's three senses of social rule as independent functional categories. We also want to know if Black somehow overlooked a sense of rule. The point is to establish—insofar as anything constructed is ever established in this sense—that Black's three senses of social rule are the only possible ones, indeed that they are inclusive functional categories.

I believe that some fairly recent developments in the philosophy of language provide independent support for the three functional categories I attribute to Black. I have in mind the theory of speech acts, the relevance of which is immediately evident if we substitute "speakers" for the "authors" of the preceding discussion. The theory (more properly, it is a codificatory paradigm) systematically relates speakers' (authors') intentions to linguistic activity. Hearers make (correct) inferences as to speakers' intentions by noting the illocutionary force as well as propositional content of (well-formed) utterances. Illocutionary force refers to the part of speech constituting an action of social consequence. By fixing "the communicative function of content uttered" (Habermas 1979: 34; see further pp. 59–65), it turns words into deeds.

To invoke some property of language called illocutionary force is
indeed to leave behind the longstanding view, on which positivism
depends, that the (only) function of language is to represent reality.
The distinctive claim of the theory of speech acts is that language
is both representative and performative. People use words to represent deeds and they can use words, and words alone, to perform
deeds. Clearly the theory of speech acts comports with the constructivist premises of this book and warrants any emphasis on social
rules, and not just public rules of language, in the constitution of
reality.

J. L. Austin was first to recognize the performative aspect of language for what it is (1963). He and other Philosophers working in
the ordinary language tradition were attracted to particular cases
and not the general features of language use.[10] Only with John Searle
(1969) did consideration of speech acts locate itself in a codificatory
paradigm. Searle's starting point is both familiar and, for our purposes, appropriate. "Speaking a language is engaging in a (highly
complex) rule-governed form of behavior"[11] (1969: 12). Searle brought
speech acts to the door of social theory.

To my knowledge, only one social theorist, Jürgen Habermas,
has grasped the importance of speech act theory and explored its implications with any care. In his view, "the illocutionary lexicon is,
as it were, the sectional plane in which language and institutional
order of society interpenetrate" (1984: 321). My efforts parallel Habermas' in a number of respects, but also depart from his, just as our objectives in developing speech act theory diverge. While I hope to

---

10. Because Austin was against Philosophy as then constituted, I am tempted to call
    him a philosopher, not Philosopher. His procedure was to select cases of ordinary
    language use that are exemplary in their complexity. Disciplinary paradigms treat
    exemplars (examples of a theory at work) and puzzles (problems for a theory to
    address) as necessarily different. Austin disregarded theory and saw all worthy
    examples as puzzling. See as an example his famous exposition on excuses (1964)
    and their relation to accidents, mistakes and the like.
11. Not everyone approaches speech acts this way. An alternative uses intentionalist
    semantics to simplify the analysis of speech acts by eliminating rules. It succeeds
    by (I would say, suffers from) defining rules in a naively limited way (Bach and
    Harnish 1979).

ground functional categories of rules in certain properties of language, he has sought a theory of uncoerced communicative competence.[12]

We need now to locate illocutionary acts in the scheme of speech acts first worked out by Austin and orienting all subsequent discussions (a second Austinian tradition, though I will not call it that to avoid confusion). Habermas has provided a helpful summary (1984: 288–289):

> Through *locutionary* acts the speaker expresses states of affairs; he says something. Through *illocutionary acts* the speaker performs an action in saying something. The illocutionary role establishes the mode of a sentence . . . employed as a statement, promise, command, avowal, or the like. Under standard conditions, the mode is expressed by means of a performative verb in the first person present; the action meaning can be seen particularly in the fact that "hereby" can be added to the illocutionary component of the speech act: "I hereby promise you (command you, confess to you) that [propositional content— state of affairs]." Finally, through *perlocutionary acts* the speaker produces an effect upon the hearer. By carrying out a speech he brings about something in the world. Thus the three acts that Austin distinguishes can be characterized in the following catch-phrases: to say *something,* to act *in* saying something, to bring about something *through* acting in saying something.

By following rules on forming sentences, any speaker makes it possible for any hearer to know what the former intends. Observe that rules for establishing illocutionary force, by enabling a sentence to take the form, I hereby act by using some rule-specified word for action, produce sentences that are themselves in the form of rules. That is to say, these sentences require or permit an inference about their speakers' intentions. Though all rules have an illocutionary

---

12. Habermas has argued that such a theory, based on the "paradigm of linguistic philosophy" which is replacing the representational view of language, would reverse the centuries-long growth of instrumental reason as the sine qua non of rationality and constitute what I would call an operative paradigm for society (1984: 386–399.)

component, it is not true that all sentences endowed with illocution-ary force are rules. At best we can say that they are rule-candidates.

Whether such rule-candidates become rules depends on their re-ception. If the hearer understands the intentions of the speaker, and so indicates with an affirmative, then she "accepts a speech act offer and grounds an agreement: this agreement concerns the *content of the utterance* on the one hand, and on the other hand, certain *guarantees immanent to speech acts* and certain *obligations relevant to the sequel of interaction*" (Habermas 1984: 296, emphasis on original). Habermas considered this, as do I, "a weak normative bond . . ." (p. 304; see also 1979: 62–63). Though weak, it is never-theless decisive in giving speech acts with an illocutionary compo-nent the function as well as the form of a rule. To say that norma-tively is weak means it is immanent in the speech act and, therefore, confined to the speaker and hearer.

One might object that normativity thus conferred is insufficient to establish a rule because the latter must refer to a "class of actions" (Black 1962: 108, as quoted above), which a single interaction is not. The objection need not present Habermas with difficulty, because he called the result of the interaction a "norm," which may be in-dividual and thus not a rule (compare chapter 4, footnote 2). In my case, to avoid trouble I should say that normativity is confined to the initiating interaction of speaker and hearer *and* all subsequent interactions that they accept as belonging to the class of interactions for which their initiating interaction is exemplary. Perhaps this is what Habermas meant by "the sequel of interaction."

Such weak normativity explains how instructions can be rules. If I hereby state that X counts as Y, and you accept this statement as operative between us, without qualifications (which, if offered, I may accept in turn), then that statement rules our intersubjective situation a propos the relation of X to Y. We can always agree to change a rule; others can join in the agreement; it may become gen-erally accepted. Were such to happen, through the play of additional speech acts with complementary illocutionary force, we speak of a convention emerging. Conventions are no less weak normatively speaking than the original agreement — normativity is immanent in each complementary speech act — but it is wider because more speak-ers and hearers are involved.

Conventions once established in this fashion begin to substitute for new sets of agreements. Rather than saying, I hereby state that X counts as Y, I am inclined to say, it is the convention that X counts as Y, don't you agree? Eventually I feel no obligation to seek your agreement; I merely invoke the convention. We may say that conventions have become institutionalized and, in this process, acquire additional normativity, that is, they generate expectations not dependent on fresh agreement. Institutionalized conventions are not more rule-like for being normatively stronger. They are merely more visible and harder to ignore. Because they are normatively stronger, it is more difficult to change the content of the instruction contained in the convention, but it is not impossible.

A special case of rules in the instruction sense has X count as Y, where Y is a value. These are principles, though not in Black's sense of the term. Consider the statement, nice guys, as a rule, finish last. If being a nice person or finishing last is asserted to have a value, good or bad, the instruction is not merely to avoid finishing last, don't be nice. The full reading is: Success is better than niceness, so don't be nice and avoid finishing last.

Institutionalization expedites the assignment of value to and through rules offering instruction. That principles tend to be well-institutionalized helps to explain the impression that they stand apart from other instructions in their normative power. Nevertheless, their ruleness, on which any normativity hinges, begins in speech. "The moral of this is chastening, even disturbing: institutions are no more than the (temporary) effects of speech act agreements, and they are as fragile as the decision, always capable of being revoked, to abide by them." I would add to this acute observation by Stanley Fish (1980: 213) that institutionalization and valuation serve to inhibit casual revocation (compare pp. 318–321).

For convenience I have proceeded with just one sense of rule, rules that instruct. I believe they constitute a functional category of rules, which I will hereinafter call instruction-rules. Some writers have denied that instructions and conventions are rules at all (for example, Bach and Harnish 1979: 108–110, 120–127). Others, like Habermas, have acknowledged their normativity but not their regulative character (1979: 54–55, 1984: 303–305). Such denials recall the forced distinction between constitutive and regulative rules. A constructivist always sees this distinction as arbitrary and unhelpful. Nothing in speech act theory supports it. The preceding remarks show that when assertive speech acts are successful (their reception confirmed, with normativity attaching), they produce rules, however fragile their constitution and tenuous their normativity. When any such rule becomes a convention, constitution of the rule by speech acts accepting its status as a rule begins to supplant its constitution by the repetition of speech acts with complementary propositional content. Then the rule is normatively stronger, its regulative character supporting its independent constitution, and conversely. The change in condition is signified by a change in nomenclature: constitution becomes institution.

All social rules, and not just instruction-rules, are necessarily and simultaneously constitutive and regulative. If in producing instruction-rules assertive speech acts account for both their constitutive and regulative character, at least in the last instance, one might wonder if all speech acts have this effect, or only those making assertions. Here we should recall that speech acts make language performative. By making an assertion, one does something social, at least if one's utterance meets with a response—any response. Yet making assertions can hardly exhaust the range of possible speech acts, any more than all social rules give instructions.

It would seem to follow that speech acts other than those asserting some state of affairs (in Habermas' terms, having other illocutionary roles) can produce rules by endowing utterances with constitutive and regulative consequences. It does not follow that *all* speech acts can produce rules. This would depend on the verbs chosen and the effects their utterance is intended to secure. To know what speech acts other than assertives are rule candidates, we need a list of verbs used in linguistically effected social performances or, better, a scheme classifying them into categories of speech acts.

Beginning with J. L. Austin (1963: 150–162), Philosophers have listed verbs to be found in performative utterances and grouped them into what they took to be distinctive categories. Because these performances are social, the categories are implicitly functional. Thus is explained the credibility and influence of the scheme Searle introduced (1979) for classifying speech acts. He got the categories right, at least as far as his audience is concerned. Searle's scheme is the keystone in the doorway through which the theory of speech acts can proceed to be social theory. And, for the purposes of social theory, it is a manageable scheme. Searle offered five categories of speech acts: assertives, directives, commissives, expressives, and declarations.

Assertives, as we have already seen, are speech acts stating a belief, coupled of course to the speaker's wish or intention that the hearer accept this belief. Neither intends the regulative consequences their acts jointly produce. Representative verbs used in assertive speech acts are: state, affirm, report, characterize, attribute, insist, dissent. While instruction-rules obviously issue from assertives, Black confused matters a bit by suggesting that directions and instructions are synonyms for rules in an instruction-sense. Because directions so understood do not issue from directive speech acts, which is Searle's next category, it is better to avoid using the term "directions" at all (recall introduction, footnote 4).

Directive speech acts also present the hearer with a speaker's intention as to some act the speaker would like to have performed. Typical directive verbs are: ask, command, demand, permit, caution. Even though all directives are not imperative, imperatives are the model case for rules seen as commands. Nevertheless, the intent of all directives and not just imperatives is to place a regulative burden on hearers. It is this feature of directive speech acts which leads us to think, though mistakenly, that the rules they give rise to are particularly or even uniquely regulative. Thus Black's rules in a regulation-sense correspond to directives inclusively. Successful requests and commands have the same kind, though not the same degree, of regulative effect. Put otherwise, illocutionary force varies from verb to verb, even when the perlocutionary subject remains the same.

Here again Black's choice of terms confuses matters. All speech acts producing rules must have some kind of regulative effect, because all rules are regulative. If all rules are "regulations," then those produced by directive speech acts need a name of their own. I will call them "directive-rules."

Commissives reveal the speaker's intention of being committed to a stated course of action. To promise and offer are usual examples. For a hearer to accept any speaker's offer or promise constitutes a commitment on the speaker's part. The term "commitment" itself suggests the deliberate creation of a normative bond far stronger than the bond immanent in successful assertions. Directive and commissive speech acts are intended to have the same effect, which is to get the perlocutionary subject to do something. They differ on the identity of that subject—another person or one's self—and thus on the locus of obligation. Commitments made to others are rule-candidates. Commitments accepted by others provide rules for those making such commitments.

Whether commitments to one's self can also produce rules is a difficult question.[13] One can say interchangeably, I have promised myself to go to church every week, and, I make it a rule to do so. Is this private commitment a rule unless it is followed by a public statement, the latter being the proximate source of normativity? To the extent that rules need not be stated to be considered as such, I take it as sufficient that the commitment is capable of public statement and the person making the commitment would not shirk from making it publicly. Wishing to keep the commitment private suggests insincerity about being committed and withholds normative consequences. If one accepts promises to one's self, then it is indeed (in deed) a rule for that person because it is constitutive and regulative at one and the same time.

Most writers either ignore rules arising from commitments or relegate them to the category of directive-rules. Perhaps this is because they tend to see rules as either constitutive or regulative, the former offering guidance and the latter requiring compliance. Yet acknowledgement of a third category is implicit in the language of rights and duties. To state a duty—It is my duty to go to church every week—is a way of saying, I promised (my parents, the preacher, myself) to go to church every week. To state a right—It is my right to go to church—can be restated, somebody promised me that I can go to church. My promises confer duties on me that are simultaneously rights others claim I have conferred on them. The same holds for others' promises as they affect me. Commitment-rules, as I will call them here, always distribute consequences this way.

One might assume that the commitment-rules are the same as Black's rules in the sense of precepts. This turns out not quite the

---

13. Jon Elster has called the act of binding oneself a "precommitment" (1979: 36–111). I find this a peculiar coinage because it suggests an act prior to commitment. Indeed Elster's elaborate discussion centers on strategic concerns, which necessarily require the presence of others. It is to these others that the prior act serves as instruction or direction (p. 38). Commitments as such are of negligible interest in Elster's discussion.

case. To start with, Black identified two senses for precepts, one refer-ring to prudential rules, the second to moral rules (1962: 111). Black thought that prudential rules are plausibly regarded as instructions of the sort in which values are asserted. These are what I have called principles. Moral rules he held to be different because we cannot choose not to have them not applied to ourselves (pp. 111–112). This is unconvincing. One may be exempt from such a rule at great social cost, but then the rule is an instruction-rule or directive-rule.

What Black was groping for is revealed in his two illustrations of precepts. "It is a good rule to pay one's debts promptly," and "A good rule is: to put charity ahead of justice" (1962: 111). In the first, a prudential rule, having a debt bespeaks of having made a commit-ment to pay it, and the rule has to do with keeping promises. The second, a moral rule, is clearly contestable (and hardly the example Black thought it is of a rule from which exemption cannot be had), but its point is (I think) that if someone has failed on a promise, we should be forgiving or understanding rather than act on an in-dependent rule that tells us what in justice we can do about this kind of conduct. Both illustrations are about commitments and thus about the category of speech acts called commissives. The rules themselves happen to be principles that people assert in circumstances produced by commitment-rules and their breach. Black presupposed commitment-rules in trying to get at the sense of precepts. In the process, he wrongly imputed the former's distinctiveness to the latter.

The correspondence between assertive, directive, and commissive speech acts and Black's functional categories of rule (once they have been renamed and the third reconstructed) suggests that Searle's two remaining categories of speech acts — expressives and declarations — do not produce rules. This a brief examination of each confirms. More precisely, it confirms that speech acts in neither category can produce rules on their own.

Expressives serve to convey an emotion or attitude toward a state of affairs. Illustrative are apologies and congratulations. They are not rule-candidates because their reception is sufficient from the speaker's point of view to fulfill her intentions in having made the statement. If I say, I hereby apologize to you, and you accept, noth-ing further need transpire between us for the reason of my having apologized. Upon acceptance, the speech act has completely per-formed the action intended — it has no extended perlocutionary effects. To the extent that expressives become courtesies, they acquire regulative character by parasitic associations with other kinds of speech acts.

Declarations would appear not even to require acceptance to have completely performed the speaker's intentions. To say, I hereby declare that you are fired, does not require acknowledgment to be successful, at least as Searle saw it. Declarations are thus regulative in a more immediate sense than other speech acts. Actually, as my illustration shows, insufficient information has been provided (Compare Hancher 1979). Can the speaker fire the hearer because she has the authority to do so? If so, rules exist stating such, and these rules give the speech act its regulative effect. If not, then the act of firing the hearer becomes regulative only when the speaker assents. The former case is a directive speech act involving a high degree of institutionalization. The latter case is an assertive speech act and nothing more. Other common examples — I hereby declare you married, I hereby declare war — suggest that the former case is usually the operative one for declarations, and they should be seen achieving illucutionary force and performative sufficiency, not through perlocutionary effects, but by parasitic association with institutionalized rules. If firing someone is directive, then declaring war is assertive, and bidding at an auction commissive. Declarative forms exist for those categories of speech acts with rule potential.

Stated differently, all rules are either assertives of the form, I state that X counts as Y, or directives of the form, I state that X person (should, must, may) do Y, or commissives of the form, I state that I (can, will, should) do Y. While each is a distinctive category, all three play on each other in the production of rules. People make assertions about others' promises, respond to assertives with directives and so on. Let me illustrate with the word "claim," which I used a few pages ago.

Take the statement, I hereby claim that it is my money. Depending on the context, such a statement might have an assertive meaning: This money counts as mine. To add, because my uncle's will says so, is to try an assertive declaration. A second possibility has a directive meaning: I request that I be allowed to have what is mine. To add, because I am king, is to make a directive declaration (or to entertain a delusion). Note that both the assertives and directives conveyed by the word "claim" depend on the existence of a prior commissive giving me a right to the money. The core of my claim, whatever form I offer it in, is that I was promised money. I may even have made the promise to myself, thereby committing myself to getting the money. In this case, I do not promise in advance what I will do to secure it; that depends on what you do on hearing my claim.

The contingent character of the promise in this instance is an invitation for strategic interaction (defined in chapter 6, footnote 14). As Habermas would say, it is not understanding-oriented. It is success-oriented, and it deliberately manipulates perlocutionary possibilities to shift the direction of illocutionary force from the speaker to the hearer — you will end up being committed to (at least something of) what I have promised myself. The hearer normally responds with a counter-claim. The process of interacting over these claims is a particularly fertile one for new rules in the form of agreed outcomes (see Kratochwil 1983: 17–21; 1984: 691–697). Such rules stem from joint commissives — we both promise. . . . If they are joint commissive declarations, we should call them contracts.[14] Under highly institutionalized circumstances, in which known legal rules are invoked in support of claims, we have the adversarial setting and reasoned argument Kennedy and Kratochwil find emblematic of the legal situation. Note, however, that claims of other sorts are no less appropriate for legal consideration.

I suggest that no legally relevant use of the term "claim" falls outside the categories offered by speech act theory, and all uses fit one or another category or compound categories in complex systems of use. Behind all such uses stands an original, or initiating speech act, which is a commissive. Comparably, assertives and directives initiate the making of rules. No other speech acts can. That this is so leads me to a final, rule-aspiring assertion of my own: Starting with assertives, directives, and commissive speech acts, we have an inclusive classificatory scheme for *all* social rules.

A question remains. As noted, Searle's scheme is implicitly functional. It sorts speech acts by reference to speaker's intentions, meaning the purposes they serve speakers. Now, how do we know that he

---

14. Michael Hancher (1979) pursued a similar line of reasoning but saw contracts and other cooperative speech acts as hybrids of the generic categories rather than declarations.

has fixed on fundamental categories of human linguistic activity? Habermas observed that Searle's is "a clear and intuitively evident classification. . . ." (1984: 320). On this I quite agree, but it is still less than the complete answer we need. Happily, Searle identified an ontological principle underlying his scheme. Not so happily, I think his categories of being are improperly worked out and thus result in what Searle himself called an "inelegant solution . . ." [1979: 15].

Searle held that speech acts involve the fit between words a speaker uses to have her intentions realized and the world, or state of affairs, the speaker refers to. He then argued that assertives as a class intend to fit words to world; conversely, directives fit the world to the speaker's words by intending hearers to act on and thus change the world. In the case of commissives, Searle also saw the speaker trying to fit the world to words, as with directives, by committing herself to doing what is required, rather than having someone else do it. Searle wanted to show that directives and commissives "are really members of the same category," but found no good reason to make either one a subject of the other (1979: 14).

Habermas approached the problem somewhat differently. He argued, with Searle, that assertives attempt to fit words to world. He then detached "mere imperatives" from other directives which he called "normatively authorized . . ." (1984: 324). His treatment of commissives argues in effect that mere promises fit the world to words. But, in so doing, "the speaker *binds* his will in the sense of *normative* obligation; . . ." (1984: 324). I read Habermas to mean that the normativity immanent in commissives reverses their apparent fit to the world. On his assessment they are words-to-world in fit. Thus Habermas reoriented Searle's tripartite scheme to label imperatives and, we might infer, promises to oneself, as efforts at changing the world through speech acts, while assertives and most directives and commissives are efforts at the converse. For Habermas, the latter condition is the road to intersubjective recognition of the legitimacy of states of affairs and intentions.

Habermas has altered Searle's ontological principle for his own normative purposes. Direction of fit matters—words-to-world is desirable and the other way is not, at least for individual speech acts. Only when the world-to-words fit is a product of legitimate (words-to-world) exchanges is it desirable. Those speech acts that have regulative properties (which does not include imperatives) or are normatively inoffensive (assertives) have the right direction of fit. Discriminating between imperatives and other directives substitutes degree of institutionalization (what else can normative authorization be?) for the original ontological principle.

We must return to the question of direction of fit ontologically understood, and ask if Searle has chosen his words correctly. Some words fit the world without being fit to it, or having the world fit to them. I think this is generally true of assertives. They either reflect an existing words-to-world fit or propose a new one.[15] They do not endeavor to change an existing arrangement. Against Habermas, I do agree with Searle that directives as a class fit the world to words. Take as an example, I request that you fix the stairs. The state of affairs here is a problem with the stairs. Your actions, prompted by my request, will correct the problem. My words (set in train actions that) change the world.

Against Searle's position, I believe commissives as a class fit words to the world. To commit oneself is to project a desired state of affairs and bring it to bear on oneself. Consider my saying, I promise that I will fix the stairs. I commit myself to a state of affairs in which the stairs are no longer a problem. My actions, prompted by my commitment, will be directed toward realization of that anticipated state of affairs. My commitment will then be discharged. My words — making a commitment — are fit to a state of affairs — with the stairs fixed, my commitment is discharged — as a way of changing the world as it is — the stairs are broken, need fixing. The "world as it is" is not the "world as a state of affairs" indicated in a commissive speech act.[16]

---

15. Searle saw expressives as having no direction of fit because "the truth of the proposition expressed in an expressive is presupposed" (1979: 16). Better to say, no fit at all, because nothing is being related to anything else. He also saw declarations as having a two-way fit because an "extra-linguistic institution" is required for illocutionary force (pp. 18–19). Institutionalization, though prior, is hardly extra-linguistic, and the connection to direction of fit is obscure (Habermas 1984: 324–325).

16. Direction of fit may be cast in terms of an anticipated state of affairs. I request that you fix the stairs, could mean, I want the stairs fixed. Will you undertake to fix them? This is a two-step speech act. I fit the world into my words (try to

If I am right in this reconstruction of the ways in which words and worlds fit, ontological categories match functional categories of speech acts and rules. Reassuring as this is, it is in one crucial respect a bogus accomplishment. Searle's ontological principle, in any version, relies on positivism and a representational view of language. The term "fit" presupposes the independence of positivities, in this instance words and world, about which questions of fit are being asked. A constructivist view denies that world and words are independent; it sees them as mutually constitutive. If categories of being are linguistically constituted, then they may be said to have social origins.

As I observe at the beginning of chapter 1, the search for grounding may lead in circles. What then is reassuring about the correspondence of functional and ontological categories, when one finds that each set does indeed lead to the other? The answer, at least for me, is the accumulation of congruent categories. No one set is ever fundamental, "transcendental," or primary. We mis(use) such terms when we find what we are looking for in the next place we look hard. I find that there are three categories of words-to-world fit. I style my efforts as going "deeper" or back toward a putative "beginning." Each new set is more "fundamental" than the last.

I would do better to say that I choose to go in one direction, by relating words and worlds, speech and rules, before going in another. Legal theory, with which I begin this chapter, takes that other path, by relating rules to law and order. I take a more circuitous route, because I think legal theory ignores language and fails to connect individual conduct and social rules adequately. Speech acts supply the connection, but not sufficiently.

---

have you do something like fix the stairs) by having you fit your words to the world (make a commitment as to a state of affairs I prefer). But I do not *need* to make my request contingent on your willingness to commit yourself, though I may do so to enhance prospects for the perlocutionary effects I desire. I can simply order you to fix the stairs, without concern for your willingness to be committed, and you *may* do so independently of any such commitment. The differences between requests so understood and other directives may be what Habermas had in mind in arguing that simple imperatives are distinguishable from normatively authorized directives. The latter are commissives, not directives, for the purpose of establishing direction of fit, which Habermas wrongly saw as their normativizing trait.

More need be said about individual conduct, and particularly about how people learn what rules are and when to follow them. This is the subject of the next chapter, as is culture, by which I mean the general pattern is individuals' conduct. If legal theory fails to connect individual conduct and social rules, it does no better with rules in use and social arrangements — "the problem of order," as chapter 4 is entitled. In that chapter, I conclude with a discussion of rhetoric, but not as conduct within arenas preconceived as legal. Instead figurative speech shares with rules in the construction of social arrangements, not least the ones we dignify as legal.

3

COGNITION, JUDGMENT, CULTURE

Categories of performative language and rules match modes of reasoning. I support this assertion by further consideration of the question of "direction of fit," introduced in the preceding chapter, and by a constructivist demonstration that modes of reasoning arise from longstanding human practices situated in generally present material circumstances. I argue more particularly that "ancestral institutions," and not logic or genes, make modes of reasoning what they are. Reasoning takes practice; cognition is conduct.[1]

A constructivist interpretation of reasoning extends to learning

---

1. I understand "cognition" to refer broadly to mindful behavior—behavior dependent on "higher brain function." This inclusive conception of cognition is also preferred in the transdisciplinary movement, known as the cognitive sciences, which "seeks to develop mental processes and representations that are biologically founded, logically justifiable, psychologically real, and capable of being programmed on a computer" (Gardner 1981: 265). I take this strikingly positivist-objectivist program to be valuable within the limits of its physicalist assumptions. Whether all activities of mind can finally be reduced to binary operations, the metaphorical equation of mind and computer so simplifies what goes on in and among minds that it ill suits the constructivist view of cognition as conduct. See further footnotes 14 and 15 below.

and knowing, not just in the sense of acquiring propositional knowledge, but learning and knowing how to use that knowledge, including knowledge of rules. I call this learning how to exercise judgment, and in effect I endorse Harold Garfinckel's view that people are not "judgmental dopes" (1967: 68; see also Heritage 1984: 110–115). Instead they learn as children how to exercise judgment in successive, well-defined stages of individual social and physical growth—the stages, or levels, of "moral development" respectively described by Jean Piaget and Lawrence Kohlberg. In my constructivist rendition of their work, I associate a first stage with the acquisition of knowledge about, and competence in using, instruction-rules, a second stage with directive-rules, and a third stage with commitment-rules.

Categories of rules in use are subject both to practice and consciousness, as Piaget pointed out. Consciousness is the internal dimension of support for rules, which, in each category, also have a characteristic external dimension of support. These ensembles of support for each category of rule along with the rules that people have internalized and use in practice, constitute culture. Cultures mix rules, sorted by category, and the correlative modalities of support those rules elicit, in different proportions. Although any culture's mix is subject to change, no necessary or preferred developmental sequence is implied. As culture relates to categories of rules, so gender relates to categories of reasoning. The chapter concludes with remarks on this proposition.

COGNITIVE UNIVERSALS

Whether given categories of human conduct are fundamental is an unanswerable question. A different question—whether any such categories are universal—may not be. "Universal" in this context describes any distinguishable attribute or activity common to humanity or, more particularly, common to all competent human beings, wherever and in whatever circumstances they are found. "Competence" refers to a level of cognitive development achieved by most adult members of the species. Obviously individuals may not be able to do something most other adults can do—speak, for example, yet otherwise they are competent—say, to care for themselves.

Language, including performative language, is a human universal. It is difficult to imagine that the three categories of speech acts—assertive, directive, and commissive—and the correlative categories of rules, which I identify in the preceding chapter, are not. Nevertheless, their universality is not to be taken for granted. The Yimas of New Guinea are said to have only ninety verbs in their language, just one of them performative—to say.[2] However surprising this is, I consider it likely that the Yimas put that one verb to service in other than assertive speech acts. The sentence, I say that you, or I (should, must, will) leave, can have directive or commissive force *if* the Yimas possess any notion of temporality. They must if they are capable of reasoning.

On empirical grounds, there is little doubt that reasoning, like language, is universal. Indeed the capacity to reason is a standard criterion for cognitive competence. Two categories of reasoning are widely acknowledged—deductive and inductive reasoning. C. S. Peirce introduced a third category, abduction, only a century ago (Buchler 1955: 150–156, Habermas 1971: 113–139, Eco and Sebeok 1983). I find it no less plausibly a universal category (compare Sebeok 1983). I am also satisfied that these three categories are inclusive. To see why this should be so, let us revert to the question of "direction of fit" of categories of speech acts.

The point of a speech act is to have an effect on some state of affairs. In the case of assertives, one state of affairs is held to count for another. With directives, the intent is to alter some circumscribed part of an initial, larger state of affairs. With commissives, the intent is to take a circumscribed state of affairs and have it alter a resulting, larger state of affairs. Assertives relate wholes to wholes,

---

2. I quote an account of a lunch-time conversation at the University of California's Berkeley campus.

> People were skeptical. Ninety verb stems? . . . You couldn't say "she wanted him to leave but she didn't say anything". . . . You could only say, "she told him to leave" but you couldn't say that either, because there is no indirect quotation in Yimas, and only a single verb to describe [better to say, perform] speech acts. "What's the speech act verb?" "To say." A hush fell across the room. People shook their heads and exhaled slowly. "That's incredible." "I don't believe it" (Rose 1984: 133–134).

whether spatially or temporally. Directives relate wholes to parts, and commissive parts to wholes. In the latter two cases, temporality is presupposed—these speech acts lead from one state of affairs, in whole or part, to the next, in part or whole.[3]

So understood, speech acts are instances of applied reasoning. To proceed from a whole to its parts is what one normally describes as deductive reasoning. To proceed from parts to whole is inductive. Peirce's abduction is a matter of leaping from one whole to another without having to proceed down to the parts and up to the next whole. These three categories exhaust the possible ways wholes and parts can be related, for part-to-part relations, in which no connection to a whole is presumed, are then whole-to-whole relations.

Deduction has the longest recognition as a distinctive form of reasoning because it appears to be so conclusive: A whole can only be its parts, and parts must relate to each other in determinate ways, or they are not parts at all. Take A, B, and C as symbols expressing ratios of parts to a whole. If A equals B, but B does not equal C in some defined respect (defined for the whole), then A cannot equal C in that same respect. Notice, however, if the whole is indeterminate and thus possibly variable, A might equal C. Induction rarely gets credit for having the same logical rigor as deduction because the contents of the whole cannot be known or fixed in advance. Most problematical of all is abduction, since the content of wholes, left as such, are indeterminately different. If the wholes are rendered determinate, then they are but parts of a known whole (consisting

---

3. The presumption of temporality brings to mind Immanuel Kant's famous discussion of "the analogies of experience" (1933: 208–238). "The three modes of time are *duration, succession,* and *coexistence.* There will, therefore, be three rules of all relations of appearances in time, and these rules will be prior to all experience, and indeed make it possible" (p. 209; emphasis in original). Relations of time viewed dynamically ("dynamical relations") yield "inherence, consequence, and composition" (p. 236). Kant's proofs for the three analogies, formulated as principles, are flawed and inconsistent (Wolff 1969: 238–292) Furthermore, permanence is not a relation of time at all (p. 246), although it is perhaps a relation of space in time. The parallels between the three categories of directionality and Kant's three categories of (space and) time relations can hardly be coincidental. Thus the problem is not with Kant's categories but his effort to prove that they alone are necessary and sufficient for experience and, as such, fundamental.

of those two parts) to which they are determinately related. Otherwise the relation of wholes is a matter of conjecture.

If abduction is the last category of reasoning to gain recognition as such, it is only because conjecture is so inconclusive. When conjecture is harnessed to other modes of reasoning, we dignify it as the creative part of the theory enterprise. More than that, it is central to any such enterprise, which is generally modeled as parts to whole (induction), whole to (simpler) whole, whole to parts (deduction), the determinate relation of the latter set of parts clarifying the ambiguous relation of the initiating set of parts. Conjecture in the absence of such supporting activities is always open to challenge and counter-conjecture, unless of course it has become accepted on faith. Karl Popper's warning (1968: 40–42) that theories are never verifiable is sophisticated acknowledgment that conjecture retains its inconclusive character even where it is supported by other modes of reasoning (although he disallowed induction).

Deduction, induction, and abduction are human practices, apparently universal, antedating their abstract characterization as distinctive realms of cognitive activity. Are they natural, in the sense of being genetically mandated or physically necessitated? The case of deduction misleads here. That the brain, as a physico-chemical system, undoubtedly uses the same kind of on/off, either/or operations that characterize deduction does not make it necessary for the brain, cognitively speaking, to use, prefer, or even be able to use those same operations in the absence of practice. Whether nature presupposes us to reason as we do, reasoning itself is a social matter.

The case of induction better suits an examination of this proposition. If deduction seems to be compelled by nature (accessible nature seems never to violate the laws of deductive logic), the same cannot be said for induction. We choose to proceed inductively because we have learned that it helps in our endeavors. Indeed induction is a way of talking about the cumulative effect of our experiences. Our endeavors and experiences are less decreed by nature than made what they are by society.

Max Black has elaborated on much the same point in this striking passage:

> It is, therefore, not fanciful to conceive of all adult human beings as participating in a complex system of ways of learning

that might be called an inductive institution. Like other institutions (warfare, the law, and so on), it has a relatively fixed, though not immutable structure transmitted from one generation to the next and crystallized in the form of prohibitions and licenses, maxims of conduct, and informal precepts of performance. Like other institutions, the inductive institution requires that its participants have mastered a system of distinctive concepts having both descriptive and normative aspects (1970: 86–87).

I cannot see that deduction is any less an institution. We engage in it because it works for us, even if we feel that nature leaves us no choice. At the other extreme, conjecture, as the word suggests, is never compelled, always spontaneous. Yet it too is an institution. As such, conjecture stabilizes as reasoning warranted for the results it gets. With practice we change the rules and alter results.

Black argued that "we cannot regard inductive inference as something merely 'given,' as a natural fact, like the Milky Way, that would be absurd to criticize. To understand induction is necessarily to accept its authority" (p. 89). Black's point is telling. Even if we regard deduction as "given," that we understand how to do it, just as we know how to proceed inductively and conjecturally, means accepting "its authority." The "it" in question is an institution: Whether deductive, inductive, abductive, its authority is social.

Authority, as Black used the term, refers to the history of normativity authors have succeeded in bestowing on rules. That individual authors are unknown and a detailed history beyond recovery makes them no less potent normatively. To the contrary, universal, anonymous authorship contributes to their authority.[4] This does not mean, however, that we cannot plausibly reconstruct, at least in broad

---

4. Black observed that his "linguistic approach" to induction "may be usefully compared with Hume's view of induction as a habit or custom" (p. 89). I think this comparison is apt, and it suggests that Black was indeed wrong, as I assert in the preceding chapter (pp. 122–123), to claim that instruction-rules have neither authors nor histories. Not only is the instruction, Do not plant tomatoes until the first frost, a convention produced by many unknown authors, their assertions to this effect, at least before institutionalization of the convention, are born of their common participation in the institution of induction: Each determined the appropriate time of planting inductively. See also chapter 1, footnote 12.

outline, the history of institutions, the authority and relevance of which are such that we treat them as cognitive universals.

If we recall that people reason in particular ways because it helps them in their endeavors, then we might ask what kinds of endeavors are likely to be promoted by the three kinds of reasoning we know virtually everyone engages in. These doings must be recurrent in the human experience, and we may guess that they are repeatedly discovered, widely diffused, or both. Not everyone must participate in these endeavors directly, but everyone is likely to be aware of them and their import across their own social unit. Apart from the kind of reasoning they promote, they are subject to articulation, generalization, institutionalization—they are ruled constructions of deeds.

Black gave a clue to one constellation of practices meeting all these conditions: the institution of warfare. Warriors may be said to proceed preferentially from the whole to the parts, that is, deductively. Given a situation, they proceed to break it down, to analyze it, so as to be able to recommend or pursue promising lines of attack. The metaphor "attack" reveals the definition of the situation. There exist both an adversary and an objective, the objective being to defeat, even destroy, the adversary. Note also that this metaphor is unembarrassedly military. Even if there is no actual adversary—no one to beat—one is imagined. We attack problems; we assault nature. This we recognize as the language of science, in which the adversary is whatever we define as unknown or intractable. (On the metaphorical complex, "argument is war," see Lakoff and Johnson 1980: 4–6.)

The conjunction of analytico-deductive methods, escalating efforts to exercise control over nature, the development of machines to assist and substitute for human labor, the employment of human labor in social machines modeled on analytic practices (what we call the division of labor)—this conjunction is but the contemporary realization of warfare, beyond actual warfare, as an institution. It refines and amplifies the way warriors think so successfully that it captures the way many of us think about the way we think—only the rational-instrumental pattern of thought, of speaking, is "rational."[5]

---

5. Made famous by Herbert Marcuse (1964), this is one of the Frankfurt School's major themes (Held 1980: 65–70).

Under the circumstances, it is no great surprise that staff planning is a military invention, that military personnel today rarely fight but are found in the front rank of "modernizers" in new countries,[6] that the term "military-industrial complex" has a potency far beyond its descriptive utility. Nor is it surprising that organizational functionaries of all sorts occupy ranks, enforce discipline, and talk as if they were fighting. Organizational functionaries, and not the renegades and mercenaries romanticized on film, are the paradigm case of warriors in our time.

The second constellation of practices meeting all the conditions necessary to be plausibly implicated in the history of the ways we reason has to do with hunting—hunting for food, in the first instance. Hunting stands in marked contrast to attacking, which is the prime metaphor for those who proceed from the whole to parts. Hunting describes those who reverse this procedure and go from parts to whole. They hunt for clues, diagnose a condition, put together discrete signs to form a concrete mental picture (compare Ginsburg 1983). Abstracted as reasoning, this is induction.

Not to confuse the violence incidental to hunting with the violent dismemberment of an attack, we should recall that the simple societies in which such doings are paramount are usually called "hunting and gathering" societies. Gathering a material of any sort to suit a human need is always a matter of hunting for evidence of the availability of whatever is needed. The practices of hunting and gathering suit many circumstances that human beings encounter as they expand the range of socially consequential activities.

Registering clues about the natural behavior of plants and animals fosters conjectures about the possibility of fruitful intervention and attempts at simulation, with agriculture and husbandry the result. The neolithic revolution was after all a revolution in, or more accurately, to production to meet material needs.[7] Farmers are systematic gatherers; no longer do they need to "hunt" as they once did, al-

---

6. See Trimberger (1978) on "Military Bureaucrats and Development in Japan, Turkey, Egypt and Peru," as this book is subtitled.
7. Jürgen Habermas (1979: 135–151) has dated the first mode of production from before the neolithic revolution because of the cooperative implications of hunting in bands. He did note the controversy on this issue, including the argument that hunting, unlike farming, is appropriative rather than productive.

though they still must look for clues — clues about incipient weather, diseased plants and animals, replenishment of the soil and so on.

Perhaps the distinctive method of the hunter is clearest for those who deal with maladies, human and otherwise. Diagnosing a condition is the sine qua non of medicine. It is customary to dignify medicine as a science, but doing so promotes a methodological confusion.[8] Physicians do not depend in the first instance on scientific method. After hunting for symptoms in an individual, the physician attempts to match those symptoms against available model sets of symptoms, canonically described as diseases. The best fit is conjectured as the patient's disease, with procedures recommended on the basis of past experience with other patients similarly diagnosed.[9] Failure of the patient to respond means further hunting for symptoms, evaluation of changes in the patient's condition, sorting through other possible models for fit, and the rest. Science dramatically expedites this process but cannot replace diagnosis as the key to medicine.[10]

The third constellation of practices implicated in the history of

---

8. The more so because the "low" sciences, like alchemy, were historically allied to medicine and the interpretation of signs; "high" Galilean science discredited the former as science. Deduction was coupled to experiment and induction, as the implied method of the low sciences and medicine, had to wait for Hume for methodological validation (Hacking 1975).

9. At first glance, Michel Foucault's arresting discussion of the "observing gaze" in medical practice (1973) ill suits my emphasis on diagnosis as a matter of hunting for clues. Foucault described this activity in visual terms (the chapter beginning on p. 107 is entitled "Seeing and Knowing), while I take it as aural in the first instance: In making a diagnosis, the physician must listen and, insofar as other clues become available to the other senses, integrate all the evidence. Foucault knew this. "In the clinician's catalogue, the purity of the gaze is bound up with a certain silence that enables him to listen. The prolix discourses of systems must be interrupted: 'All theory is always silent or vanishes at the patient's bedside' . . ." (p. 107, footnote deleted). Foucault's concern, no less than mine, is with "Signs and Cases" (title of the preceding chapter, pp. 88–106), signs to be "read," whether experienced aurally, visually, or by other senses, cases to be recalled. For Foucault the birth of the clinic in the late eighteenth century imposed "the sovereignty of the gaze," by making medicine a regime of science, of catalogues and systems. "The clinic was probably the first attempt to order a science on the exercise and decisions of the gaze" p. 89.

10. In this, medicine resembles *bricolage,* an activity made famous by Claude Levi-Strauss (1966: 16–36), for which there is no exact equivalent term in English. "A

reasoning are those of priests. Our general image of priests is that, to protect and disseminate the central beliefs of a society, they repeat the same limited repertory of beliefs endlessly, elaborating on them, sometimes extravagantly, amplifying them for all to hear, but rarely altering them. Ceremony traps belief and sanctification ensures their timelessness. To offset this familiar construction of priestly skill, we must consider the practice of priests in simple, egalitarian settings, in which we consistently find divination and conjuration preeminent.[11] Priests are indeed by origin specialists in conjecture, association, illumination. Their talk establishes meaning and verifies the significance of what goes on in the world. Repeated invocation and ritualization lends credibility to their conjectures by obscuring their associative origins.[12]

In the secular circumstances of our own day, psychotherapists substitute for priests. Even more do teachers. Like priests, teachers experience the tension between the associative freedom of conjecture and the constraining effects of inculcating beliefs. Notice that professors like me normally feel obligated to cloak their conjectures in the guarded language of hypothesis, buttress them by invoking earlier authorities or the apparatus of science and analytic procedure, or excuse them as the humble opinion of private persons. Notice also that such accompaniments to conjecture are credulously accepted or ignored, and our conjectures accorded extraordinary stature. Some of us become all-purpose public commentators or advisors to officials. Others are busy selling intellectual fashions or prompting mildly subversive thoughts in young minds.

'bricoleur' is adept at performing a large number of diverse tasks, but unlike the engineer, he does not subordinate each of them to the availability of raw materials and tools conceived and procured for the purpose of the project." Instead the bricoleur collects and retains material and tools for "potential use . . . on the principle that 'they may come in handy'" (pp. 17–18). Indicatively, "the engineer works by means of concepts and the 'bricoleur' by means of signs" (p. 20).

11. On the magical, creative aspects of the human experience in hunting and gathering societies, and the incidence of shamanism, see for example Eliade (1978: 16–28). Durkheim's well-known separation of religion and magic, the former being collective and system-functional by creating group solidarity, the latter being clientelistic and transitory, may explain the functionalist emphasis on ceremony and consequent disregard of the creative side of priestly behavior (1915: 42–47).

12. At which time we may speak of religion: "(1) a system of symbols which acts to (2) establish powerful, pervasive, and long-lasting moods and motivations in men by (3) formulating concepts of a general order of existence and (4) clothing these conceptions with such an aura of factuality that (5) the moods and motivations seem uniquely realistic" (Geertz 1973: 90, emphasis deleted).

Whether professors profess an interest in shaping social reality with their conjectures, shape it they do. When they also happen to be priests (consider Shi'a mullahs), they represent a powerful voice that calls on resources rarely mobilized by warriors. The conjunction of prophecy, inculcated belief, and unleashed popular support is a common element in the mass movements of today and perhaps a necessary condition for totalitarianism. Because teachers in the West are so deeply imbued with respect for analytic procedures, those of us attempting to find the meaning in such events cannot hear their source in voices like our own. As we extol the virtues of analysis, inculcate procedural mastery, conduct wars against war, crime, poverty, cancer, illiteracy and superstition (the last being the concrete conjectural world of ordinary people), we lace these pursuits with conjecture. If priests are professors of the sacred, professors are priests of the profane.

To recapitulate, people make sense of their situation through conjecture and ceremony, confront their adversaries by using techniques of destruction, and provide for their needs by hunting and gathering. If we construe these practices broadly, almost everyone is competent to do them. Specialization also occurs. Some people become adept in one or another mode of reasoning and skilled in the practices to which they apply. They constitute themselves into groups and institutionalize them to control membership, secure patronage, standardize practices, and pass on their skills. Such groups become professions, corporations, and castes. Following Harold D. Lasswell (1965a: 3–20), I call these, "skill groups." I return to them in chapter 7.

However many there are, however specialized skill groups become, all of them trace back to just three ancestral institutions, respectively concerned with prophecy, war, and provisioning. Yet specialized secondary institutions have their own peremptory histories. Not only are distant connections forgotten, even suppressed, new connections are proposed, acquire practical significance, become institutions, and lose their histories. To give an example, hypothetico-deductive and inducto-hypotheticative modes of reasoning are complementary opposites in an institution called formal reasoning. Hypotheses are domesticated conjectures, free conjecture is demoted to speculation, imagination, superstition—it is no longer reasoning at all. On rediscovery as a mode of reasoning, conjecture acquired a new name, "abduction," so that it could rejoin deduction and induction on more or less equal terms.

Set against the tendency for people to borrow, revise, combine, and reduce other people's practices and then forget or deny having done so is the remarkable institution of language. No doubt language in use is as protean as any other institution, but language at rest is laden with the past its current use serves to obliterate. This is notably so with the Indo-European language group, a large, successful family of languages, including the one I write in now, reaching across Europe to South Asia and back to an early agrarian period in human history. Because there are a number of Indo-European languages, historic and contemporary, and a large body of tales, myths, and practices articulated in them, comparison expedites informed inference. My conjectures can be formed as hypotheses and checked against the record.

Fortunately, I do not have to do so myself. Indo-European Comparative Philology provides both the raw materials and their reconstruction, the latter undertaken chiefly by George Dumézil. Let me quote an excellent introduction to Dumézil's work (Littleton 1982: 6):

> In sum, on the basis of his comparative analysis of the varied social and mythological forms presented by the ancient I-E [Indo-European]-speaking world, Dumézil has concluded (1) that the parent or Proto-I-E society, before it broke up, was characterized by a triparite ideology; (2) that elements of this ideology were carried by the inheritors of that society across the length and breadth of what was to become the historic I-E domain; and (3) that these elements can be discovered in most, but by no means all, of the early I-E mythical and epical literature, from the *Vedas* of ancient India to the *Eddas* of pre-Christian Iceland, from the *Mahābhārata* to the *Heimskringla.* Moreover, this ideology, whether expressed in myth, epic, or social organization, is asserted to be uniquely I-E, having no parallels among the ancient civilizations of the Near East, the Nile Valley, China or any other region of the Old World prior to the I-E migrations in the second millennium B.C.

The reader will now have guessed that Indo-European "tripartite ideology" is nothing more than the three ancestral institutions I have identified, linked together as a meta-institution. Perhaps the clearest expression is to be found in classical Indic social arrangements, myth, and religion. From the earliest time from which there is evidence, we find three main castes, respectively consisting of priests, warriors, and cultivators, with everyone else being out-castes. Throughout the classical literature of India; the pantheon of the gods mirrored and, we may suppose, supported this arrangement.

The same threefold division (with artisans joining cultivators) is repeated endlessly in the evidence from Indo-Iranian, Greek, Latin, Germanic, Norse, and Celtic parts of the ancient world (pp. 17–19). To give but one obvious example, the three orders of European society reproduce the threefold division organizing India's castes (Duby 1980), without any substantial direct connection between the two sets of practices. Europeans did not have to learn from India what they already did for themselves.[13]

Yet, as the passage I just quoted indicates, not all people have accorded such significance to the three ancestral institutions of conjuration and ceremony, combat, and clue-finding. They do not shape and sort their practices in categories of three. This should not be taken to mean that they cannot reason the way Indo-Europeans do, or that their rules are not of three kinds. It means that they do not characterize what they do competently the same way I would. Characterization is constitution, however, so I am obligated to say something ambiguously unhelpful, such as: They make less of their ancestral institutions than we do.

My efforts to construct a people's practices in the categories that work as a template for my mind, but not theirs, impose my categories upon them. Indo-European peoples have pressed over the planet, always imposing themselves and their practices on others. Perhaps the clarity and efficiency of their tripartite ideology helps to account for millenia of successful expansion. In any event, it is no longer the case that any substantial group of people is spared the

---

13. Thus Europeans rarely ranked these three institutions and their adepts as Indians did. In European agrarian societies, warriors typically subordinated priests, appropriated their services, and secured "religious authentication" of the institution of kingship (Bendix 1978: 22). Chapter 8, below, attends to questions of rank and ranking.

effects of tripartite thinking and speaking on what they do. In a constitutive view, thinking and speaking begin in deeds: What they do differently because of us become ways of thinking and speaking closer to our own.

Constituting practices in categories (even perception takes practice) is not just universal, it is fundamental. Immanuel Kant made this case by reasoning back from the materials of experience as well as it can be made.[14] In the last decade, Gerard M. Edelman has developed a theory that makes categorization fundamental to higher brain function—cognition in the broadest sense—in the same way that binary operations are fundamental to the brain as a physico-chemical system in receipt of sensory information (1987; note however that, "at the level of concepts, categorization is carried out neither by rigorous, nor by logical, nor by universal criteria" (p. 246; see also Lakoff 1987)[15]

If categorization is fundamental, no set of categories is. Binarism—

---

14. Of course Kant could not escape the effects of social constitution on his description and defense of a priori relations. This is conspicuously illustrated in his treatment of the third analogy of experience, the principle of community (*Gemeinschaft*). "The word community is in the German language ambiguous. It may mean either *communio* or *commercium*. We here employ it in the latter sense, as signifying a dynamical community, without which even local community (*communio spatii*) could never be empirically known" (Kant 1933: 235). It is difficult to imagine a word more redolent of social associations than *commercium*. Even if Kant's relations of and in time constitute fundamental categories, his construction of them is necessarily contingent, local, and arguable.

15. I offer Israel Rosenberg's convenient summary of Edelman's work. During embryonic development human brain cells are organized into an enormous number of "neuronal groups." "Groups are arranged in 'maps' that 'speak' back and forth to each other so as to create different categories of things and events" (Rosenfield 1986: 25).

> This suggests that memory is not an exact repetition of an image of events in one's brain, but a recategorization. Recategorizations occur when the connections between the neuronal groups in different maps are temporarily strengthened. Recategorization of objects or events depends upon motion as well as upon sensation, and it is a skill acquired in the course of experience. We recollect information in different maps interacting in different ways from those of our initial encounter with the information and it leads to its recategorization. We do not simply store images or bits but become more richly endowed with the *capacity to categorize* in connected ways (p. 27; emphasis in original).

the universal resort to paired categories—is a cognitive universal. The existence of rules is predicated on it, because rules always offer a choice, either to follow them or not. The tripartite categorization that I dwell on in these pages may be universal in origin. It has become universal, or nearly so, in the human practices of today. If these categories are universal in practice, they must be cognitive universals, apart from any one of the institutions which they shape and in which they are conveyed.

COMPETENCE WITH RULES

Psychologists and sociologists long shared, and most still share, a simple, plausible account of how people become competent in using rules. This account is positivist and, more particularly, behaviorist. People learn, and then know what rules require of them by noting the consequences of their actions. Regularities are the key. If a repeated action secures the same response on every occasion, then the regularity thus manifested bespeaks of a rule that the agent has learned—learned to comply with, whether she can articulate its content. In a word, she has internalized the rule. Her behavior is rule-governed, as that phrase is commonly, and loosely, used.

Obviously the problem with this account is that some human behavior is the result of informed judgment, based on the context of relevant rules and of the consequences of choosing to follow some, all, or none of them. Such conduct would seem to override the simple mechanism of an automatic response to a situation governed by an internalized rule. As Black has pointed out, even this "stark choice between blind, unconscious mastery ('rule-covered behavior' or the even more primitive outcome of 'conditioning') and self-conscious adherence to explicitly formulated principles ('rule-invoking behavior')" unduly simplifies the range of responses to rules. "Between these extremes, we have been able to discern types of intelligent and skillful performance ('rule-accepting' and 'rule-guided' behavior), . . ." (1970: 55, see generally pp. 41–56). Undoubtedly people learn, and know, what rules require of them. Beyond that they learn, and know, how to use rules. Jeff Coulter described this as *"non*-propositional learning how."[16] I would call it learning how to exercise judgment.

Evidently learning how to use rules is cognitively more complex and demanding than learning what rules say. It is equally evident that children become competent both in knowing the rules and exercising judgment in their use as they grow physically and socially. Given the fundamental human propensity to categorize, incremental changes in a particular direction (growth) are seen as movement through stages. Insofar as children internalize rules by learning from the consequences of not knowing them, stages register gains in knowledge — not just gains in memory but gains in the capacity to generalize from specific experiences and categorize them aptly. Insofar as children learn how to use rules, stages register the emergence of new capabilities to override propositional learning and substitute more skillful performances.

That cognitive development proceeds in stages is not a matter of controversy. What we might mean by "stage" is. In the instance of learning what rules say, stages are observers' benchmarks in the growth of children's mastery of the propositional content of rules. In the instance of learning how to use rules, stages represent successive transformations in children's cognitive organization. Com-

---

16. He did so in the context of arguing that the behaviorist account of learning construes the mind as a computer (Coulter 1983: 57–60). This is a programming metaphor in his terms, which conveys what I have been calling the binary view of cognition.

> The programming metaphor for acculturation in humans is precisely a *metaphor* because much of the learning which it construes as programming-with-rules is, in fact, *non*-propositional learning *how.* Of course, there is a great deal of learning-that characteristic of early socialization (given a rich enough basis in language-acquisition on the part of the learner), and some of this propositional learning is indeed the learning of discursive statements about conduct, categorical declaratives, proverbs, principles and rules of various sorts. However, for those accomplishments of the child for which the programming metaphor has been so literally construed in modern cognitivism and philosophy of psychology, there is very little actual rule-learning going on at all (p. 59, his emphases).

See also Johnson (1987) on the connection between "nonpropositional meaning and metaphorical structures . . ." (pp. 1–40, quoting p. 5).

petence means to have passed through a necessary and invariant sequence of stages.

From a constructivist perspective, these positions can be reconciled. Children grow in competence to deal with socially constituted reality. That reality is not just a collection of rules, but a variety of practices, all of which sort into three categories. It would not be surprising if children developed competence in each inclusive category — category of speech act, rules, and reasoning — at a different time in their cognitive development, which is ineluctibly associated with their physical and social development. If this is so (and I think it is), then stages of growth would appear to the observer as necessary and invariant in their relation. Yet the stages are still nothing other than benchmarks in the acquisition of particular categories of competence, which children universally achieve in the same sequence. No logic of stages is needed for stages always appear in the same order.

These matters are brought to the fore in the study of "moral development" in children. Jean Piaget (1932) initiated study of the emergence of judgment as an aspect of cognitive development. More recently Lawrence Kohlberg has been the dominant figure. In his first published work, Kohlberg identified two opposed positions on stages of moral develpment. They are seen as either "successive acquisitions or internalizations of cultural moral concepts," or "structures emerging from the interaction of the child with his social environment, rather than directly reflecting external structures given by the child's culture" (1963: 30). Kohlberg himself undeviatingly adhered to the second position, calling it constructivist.

Both the label and inspiration for Kohlberg's position come from Piaget (Kohlberg 1984: 301). Notwithstanding, Kohlberg's work is not really constructivist. He has always maintained that moral development proceeds "stepwise through an invariant sequence" (1963: 31). This sequence has an "inner logic": "later stages not only *replace,* but also *transform* earlier stages" (1984: 246, emphasis in original).

Kohlberg's move from an invariant sequence to an inner logic trades constructivism for structuralism. This is Piaget's ambiguous legacy, for he was an exponent of both (1970). Structuralist models associated with Piaget, Claude Levi-Strauss, and Noam Chomsky depend on invariant transformation rules for endogenous changes in state and behind them a postulate of binarism as the fundamental

structural principle—or primary mental operation, which human beings are not just competent, but genetically mandated, to perform.

Piaget's structuralism provides a concise way of summarizing
stages of development, because constructions are structures, even if
they are not generated by a structural principle. Kohlberg need not
have accepted the structuralist explanation for the relation of structures to have profited from structuralist description. Even Piaget
showed little interest in structuralist logic when he came to describing stages as structures.

To Kohlberg's credit, his own descriptive efforts prompted him to
look for a constructivist release from the undue rigidity of a presumed inner logic of development. The issue for Kohlberg is posed
by evidence that most people fail to achieve what he has identified
as a last (sixth) stage of moral development. That some people do
achieve this stage is due to their powers of construction and the
favored circumstances of their social reality. Because Kohlberg described the content of a sixth stage in terms of personal autonomy
and principled conduct (Black's rule-invoking behavior), he turned
in his constructivist quest to the moral tradition of Kant and contemporary Kantians like John Rawls and Jürgen Habermas[17] (1984:
217–224, 300–304). Nevertheless, all that Kohlberg can have gained
by this is support for construction of the last stage, which, his critics
have advised, is nothing more than support for his liberal sentiments
(Reid and Yanarella 1980, Shweder 1982).

There is an alternative which, were Kohlberg to have adopted it,
would substitute a constructivist rendition of invariant stages in
moral development for a problematic inner logic. Ironically it means
returning to Piaget's pioneering work on the subject (1932), one element of which—rules—is conspicuously absent from Kohlberg's
characterization of the stages of development. For Piaget the con-

---

17. Kohlberg's recourse to Habermas and his ambitious program of "reconstructive
science" (1979, 1984) may seem a bit quixotic, given that Habermas, despite Kantian sympathies, has been a leading critic of liberal values to which Kohlberg was
committed (1981: 227–230). Furthermore, Habermas' program is not constructivist in any sense that helps Kohlberg—in effect it rejects categories of representation imposed by systematic science in favor of the clarification of categories
already informing ordinary language, thereby emancipating the everyday world
by restoring its capacity to represent itself (Alford 1985).

structivist, rules mediate the interaction between a child and her environment. "All morality consists of a system of rules, and the essence of all morality is to be sought for in the respect that the individual acquires for these rules." (Piaget 1932: 11).

Piaget distinguished between the practice of rules and consciousness of rules, and identified four stages of development in practice and three stages of development in consciousness. The first stage of rule practice he decided was "of a purely motor and individual character," and can be dispensed with because the rules in question are not "truly collective rules" (Piaget 1932: 16, his emphasis). Certainly this is the case with infants, and Piaget was correct not to infer rules from mere behavioral regularities. Thereafter stages of rule consciousness parallel, but lag somewhat behind, stages of rule practice.

Kohlberg started with six stages of moral development, none of them defined by reference to rules. Soon, however, he and his associates had organized invariant stages into three levels (Kohlberg 1981: 16–17, Kohlberg and Gilligan 1971: 1066–1068, Tapp and Kohlberg 1971: 68–70). In his canonical statement of 1976, Kohlberg recommended thinking of levels "as different types of relationships between the *self* and *society's rules and expectations*" (1984: 173, his emphasis). The three levels, I, II, and III, are rather unhelpfully labeled preconventional, conventional, and postconventional, a convention apparently being an external rule that an individual has successfully internalized. The preconventional level of development finds rules external to the self, and the postconventional level finds the individual having "differentiated his or her self from the rules and expectations of others and define[d] his or her values in terms of self-chosen principles" (p. 173).

Observe that Kohlberg recovered the rule element at great cost to his claim to a constructivist position; the first two levels reproduce the conventional internalization scheme of his adversaries, and the third level extends it by showing that internalized rules can be thrown back to the external world and then replaced with new rules (self-chosen principles) that are internally created. If constructivism means, as I think it must, that the individual actively participates in the construction of her own social reality, then choices are never just internally created, any more than they are just internalized. Constructivists want to overcome the dualism of self and world by denying priority to either. Yet I get a different impression in reading, for example, that the individual's "social perspective" at level III is "prior-to-society" (Kohlberg 1984: 177).

None of this means that Kohlberg was wrong to have organized stages into levels. His doing so brings rules back into the picture, though hardly to good effect. It also raises a question—two questions actually: Does it bring Piaget back into the picture and, if so, what is the exact relation of Kohlberg's stages to Piaget's? Were both men employing the same inner logic, then their stages should also be the same. Yet Piaget had three stages of practice, if we forget the nonsocial, premoral first stage, and, inasmuch as Kohlberg ignored consciousness of rules altogether, the latter's six stages double that number. Kohlberg's interpretation of this inconsistency is itself inconsistent. A chart Kohlberg published in 1969 shows his first two stages aligned with Piaget's first two, his third and fourth without counterpart in Piaget's sequence, and his fifth and sixth stages aligned with Piaget's last stage (1984: 45). A decade later he remarked in passing that from the beginning he had added fourth, fifth, and sixth stages to Piaget's original three (1979: viii).

The inconsistency disappears if we think of Kohlberg as having stretched Piaget's third stage to include the last four stages in the sequence of six. This is plausible only if we attribute to Piaget a thoroughgoing indifference to moral development in children after the age of thirteen or so, presumably because their cognitive development is substantially complete by then. Kohlberg would then be correct in his argument that Kohlbergian educators could speed up moral development after that age (Kohlberg 1981: 55–59). It also follows that any movement that does occur in the second half of a child's development has no explanation. Kohlberg's description of development as proceeding through invariant stages after the halfway point is just that: a description.

Introducing rules as the medium connecting children and their environment is a necessary step in a constructivist interpretation of moral development. Without a second step, the result is still unsatisfactory because Piaget's and Kohlberg's descriptions of the developmental sequence come out in different places. The problem is their joint acceptance of the view, which serves the internalization position well enough, that rules constitute a passive and transparent medium between people and environment. Consequently nothing in the environment is systematically differentiated for developmental purposes, and moral development can only be driven by an hypothesized inner logic of genetically supplied cognitive transformations.

Rules are not simply passive conduits of the contents of an environment. They perform constitutive and regulative tasks, as revealed in the speech acts they employ. A necessary second step for a constructivist interpretation of moral development requires the introduction of categories of rules in relation to Piaget's stages and Kohlberg's levels. Only then can their descriptions of an invariant developmental sequence be reconciled, while avoiding the gratuitous postulation of an inner logic of development. Only then is it possible to understand the construction of judgment, and the possible constructions of judgment.

When children are between the age of three to five years, Piaget discovered that they cannot play games without following rules. These are instruction-rules which help the child play "in an individualistic manner with material that is social" (Piaget 1932: 271). This is the first stage of rule practice that can properly be called moral, and, even then, Piaget called it "the stage of *egocentrism*" (Piaget 1932: 26, his emphasis). Kohlberg also found the preconventional level marked by egocentric behavior and a "concrete individual" perspective (Kohlberg 1984: 177). Nevertheless, he asserted that the object of egocentric behavior is to avoid punishment. The child is *"rule-obeying"* (Tapp and Kohlberg 1971: 69, their emphasis). Such behavior implies rules issued and enforced by others, which are directive-rules and not instructions. Evidently Piaget and Kohlberg were talking about different kinds of rules at level I.

An example will shed some light on the difference. The instruction, Don't touch the stove, need not be accompanied by threats of punishment to become a rule practiced by the young child. That child still learns from diverse experiences why instructions ought to be followed. Faced with a directive (directive speech act or directive-rule), the child treats its content as an instruction and responds accordingly. Indeed all rules are external to the child at that early age (See also Piaget 1932: 42, fn. 1). That this is so led Kohlberg to conflate two different rule practices at the first level, because that is what parents often do in their rule practice toward young children.

Piaget did not make this mistake, because he was not interested in the proximate origin of the rules, but only in their use by children. Punishment is not a consideration. As with practice, so with consciousness. Here again the first stage is not oriented to authority. Indeed Piaget found the contrary: "The child more or less pleases himself in the application of the rules" (Piaget 1932: 49). What then, as Piaget himself asked, is the role of the adult authority? For the child, it simply "affirms a continuous communion between the ego and the World of the Elder or Adult, . . ." If punishment is not a consideration in rule practice at level I, it is because consciousness at that level assigns no place or meaning to punishment as adults understand it.

Piaget's characterization of the practice of rules at level II emphasizes goal-oriented behavior within bounds set by common rules. Thus activity is fully social, for it involves comparing performances with competitors playing by the same rules. Cooperation is insured by the existence of rules, which tend to be seen as inviolate or sacred (a matter of consciousness) and which have been completely internalized — everyone knows them by heart (Piaget 1932: 45–46). Hence Kohlberg's designation of rules at this level as conventional seems right, but not the inference that compliance with rules is assured because they are internalized. I read just such an inference in the statement that "at the conventional level (II), a *rule-maintaining* perspective prevails. The main concern is law and order. . . ." (Tapp and Kohlberg 1971: 69, their emphasis).

Children will break rules and then deny or justify their actions. Other children will respond to violations and their justification by calling on authority. Asking older children or adults to evaluate transgressions, clarify rules, and punish malfeasants shows the emergence of an understanding of authority as a social matter and not just a matter of adult whimsy. The conventional attitude fosters an appreciation of directive-rules. Because they are also internalized, behavior also tends to be conventional, that is, consistent with what the rule requires. Unconventional behavior, though infrequent, meets with a public outcry and the invocation of authority. Punishment is brought into the picture because it is part of the received cultural apparatus of authority (if it is — in some cultures it may be very little present). Fear of punishment is an entailment of the disposition of authorities to punish; that fear be a deterrent does not require it be specifically a fear of punishment. Rather it is fear of having to deal with a public situation of alleged violation and justification, not to mention disruption of whatever activity is at hand. To see fear more narrowly in terms of punishment is to see the world of children only through adult eyes.

At level II children also learn to act authoritatively, that is, issue directive-rules, specify conditions of applicability and, if disregarded, act accordingly. Piaget noted that to resolve the contradiction between creating a new rule and thinking it sacred and timeless, the child imagines "that he has merely rediscovered a rule that was already in existence" (Piaget 1932: 48). Wielding authority is consonant with a conventional attitude. The result is indeed consciousness of being a "member-of-society," in Kohlberg's words (1984: 177), and not just in the passive sense of responding to rules.

Kohlberg's description of moral conduct at level III comports nicely with Piaget's fourth stage of rule practice, dominated by "interest in rules themselves," and his third stage of consciousness, in which "there are no more crises of opinion, but only breaches in procedure" (Piaget 1932: 41, 57). Self-consciousness about negotiating rules, accepting innovations, and bowing to reasonably expressed public opinion presupposes knowing that some rules specify conditions under which one commits oneself on the understanding that other people, whether adults or children, are making commitments too.

Of all rules, commitment-rules are the most difficult to practice because they require a correlative consciousness about the social meaning of such practices. Obviously some people may not easily solve the chicken-and-egg dilemma implied here. How does one get the requisite consciousness without relevant practice; why would one risk rule practice in the absence of rule consciousness? The paradigm for this situation is the Prisoner's Dilemma (discussed in chapter 8), which offers conditions under which commitment-rules may be practiced to mutual advantage only if partners impute an appropriate rule-consciousness to each other.

It is no wonder then that Kohlberg and his colleagues have had some empirical difficulties with A and B stages of level III (stages 5 and 6) (Kohlberg 1984: 270–74). Stage 6 cannot be extricated from stage 5 because practices and consciousness are interdependent. Kohlberg's level III social perspective should be maker-of-society, not prior-to-society. Tapp and Kohlberg came closer by calling it the "*rule-making* perspective," then vitiated the point by having rules made rationally, "*ex nihilo*," out of nothing (1971: 69–70, their emphasis). To be fully conscious of the implications of making society by making commitments, not rules as such, is to be constructivist. Gone is the autonomous individual – she is an artifact of lower levels of rule experience.

At each level, Kohlberg's A and B stages correspond closely to Piaget's division between practice and consciousness. Thus stages 1, 3, and 5 are levels of development in the practice of rules; levels 2, 4, and 6 are lagging levels of consciousness about rule practices. Kohlberg is therefore almost right in saying that the "second stage is a more advanced and organized form of the general perspective at each major level" (Kohlberg 1984: 173). Stage B appears to be more advanced because it requires organization, but second-order activity can also be seen as secondary – cleaning things up, so to speak.

Stage 6 (level IIIB) would seem to require more than organization. It calls for an ability to think abstractly. Yet children who reach the needed cognitive level do so years before Kohlberg found them achieving stage 6 consciousness. More generally Kohlberg's stages come later in children's lives than do Piaget's. This age gap must relate to different substantive foci of structurally parallel schemes. Piaget focused on rules as used by children; Kohlberg on situations hypothesized by adults (see further Damon 1977: 36–46). The absence of rule-talk in his adult-to-child settings temporally shifts the whole pattern of development as it is discerned empirically.

Kohlberg's version of the developmental sequence holds up less well to inspection than does Piaget's. By resorting to the language of internalization to define his levels, Kohlberg has made a series of category mistakes, such as putting consciousness of authority at the wrong level. Levels are not just degrees to which rules have become internalized. Instead they are levels of practice and consciousness about categories of rules that are successively more complex in their cognitive demands. Practice and consciousness taken together yield judgment. We do not simply learn to respond to instruction-, directive-, and commitment-rules, having learned to recognize them in successive stages of development. We judge them differently, once we have learned how to, and respond accordingly.

CULTURAL DIFFERENCES

The conventional belief that only performatively directive rules are really rules stems, I think, from the presumption that rules count as such only when their propositional content is rejected or resisted, and they must therefore be imposed. On this view, rules are effective because they are enforced, or at least the possibility of their enforcement is seen as real by those to whom these rules are directed. Because directive-rules are so obviously imposed and resisted, they alone require a continuous, external structure of support in the form of sanctions. Sanctions figure decisively in positivist thought since Bentham (1948: 24–28; see also chapter 5). Except for allowing a place for inducements, or positive sanctions, nothing has changed in this view.[18]

Nevertheless, I find it unduly restrictive. Both instruction-rules and commitment-rules must also have some external dimension. No less, or more, than do directive-rules, can these rules be supposed to incur rejection or resistance and require imposition. In the case of instruction-rules, including the special case of principles, I would argue that the external structure parallel to enforcement involves denigration, mockery, and ostracism. If an instruction-rule has a material component — an example being, Don't touch the stove — to respond with an "I told you so" after the child has burned herself is a simple, and sufficient, application of the external structure. If the rule is strictly a social construction — an example being, Don't eat with your hands — the response is likely to be something like: People will laugh at you. To resort to punishment (or bribery) is to have converted the instruction into a directive, and thus to have augmented or substituted bases for securing compliance. This means that the child will add fear (or greed) to embarrassment and humiliation.

In the case of a commitment-rule, the external element parallel to enforcement is the structure of rights and duties, or reciprocities, upon which notions like person, or property, depend. Thus a commitment-rule saying, Don't snitch on your friends, is accompanied by a power-

---

18. "The sanction is *positive* when it enhances values for the actor to whom it has been applied, negative when it deprives him of values" (Lasswell and Kaplan 1950: 48–49, their emphasis).

ful sanction: Or they will do it to you, and what would it be like not to be able to trust anybody? Of course this rule is capable of being converted into a directive (Or we will beat you up) or an instruction (Or you will lose your friends). Given the difficulty of acquiring a "correct" consciousness of the connection between an exterior reality (a world of trust, for example) and the practice of specific commitment-rules (don't snitch), we may expect that commitment-rules will typically be converted to instructions and directives, with their respective external domains being brought to bear. Yet no rule necessarily loses its original character by being treated as a rule of a different sort for purposes of social convenience or effective internalization.

A proper constructivist view of rules, once they have been sorted into the three categories advanced here, would acknowledge the likelihood that instruction-, directive-, and commitment-rules are likely to be combined in different proportions in historically distinct cultural experiences. Rules in all three categories and associated levels of practice and consciousness are doubtless present in all cultures, though in different mixes. Cultures in which elaborate and highly ritualized instructions, along with much show and pageantry, form the basis of stable social arrangements exemplified by classical Indic societies, as Clifford Geertz (1980) has persuasively demonstrated. A characteristic internalized response in these cultures is what Geertz calls "stage-fright" (1973: 400–403), which I take to be a highly evolved anticipation of the consequences of the failure to perform instructions—a feeling we in the culture of the West share only when on stage.

That culture which has the greatest proportion of commitment-rules in its mix may be our own liberal world. Some of these rules constitute the structure of rights and duties defining our cherished individuality. That which makes us individuals — "possessive individuals" in the specific liberal sense (see also chapter 5) — also creates in us a sense of responsibility, guilt over performance failures, and rage at others' willful disregard of such rules and imperfect consciousness that society depends on them.

Cultures with a substantial proportion of directive-rules include our own, with its police and penal apparatus, its prevailing legal theory, its childrearing practices, and its analytic and reductive tendencies. The techniques of securing compliance to directive-rules are all too well known to us, not to mention the response they elicit (which is, crudely, fear and greed) and the propensity of human beings to internalize both these rules and the consequences of their violation in an abstract and retrievable form.

What the proportion of directive- and commitment-rules might be in Western culture is a difficult empirical question, and whether we have seen a long-run shift in the latter's favor is an ideologically explosive issue, the more so because of the progressive substitution of supervision for punishment. The correlative increase in public spectacles and policies as theater also suggests a shift toward instruction-rules and their cultural concomitants. Technologically enabled possibilities of combining directive- and instruction-rules for control purposes may be sufficiently potent to threaten the long-term balance between directive- and commitment-rules, and fulfill prophecies of a dystopic future (Onuf 1984). Or the counter-tendency toward *embourgeoisement* accompanying global capitalist growth may strengthen the commissive culture of liberalism (Kahn and others 1976).

Others might doubt whether a long-term increase in commitment-rules, at the expense of instruction- and directive-rules, is warranted. They see in liberal culture and its structure of compliance untoward distributive consequences, an exceptionally elusive false consciousness about who's in control because of its depersonalized emphasis on rights and duties, and dire effects on the psychic well-being of its primary beneficiaries—effects in the form of misdirected anger, anxiety, and guilt.

On examination we find that rules in all three categories make stable social arrangements possible by privileging some people over others. We also find that they do so in characteristically different ways and that cultures vary substantially in how they deal with the mix and who ends up with what kind of privilege. To speak in terms that Ruth Benedict made famous (1946: 222–227), a shame culture is one in which the proportion of instruction-rules is relatively high. Also conspicuous are public, even theatrical, responses to questions of competence, comportment, and compliance (rites of passage, ceremonial observances, elaborate courtesies, confessions, and displays of remorse). The holders of privilege tend to be elders, priests, and those upon whom honorifics are bestowed. To define shame as a response to having violated an external rule, as Benedict did (p. 223), and then hang a whole cultural complex on such a thread asks too much of the distinction, fostered by the internalization thesis, between external and internalized rules.

No differently a guilt culture, in which commitment-rules, a sense of responsibility and concern over performance failures (one's own and others'), and the privileging of merchants and property owners implies a great deal more than would guilt as a response to internalized rules (again Benedict, p. 223). To the extent that a guilt culture, like that of the West, creates a conspicuous public place for rights, the point is not just that such rules need not be internalized, but that the response to their violation is indignation and the mobilization of public sentiment, just as we would expect in a shame culture. Conversely, to the extent that a shame culture, like that of Shi'ism, places such principles as the identity of self and community at its center, these principles are so completely internalized that martyrdom does not demand an audience.

Not only does the shame/guilt distinction unduly simplify the relation of rules to cultures, it falsely portrays the world as having only two types of cultures. The third possibility consists in cultures of fear and dread, in which we find directive-rules, calculating conduct, fear of mistakes, and the privileging of warriors and those who are brazen or wily (lions and foxes, in Niccolò Machiavelli's vocabulary). Because our own highly instrumental, analytic culture depends on the internalization of directive-rules and a calculating response, we minimize the extent that ours is as much, or more, a culture of fear as it is of guilt. We do not think we are afraid of punishment because we spend so much time avoiding it; we do not find our prudence remarkable because much of it is discharged in an organizational environment in which punishments and rewards are depersonalized and palpable fears are transmuted into a generalized performance anxiety.

That every culture displays rules in all three categories, though in different proportions, does not deny the possibility of developmental tendencies in any real culture. Development can only mean a change in the mix. As an acknowledged liberal, Kohlberg obviously preferred any development toward the ideal type of culture consisting of commitment-rules, responsibility, and guilt, and the privileging of property. A Confucian philosopher might well prefer the ideal type of culture consisting of principles, honor, and shame, and the privileging of the old and wise. Behaviorists as philosophers no less than organization theorists can be seen to prefer directive-rules disguised as objectives, efficiency and calculation, and the privileging of the instrumentally skilled.[19] Each is more aware of the limitations of the others' ideal culture than of her own, but we are entitled (to use the language of commissives) to fault them all for their purity.

The alternative is to prefer a balance in the proportion of rules by category and associated cultural propensities. Were the term "pluralist" not already appropriated by people like Kohlberg, who prefer a multiplicity of rights (as they see it) or tyranny of property (as their critics say), it might suit this alternative. Albeit unconsciously, most of us prefer the rule mix that privileges us or that we are comfortable with because it is ours. The best case I can make for the last alternative is that it fairly describes my own culture, which indeed privileges me. It would also seem to ensure a degree of cultural diversity that most of us who value it unduly attribute to the cultural complex of rights, responsibilities, and material achievement.

These exceedingly sketchy remarks about culture do not make the particular material circumstances in which the members of a social unit find themselves "immaterial" for their culture. Even if such circumstances significantly affect productive activities—intensive rice cultivation in Bali, for example—and tend even to exclude certain social arrangements—commitment-rules constituting exclusive prop-

---

19. B. F. Skinner is exemplary (1971). In *Verbal Behavior* (1957), Skinner's preoccupation with directives prompted him to introduce the term "mand" for the "mnemonic value derived from a 'command,' 'demand,' 'countermand,' and so on. . . . A 'mand,' then may be defined as a verbal operant in which the response is reinforced by a characteristic consequence and is therefore under the functional control of relevant conditions of deprivation and aversive stimulation" (p. 35). Skinner also invented the term "tact." "The term carries the mnemonic suggestion of behavior which 'makes contact with' the physical world" (p. 81). Despite this apparent acknowledgement of language's representational function, Skinner resisted the temptation "to say that in a tact the response 'refers to,' 'mentions,' 'announces,' 'talks about,' 'names,' 'denotes,' or 'describes' its stimulus." In asserting states of affairs, tacts function only to reinforce behavior (pp. 83–90), which makes them nothing more than directives. The sanctions for tacts are positive, for mands negative. In his singleminded commitment to behaviorism, even in matters of language, Skinner rejected the long-prevailing representational view of language and, by providing nothing in its place, implied a radical materialist position denying the existence of knowledge. There are only behavior, deprivation, and reinforcement.

erty rights, in this example—other arrangements and cultural consequences than those that Geertz found so prominent in Bali, with its
instruction-rules and theatrical display, are not ruled out. The main-
tenance of waterworks for purposes of irrigation could have resulted
in the directive-rule complex of "hydraulic societies" (Wittfogel 1957,
which considers Bali a "well-integrated hydraulic order," p. 53; see
Geertz 1980: 45–46, against this view) or the interdependence of
tasks in an Owenite community self-consciously founded on a social
contract of mutual aid and responsibility.

I would say the same for gender. The categories of man and woman
obviously depend on what one might call a material condition, namely,
that women alone have the capacity to bear and nurse children. This
differentiating condition promotes a near universal tendency to associate other activities with "mothering" and assign them to women.
Gender is substantially a social construction, and gender differentiation an instruction-rule, or principle, as to who is responsible for
mothering, not just as reproduction, but as social practice.

"Maternal practice," to borrow Sara Ruddick's useful phrase, is
caring for children and, by extension, the household, the infirm, the
incompetent, the needy, the world. It is "the work of 'world *protection,* world *preservation,* world *repair* . . .'" (Ruddick 1983a: 217,
quoting Adrienne Rich; Ruddick's emphases). Maternal practice is
also a way of thinking about the world. For Ruddick, it is "maternal
thinking" (1983a) and "preservative love" (1983b); for Carol Gilligan
(1982) and Nel Noddings (1984), it is simply "caring."

Evidently gender assignment disposes men and women to reason
differently and, when they reason about rules, with consequences we
see as ethically freighted. Gilligan's work supports the conclusion
that, at least in liberal culture, boys learn to use deductive reasoning
when faced with moral dilemmas, while girls rely on inductive reasoning[20] (1982: 24–63). In Ruddick's formulation, men think "warfully,"
or, more abstractly, they are given to abstraction (1983b: 249–252).

---

20. Gilligan used Kohlberg's scheme for the moral development of children and the
    moral dilemmas he devised for rating the development of particular children. She
    found that Kohlberg's predilection for deductive reasoning resulted in girls being
    rated behind boys because they reason differently and not because they differ in
    rule competence. In studying adolescent women, Gilligan sketched a counterpart
    scheme to Kohlberg's oriented to inductive reasoning (1982: 64–105).

Women think concretely. Maternal thinking "respects complexity, connection, particularity, and ambiguity" (p. 249; see also Gilligan 1982: 101 and Noddings 1984: 36–37).

In this line of feminist thought, "cognitive style" (Ruddick 1983b: 249) yields correlative ethical styles, respectively for men and women, austere judgment and (with apologies to Geertz) thick prescription. According to Gilligan, the former emphasizes rights, the latter responsibilities. This they do when moral dilemmas involve conflicts over commitment-rules—the moral dilemmas Gilligan, for example, took for granted. If instruction-rules are at stake, an analytic cognitive style would emphasize clarity and directness; a concrete, integrative style would emphasize empathy. When Ruddick charged men with disregard for "the details of suffering" (1983b: 250), directive-rules figure in the equation. Yet if women are sensitive to details, abstraction fosters an appreciation of the magnitude of suffering.

Perhaps we may summarize women's concerns as "an ethic of care" and men's "a principled conception of justice", as Gilligan did (1982: 30). Nevertheless, I hesitate to say that the former is always to be preferred to the latter. Nor does a particular cognitive style necessarily lead in a direction I find ethically attractive. Abstraction can lead to absolutism and arrogance, concreteness to triviality and smugness. Furthermore, abductive thinking is a third cognitive style not to be found in these discussions (I suppose, because abduction is so generally underestimated and because it poorly correlates with gender). Abduction is associative, instead of analytic or integrative. It support an ethic of affect, of honor and pity. Acknowledgment of abduction and its consequences is a useful antidote to binarism and social polarization.

Obviously many factors intrude when people choose different categories of reasoning to deal with moral dilemmas. Gender contributes one such factor. So does culture and its distinctive mix of rules and thus of moral dilemmas. Material conditions play their part. Children must be cared for; caring is a consequence. People can kill each other; war is a consequence. If cultures mix rules, differentiated by category, in different proportions, people, differentiated by gender, culture, life circumstances, and material conditions, resort to categories of reasoning in different and ever changing proportions. That the Balinese favor instruction-rules, or men abstraction, are generalizations admitting to significant individual variation, and not categorical statements.

4

THE PROBLEM
OF ORDER

Culture provides support for rules. In the culture of the West, the
prominence of directive-rules has inspired in political and legal
theory a preoccupation with enforcement as the external dimension
of support for rules. (The abundance of commitment-rules matches
a preoccupation with obligation, which, as this culture's preferred
abstraction for the support of such rules, does not discriminate
clearly between internal and external dimensions of support.) Order
breaks down in the absence of rules that are effective because they
are enforced. Talcott Parsons called this "the problem of order,"
concern for which he dated from Thomas Hobbes (although Hobbes
used the term "order" and its cognates infrequently). Parsons rejected Hobbes' contractarian solution and ignored his successors,
emphasizing instead the internal dimension of support for rules.
For this, he drew on Emile Durkheim, but not, as he should have,
on Max Weber.

Had Parsons fully appreciated the Sociology of Law initiated by
Durkheim and Weber, not to mention the tradition of thought he
ascribed to Hobbes, he would have realized that all rules, whether
bearing instructions, directives or commitments, depend for their effectiveness on internalization, as the last chapter concludes, and on
such external features of rules and their support as formality and
institutionalization. The presence of such features are criteria of

legality. Orders are legal in the degree that their rules are effectively supported. Whether the international order is indeed a legal one is a subtle question. That "international regimes," as well-supported rule complexes, are legal is a conclusion that helps to sort out the many and diverse regimes constituting perhaps the bulk of international relations.

For the better part of this discussion, I accept the problem of order as asserted, because those assertions rule our thought. I do so only provisionally. I conclude the chapter with the claim that invoking the problem of order is a rhetorical strategy which, by metaphorically associating order, nature, and social arrangements, serves to disguise another problem, no less "real" (once we understand the construction of reality) than the problem of order. This is the problem of privilege: By constituting conditions of rule, rules always distribute privilege, and always preferentially.

LAW AND ORDER

Hobbes posed the problem of order in its definitive form, as Parsons reminded social scientists in his landmark reconstruction of social theory produced by the generation preceding his own (1937: 89–94). Autonomous agents, as utility maximizers, clash in their pursuit of scarce values, with dire results. Parsons correctly maintained that "Hobbes' system of social theory is almost a pure case of utilitarianism" (p. 90)—almost pure, because Hobbes's statement of the problem of order is consistent with utilitarian premises, but his social contract solution is not. Nor did Parsons find Hobbes' solution persuasive (1937: 93). Furthermore, John Locke weakened Hobbes' utilitarian rendition of the human situation with a "more or less wishful postulation of the natural identity of interests," thereby making the idea of social contract more plausible but "minimizing the importance of the problem of order" (pp. 96–97).

Parsons appears to have thought that the problem went unaddressed until Vilfredo Pareto, Durkheim, and Weber—the prime subjects of his study—lay the foundations for the discipline of Sociology then emerging with Parsons' codificatory assistance (compare introduction, footnote 14). Yet Parsons was wrong to think that the

Hobbesian problem and its solution receded in importance after Hobbes. One must remember that the social contract is not itself the solution to the Hobbesian problem, but instead the means to a solution, which is of course the Leviathan. Utilitarians like David Hume, Jeremy Bentham, James Mill, and John Austin progressively saw the social contract as an unneeded artifice and transformed the Leviathan from a too easily caricatured despot to a legal order. The Lockean tradition, which finds limits to calculation in the play of rights and duties, points in the same direction: the rule of law, as our liberal-constitutional rhetoric would have it. Parsons neglected both the practical successes and theoretical sophistication which the original solution subsequently achieved because he had a different solution, one he attributed to Durkheim more than anyone else.[1]

As related by Parsons, Durkheim's solution to the problem of order was to emphasize the internalization of norms—"they enter directly into the constitution of the actors' ends themselves" (1937: 382; see generally pp. 378–390). I want to pause here to consider Parsons' word choices. In the preceding chapter, I referred to the internalization of the propositional content of rules. Durkheim wrote of "rules" (*règles*), whether in reference to method or conduct. In assessing Durkheim's solution to the problem of order, Parsons observed that "it opens the door to a new conception of the relation of the individual, and hence of constraint, to the normative rule" (p. 382). Throughout his discussion of Durkheim, Parsons often substituted "norm" for "rule."[2]

---

1. Perhaps it would be better to say that Parsons collapsed the Hobbesian solution as it had developed into the concept of authority, which he famously but incorrectly used to translate Weber's "*Herrschaft*," or rule. The latter term comes from an altogether different intellectual tradition, in which nothing resembling Hobbes's problem is to be found. Symptomatically Parsons all but ignored the matter of authority in the work I examine here, notwithstanding his attention to Weber (1937: 500–697). See chapter 6 for a detailed discussion of *Herrschaft*.
2. One might argue the terms are interchangeable. Weber appears to have thought they were. He used both, though favoring "norm" throughout *Economy and Society* (1968). Nevertheless, German scholarship shows a decided preference for "rule" (*Regel*) in the instance of rules of language or method (Ludwig Wittgenstein being an example) and for "norm" (*Norm*) in the instance of rules of law (Hans Kelsen an example). I should also note that I do not find Kelsen's reasons for preferring "norm" to "rule" very convincing. The first is that the term "rules" is too inclusive, referring as it does to "laws of nature (in the sense of physics)"

Yet there is a method to Parsons' choice of terms. When he, or Durkheim, had constraints in mind, the term "rule" is preferred. When the subject is some "sentiment attributable to one or more actors that something is an end in itself" (1937: 75), then "norm" is the proper term. The first is the external, the second the internalized manifestation of prescribed propositional content. Because Durkheim saw these as twin aspects of the same phenomenon, "normative rule" is an appropriate term for Parsons' use, with rule and norm interchangeable shorthand versions.

In the remainder of Parsons' 1937 book, we find the terms "norm" and especially "normative" frequently, the term "rule" rarely. His next major work (1951) repeats this pattern. Some descriptively oriented passages make reference to "rules" (e.g., pp. 270–271). For conceptual purposes, though, rules become "standards of behavior" (p. 38), which are nothing other than the expectations of others. One's expectations of oneself ("role expectations", p. 38; Parsons' quotation marks) come from "internalization of the standard" (p. 38). "Normative order," normative orientation" (pp. 11–12), and "normative pattern system" (pp. 271–273) are synonyms for the "expectation system" of self and others.

I see in all this a decided tendency on Parsons' part to favor the internalized aspect of rules over their external aspect. Durkheim's "solution" was to see constraint and conformity as complementary in explaining order. Parsons acknowledged this (1937: 365, 403). But when Parsons developed the Durkheimian solution systematically, his concern was why people conform when they are not actively forced to. Reducing everything to expectations imputes primacy to what is

---

(1945: 37). Obviously rules in this sense are different from other rules, all of which, because they have authors and histories, are "normative." Notice, however, that "laws of nature" are different from all human laws (legal rules) in just the same way, yet Kelsen failed to propose that we also abandon the term "laws" to Physicists. Kelsen's second reason for preferring "norms" is that rules must always be general, referring to "a whole class of similar events' (p. 38, compare Black 1962: 108), while some norms refer to specific individuals and situations and yet are clearly legal. Notice though that if the circumstances specified by any such norm were to be repeated, however unlikely this may be, then that norm would apply in this instance also. Otherwise it is difficult to see what is "normative" about the putative norm.

already internal—to be found in oneself and others. In effect Parsons reversed the presumption that externally manifest propositional content is internalized. For him, internally manifest content is externalized as expectations of others.

I am not suggesting that Parsons' reversal is wrong-headed. On the contrary, internalization and externalization should be seen as two phases of a single process.[3] My reservation is this: No less than those who posit internalization of externally manifest content, Parsons treated rules as a transparent medium and all behavior as governed by the content of rules. The result is not just that the agent is rendered passive and conflicts among agents minimized, to repeat well-known (and well-deserved) criticisms of Parsons (Coser 1956: 20–23, Mills 1959b: 25–44, Gouldner 1970: 199–245; compare Alexander's "revisionist" assessment, 1983b, quoting p. 5). More importantly, society itself disappears. In its place is the "social system," which is a brief for methodological collectivism masquerading as a description of social reality. Parsons believed that with Durkheim's help he had saved positivism from the excesses of utilitarian individualism. Perhaps Durkheim's balanced treatment of constraint and conformity achieved this goal, but Parsons erred in the other direction. For all his talk of action—"The Action Frame of Reference and the General Theory of Action" (1951: title of chapter I)—nothing happens.

---

3. Weber took exactly this position:

> The 'adjustment' which arises from the habituation to an action causes conduct that in the beginning constituted plain habit later to be experienced as binding; then, with the awareness of the diffusion of such conduct among a plurality of individuals, it comes to be incorporated as "consensus" into people's semi- or wholly conscious "expectations" as to the meaningfully corresponding conduct of others (Weber 1968: 754).

In constructivist terms, neither phase should be seen as having temporal (or causal) priority. In view of Parsons's careful study of Weber, it is surprising that he gave credit only to Durkheim for seeing internalization as necessary to the solution of the problem of order. Perhaps Weber's emphatic attachment to positivist legal theory distracted Parsons. Thus in the passage just quoted, Weber went on to say: "Finally these 'consensual understandings' acquire the guaranty of coercive enforcement by which they are distinguished from mere 'conventions'." Yet, I argue below, Parsons took the same position despite himself.

That nothing happens in Parsons' system (meaning his system of
ideas and the social system, which are the same) is nicely illustrated
by the way he handled the phenomenon of institutionalization. Given
Parsons' emphasis on propositional content which, upon being internalized, explains conformity and yields order, he was bound to
acknowledge the regularities of conduct thus manifest. Externalized
as behavior, content affects others through expectations. In its externalized form, such behavior is subject to institutionalization.

For Parsons, "a value-orientation standard" is institutionalized
when two conditions are fulfilled.

> In the first place, by virtue of internalization of the standard,
> uniformity with it tends to be of personal, expressive and/or
> instrumental significance to ego [the self]. In the second place,
> the structuring of reactions of alter [other] to ego's action as
> sanctions is a function of his conformity with the standard
> (1951: 38).

These two conditions tell us nothing, for they must already obtain
if propositional content is to be construed as a value-orientation
standard, as Parsons specified.

Parsons explained that institutionalization is marked by "the fulfillment of . . . need dispositions and a condition of 'optimizing' the
reactions of other significant actors, . . ." (1951: 38). But when are
someone's needs fulfilled and others' reactions optimized? That no
general answer is possible warrants Parsons' assertion that "institutionalization of a set of role expectations and of corresponding sanctions is clearly a matter of degree" (p. 39). More than this, however,
institutionalization must, as a matter of degree, vary from person
to person. By Parsons' reckoning, institutionalization cannot be a
social phenomenon at all.

It might be said in Parsons' defense that he brought the system
into the realm of the social by including sanctions as well as expectations in the abstract formulations I have just quoted. Sanctions, and
the expectations that they will be applied, could supply the system
with an external and dynamic element. These formulations recapitulate Parsons' earlier discussion of Durkheim's solution to the problem of order, which Durkheim in turn had lodged in a discussion
of rules of contract. For Durkheim such rules were legal despite not

being the usual sort of directive-rule backed by coercion. He did use the term "sanction," which is of course an integral part of the utilitarian formula for law. In the instance of contract rules, however, sanctions were not "repressive" but "restitutive" (1933: 69). Durkheim's contract rules are, in my vocabulary, commitment-rules, which have their own distinctive external dimension of support, as I argue in the preceding chapter.

Parsons misinterpreted Durkheim on this point because of the way he, Parsons, defined sanctions. "*What are expectations to ego are sanctions to alter and vice*" (1951: 40, his emphasis). Parsons has gone back to the point where nothing really happens, because expectations are everything. Nominally external, sanctions so defined have no institutional character or social reality. This is obviously untenable. Parsons, sensing as much, defended himself by holding that the "intention" of the sanction "to influence the behavior of the other, or to 'reward' his conformity and to 'punish' his deviance," was not a criterion of his concept of sanction (p. 40). But punishment and reward are its content, as his long subsequent discussion of "Deviant Behavior and the Mechanisms of Social Control" (title of chapter VII, pp. 249–311) makes evident. Even approval and disapproval are but instances of reward and punishment (p. 422; compare chapter 3, footnote 19, on B. F. Skinner).

Parsons escaped from his empty definition of sanction by adopting, albeit unconsciously, the legal positivist definition of the term, and not Durkheim's differentiated conception. Thus a commendable effort to reach beyond the utilitarian solution to the problem of order led Parsons to reject that solution while succumbing to one of its most conspicuous flaws: If rules are more than internalized propositional content, then they must be directive-rules backed by coercive sanctions (rewards and punishment).[4]

For Parsons there is an unbridgeable divide between the social system as a collective representation of internalized content, explaining nothing because nothing happens, and a panoply of institutions (an institution being "a higher order unit of social structure which

---

4. At least Parsons avoided the tendency in legal positivism to define such sanctions exclusively in terms of punishment. As terms like "repressive sanction" and "coercive enforcement" indicate, Durkheim and Weber did not.

is of strategic significance for the social system in question," 1951: 39), the unexplained presence of which is the only available explanation for regularities of conduct.[5] Institutionalization, but not Parsons' conception of it, and the differentiation of ways rules are supported, such as we see in Durkheim's conception of sanction, but not in Parsons', together constitute a bridge across the divide.

Parsons expressly rejected Durkheim's distinction between repressive and restitutive sanctions, yielding "two types of law" and "two types of society" (1937: 318). According to Parsons, this distinction is an artifact of Durkheim's early schematic work, which gave way to the development of the idea of *"collective conscience,"* initially thought by Durkheim to underlie repressive law, but later recognized by him to underlie the division of labor and restitution as well. Parsons saw in Durkheim's shift a clear repudiation of utilitarian individualism and a warrant for his own program of methodological collectivism. I see no evidence myself that Durkheim thought the less of his work on law just because his interests changed. Parsons simply underestimated that work by seeing it only in reference to the problem of order and an allegedly collectivist solution.

Durkheim differentiated law into two categories by reference to what laws in each category do in society and how they do it. In one, laws promote orderly individual behavior by threatening to constrain individuals whose behavior warrants this response. In the other,

---

5. Indicatively, Parsons' illustrations of institutions—property, marriage, parenthood—are legal institutions, by which I mean that some of their central rules are legal. The institution of the law would seem to have been presupposed. We see the same problem with Paul Bohannan's otherwise useful concept of "double institutionalization," which distinguishes custom from law.

> All social institutions are marked by "customs" and these "customs" exhibit most of the stigmata cited by any definition of law. But there is one salient difference. Whereas custom continues to inhere in, and only in, those institutions which it governs (and which in turn govern it), law is specifically recreated, by agents of society, in a narrow and recognizable context—that is, in the context of institutions that are legal in character and, to some degree at least, discrete from all others (1967: 45).

The reader will recognize this as another of legal positivism's conspicuous flaws: The theory stipulates what it endeavors to explain, namely, the existence of legal order.

laws promote orderly exchange among individuals by spelling out conditions for exchange and consequences for their nonfulfillment. Weber also proposed two categories of law. Parsons evinced far less interest in Weber's work on law than in Durkheim's, and so he failed even to recognize Weber's contribution. One category, understandably enough, is the same as Durkheim's repressive law and the one category admitted in positivist legal theory. The second acknowledges the legal character of the pronouncements of high dignitaries (*honoratiores*; Weber 1968: 648–649, 784–802), even when no particular actor is subject to constraint. These pronouncements are of course principles, which I define in chapter 2 as instruction-rules in which some value is articulated. They promote general conformity of behavior by reference to shared values. This is done by example, by appeal and, if necessary, discrimination. Discriminating against nonconforming individuals or groups is only part of the external dimension of support for principle. Yet it is the part most resembling a sanction as Durkheim, Weber, and utilitarian positivists have understood that term.

It should now be clear that together Durkheim and Weber differentiated legal rules into the three categories of rules I ascertain in chapter 2. Weber's "abstract legal concepts" (1968: 799) are instruction-rules, laws in the usual sense of criminal law are directive-rules, and the rules of Durkheim's "cooperative law" (1933: 127) are commitment-rules. Obviously not all rules are legal rules. Certain conditions must be fulfilled. The point of the Sociology of law developed by Durkheim and Weber is to describe those conditions in general and comparative terms. I have examined their work on law elsewhere (1982b: 31–39). Here I wish to summarize it as a set of propositions which Durkheim and Weber either state or imply. From these propositions I will draw some more general conclusions.

First, principles are legal when they are enunciated by dignitaries of sufficiently high station and on occasions of such solemnity that their principled content cannot be impugned without also impugning the source and circumstances of their enunciation. Weber implied that legality is indistinguishable from the sanctity of principles, sanctity resulting from the independence, integrity, and prestige of those responsible for announcing or more typically affirming principles. Second, positivist legal theory, to which both Durkheim and Weber subscribed in the instance of directive-rules, assumes a clear point demarcating those rules to be considered legal. Rules are legal when they are effective, which in turn depends on their enforcement. Weber further required that such enforcement be in the hands of an autonomous staff. Third, commitment-rules could only be considered legal when their application results in fair and thus generally accepted consequences. Durkheim saw this result in the availability of established means of recourse to address complaints and remedy defects. He implied the existence of impartial administration for this purpose.

Generalizing, legality is a function of the degree to which (1) rules are formally stated, (2) their external dimension of support is institutionalized, and (3) the personnel responsible for formalizing and institutionally supporting rules are specifically and formally assigned these tasks, for which they are often also specifically trained. Though related in complex ways, these three criteria are separable. The extent to which each is fulfilled in the instance of a particular rule may, but need not, coincide. Such incongruities are especially evident in what we might call (at least for the moment) the international order and raise the vexing question, Is that order a legal one? Let me take each criterion of legality in turn, to see if this question is answerable.

Formality can be given a functional interpretation. The formal statement of principles gives them weight—the more formal the weightier. This property enables people to rank and choose among large numbers of sometimes incompatible rules.[6] The formal statement of directive-rules makes them more abstract, often by casting them in the passive voice. This is likely to produce a detached response—one as impersonal as the rule—which eases the burden of making the rule work onto those whom it directs. Finally the formal statement of an ensemble of commitment-rules requires their compilation, with conflicts resolved and gaps filled, so as to provide routine access to what would otherwise be a confusing and inconsistent mass of rules.

Performative speech formalizes rules. Those rules that are legal in function take the form of declarative speech acts, i.e., those that

---

6. On the weightiness of principles, see Ronald Dworkin (1977: 22–28), although he saw this property as barring them from being rules, thus too narrowly defined.

are successful, or performatively sufficient, without depending on hearers' assent to implicate hearers in their normativity. Most such speech acts assume the characteristics of declarations because they conform to perlocutionary requirements stipulated by speech acts of the same character. Said otherwise, the speech act, I declare war, acquires its performative sufficiency because some other declaration (a constitution, for example) specifies as one of its perlocutionary effects that I may do so. Regress takes us to rules that are declarations because they are stated with that specific intention in mind — They are intended to be rules with the specific perlocutionary effect of authorizing persons to perform certain speech acts which will then be declarations on performance. And they are guaranteed success as speech acts because assent is either formally accorded prior to their declarative statement (e.g., vote, signature) or can be inferred from circumstances (custom).

Most declarations have their source as law in other declarations. Those that have no such source are self-referential, in the sense that they refer back only to their own authorship for legal standing. This explains the difference between rules based on precedent and those based on custom, as well as between contracts and treaties. As they develop, legal orders do away with self-referential declarations. In this connection, however, principles present a special case. Self-referential assertive declarations do exist in highly developed orders, but they are not easily assimilated into the usual positivist conception of law (as Ronald Dworkin demonstrated, 1977: 14–45). But law they are, whatever damage this does to the positivist conception of a properly legal order.

Readers may observe a parallel in this discussion to H. L. A. Hart's famous distinction between primary and secondary rules (1961: 77–120; regress implies the possibility of tertiary rules, Kratochwil 1983: 25–27). In Hart's language, self-referential declarations are secondary rules recognizing the legal character of primary rules — the bulk of rules specifying conduct. If the order is without secondary rules, then, according to Hart, it is not genuinely legal, and primary rules are necessarily self-referential declarations. I might not want to call an order "constitutional" in the usual sense if most or all of its rules are self-referential. All the same, those rules are legal if they are performatively sufficient, that is, invoking them is a successfully performed speech act independent of hearers' reception. If rules in an order are legal, how can the legal order not be legal? To the degree that rules are legal, it follows then that the order is legal to the same degree.

Consider the international order. Hart's willingness to call it legal on grounds of similarity to constitutional orders (1961: 208–231) is persuasive only if one accepts the doctrine of a hierarchy of sources of international law, which leaves little room for self-referential declarations. (On sources doctrine, see Onuf 1982b: 8–27.) Yet, if one does accept this doctrine, the international order has an abundance of rules of doubtful legality, for they lack a source in law. Better to say that the international order is legal to a degree that it would not be if it were to resemble a constitutional order.

The degree to which rules are formalized is one criterion of their legality. A second criterion, rarely completely dissociated from the first, is the degree to which the external dimension of support for rules is institutionalized. There are two features of interest in the institutionalization of support. The first is that supports for rules are also rules, always derived from three categories of speech acts. The second feature of these supports as ruled constructions is that they specify roles, the occupants of which act in support of legal rules.[7] For the most part, these acts are speech acts.

Taking principles first, their support typically takes the form of exhortation. This is clearest when a system of rules attains the formality associated with religion (see chapter 3, footnote 12.) Exhortations are directive speech acts, which become institutionalized as the injunctions and imprecations of role occupants performing liturgical and pastoral duties. The support typically accompanying directive speech acts takes the form of a threat. At least when the word is used transitively, a threat is a contingent promise expressed in a commissive speech act. Role occupants are capable of keeping these promises, with recognition that their willingness to do so deters con-

---

7. I use the term "role" narrowly for positions in a society which have fully and formally stated qualifications and duties. I do not mean all conceivable social positions, or "'points of articulation' between actors and structures." (Giddens 1979: 117, quoting Parsons; see generally pp. 115–120 for a critique of the broad, Parsonsian view of role.)

duct warranting the promised response.[8] Finally commitment-rules find support in the issuance of opinions and interpretations as to their scope and application. Role occupants responsible for issuing these instructions are presumably personally disinterested in the consequences of their acts—They are impartial third parties. (On impartiality and its relation to "third-party law," see Franck 1968.) Cumulatively these acts become institutionalized as procedural guidelines and collations of precedents.

Roles supporting formal rules are found in religions, as I have already suggested, in gangs and clubs which have enforcers, and in systems of third-party dispute settlement. Are these legal orders? I am inclined to think they are. Such doubts as are raised I would attribute to the likelihood that formalization of rules has not (or does not appear to have) proceeded apace with institutionalization of supporting rules. Thus a "folk" religion may well have well-institutionalized support for rules which is nonetheless difficult (at least for an outsider) to ascertain. Because the outsider in question almost certainly comes from a culture in which formalization is closely and unduly associated with literacy and record-keeping, the formality of orally transmitted rules goes unrecognized and their legality denied, notwithstanding an evidently high level of institutionalized support for those rules.[9]

No such difficulty arises in the case of international relations. Many rules are written down—in treaties, treatises, proceedings of tribunals, codificatory texts—and described in such writings as legal or binding. Instead international relations produce relatively few

8. Thomas C. Schelling's memorable discussion of threats and promises identifies one difference between them. "The difference is that a promise is costly when it succeeds, and a threat is costly when it fails" (1960: 177). This is, however, not a difference in what threats and promises do, but what their content is. Threats might be defined as commissive speech acts the perlocutionary content of which consists of deprivations and not rewards. As promised states of affairs, rewards and deprivations both incur costs, but only if the promise must be kept.

9. Recognition is hampered by a baffling feature of unwritten, customary rules of law. They are vaguely general in statement but specific in application, with repeated application never making the verbal statement of the rule more specific: "the law returns, as it were, from its brief excursion into detail and reverts to its normal condition of generality." (Hamnett 1975: 11; see also Comaroff and Roberts 1981: 70–84, 231–240, Geertz 1983: 207–214)

rules institutionalizing support for formal rules oriented to conduct. In effect, roles are relegated to the very agents whose conduct is at stake. The result is called a "self-help" system (Kelsen 1952: 14–17, Tucker 1977: 3–15).

Doubts that such a system constitutes a legal order are hardly unexpected. Scholars nonetheless convinced that an international legal order does exist have an ingenious response. They claim the agents in question are "double-functionaries"—They act simultaneously, and more or less self-consciously, on behalf of the legal order known as the state and the international legal order. In so doing, they can be expected to minimize the conflict incipient in their dual responsibilities.[10] It would not do to dismiss this response as nothing more than clever semantics, but I must save its defense until later.

Rules specifying roles in support of formal rules are themselves susceptible to formalization and institutional support from yet other rules. Following Hart, I would call rules so formalized "power-conferring rules" or, more simply, "powers" (1962: 32–43). They constitute supporting roles legally, endowing acts thus prescribed—exhortations, promises, opinions—with the force of law. Occupants of such roles are officers—"officers of the law." Furthermore, personnel so empowered are likely to be trained, often rigorously, in the performance of their legal duties.[11]

The presence of officers, as understood here, is the third criterion of legality. If it is met, any uncertainty left by the application of the other two criteria—formality and institutionalized support of rules—is likely to be dispelled for the participants in that order. Thus "organized" religions, criminal syndicates, and systems of third-party dispute settlement are readily acknowledged as legal orders because their officers, be they priests, *capi* or judges, speak within the order with the force of law.[12] Again, the outsider may be skeptical because

---

10. This is the well-known concept of *dédoublement fonctionnel"* offered by Georges Scelle and extended by Myres S. McDougal. For critical discussion, see Nardin (1983: 162 n. 14, 206–207).

11. Devotees of old cowboy movies will recognize a posse deputized to apprehend an "outlaw" as an exceptional instance demanded by the unsettled circumstances of the frontier.

12. Weber defined "organization (*Verband*)" as "a social relationship" in which "regu-

she fails for cultural reasons to recognize the formality of power-conferring rules. Or the outsider may doubt the legality of the order because its officers violate the rules of some other, allegedly encompassing legal order with their acts. Such a view is persuasive, however, only if one holds that agents may participate in just one legal order at a time, or that all legal orders are nested, so that rules of one are granted legality by the rules of a "higher" order.

Evidently, even after all three criteria of rules in an order have been met, it is possible to object that the order is not a legal one. This objection follows from Austin's identification of law with the command of a sovereign (see chapter 2, footnote 2). We may dispatch the legal positivist's demand that rules must be directive (commands), and still be left with sovereignty as a condition that must obtain for the order if its rules are to be considered legal. For legal positivists, a final test of a legal order is the possession of sovereignty.

The condition of sovereignty requires that a formally connected set of rules operates exclusively in some manifold of space and time. The state is that rule set and its material correlates – the resources of territory and population. From an individual's perspective, a sovereign legal order excludes participation in any other legal order in the same place and at the same time. Competing orders are legal only if the sovereign legal order makes them so by incorporating them into itself. For a given space-time manifold, there can be one legal order, but never more than one.

For legal positivists, and no less so for political realists, sovereignty is indivisible. (Morgenthau 1967: 312–317) Yet the exclusive sway of a sovereign legal order requires the strenuous and unremitting application of directive-rules and coercive sanctions. The result is the state, rendered abstractly as "a monopoly of organized violence" (p. 487; see also Claude 1962: 222–242). Sovereignty,

---

lations are enforced by specific individuals: a chief and, possibly, an administrative staff, which normally also has representative powers. The incumbency of a policy-making position or participation in the functions of a staff constitute 'executive powers' (*Regierungsgewalten*)" (1968: 48). Even if we drop Weber's emphasis on directive-rules and their enforcement, the presence of officers remains the defining characteristic of "organized" social relations.

directive-rules and the state—Each necessitates the other in a tight, unbroken circle.[13]

Sovereignty is not a condition that just happens to rule sets. Instead it is an ideal that is never reached, in a world where each step toward the ideal takes effort and costs resources, possibly in increasing increments, to prevent ever smaller amounts of unwanted behavior (Young 1979: 122–124). Formalization of the rule set promotes the fiction of sovereignty, rather than the independence of the order; but the ideal of a self-encapsulated set of rules, ordered by principle, abstractly rendered and exhaustively explicated is, again, the more difficult to achieve as it is approached. Practically speaking, officers of legal orders must be satisfied with something less than sovereignty.

State sovereignty can, but does not automatically, prevent religions, criminal syndicates, or systems of dispute settlement to be found within the space-time manifold of the state from being legal. Indeed, states' officers protect the fiction of state sovereignty by granting formal legal autonomy to religions, or labor unions, for example, by incorporating them into the legal order of the state. Criminal syndicates cannot be treated this way, because these rule sets, like that of the state, center on strenuously applied directive-rules, formal

---

13. There is nothing logically necessary about this circle, however. One can imagine a legal order in which sovereignty is approximated by strenuous indoctrination and exhaustive discussion. Either could prove to be materially less expensive than systematic coercion. An example of the former might be the Chinese "preceptoral system" under Mao. "A preceptoral system is a system of social control through highly unilateral governmental persuasion addressed . . . to an entire population" (Lindblom 1977: 55, see generally pp. 55–59). An example of the latter might be the endless discussion of group differences by the Kalihari's !Kung San. "Conflicts within the group are resolved by talking, sometimes half or all of the night, for nights, weeks on end." Melvin Konner, whose words these are, went on to observe: "After two years with the San, I came to think of the Pleistocene epoch of human history . . . as one interminable marathon encounter group" (1982: 7). The legal positivist penchant for directive-rules is partly a cultural bias, given the large proportion of directive-rules in Western practice and partly an appreciation of the problem of securing a legal order from external threats to its independence. Absence of such threats lessens the pressure on officers of the legal order to develop coercive capabilities that can be deployed within the order at little additional cost.

acknowledgement of which would be tantamount to a conferral of sovereignty, at least in legal positivist terms.

We find much the same situation in international relations. States' officers are persuaded that many rules outside of the legal order of the state are nonetheless legal. They give formal acknowledgement and institutional support to a number of limited, more or less coherent rule sets constituting and regulating particularly dense, complex patches of international relations. Each is a legal order in its own right, no less than, say, a religion organized within and tolerated by the state is, and often more so. Current scholarly fashion calls these legal orders "international regimes," and I turn to them presently. Finally, states' officers even regard the full set of rules constituting international relations — conventionally taken to mean all relations of states — as a legal order. This they do despite the incoherence of this rule set and the logical inconsistency that results for legal positivism. As a test for an order's legality, sovereignty is honored in the breach.

When I am unsure of the legal implications of some endeavor of mine, I rarely trouble myself with the subtle question of sovereignty. I do seek the advice of someone who knows more about the relevant rules than I do (D'Amato 1984: 5–55). Were I a duly trained and empowered officer of the law, I would do the same. The help I need is provided by lawyers — a group trained in the law, skilled with the materials and tools of the law, and entitled, sometimes empowered, to render advice on the law. Lawyers may settle the skeptical outsider's question about sovereignty. (It is, after all, not my question.) This, however, is the lesser part of what they do. They answer my question about the legality of particular rules. They do the same in institutionally fixed ways for any number of individuals with similar questions. My activities presuppose what lawyers would have difficulty establishing to the satisfaction of a legal positivist: The rules in question, and the many correlative institutionalized practices they, as lawyers, engage in and attend to, constitute the legal order.

Ordinarily the activities of lawyers and of officers are highly complementary. These activities together make the legal order what it is, and they cannot be dissociated. Here again the international order is anomalous, but less so than it seems. Lawyers, trained to recognize as law the many rules of high formality in international relations, are as abundant as agents acting solely on behalf of the international legal order (much less officers empowered to do so) are scarce. Not only have these lawyers established, more or less successfully, the legal character of a substantial proportion of international relations' rules, they function as advisers to the double functionaries who stand in as the order's institutionalized support.

The legal adviser serves her client, the double functionary, *and* the international legal order, through her advice on what the order demands of her client. She too is a double-functionary, whose commitment to law and the idea of legal order tends to offset the inevitable parochialism of the officer she advises. It is the complementarity of their activities that lends credibility to the argument that officers can act on behalf of two (or more) orders. If rules are legal in the international order to the degree that lawyers say so and other agree (compare Onuf 1982b: 66–73), that order is a legal one to the degree that legal advisers and their clients act as if it is (compare Onuf 1979: 265).

REGIMES

The international legal order is a set of rules, the coherence of which derives from practices associated with the formality and institutionalized support of rules in any legal order. Above all, the international legal order is a lawyerly construction. Lawyers give the rule set whatever coherence it possesses. Those less expansive but more coherent sets of rules to be found throughout international relations — international regimes, as noted above — owe their character, meaning their scope and coherence, to the fact that they are confined to "a given area of international relations." At least, this is what the now standard definition tells us.[14]

---

14. "Regimes can be defined as sets of implicit or explicit principles, norms, rules and decision-making procedures, around which actors' expectations converge in a given area of international relations" (Krasner 1982: 185). Some scholars have emphasized the sets of rules, others convergent expectations (Haggard and Simmons 1987: 493–495). The former are ill served by the uselessly imprecise definitions offered for principle, norm, rule and decision-making procedure. The latter are stuck, like Parsons and his social system, with notional regimes in which nothing happens.

Who decides what "a given area" is? Scholars typically take "given" to mean "objectively given," as in objectively available to anyone who cares to look. This is of course the baldest kind of positivism, which, contrary to Kratochwil and Ruggie's claim (1986: 764), denies regimes any "element of intersubjectivity." As such, it warrants the response that regimes are what those people whose activities constitute them think they are. In effect, regime role occupants give the regime the scope and coherence that scholars see as an objection condition.

One version of this response is Ernst B. Haas' concern for "the ways actors order their knowledge and apply knowledge in the construction of regimes" (1980: 375). Haas focused on occupants more than roles. By virtue of training and professional orientation, the individuals filling such roles impose coherence on their activities—cognition precedes constitution (1980, 1982; compare Haggard and Simmons 1987: 509–513, on the "cognitivist" view of regimes). My inclination runs in the other direction. Roles come first, because regimes are ruled constructions. The rules themselves come from activities, not just of the regime's role occupants, but as well of scholars, lawyers, officers of legal orders served by the fiction of sovereignty, and the many and diverse individuals, beyond those whose roles I just named, who are associated with institutions for which the regime matters.

Rules "give" any regime its scope and coherence by demarcating roles. The more formal these roles are and the better supported institutionally, the more confidently we (role occupants, scholars, lawyers, officers) say a regime exists. For all intents and purposes, any regime known as such must have enough legal rules to qualify, at least in my terms, as a legal order in its own right. International lawyers have long acknowledged the existence of international regimes, but account for their legality by mere incorporation into the international legal order. International Relations scholars, who discovered international regimes only recently and without much awareness of lawyers' concerns, have assiduously avoided calling them legal. Both groups miss the central feature of regimes: They are sets of rules, a substantial number of which (especially those giving the regime its scope and coherence) are legal rules. Both groups miss this point because of their joint attachment to legal positivism, which accords or denies legality to rules by the set and not rule by rule.

As more or less self-contained rule sets, international regimes mix instruction-, directive-, and commitment-rules, each doing so in different proportions. As noted, many of the rules in a regime will be sufficiently formal and institutionally well-supported to be called law. Again, the ratio of formal to informal rules will vary from regime to regime, as will the distribution of formal instruction-, directive-, and commitment-rules. Clearly regimes do not fall into categories, as rules do. Nonetheless, they can be typed, perhaps crudely, by comparing them to ideal types of regimes, defined by reference to the prominence of instruction-, directive-, and commitment-rules in their constitution. This is not simply a quantitative measure of the distribution of formal rules. Rather it involves a judgment about the necessarily small number of rules providing all other regime rules, formal and informal, with a point of reference, and thereby granting the regime its identity as a coherent rule set. Usually these rules will be self-referential declarations, or secondary rules in Hart's sense, though obviously they are any regime's primary rules, or "constitution," in the usual sense of these terms.

As a type, regimes in which formal instruction-rules are primary I would call "monitory regimes." They are constituted around a small number of principles which have achieved a high level of formality through enunciation in plenary forums. Regime principles are supported through a great deal of conventional, indeed ritualized, exhortation. These admonitions seldom receive the institutional support necessary for directive-rules to become laws. In the absence of a formal, directive apparatus to supervise conduct, the monitory flow reminds regime participants that their conduct is being monitored, however informally. That the bulk of regime rules are informal makes it difficult even to be sure that a regime exists, and they are rarely discussed as such in the literature.[15]

Let me offer some examples of monitory international regimes. One is the regime organized under General Assembly Resolution 1514(XV), "Declaration on the Granting of Independence to Colonial Countries and Peoples" (1960), and its many iterations (Bleicher

---

15. In earlier work (1982b: 78), I called regimes of this type "management regimes," with international resource regimes in mind as examples. Later Peterson and I (1984: 332) called this type "tutelary regimes," with the United Nations' human rights regime the subject of our attention. Both "management" and "tutelage," I now think, are regime activities too narrowly associated with the specific examples then under consideration.

1969), to expedite the process of decolonization then underway. The United Nations Special Committee on Colonialism has issued a stream of directive-rules, many of them singling out United Nations members not conforming to the principle of decolonization. Because these directive-rules tend to be individualized and weakly supported, they have never achieved legal standing. When resisted, the committee has resorted to fact-finding, and produced detailed reports, thereby adding credibility to its charges against specific regime participants.

These tactics sacrifice the abstraction generally necessary for directive-rules to become legal in favor of an increase in the external support for a legal principle. By naming names and documenting practices, the committee supports the principle by embarrassing non-conforming members and even subjecting them to a hint of ostracism. Consider the committee's recent preoccupation with the status of Puerto Rico (Franck 1985: 195–204). The angry reaction in the United States suggests that no regime participant is completely immune to the committee's endeavors.

A second example of a monitory regime is the one constituted on the principle that *Apartheid* is such an egregious offense to humanity that its practice anywhere cannot be condoned. Because the Republic of South Africa is alone in practicing *Apartheid* in flagrant disregard for the principle, the United Nations membership has dedicated itself to supporting that principle, at first with resolutions deploring South Africa's conduct and appealing for a change of policies, and then with a general and abstract rule—a rule of law—directing any regime to cease complicity in the practice of *Apartheid*.[16] Insofar as

---

Insofar as these regimes are all constituted to elicit conformity to principle, they can do so only by combining formal exhortation and informal supervision. But for the informality of directive-rules supporting principles, I would have called these regimes "supervisory." Alternatively I might have called them "disciplinary" but for my extensive use of this term in an unrelated context (Introduction). Both possibilities, and my thoughts on this type of regime, owe to Michel Foucault's *Discipline and Punish* (1979).

16. Of particular consequence for the emergence of this general rule is General Assembly Resolution 1904 (XVIII), "United Nations Declaration on the Elimination of All Forms of Racial Discrimination" (1963), Article 5 of which directs: "An end shall be put without delay to governmental and other public policies of racial segregation and especially policies of *apartheid,* as well as all forms of racial discrimination and separation resulting from such policies."

this effort has succeeded in legal terms (I think it has; see also Henkin 1979: 126, 178), South Africa cannot claim to be excluded, by its own choice, from participation in the regime. Even the progressive ostracism of South Africa, effected by expulsion from other regimes, supports the legal principle against *Apartheid* without adversely affecting the general directive-rule that no officer for any legal order may practice *Apartheid*.

Other, perhaps more typical examples of monitory international regimes can be found in the area of resource conservation and use. Thus the international whaling regime is organized around the principle of maximum sustainable yield in harvesting whales (Birnie 1985: 168–170). The principle's success depends on the adoption by regime participants of an annual quota (reduced to zero in 1985), which is then supervised by the International Whaling Commission as a permanent fact-finding apparatus. Failure of the regime to guarantee the principle of sustaining whale populations has prompted some private groups to interfere with whaling operations of some regime participants (Day 1987). Whether this means a broadening of the regime to include directive-rules of extreme informality or the disappearance of the regime, as incoherence sets in, remains to be seen.

Despite the tendency for directive-rules to seep into monitory regimes which have proven to be weak and ineffective systems of support for principles, these rules are unlikely to acquire a meaningful degree of formality and institutional support. Were this to happen, and furthermore these rules substitute for principles in defining a regime's activities, then we could say that the regime had changed to a new type. Indeed, we may say in the exceptional case of *Apartheid* that the emergence of a formal directive-rule against *Apartheid* constitutes a second, minimally developed regime working in parallel with the monitory regime against *Apartheid*. In general, however, we would expect few international regimes to be constituted on formal directive-rules, and for the same reason that criminal syndicates are denied legal standing: Regimes dependent on formal directive-rules for their identity—executive regimes, we might call them—threaten the fiction that states alone are sovereign legal orders. If these regimes do not threaten the fiction of sovereignty, it is because they have been incorporated into the ensemble of regimes authorized by the state and constituting its government.[17]

Executive regimes linked as a state's government individually exhibit a marked degree of coherence in the form of governmental ministries and agencies. What seem to be objectively given areas of international relations for which regimes can be identified correspond to the areas of responsibility typically demarcating governmental ministries. Comparably demarcated international regimes are nevertheless endowed with few if any of the directive-rules applicable to the states' officers participating in the regime. Instead many international regimes have been endowed with organizations resembling ministries, within which directive-rules apply to the organization's officers. This enables the organization to carry out responsibilities assigned to it under the regime's instruction-rules and especially commitment-rules, as we shall see presently.

There are instances, however, in which states' officers agree to give a tightly circumscribed area of international relations a set of formal directive-rules, affecting themselves, lodged in a matrix of rules offering considerable institutional support. Such is the case with the European Community and the parallel system for deep seabed mining in the Law of the Sea Convention. In both cases, the institutional support provided for directive-rules is complicated to the point of ambiguity. The practical implications of divided sovereignty could hardly make it otherwise. The conceptual problem raised by dividing the indivisible is more readily solved by constructing a new category for regimes of this character: They are supranational (Haas 1968: 32–59).

Collective security is also an attempt to build a system of support, or legal regime, around a few directive-rules (see generally Claude 1962: 94–204). In this case, however, the practical and conceptual

---

17. In my earlier work with Peterson (1984: 332), we referred to regimes organized around directive-rules as "governmental regimes." I now prefer to think of them as executive regimes so as to note what such regimes empower officers to do, namely, carry out or "execute" commitments institutionally supporting formal directive-rules. The term "governmental regime" describes what a regime is, not what it does, but confusingly, because the term "government" may be used interchangeably with regime to mean the officers of a sovereign legal order, or comprehensively to mean the largest possible set of regimes within a legal order.

problem of sovereignty cannot be finessed, disguised, or ignored, because of the area of international relations to which the directive-rules in question apply. Collective security would smuggle the Hobbesian solution to the problem of order into the disorderly world of states. True to Hobbes, a collective security system precludes self-referential directive declarations. Instead some executive body, itself constituted by a commissive declaration of the highest formality (indeed a social contract) decides on specific directive-rules. No one can anticipate whose conduct is subject to decision. That depends on how participants, knowing the consequences all have promised each other, decide to conduct themselves. Furthermore, every participant must be committed to the support of such decisions. Experience indicates that these commitments are more likely to be honored if they are supported in turn by detailed instruction-rules. Thus is explained the fifty-year quest in the League of Nations and the United Nations for a workable definition of aggression (Ferencz 1975).

The more thoroughgoing the system of support for collective security, the more closely it resembles a sovereign legal order. If the state is Hobbes' solution to the problem of order, the same solution, when applied to the relations of states, would yield a state above states. Obviously this challenges the practical need for states as collective security systems in their own right. This outcome states' officers cannot afford and will not permit, no matter how ingenious and sincere their efforts to become collectively secure.

Collective security demands the formalization of rules if it is to fulfill its promise, whether within or among states. This is a paradox of competing formalizations. It disappears if conditions allow an international regime's directive-rules to work even when, or precisely because, they lack formality. The system of mutual nuclear deterrence is a case in point. Officers of the two states possessing abundant nuclear arsenals and delivery capabilities—the superpowers as they are commonly known—have issued the same directive to each other. They are directed not to engage in a number of more or less clearly specified activities. Should either do so, a devastating response is promised. Each side, knowing itself deterred, presumes the other is also.

The language of deterrence, which dominates all strategic considerations between these two states, is of course the language of positivist legal theory. Bentham's rules on how to prevent mischief with mischief distinguish the idea of punishment from punishment itself: "It is the idea only . . . that really acts on the mind, . . ." (1948: 171–203, quoting p. 193). The rules center on the principle of proportionality. Deterrence increases as preventive mischief, or sanctions, becomes ever more "real" an idea, which is a trait enhanced by increased formality and institutional support. In an ideal legal order, sanctions have been perfected and therefore need never be used—Knowing the inevitable consequences, no one would be foolish enough to bring about their employment. (Compare Schelling 1960: 9: "A theory of deterrence would be, in effect, a theory of the skillful *nonuse* of military forces," his emphasis.) This ideal has never been achieved in practice, except (so far) in the mutual insecurity system operated by officers of the superpowers. In this system both sides have refrained from formalizing the directive-rules so effectively deterring them. This is legal positivism stood on its head, and it raises suspicion that formalization could introduce flaws into what has proved to be a perfect system of deterrence.

This suspicion is widely shared (but not universally; see Falk 1985). Even the effort to formalize a principle—the principle of no-first use of nuclear weapons—to serve as an umbrella for the reciprocal directive-rules issued by officers of the superpowers, has been resisted[18] (Beres 1980: 217–220). The principle itself is only half stated, for it cannot affirm what must be accepted, namely, that the retaliatory use of nuclear weapons is essential to the system of deterrence. Obviously this first, faltering step toward formalization of the rules in this system of deterrence is no great threat to its stability. Yet other, more problematic efforts are not difficult to imagine.

Whether this mutual insecurity system should be called an inter-

---

18. Nevertheless the principle is acknowledged in strategic doctrine as a "limit" (Schelling 1960: 257–266) or "threshold" (Kahn 1965: 94–101).

> If everybody believes, and expect everybody else to believe, that things get more dangerous when the first nuclear weapon goes off, whatever his belief is based on he is going to be reluctant to authorize nuclear weapons, will expect the other side to be reluctant, and in the event nuclear weapons are used will be expectant about rapid escalation in a way that could make escalation more likely (Schelling 1966: 158).

national regime is doubtful (Jervis 1982). That its directive-rules are too informal to be considered legal suggests that it is not a regime in its own right. Insofar as officers for the superpowers have come to recognize that changes in nuclear capabilities could upset the system (recognition abetted by such influential analyses as Schelling and Halperin 1961: 49–61), they have devised an increasingly elaborate legal regime to control such changes — a nuclear arms control regime. Thus rules assuring the integrity of the mutual insecurity system are subject to a degree of formalization not considered appropriate for the rules constituting that system.

Collective security and mutual insecurity systems represent extremes on a continuum of rule sets in which directive-rules figure prominently. Collective security requires such formality that it becomes indistinguishable from one of the key regimes constituting the state, while the mutual insecurity system is so lacking in formality that one has difficulty considering it a regime at all. In between are regimes that lodge a few directive-rules in a larger ensemble of formal instruction- and commitment-rules. Certainly the most important example is the regime, constructed after World War II, which is said to provide officers of the United States with the means of controlling the world economy.[19]

Inasmuch as the United States held a dominating position in the world economy (accounting for nearly half of the world's Gross National Product in 1950; Russett 1965: 121), and in particular was its chief creditor, it could have used informal directive-rules to control credit flows and thus world trade, all the time espousing the principle of free trade. It could even have constructed a minimal free trade

---

19. Whether one or several regimes were constructed for this purpose is arguable. Many scholars identify regimes for each of three well-organized institutions, the General Agreement on Tariffs and Trade (successor to the failed International Trade Organization), International Monetary Fund and International Bank for Reconstruction and Development and its affiliates. I view these three institutions as linked in a larger ensemble of rules, many of them informal, which nevertheless exhibit the coherence of a single, overarching regime for the world economy. The emergence in recent years of other institutions, including private banks, as indispensable regime elements supports the latter view. There is no reason why regimes cannot be nested within regimes (Aggarwal 1985: 32), and no one need fall prey to the legal positivist presumption that nesting confers legality on nested regimes.

regime from innumerable commercial treaties, each containing a most favored nation clause, and still have had control. Yet for complicated reasons, officers of the United States chose an institutional approach in which formal principles and collective pecuniary commitments support a core of directive-rules substitutes for what would otherwise have been an informal rule set, and indeed had been an informal rule set during an earlier period of British ascendancy (compare Ruggie 1982, whose explication of this is unrivaled.)

Even as officers of the United States found their state facing relative decline, the regime continued to operate. Its dense network of supporting rules permitted the issuance of new directive-rules, most prominently in 1971, adapting the regime to changing circumstances.[20] The conditions that officers of the International Monetary Fund often impose when making loans amply testify to continuing reliance on directive-rules. (On "conditionality," see Dell 1981, Guitián 1981; Kenen 1986.) These rules are augmented with detailed instructions and are formally stated and accepted even before they are embedded in loan agreements—joint commissive declarations ostensibly freely decided upon by both parties under formal regime rules.

Finally, and briefly, let me consider international regimes organized around a primary set of commitment-rules. Especially in recent practice, these rules are likely to take the form of a multilateral treaty (self-referential commissive declaration). Such treaties frequently state principles, which then set these treaties apart from the many other agreements officers make on behalf of states and underscore the central place of treaties in the constitution of regimes. These same treaties also constitute periodic forums for regime participants to assess, revise, and extend their formal commitments, as well as permanent bureaux to assist participants in carrying out those commitments. Regime officers whose roles are constituted for this purpose direct a great deal of their attention to the elaboration of detailed instructions. Finally such treaties may constitute forums

---

20. The persistence of this one regime beyond the conditions enabling its constitution spurred recent scholarly attention to regimes. The literature is voluminous, but see especially Robert O. Keohane's development (1980, 1982, 1984), and Duncan Snidal's critical assessment (1985b), of the "theory of hegemonic stability." Chapter 6 treats the misleading use of the term "hegemony" in this context.

to hear complaints about the interpretations and performance of commitments.

After much deliberation, I have decided to call regimes of this type "administrative regimes."[21] One might wonder about this choice of terms in the instance of an international regime minimally constituted around some commitment-rules, such as the "long-established régime" on the privileges and immunities of diplomats (International Court of Justice 1980: 777). Although the legal rules of this regime, clearly stating reciprocal commitments, were formed into multilateral treaties only recently (1961 and 1963) and even now have no bureau to provide them administrative support, the regime is administered, for the most part, quite successfully. The regime's officers are also officers of the legal orders which are regime participants. Diplomats and their legal advisers are double-functionaries. Because the professional position of diplomats depends on the effective administration of commitments made on their behalf, they are more than willing to assume this responsibility.

Most international regimes of the administrative type are not so modestly constituted. Instead they feature bureaux with a decided tendency to expand and, in so doing, acquire the internal support of directive-rules. They become bureaucracies. We need look no further than the United Nations' system of specialized agencies and the General Assembly's subsidiary bodies for examples of administrative regimes prone to expansion. Administrative growth is a hallmark of modernity in social relations generally. Endless growth threatens any administrative regime with eutrophy. The many administrative regimes operating above, among, across, within and around states, including prominently those of the United Nations, are a distinctive feature of modernity and, as they collectively reach the point of eutrophy, the hallmark of the world to come.

---

21. Earlier I had called them "regulatory regimes" (Onuf 1982b: 77–78, Onuf and Peterson 1984: 332), because the codification of entitlements and detailed supporting instructions typical of such regimes produces sets of rules commonly called regulations. In that all rules regulate, I now prefer a term describing the regime's function, which is to provide administrative support for carrying out commitments. This includes administration under sponsorship of executive officers that they may carry out their commitments in support of directive-rules.

RHETORIC AND PRIVILEGE

In the Hobbesian tradition the problem of order is the problem of
achieving and maintaining order. There is nothing problematic about
order as such. Indeed, order is taken as an objective condition, the
stable arrangement of phenomena such as is achieved in nature. It
bears recalling that the Greek word for order, "cosmos," is no less
the term for nature in the largest sense (compare Hayek 1973: 36–
46). Yet "order" is not a strict, literal representation of the condition
of the universe as apprehended by human beings who, after all,
observe a great deal of instability and disarrangement in what they
are capable of apprehending. They could just as well represent what
they see with another Greek word, "chaos."

Those of us whose conception of order is influenced by Greek
thought — which is to say, anyone using the term — use it only figuratively, wishfully perhaps, to represent what is at best imperfectly
achieved and never sustained. When we speak of order, we choose
a fiction to believe in. "Order" is a metaphor, a figure of speech, a
disguise. It is constituted by performative speech and constitutes
propositional content for such speech. One asserts that "order" stands
for, or counts as, the way the world is, can be, should be, will be.
The assertion that order represents something else is also a misrepre-
sentation, because the fit between the one and the other is imperfect.
If indeed the fit is perfect, then it is pointless: a tautology. The point
is clearer if we return again to the question of direction of fit between speech acts and the world as states of affairs.

Note that "world" is also a metaphor, (mis)representing propositional content, which consists of words, as an objective condition. Fit
must refer to the relation between sets of words, not words and "reality." The fit between words describing a state of affairs and the words
used to describe a second state of affairs logically has to be directionless. The whole thing represented by X counts as (stands for, is equivalent to) the whole thing represented by Y. Because X and Y are likely
to differ in specificity or complexity, we may resist saying, Y counts as
X, even if this is the point of the assertion. The directionless fit of assertives is always recognizable as a metaphorical construction.

If the fit is world-to-words, we could also say that part of a state of affairs can change the whole — You are a part of a state of affairs and I direct you to change it and yourself through your actions. This relation of part to whole is a metonymical construction. Finally, a state of affairs as a whole can have an impact on parts: I commit myself, a part, to the creation of a desired state of affairs; I want my actions to be a part of what it becomes. This is a synecdochal construction.

Metaphor, metonymy, and synecdoche are the three basic figures of speech known to rhetoric. They exhaust the possible relations of parts and wholes: whole-to-whole which is the same as part-to-part, for the parts are then operating as wholes, whole-to-part, and part-to-whole (White 1973: 31–36). Three categories of speech acts necessarily result in three categories of rhetorical strategies.[22]

Metaphors are representational, yet they misrepresent. They always want us to construe something in doubt as partaking of the reality of something that we are confident about.[23] In the same way, reduction effectuated through metonymy as a rhetorical strategy does not make the parts more "real," fundamental, or essential, though this is how they appear. Integration does not yield a whole greater than the sum of the parts, though this is the conviction of

---

22. Since Aristotle, irony has been held to be the fourth basic figure of speech, use of which is said to distance the speaker from the subject of speech (White 1973: 36–38). As such, it would seem to be an expressive speech act, and not basic, inasmuch as a number of speaker's stances toward the subject can be imagined, and stated expressively, probably in parasitic association with other categories of speech acts. In the structuralist tradition, metaphor and metonymy are taken to be the primary figures of speech, standing in opposition. Synecdoche and irony are disregarded (Jakobson and Halle 1971: 90–96, Levi-Strauss 1966: 204–208, 224–228). By contrast, poststructuralists privilege irony, but do so ironically, in their acts of deconstruction (Nelson 1983: 184; see also chapter 1).

23. Symptomatically this position resembles, but also departs from, that taken by John Searle (1979: 76–103), whose discussion of speech acts and states of affairs prompts my own. Searle held that metaphors cannot be "comparisons" (the usual view; see Johnson 1987: 66–68), because the introduction of difference, on which the metaphor depends for meaning, is incompatible with the presumption of similarity underlying comparison. Searle posited the model assertive as a literal representation of the world and thus strictly a matter of comparison. Any such comparison can be restated metaphorically, in figurative terms, so that the assertive, as spoken, differs from what the speakers means the hearer to understand. Searle was therefore obliged to put metaphors in a special class of indirect speech acts.

those subject to synecdoche as a rhetorical strategy. If I may speak paradoxically, all figures of speech extend the fiction of their reality to social construction. Insofar as any figure of speech is persuasive — it persuades us to see what we hear — it shifts whatever is undergoing construction into the realm of what the speaker guesses is already "real" to the hearer. When human beings speak performatively, we also speak figuratively, thereby shielding ourselves and others from the provisional nature of our assertions, directives and commitments. That performative speech is also figurative speech means that the ongoing (re)construction of reality is rarely distinguishable from the known, felt, lived-in world we "really" inhabit.

To assert that order is a problem is to propose that the speaker thinks, and the hearer accepts, that order is a natural condition which is both desirable and achievable as a social condition. Figuratively "real," the natural condition of order is different from, but still subject to comparison with, an implied, necessarily figurative representation of a state of affairs we might call "disorder" or "anarchy" (but not "chaos", which would be incomparably different). The presumption that the two conditions are similar enough to be meaningfully compared, but different enough to be worth comparing is fixed by the metaphor "problem," which suggests that the comparison can lead to a solution, also figuratively understood — for Hobbes, the Leviathan and, for Parsons, the internalization of expectations.

The former is a metonymical move because it reduces a whole, "the problem," or disorder, into a part, the Leviathan, which changes the whole from disorder to something that more closely resembles

---

Compare this with my position, which clearly implies that metaphors are not a special class of speech acts, because assertives are always metaphorical constructions. (See Johnson 1987: 68–71 and 220 n. 18 on "the strong constitutive view of metaphor.") If we reject Searle's claim that assertives can literally represent the world, as if the words constituting their propositional content were a perfectly transparent medium, then his position collapses into mine. Searle was right to think that assertives, as speech acts, always presume similarity and metaphors always manipulate differences. Yet similarity necessarily implies difference, or there would be nothing to compare. By asserting that X is similar enough to Y to count as Y, in order to mark (exaggerate, minimize) the difference between X and Y, the speaker represents X and Y conventionally (nonliterally) and then expects the hearer to accept it as literal (literally what the speaker means), thus creating a provisional, negotiated reality between them.

an order. Indicatively, the Leviathan does this with directive-rules. By contrast, Parsons' solution is a synecdochal move because it takes the problem of disorder as a failure of parts (individuals) to function properly as a whole. Internalization of expectations, insofar as it succeeds, integrates parts into a whole, or order, which is then ontologically more real than the parts. Again, indicatively, Parsons' work is replete with terms like "integration" and of course "system," all of which deny the need for, or efficacy of, active direction.

In keeping with my assertion that social construction proceeds with aid from three categories of figurative language, I propose a third solution to the problem of order, which is (need I say?) dependent on a metaphorical move. This solution to the problem of order substitutes a different metaphor for comparison with the state of affairs constituting the problem. The metaphor "order" suggests a stable social arrangement comparable to stable arrangements of the physical world, or nature. Notice that order then is a two-part metaphor. Order is compared to a stable arrangement, which is in turn compared to nature. My metaphor is also constructed in two parts: Order is a stable arrangement, and such arrangements are stable not because they resemble nature, which is also stable, but because they benefit those whose arrangements they are.

The problem then is not to make social arrangements more stable, for they "really" are stable (my metaphor makes them so). Instead the problem is to find out why they are stable. This is the same as asking, who benefits from any given set of arrangements? To speak of a "problem" problematizes whatever is asserted. My metaphorical move from order to arrangement shifts the normative weight invested in the term "problem" away from stability and toward the facticity of "arrangements" as having been arranged.[24]

Most people do not see arrangements as a problem, unless one goes on to suggest collusion or conspiracy, which I do not, at least

---

24. Friedrich von Hayek understood exactly the ideological implications of this choice of metaphors, but he felt that "authoritarians" had already succeeded in interpreting order as "a deliberate *arrangement* by somebody," thus making the concept "unpopular among friends of liberty . . ." (1973: 36, his emphasis). He then sought to rescue the concept of order from this fate by restoring its metaphorical association with nature.

as the invariable or even the usual case. I have an alternative. I can substitute a term like "privilege" for "order": The problem of order becomes the problem of privilege. Yet even this metaphorical move loses its force against the "reality" of order understood as Parsons, among so many others, had wanted us to understand it.

Under the circumstances, I would do well not to use the term "order" at all. To the extent that I can count on others thinking of arrangements as having been arranged (once I point this out), then it suffices to speak of "social arrangements" instead of order, and "legal arrangements" instead of legal order. Orders are institutionalized; arrangements are instituted (compare Polanyi, Arensberg, and Pearson 1971). Because I do not think this move suffices entirely, I will freely speak of privilege in such a way as to problematize it. The rhetorical potency of "order" warrants this strategy, with results no more deceptive than any metaphor, any assertion, secures.

Michael Oakeshott preferred arrangement to order in his well-known definition of politics: "Politics I take to be the activity of attending to the general arrangements of a set of people whom chance or choice have brought together" (1962: 112). Oakeshott's conservatism had him choose "attending to arrangements," because "the arrangements which are enjoyed always far exceed those which are recognized to stand in need of attention, . . ." (p. 112). Normative concerns aside, I quite concur with Oakeshott's empirical judgment and find the idea that arrangements are attended to fully consistent with the position that arrangements are arranged. I also take this definition to support the one I offer above in the introduction.

PART 2: RULE

Rules are empty in themselves, violent and unfinalized; they are impersonal and can be bent to any purpose. The successes of history belong to those who are capable of seizing these rules . . .

Michel Foucault
Language, Counter-Memory,
Practice (1977a: 151)

5

THE PRESUMPTION OF ANARCHY

How any collection of self-interested agents might be capable of co-existence is one of the central substantive questions for social science paradigms in the positivist ontological mode. As the problem of individualism versus collectivism, it is the one procedural problem they all share. For there to be a problem, one must grant its terms. Agents are free; cooperative undertakings are calculated, and they are difficult. These are the terms of liberalism.

I begin this chapter with a discussion of liberalism, in which I argue that international relations considered as a condition of anarchy, a virtual state of nature, is liberalism's paradigm case. Current scholarship tends to view domestic societies as having progressively solved the problem of order by developing as states, while international relations persists in anarchy. I take a contrary view, namely, that international relations was never a matter of anarchy, any more than domestic societies could have been.

Thomas Hobbes notwithstanding, social and political thought during his time drew no sharp distinction between the state and the state of nature. Social relations, including international relations, could and did display evidence of being ruled arrangements. Virtue, rights, and manners describe important features of arrangements lacking central authority and thus formally anarchic. A century after Hobbes, political theorists began to substitute utility for virtue, law for rights, and conventions for manners. The result was to empty anarchy of content and give it today's entirely negative sense: formally, the absence of the central authority of the state; substantively, the absence of guidance provided by virtue, rights and manners.

LIBERALISM

In J. G. A. Pocock's *Virtue, Commerce and History,* we find that liberalism is "a tormented yet oddly triumphant entity . . ." (1985: 38). The term "entity" suggests an operative paradigm, contributing to which is a line of thought—social and political thought in the liberal tradition (recall introduction). Liberal thought attempts to account for important features of liberalism as an ensemble of practices. Yet clearly for Pocock, "tormented" and "triumphant" are words to describe the line of thought rather more than the ensemble of practices. Thus the sentence quoted goes on to say that liberalism has been

> denounced by naturalists as insufficiently natural and by historicists as insufficiently historical, vindicated by some of its defenders on grounds robustly independent of either nature or history, yet accorded by all three—in consequence of their centralizing concern with it—a place in history a good deal more central (I shall argue) than it has in fact occupied (Pocock 1985: 38).

Whatever else it has become, liberalism is a judgment about human nature and its social consequences. C. B. Mcpherson has provided what is by now the standard account of liberalism so considered (part of which I also quote in the introduction, footnote 10):

The individual is free inasmuch as he is the proprietor of his person and capacities. The human essence is freedom from dependence on the will of others, and freedom is a function of possession. Society has a lot of free individuals related to each other as proprietors of their own capacities and of what they have acquired by their exercise (1962: 3).

Liberalism as "possessive individualism" is an altogether apt phrase for this minimal account. Pocock took issue, not with the account as such, but with Mcpherson's having attributed it to Thomas Hobbes and John Locke. Instead Pocock dated its origins a century after Locke's work had appeared (1985: 59–71, 121–123). Nevertheless, Hobbes' and Locke's construction of the individual as free agent is essential to liberal thought. On this Mcpherson was right. Locke made an additional, all too familiar assumption, namely, that the pursuit by many individuals of their self-interest is fundamentally harmonious. While Hobbes did not grant this assumption, he and Locke made quite another assumption, one that Pocock would associate with naturalism. Other assumptions that liberalism has accumulated along the way are historicist, as Pocock noted, or conventionalist, as I will describe Pocock's "robustly independent" grounds for vindicating liberalism.

These additional assumptions tormented liberal thought, if I understand Pocock here, by complicating it, but in doing so they made its triumph possible. Practice found self-interested individuals cooperating, and not just incidentally, to provide such general interests as justice and security. Liberal thought has had to account for these complicating features of liberal practice. It did so by adding auxilliary assumptions qualifying the central belief of possessive individualism and thus protecting it from serious challenge on grounds of practice. The tormenting of liberal thought contributed to the triumph of liberalism as an operative paradigm.[1]

Liberal thought is not, and never was, a simple statement of the

---

1. The reader may recognize in this formulation the influence of Imre Lakatos' account of the growth of scientific knowledge; I did not until a reader of an earlier version pointed it out to me (Lakatos 1978: 47–51). Lakatos divided "research programmes" into a "hard core" of unchallengeable assumptions and a "protec-

social implications of possessive individualism, notwithstanding occasional, sometimes brilliant efforts to make it so (for example,
Nozick 1974). International Relations constitutes the only substantial exception to this generalization. Instead International Relations
is dominated by the presumption of anarchy.[2] Thus Kenneth A. Oye
introduced *World Politics'* recent symposium issue on "cooperation
under anarchy" with this forceful declaration: "Nations dwell in
perpetual anarchy, for no central authority imposes limits on the pursuit of sovereign interests" (1985b: 1).

States are granted just those properties that liberalism grants to
individuals. The presumption of anarchy need not be stripped of additional assumptions and practices, for it is the bare-bones account
of society as "a lot of free individuals. . . ." Everything that has been
added on to that account in the name of liberalism is thought to differentiate domestic political society from the circumstances of international life, which are said therefore to constitute a generalized
state of war. Hobbes reigns, not simply as author of liberalism but
guarantor of an uncontaminated rendition of it in the form of international relations as a state of nature. The presumption of anarchy
necessitates the problematique with which Oye and his colleagues
have concerned themselves: The presence of cooperation is indeed
a problem for theory when the conditions making cooperation possible have been defined away.

The problem with this characterization—one in which liberalism
and anarchy start off pretty much the same but take different paths,
liberalism developing within states and anarchy prevented from doing so by the existence of many states—comes at the starting point.

---

tive belt" of auxilliary hypotheses. Lakatos also indentified progressive or degenerative "problemshifts," depending on whether added material enables a theory
to make more powerful predictions. Shifts in liberal thought are degenerative insofar as the model for that thought is theory with predictive capability. If the
model is an adequate account of liberal practice, itself shifting, then shifts in
liberal thought are progressive.
2. I owe this phrase to Hayward R. Alker, Jr., who used it as a title for a paper
which, along with one by Richard K. Ashley, prompted my thoughts on anarchy
and its career. Later versions of their papers, and another version of this chapter,
are to be found in Alker and Ashley (forthcoming).

At the time liberalism emerged, international relations were not anarchical, if we mean by that a primal world of possessive sovereigns. Instead international relations have always constituted a political society, by which I mean any social arrangement limiting conduct and distributing privilege (see further chapter 6). Notice that the presence of politics does not deny the possibility, or even pervasiveness, of individually possessive conduct, only the presumption that such conduct sufficiently constitutes society.

Political thought from Niccolò Machiavelli to the end of the eighteenth century developed liberal tenets without presuming international anarchy. Only gradually has the image of international relations as state of nature come to dominate thinking, and we now read Machiavelli, Hobbes, and their successors accordingly. If international relations have changed less than the image we hold, what has changed far more is the contrast between international relations and domestic political societies. While this may be a reason to enrich liberal thought with additional assumptions and qualifications, as indeed has been the case, it hardly justifies the judgment that international relations no longer, or never did, constitute a political society.

This is not to say that international relations are never anarchic. They often are. My point is different: The incidence of anarchy is not the same as a condition of anarchy, that is, an absence of rule. For all the exceptions, the large pattern of international relations is one of asymmetric and involuntary relations among ostensibly free and equal actors. To quote Oran Young:

> Virtually everything capable of being allocated among members of the international polity is distributed in a highly inegalitarian fashion. This is true whether the value at stake is population, natural resources, wealth, power, or prestige. Thus, the level of between-unit inequalities in this political system rivals the level of within-unit inequalities (1978: 244).

If this is a tenable empirical judgment, it does no good to rescue anarchy from exceptional instances, because exceptions are the rule. To put it the other way around, social arrangements need not possess sovereignty or any other formal feature of the state, much less a high degree of centralization in enforcement capacities, to qualify as political societies. International relations are by no means a special case. Rather, the state is the special case, one to have become paradigmatic for political society only recently.

Lost are conceptions of political society predating the state as the dominant social reality. Domestic political society in Europe of the seventeenth and eighteenth centuries was hardly absolutist, labels notwithstanding—the term "absolutist" refers more to the ascendancy of the king in court society than to the state as centralized coercive machinery (Elias 1982). Hobbes' description of the Leviathan was no less heuristically intended than was his unforgettable description of the state of nature. For political philosophers of that time, state and anarchy were limiting conditions of political society, rules and rulers the norm. Only in the nineteenth century did political philosophy begin to equate the centralization of politics in the state with the centrality of the state for politics.

It would appear that anarchy was never a primal condition. Pure liberal theory was no more suitable for understanding international relations in the seventeenth and eighteenth centuries than it is today. Conceptions of political society have always countenanced international relations. It is these conceptions that had to be tormented—by eliminating features integral to them—before anarchy could triumph as the dominant conception of international relations. Thus the historical sequence is quite different from liberalism's triumph. The latter prevailed, as thought and practice, by becoming more complex. The former prevailed by becoming more simplified and thus ever more sharply contrasted with the latter.

For expository reasons, I present these complex conceptual developments as proceeding in two distinct stages, respectively the subjects of this chapter's remaining sections. In practice the last half of the eighteenth century is when almost everything happened. Traditional conceptions of political society reached their zenith, and at the very same time came philosophical initiatives which duly resulted in the eclipse of these conceptions. It is also the period of the "great transformation" (Polanyi 1957). The idea of a naturally self-regulating market took hold, and industrial capitalism decisively altered the social relations of all those whose productive activities were affected. The paradoxical liberal practice of self-consciously reconstructing society while espousing the eternal verities of Political Economy had begun in earnest.

VIRTUES, RIGHTS, MANNERS

The quotation of Pocock which launches this chapter occurs in an essay entitled "Virtues, Rights, and Manners: A Model for Historians of Political Thought" (1981: 353–368, 1985: 37–50). Much of what I have to say about the presumption of anarchy in international relations is adapted from this essay and indeed is contained, in a remarkably compressed form, in its title. Relocating Pocock's "model for historians of political thought" to the province of international thought allows me to propose a rendition of anarchy's career over several centuries. This rendition is consistent with my presumption that political society, however much or little centralized, and not possessive individualism, however enriched, explains the complexities of international relations.

The words "virtues," "rights," and "manners" synopsize three distinctive traditions of thinking about political society before the rise of the state in anything resembling its current form. Virtue is the particular concern of Machiavelli and is integral to his conception of the *vivere civile* — not just "a way of life given over to civic concerns . . . ," but "a broadly based civic constitution" (Pocock 1975: 56–57; see further pp. 49–80, Pitkin 1984: 80–105). By no means does virtue and its expression in the *vivere civile* preempt individualism, although in Machiavelli it is a passionate rather more than possessive individualism. To repeat Machiavelli's own, often quoted words, "human appetites are insatiable, for by nature we are so constituted that there is nothing that we cannot long for . . ."[3] (1950a: 355). For Machiavelli, virtue regulates conduct driven by our longings.

Machiavelli's commentators show little agreement on how to ren-

---

3. Compare, however, this famous passage from *The Prince:* "The desire to acquire *[acquisitare]* is truly a very natural and common thing; and whenever men who can, do so, they are praised and not condemned; but when they cannot and want to do just the same, herein lies the mistake and the condemnation" (Musa 1964: 23). Indicatively the context for this assertion is the conquest of territory, for the discussion of which Machiavelli consistently used the word "acquisition" and its cognates. Possession would therefore seem to be the appropriate expression of princely appetite. Other individuals would express their appetites according to the possibilities of their situations.

der the term *"virtù,"* in part because Machiavelli used it constantly, but not consistently, for leaders, ordinary people, even institutions (Wolin 1960: 228–232, Pitkin 1984: 81–96). In *The Prince* alone, Mark Musa counted fifty-nine occurrences of the term, which he translated by using twelve different English words (Musa 1964: x–xv).[4] In a general way, *"virtù"* relates to "glory"; its antithesis is "corruption," ("virtue gone decadent") (Martines 1980: 311). More specifically the term applies to the conduct of warriors, whether to emphasize valor and manliness (Hulliung 1983: 27–30) or training and discipline (Pocock 1975: 201–202). I note that in Leslie J. Walker's translation of *The Discourses* (Machiavelli 1950a) *"virtù"* is "valor" in some martial contexts (e.g., p. 311), "efficiency" in others (e.g., p. 530; see also Walker's Introduction, pp. 99–100). Elsewhere in Machiavelli's work we see the same pattern (Pitkin 1984: 104, 85).

As Albert O. Hirschman has so persuasively demonstrated (1977: 33), absent from Machiavelli's thought is an express notion of interest. Only gradually did there emerge a sense of the difference between passions and interests, especially if the latter signifies, not "the totality of human aspirations," but instead "an element of reflection and calculation with respect to the manner in which aspirations will be pursued" (p. 32, footnote deleted). Possessive individualism, as I think Mcpherson understood the term, depends on the individual having a conception of interest in the second, narrow sense—a conception that did not emerge until the seventeenth century. Machiavelli was more directly source of the view that collectivities have interests in relation to other collectivities, so that individuals act, whether in the heat of passion or cool calculation, in the interest of some group (pp. 32–36). The multiplicity of groups leads to conflict among groups, and unity could only be achieved when "dominant interests were satisfied." "The upshot of Machiavelli's argument was to recast the notion of political unity in accordance with a new picture of political society as a diagram of interest-propelled forces" (Wolin 1960: 233). Evidently the unity of political society is not a foregone conclusion, international relations being a case in point.

4.   Machiavelli's *"virtù"* has nothing in common with the medieval concept of *"virtù"* involving contemplation and prayer; indeed, it is the reverse: a conception of action involving both the mind and the body. And when it is not specifically *capacity, strategy, virtue, courage, power, efficacy, qualities, strength, talent, resources* or *capability,* then it is *ingenuity,* a general term broad enough by its own definition to suggest some of the eleven more specific meanings of *"virtù"* (Musa 1964: xv, emphasis in original).

It is a mistake to think we must choose between valor and discipline, as if they are mutually exclusive categories, or that Machiavelli, by not choosing between them, exhibited the characteristic penchant of his time for dualities held in tension (compare Martines 1980: 310–317). For Machiavelli, valor and discipline are the complementary traits which soldiers of the Roman republic abundantly displayed. Understandably Machiavelli made much of valor as an ingredient of republican greatness, but he never assumed that valor is simply a natural talent. While "it is no doubt true" that nature makes men (men, specifically) "ardent," "it does not follow from this that the nature which makes them ardent at the start could not be so regulated by rules *[con arte]* as to keep them ardent right up to the end" (Machiavelli 1950a: 562).

Forever accused of being merely aphoristic, Machiavelli here began one of his most systematic and, for our purposes, interesting arguments.

> In proof of this let me point out that armies are of three types. In the first there is both ardour *[furore]* and order. Now order promotes both ardour and valour *[virtù]* as it did in the case of the Romans; for during the whole course of their history one finds that there was good order in their armies, which military discipline of long standing had introduced. In a well disciplined army, no one should perform any act, except in accordance with regulations. Hence in the Roman army — which, since it conquered the world, should be taken as a model by all other armies — we find that no one ate or slept or went wenching or performed any other action, military or domestic, without instructions from the consul. Armies which act otherwise are not true armies; and if they do anything of note they do it through ardour and impetuosity, not through valour (1950a: 562–563).

The second type of army has "ardour but no discipline," and the third type "is one in which there exists neither a natural ardour nor yet discipline to supplement it; . . ." (p. 563). Machiavelli did not identify a fourth type of army, in which discipline but no ardor is to be found, because nature always provides ardor, at least in the beginning, which discipline conserves and directs.[5] If discipline is present, then so must ardor be as well, yielding the first type of army. If "disciplined valor" is not available, then the second type inevitably degenerates into the third. Clearly, for Machiavelli, discipline is indispensable to virtue, even if valor is the more evident property of virtue as a model of conduct.

Observe that this is, in Sheldon Wolin's words, "a timeless model" — "Machiavelli drew the conclusion that the example of republican Rome provided later ages with a timeless model on which to base political actions and institutions" (1960: 215). Republics, empires, principalities are all subject to a world of contingency. If republican Rome is the source of Machiavelli's model of conduct, it is because Rome is "the exemplar of accidental perfection" (Mansfield 1979: 35). Unlike the timeless model of conduct that virtue, in all its connotations, describes, social arrangements are but "particular moments": "To affirm the Republic, then, was to break up the timeless continuity of the hierarchic universe into particular moments. . . ." (Pocock 1975: 54; see also Wolin 1960: 214–217).

Instead of a timeless, hierarchical universe, Machiavelli posited a common historical origin for all social arrangements, the subsequent variations among which "are due to chance" (1950a: 212).

> For in the beginning of the world, when its inhabitants are few, they lived for a time scattered like beasts. Then, with the multiplication of their offspring, they drew together and, in order to be better able to defend themselves, began to look about for a man stronger and more courageous than the rest, made him their head *[capo]*, and obeyed him (p. 212).

Evidently a hierarchical origin substitutes for timeless hierarchy. Does this mean that every historical social arrangement must have a head which others obey? On this Machiavelli was ambiguous but, I think, not deliberately. Following Polybius (Machiavelli 1950b: 7–13, Mansfield 1979: 35–41), he sorted social arrangements into six categories (in Italian, *ragioni,* "reasons"), three virtuous and three

---

5. "In the beginning" has a double meaning here. Machiavelli held that ardor diminished with age (1950a: 355) as well as in battle. Inasmuch as armies consist mostly of youth, we may presume that armies will always be ardent in the beginning.

vicious transformations of the first three (1950a: 212–216). The three virtuous arrangements are principality, aristocracy, and democracy (*"populare"*), their inversions tyranny, oligarchy, and anarchy (*"licenza"*). Now one might think that democracy and its counterpart would be headless and thus unruled, the more so because Machiavelli defined democracy negatively, as the absence from rule of "a few powerful men *[potenti]*" or a prince (p. 214). Yet Machiavelli's choice of metaphor suggests instead that popular rule swells the head, so that it includes the multitude, and rules itself.[6]

That such a situation is unlikely to persist should come as no surprise. Nor should its transformation into anarchy, in which, "as everyone did what he liked, all sorts of outrages were committed" (p. 214). Polybius called this situation "mob rule" (*"turbae potentatis"*) (Machiavelli 1950b: 8). Machiavelli would seem to have denied that anarchy is any manner of rule, because no one acts as if there are any rules. Under the circumstance, anarchy "had to be got rid of somehow," and some other arrangement is soon adopted (Machiavelli 1950a: 214). Indeed, no particular arrangement is ever stable. Barring interference from a neighbor during a periodic "state of commotion", "a commonwealth *[vivere civile]* might go on forever passing through governmental transitions" (p. 214).

I conclude that for Machiavelli the *vivere civile* is political society in general, that particular political societies are everywhere found, that all such arrangements vary from moment to moment in their particular relations of rulers and ruled, that rules mediate all social relations and that no one—prince, warrior, member of the populace, member of a mob—can count on an externally fixed, formal set of rules to guide conduct. Where there are such rules and when they codify virtue, they are to be obeyed. Machiavelli's support of

---

6. The metaphorical association of ruler with the head implies a metonymical relation of the head to the body of people, or the body politic. Because the head directs the body, we use the part figuratively for the whole. The head of a government stands in for the government, which stands in for the state, which stands in for the country. Thus we speak of "Gorbachev," say, when we mean a place and its people. When we speak instead of "Russia," it is to subvert the metonymical sequence that includes a particular state, in this instance, the Soviet Union. Insofar as the head swells to include the body of people, one could say that the metonymical relation is converted into a grotesque metaphor—The body is all head, the head all body. On such figures of speech, see chapter 4, above.

law is real enough: Even when we fight it is by law ("*con le leggi*") as well as with force (Musa 1964: 145). When laws are absent or abused, then there are less formal rules for conduct. These rules define virtue and demand discipline in circumstances where others' behavior may be excessive or reckless. Machiavelli anticipated Talcott Parsons' preoccupation with the internalization of normative content (chapter 4), although Machiavelli's model of conduct is one of civic activism, Parsons' one of passive acceptance.[7]

Political society in general consists of many political societies, a plenitude of rulers. Sometimes political society, like political societies, approximates a democracy or degenerates into anarchy (perhaps "explodes" is the better term). Sometimes it takes on the semblance of head and body, as with Rome and "its less powerful neighbors" (a phrase Machiavelli used to make the general point; Musa 1964: 15). Certainly political society in general is never free from commotion. Nor is it ever free from rules. These rules do not prescribe punishments and remedies; they advise as to consequences.

Machiavelli saw that his mission was to counter the ignorance of rulers by spelling out the consequences when rules are ignored. To do this, he wrote rule books containing detailed instructions to accompany a few maxims, or weighty principles, from which the content of virtue is to be derived. In these books we do not find Machiavelli drawing a firm line between political societies, where at most moments ruler-ruled relations are firm and clear, and political society, in which many rulers must contend with each other under the murkiest of circumstances. These respective situations provide different contexts for Machiavelli's maxims — contexts which he carefully presented. There is no pattern in these offerings, however, because he did not wish to imply that the two sets of relations are different except in the degree to which relations are stable and formal rules available. In other words Machiavelli never supposed that international relations are a permanently anarchical situation, or indeed a permanent condition of any kind.

---

7. "In the anatomy of early Roman virtue given in the *Discorsi*, Machiavelli seems to depict it as built on military discipline and civic religion, as if these were the socializing processes through which men learned to be social animals" (Pocock 1975: 201–202).

While we tend to consider Machiavelli's maxims as merely prudential — he commended them only because they work — we must not forget that he saw them as embodying virtue, albeit the austere virtue of the warrior. Failure to honor them is thus a sign of corruption, which Machiavelli held to be the problem of political society: "how easily men are corrupted . . ." (Machiavelli 1950a: 315). Rulers are corruptible, not just because they are imprudent, but because rules giving instructions depend on virtuous rulers to work, that is, to be reliable guides to the world in which rulers find themselves. In the absence of virtue, rulers read instructions to mean that anything they can get away with is permitted, imprudence is rewarded and the delicate balance of relations — the *vivere civile* — is sacrificed to avarice and aggrandizement.

Civic virtues all relate to one overarching principle. In its pure, timeless and natural form, it is the principle that one should do no harm. In a world of contingency and uncertainty, the principle of no harm translates into a number of maxims, two of which I take to be especially revealing. The first is the maxim that one must respond to injury — harm done by another to oneself (see notably 1950a: 442–444). Not only does failure to respond to any injury condone others' excesses, it is likely to induce a later act of vengeance, itself excessive and probably disastrous.

Beyond these prudential considerations, however, responding to injury is necessitated because injury is not just material harm, but also a violation of a rule which specifies the limits of harm-doing in some situation.[8] Were the injury in question not redressed, the rule as well as the injured party suffers. Not only is injurious conduct rule-relevant, but transgressions of such rules, which Machiavelli took to be commonplace, constitute the prevailing pattern of relations among individuals. Harm meets with harm, the pattern duly constituting the rule defining the occasion of harm and the occasion for a harmful response.

Often the pattern of relations is unclear, or no rule is available.

---

8. In the situation Machiavelli used to illustrate the maxim that injuries must be redressed, the Gauls alleged, and the Romans denied, an injury of the former by the latter. At contention was Rome's violation of the *jus gentium,* "the unwritten law which the Romans and other Latin people recognized as binding in their deal-

Here Machiavelli's second maxim comes to bear. This is the call for proportionality in harmful conduct. "It has been said by a wise man that if one is to hold a state by violent means, the force employed should be proportionate to the resistance offered" (Machiavelli 1950a: 529). Perhaps the wise man was Aristotle, although Harvey C. Mansfield, Jr., thought Machiavelli meant himself (1979: 380). The context is definitely ruler-ruled relations. Yet the maxim is general. The relations between autonomous individuals, including rulers, profit just as much from consideration of the requirements of proportionality. That such requirements fall into a pattern is what makes likely the presence of a rule, however informal. Proportionality and specific rules defining injury and appropriate response stand in reciprocal support. Together they constitute an "economy of violence," to use Wolin's strikingly apt phrase (1960: 220–224). As such they defeat any conception of Machiavelli's world as merely expedient or wholly aggressive.

Nowhere in Machiavelli do we find a Florentine version of the maxim "anything goes," or even of the maxim "whatever works," unless we add as a proviso that unprincipled or unruly conduct usually doesn't work. If Machiavelli's thought very little resembles the familiar interpretation of Machiavellism as unswerving dedication

---

ings with one another and sometimes with foreign states" (Walker's note, Machiavelli 1950b: 139). Walker's translation of "*jus gentium,*" as Machiavelli used it (Machiavelli 1950a: 443), is "law of nations." This is misleading insofar as it suggests the existence of something resembling international law, even if jus gentium was "one of several convenient sources of authority and material" for international law as it emerged in the sixteenth and seventeenth centuries (Corbett 1951: 7; see generally p. 3–38).

> Roman jurisprudence, which so illumined other fields of law, paid only the most fleeting attention to dealings with independent political communities. The great juristic literature is a product of the imperial period when, apart from wars with "barbarians" on remote frontiers, Rome was concerned exclusively with subordinate communities. For these, though they might be allowed to retain their own legal orders for domestic affairs, Rome's law-giving authority was final. The conditions demanding a distinct system of norms to govern the intercourse of equal states did not exist (p. 5).

Nor, as far as Machiavelli was concerned, did these conditions exist in his own time.

to *raison d'état*,[9] neither is it quite as benign as the term "civic humanism," much the vogue in current scholarship, might suggest (Hulliung 1983: 8–30). Pocock's monumental book, *The Machiavellian Moment* (1975) places Machiavelli's work in the context of emergent humanism, without painting Machiavelli, the ardent republican, a humanist too. Nevertheless Pocock lent himself to criticism by referring to the Machiavellian tradition as one of civic humanism. I think it better called the tradition of civic activism. I also think Pitkin got the Machiavelli I read as well as can be gotten in three sentences.

> Indeed, in the *vivere civile* might and right are interrelated, for law and justice are themselves partly resources of power; and conversely, a purely abstract "right" that serves no community needs and can muster no community support is politically ineffectual and wrong. Because we are simultaneously distinct and connected, politics always simultaneously concerns the distribution of costs and benefits among competitors, and the nature and direction of their shared community, both "who gets what, when, why" and "who we are." Every law or policy allocates, advantaging some and disadvantaging others; but every law or policy affects their shared common life and the principles for which they stand (1984: 300).

If these had been my sentences, I would not have used the words "right" and "might." When Pitkin wrote them, she surely was thinking of Machiavelli's famous remark that "there are two ways of fighting: one with the law, the other with force . . ." (Musa 1964: 145), which she invoked elsewhere in her book, and which I allude

---

9. *Raison d' état* can only be a persuasive interpretation of Machiavelli's message when the state is the decisive and seemingly timeless locus of politics. This is the Hegelian state of Friedrich Meinecke: "The State is an organic structure whose full power can only be maintained by allowing it in some way to continue growing; and *raison d' état* indicates both the path and the goal for such a growth" (1957: 1). How little this resembles Machiavelli's individualist way of thinking. See also Friedrich Kratochwil's demonstration (1982) that *raison d' état* acquired its contemporary sense of "unbridled self-interest as the essence of politics" only after 1870. Quotation is from p. 22.

to above. While "might" and "force" are no doubt interchangeable terms for the Italian "*forza*," "*le leggi*" is unproblematically "the law," meaning specific formal rules, and not some general category of rights that are natural to humanity or central to social arrangements.

The term "right" suggests instead the second tradition to which Pocock pointed, which is indeed the "rights" tradition, and it is not Machiavelli's. Rather it is the tradition of thought in which Hobbes and Locke are located. Pocock himself displayed a certain impatience with the tradition of thinking about political society in terms of the play of individual rights and duties because he detected a propensity among historians of political thought both classically and again since Mcpherson to adopt a "law-centered paradigm." In its devotion to rights, such an orientation effectively excludes consideration of such other basic features of political society as virtues and manners (Pocock 1985: 37). Furthermore, Pocock argued that writing "the history of political thought in law-centered terms . . . is largely equivalent to writing it as the history of liberalism" (p. 46). For Pocock, this is "a serious distortion of history" (p. 47, footnoting a paper of his own entitled "The Myth of John Locke and the Obsession with Liberalism").

Notwithstanding Pocock's resistance to the rights tradition, he has offered an exceptionally helpful recapitulation of its origins and distinctive character by juxtaposing it with the Machiavellian concern for virtue. The Machiavellian tradition of civic activism found its inspiration in the Roman Republic, the rights tradition in the Roman Empire; virtue pertains to politics, rights to commerce. Rights are generalized as rules, and they rule relations to things. "Social first and political after, the civil and common law define individuals as possessors by investing them with right and property in things, and ultimately (as in Locke) in themselves" (p. 45). Pocock has here conceded the issue of Locke's, and liberalism's, subsequent importance. Nevertheless, his point is that the rights tradition antedates early capitalism and liberal thought by centuries. As such it also antedates efforts to naturalize rights in order to render them timeless, inalienable, and constitutive of popular sovereignty and thence the state.

To the extent that the rights tradition reduces society to possession, it needs to explain self-rule through the agency of rights. The rights tradition always contained within itself such an explanation, which in due course became formalized, even stylized, by Hobbes, Locke, and their successors, as the social contract. A right is a claim as to the possession or use of things which others acknowledge in exchange for acknowledgement of their claims. Acknowledgments are exchanged — reciprocally accepted — as promises individuals make about their own future conduct. The basic principle in the rights tradition is that promises shall be kept. "Just conduct is in accord with promises given" (Brennan and Buchanan 1985: 100; see generally pp. 100–111). Inasmuch as promises will not always, and sometimes cannot, be kept, rules emerge in response to these failures.

Consider in these terms Hobbes' treatment of rights and duties in the *Leviathan* (Part I, chapters 14, 15; Hobbes 1968: 189–217), which he presented as natural. The first law of nature states "a precept, or generall rule of Reason, *that every man ought to endeavour Peace, as farre as he has hope of obtaining it; and when he cannot obtain it, that he may seek, and use, all helps, and advantages of Warre*" (p. 190, his emphasis). This of course is the Machiavellian principle of doing no harm but having no choice but to do so, as a matter of self defense, in a contingent world of harm-doers (pp. 188–189).

Hobbes' second law of nature is a procedural necessity, given his scheme: It makes the principle of no harm except in self defense an alienable right from the individual's point of view. Individuals are therefore capable of entering into binding agreements, or contracts. In Hobbes' words,

> . . . all Contract is mutuall translation, or change of Right; and therefore he that promiseth onely, because he hath already received the benefit for which he promiseth, is to be understood as if he understood the Right should passe: for unlesse he had been content to have his words so understood, the other would not have performed his Part first. And for that cause, in buying, and selling, and other acts of Contract, a Promise is equivalent to a Covenant; and therefore obligatory (1968: 194–195).

Hobbes' third natural law follows from this exposition: "*That men performe their Covenants made*: without which Covenants are in vain, and but Empty words, and the Right of all men to all things remaining, wee are still in a condition of Warre" (pp. 201–202).

Hobbes of course was sufficiently persuaded that people would

not keep their promises that he proposed the state as a solution to
the problem of political society. In this Hobbes anticipated the direction liberals have always turned when confronted by the human propensity not to be principled, or even prudent. No differently than
corruption in the civic tradition, bad faith in the rights tradition un-
dermines the integrity of political society. It also contributes to the
centralization of rule, even if it is rationalized as self-rule, as the antidote to corruption, this time not of people but of the rules people
need for mutual promising to work.

Machiavelli and Hobbes both accepted the dependence of political society on rules and rule-oriented behavior. Machiavelli was
disinclined to infer rules from promising, because people, "who are
a contemptible lot," do not hold promises in high regard (Musa
1964: 145). His one exception is revealing: Forced promises need not
be kept (Machiavelli 1950a: 574). They represent an injury that can
be redressed, appropriately and proportionally, by breaking a promise.
A different principle prevails.

Pocock identified a third tradition of thinking about political society before the emergence of the modern state, connoted by the
word "manners." Inasmuch as Pocock's particular concern in the essay I am using as a template was the eighteenth century, his exemplar
for a political society grounded in manners is Burke (Pocock 1985:
48–50). No other term would be as apt in characterizing Burke's position, which Pocock described in a different essay (published in the
same volume) as holding "that commerce is dependent on manners,
and not the other way around; a civilized society is the prerequisite
of exchange relations, and the latter cannot create the former" (p. 199).
Certainly political economists like Adam Smith had this relation the
other way around and, in Pocock's estimate, so did David Hume and
Edward Gibbon, although he elsewhere showed an inclination to include both in this tradition (pp. 101, 148).

In his first book, *The Ancient Constitution and the Feudal Law,*
Pocock concentrated his attention on an earlier period in England
and the Continent, roughly 1500–1700, in which there emerged a
sharp debate over crown prerogatives and the freedoms of people.
The latter were protected by the "ancient constitution," which was
nothing other than custom, "by its nature unwritten law, of usages
of the folk interpreted through the mouths of judges, . . . always im-
memorial and always up-to-date" (1957:15). So seen, custom is para-

doxical, and doubly so, being at once ancient and contemporary, the accretive evidence of what people want and, by virtue of having become law, a constraint on what they (the crown included) are free to do.

These paradoxes disappear if custom is codified, for a willful choice, or exercise of sovereignty, replaces a paradoxically binding but sourceless set of rules. Pocock found the origins of the concept of sovereignty in this debate. Curiously this result paves the way for the emergence of the state as we have come to know it without definitively making the crown the winner of the debate. Popular sovereignty is an exercise of the will of the people, no less an alternative to the sway of custom than the unchallengeable position of the crown.

Pocock's language for the tormenting of liberalism is equally applicable here. The ancient constitution as a matter of custom is naturalized by both sides in the debate. Thus the divine right to rule and the right of revolution are equally posed as timeless alternatives to custom, the distinctive if paradoxical feature of which is its expression of the fullness of time. The rights tradition provided the frame of reference for the common law once it had been seen as customary law predating even the feudal right to property.

When customary law is not naturalized, we find instead that it is historicized. This is how Pocock saw Burke's relation to "the great tradition of common-law thought, and in particular those men who had conceived the law of England as custom and custom as perpetual adaptation" (1957: 243). Manners are nothing other than customs seen in their historical richness. To the extent customs are divorced from law and rights in this conception, they are imbued with the mysterious capacity to refine the people whose activities produce them: They yield civilization and the rules associated with the tradition of civic activism. By veering away from the rights tradition, Burke, and Gibbon even more, verged on making manners virtuous.

Pocock seems inclined to view the manners tradition as caught between the poles represented by virtues and rights. One reason for this, I think, is that he did not establish a principle that would define this tradition in its own right. Such a principle is implicit, however, in the conservative politics associated with Burke. In a contingent world it recommends continuity and consistency. These precepts derive from a universal injunction comparable to the two principles, do no harm and keep promises, which underly the traditions organized around virtues and rights. This is the principle, tell the truth. If people act in an unprincipled way and often enough find it prudent to lie, the cumulative effect of their actions, manifest as custom or manners, does not lie. Thus a political society founded on custom or manners rests on an ethical foundation and elicits conduct in the form of consistency with what custom or manners expect. As with political society based on virtues, or rights, unethical conduct — in this instance, conduct based on the presumption that one knows more than the accumulated wisdom of the ages — will undermine the foundations of such a political society.

All three traditions have in common a basis in principle. They all recognize that political society in a world of contingency depends on maxims that translate these principles into the language of prudence. They also recognize that a willingness to honor such maxims, whether for reasons of prudence or ethical awareness (themselves converging), obviates the need for organizational apparatus associated with the state. The three principles fundamental to the three traditions of political society are well-known to classical philosophy. As Friedrich Kratochwil has adumbrated in recent work (forthcoming, chapter IV), they are especially clearly and forcefully presented as natural laws by Samuel Pufendorf.[10]

As far as I know, no one has connected these principles to the three traditions of political society, which, but for Pocock, are also unrecognized for what they are. Consider Alisdair MacIntyre's influential but misguided alternative (1981). A classical moral tradition of virtue has fallen to a modern conception of "rules," indistinguishably rules of reason and rules of law (pp. 49–50, 143, 214–216). Even Pocock did not connect the tradition of grounding political society in manners to an ethical standpoint. Among contemporary writers whose work I know, only Ronald Dworkin (1986) seems to have grasped the centrality of the principle of truth-telling as it fits the contingent (he would say, interpretive) circumstances of

---

10. Pufendorf expounded the principles, do no harm, keep promises, and tell the truth, in *De Jure Naturae et Gentium,* Book III, Chap. I; Book III, Chap. IV–VIII; Book IV, Chap. I–II (Pufendorf 1934: 313–329, 379–523).

political society. He has named it the principle of integrity and used words like "consistency" and "coherence" in describing it.

In identifying three traditions of accounting for political society, Pocock does not seem to have employed a particular conceptual scheme or even a distinctive disciplinary orientation. His work reveals an informal though highly accomplished taxonomist, who happens to have a notable fondness for tripartite formulations.[11] Beyond Pocock's sense of the record, what grounds do we have for accepting this formulation? The identification of ethical principles underlying the three traditions supports their plausibility without, however, providing any additional grounds for construing the list as complete. Indeed Hobbes, Pufendorf, and the like expound many other principles of conduct, which I take perhaps too summarily to derive from the three basic principles. Nevertheless, I am confident that Pocock's formulation, or something quite like it, is the right one, that it exhaustively lists the primary categories of political practice in any society, and that these categories are mixed or even fused in practice but fully independent and mutually exclusive in conceptual terms.

Anyone who has read the first part of this book can anticipate my defense of this claim. There are three categories of political practice, captured by the terms "virtues," "rights," and "manners," which are correlates of the three categories of speech acts and thus of rules I identify in chapter 2. If I may summarize briefly, speech acts are social performances, that is, they have direct social consequences. Such acts take the generic form, I [verb such as declare, demand, promise] that [propositional content]. Because people respond to them with their own performances, not always spoken, the pattern of speech acts and related performances constitute those practices that make the material conditions and artifacts of human experience meaningful. More specifically, the pattern of speech acts endows practices with normativity; they give rise to rules which, in synopsizing that pattern, fix preferences and expectations and shape the future against the past.

Speech acts fall into three categories for constitutive purposes—

---

11. Some examples: time, institutions, action; politics, language, time; providence, fortune, virtue; court, country, standing army. Once reordered, the last two at least are variations of the triad, virtues, rights and manners.

assertive speech acts (I state that . . .), directive (I request that . . .), and commissive (I promise that . . .). There are parallel categories of rules—instruction rules, directive-rules and, commitment-rules. Each of the three conceptions of political society is constitutively related to a particular category of speech acts and rules. The virtuous political society depends on directive speech acts, which imply the possibility of, and thus the need for restraint in, coercion. The righteous political society depends, obviously enough, on commissive speech acts, which imply rules for deciding conflicting claims of right. Finally a well-mannered political society depends on assertive speech acts, the stream of which conveys the wisdom of many voices as to appropriate conduct.

Evidently the three basic principles summarize the normative implications of preferring one over the other categories of speech acts for constituting any political society. The principles of doing no harm, keeping promises and telling the truth respectively generalize the normative content of virtue, rights, and manners. Such principles are themselves instruction-rules which relate to assertive speech acts: What they assert instructs their audience on what works and how to get along. Directive-rules and commitment-rules also bear traits reflecting their distinctive bases in speech. Rules derived from any one category of speech act can be found in political societies whose dominant complexion derives from rules of another category. As I assert in chapter 3, all political societies are mixed experiences, enjoying rules from all three categories in proportions unique to each such society.

To take advantage of Pocock's formulation of the three categories of political practice, I deviate from the invariable order in which I present categories in Part One. There I proceed from assertive speech acts to directives and then commissives, and I do the same with their correlates. No order of presentation is a priori correct. Nor is there a single historical sequence for the emergence of either ethical principles or political practices. I could just have well entitled this section, "Manners, Virtues, Rights", but for the expositional inconvenience to myself.

ANARCHY EMPTIED OF CONTENT

We are left with two questions. Why has the connection between normative considerations and political society, so evident before the rise of the state, become so tenuous and ill-understood? And why has anarchy, defined as the absence of society and thus of effective rules, come to be seen as the only alternative to the state? The answer to these questions — two versions of the same question, really — takes us to Hume, Kant, and Jeremy Bentham. Given the contributions of all three to moral philosophy, it is ironic indeed to think that they may have in some way fostered the decline of conceptions of political society not confined to the state yet still grounded in normative considerations. Yet I think this is very much the case, for reasons I can sketch only in the barest terms.

Let me take Hume first. As noted, Pocock located Hume in the tradition of thinking about political society as grounded in manners. Truer to this tradition than Burke, for example, Hume showed no inclination to either historicize or naturalize the record of human activities — neither time nor timelessness interested him directly. Instead he attended to those activities as causal chains, all of which led toward one general effect: Through repetition they become standard and predictable. In his word for it, they become conventions, meaning that they are agreements to which no one has specifically agreed. Hume found conventions to be the source of all the practices and institutions that make up society and thereby assure human survival (Aiken 1968: 55–56). Through trial and error, imitation and adjustment, people coordinate activities and by so doing accrue benefits prompting them to continue the process until it becomes standard and predictable.

Kratochwil (1981) has amply documented the intellectual power and contemporary relevance of Hume's analysis of the formation of conventions. Thomas Schelling's brilliant work on mixed games of conflict and cooperation (1960) is strikingly Humean in its premises and procedures. More generally, whenever we conceptualize a social situation as a two-party interaction, minimally structured at the outset, with additional structure generated by the interaction, we follow after Hume. While this would seem to cover the full gamut of fights, games, and debates, to borrow from Anatol Rapoport (1960), few contemporary scholars would acknowledge as much.

The point is not that Hume originated a tradition of analysis, but that he invented an analytical procedure indispensable to this tradition. Perennially reinvented in the spirit but mostly in ignorance of Hume, this procedure disaggregates society into a congeries of situations, all of them social in the same way—they have two actors responding to each other, whether constructively or destructively, in otherwise largely fixed circumstances. While we tend to focus on the disaggregation effected by this procedure, no doubt because it is entirely characteristic of the positivist worldview Hume did so much to foster, I think its other aspect is at least as important.

Hume's procedure conventionalizes a particular social situation by taking it out of time without making it timeless. Once conventionalized, that situation can be generalized. Notice that mere positivities—individuals and events—cannot be subjected to generalization, and thus to the operation of theory, until they have been conventionalized. Hume helped to lay the ground for positive social theory, such as practiced today, and staked out the single most powerful conventionalization to be found in such theory, the convention that two-party interactions are socially generative.

Beyond being a major source of positivism, Hume represents a third type of torment for anarchy. Pocock identified historicist and naturalist torments of liberalism as responses, grounded in traditional conceptions of political society, to the stark simplicity of a society of possessive individuals. The third response is conventionalist. Although it too is rooted in a tradition of political society, its effect is different. Rather than encrusting a simple account of human behavior with qualifications so that it works as a theory of political society, Hume's conventionalism eliminates political society as such and thus the need for a theory of such. In the place of political society is the aggregate of conventions enabling politics, economy and whatever else is social. For our purposes, the conventionalist response to the existence of anarchy is to see it as just another collection of conventions, mostly the result of two-party interactions themselves framed by conventions wrought the same way. Unlike historicism and naturalism, conventionalism torments anarchy by pruning and shaping, by domesticating one conception of political society, thereby rendering it in the terms of Political Economy.

The analytic attractions of conventionalism are undeniable. Nevertheless, the more conscientious its practice, the more unsatisfactory the results are. Let me illustrate by examining one of Hume's most important assertions. In *A Treatise of Human Nature,* he stated that "conventions are not of the nature of a *promise*; for even promises themselves . . . arise from human conventions" (Aiken 1968: 59, emphasis in original; see further pp. 82–90). This is of course a direct challenge to the central premise of the law-centered paradigm, which founds society in a generalized promise. The problem comes in explaining the ease and speed with which people come to agreement once conventions have created language, economy, and the other features of society. Contemporary students of anarchy follow Hume in detailing a gradual, uncertain interaction, the result of which is cooperation. Likened to a contract, such cooperation represents a final, reciprocal promise that can only have come about through, and as a conclusion to, prolonged interaction (Hardin 1982: 155–230). Each instance of cooperation must be a convention in its own right.

I do not believe that Hume intended any such conclusion. After all, language provides us with an understanding that we can make promises and expect consequences from having done so. In *The Genealogy of Morals,* Friedrich Nietzsche (1969: 57) wrote that we have a "right" to make promises and argued a thoroughly Humean case that this accomplishment, arduously produced in prehistory, "presupposes as a preparatory task that one first *makes* men to a certain degree necessary, uniform, like among like, regular, and consequently calculable" (1969: 58–59, emphasis in original). Once all this is accomplished, and codified in language, making promises to cooperate is easy.

Contemporary studies of two-party interaction typically begin with those who must calculate, if not in the dark, then in "the shadow of the future," an uncertain future of conflict and cooperation (Oye 1985b: 12–18). Hume, and Nietzsche after him, started with calculators who readily promise because, transaction costs aside, promises defer costs to their maker into the future—until the occasion stipulated for their fulfillment. As promises come due, we may infer that calculators consider strategies for breaking them to avoid consequences they incurred by promising. More often than not, prudence advises against these strategies. In short, the difficulty is not in making promises, and thus in engaging in cooperation, but in breaking them. It is the past, and not the future, casting its shadow. The convention of promising works for anarchy by making it unnecessary for new conventions to emerge in every instance in which two "sovereign individuals," to use Nietzsche's words have to deal with each other.

Hume's grounding of political society in conventions affords us a first cause explanation of how society got started. No less abstract than a social contract explanation, I nevertheless find it more persuasive (compare Onuf 1982b: 29–31). It also shows how particular practices and institutions can get started and stay with us. The danger comes in conventionalizing interactions characteristic of political society as if they alone make anarchy work. Conventionalized interactions explain the emergence of conventions and, conventions — not conventionalized interactions — explain, at least in the Humean view, why political society exists. For Hume anarchy is a political society, rich in conventions, full of cooperative endeavors, well able to provide a suitable environment for peace, prosperity, and individual accomplishment. In one of his essays, Hume went so far as to say *"That nothing is more favorable to the rise of politeness and learning, than a number of neighboring and independent states, connecting together by commerce and policy"* (1963: 120, emphasis in original).

Clearly Hume stayed well within the tradition of viewing political society, grounded in manners, as supporting a good and durable anarchy in Europe. Yet his work on disaggregating society and conventionalizing social situations contributed to the defeat of his preferred conception of anarchy. That conception gained expression in some rather modest observations about international relations — observations with little direct effect on subsequent international thought. The effect of Hume's analytical procedures, and the philosophical stance behind them, have been far greater and, in the way indicated, thoroughly deleterious for any conception of international relations as a working example of political society.

Unlike Hume, Kant seems to have thought that international relations, at least in his own time, had serious but remediable deficiencies. *Eternal Peace* offers what Kant thought were appropriate remedies, so that anarchical Europe would indeed be a flourishing political society. As with Hume, his suggestions were rather modest in comparison to his philosophical inquiries and have had little direct effect on international thought. Instead Kant's philosophical inquiries, like Hume's, have had the greater effect, although they too have been indirect and deleterious for any conception of anarchy as political society.

Kant's influence on international thought comes more particularly from his moral philosophy. In the *Metaphysical Foundations of Morals*, Kant distinguished between two human situations. The first is the situation of an autonomous and rational being. This is someone whose freedom to act is in no sense contingent and can therefore effectuate whatever she wills (Friedrich 1949: 154–191). Kant posited an "objective principle" or "command of reason" which constitutes the imperative guide for moral conduct in this situation. This of course is the famous categorical imperative: "Act *as if the maxim of your action were to become by your will a general law of nature*" (pp. 160, 171, emphasis in original). The alternative situation is one not of autonomy but of heteronomy. Here the individual faces a world of contingency and thus of uncertainty with respect to the consequences of any willful action. The categorical imperative acknowledges that this is the real situation facing any individual, which is why it formulates an imperative in the language of conditionality—"Act *as if* . . . ." Morally speaking, we can do no better.

Now I read Kant to have said that autonomy is the frame of reference to investigate morality, but that social reality does not allow for such autonomy (see also chapter 6). This does not mean that the moral conduct is impossible in the world of contingency, only that "[m]oral concepts cannot be obtained by abstraction from any empirical and hence merely contingent knowledge" (Friedrich 1949: 159). Though conceptually motivated, Kant's typology of "*rules* of skill, *counsels* of prudence, or *commands* or laws of morality" (pp. 164–165, emphasis in original) nevertheless appears to exclude prudential maxims from the realm of the moral. Many writers have subsequently tended to view prudential maxims as concerned only with self-interest and therefore necessarily lacking in moral character. A good recent example relevant to the discussion of anarchy is Charles R. Beitz (1979: 15–27).

I think this argument is Kantian—it draws its inspiration from Kant—without being Kant's. To start with, prudential maxims like Machiavelli's are not, in any limiting sense, directed only to the promotion of self-interest. No Machiavellian need reject Kant's distinctive conditions yielding autonomy and heteronomy. A Machiavellian would treat social situations in the latter terms and offer maxims for guidance in the face of a bewildering range of possible actions an individual might take. I would say that much of Machiavelli's advice to the prince warns against the conceit of autonomy. In sum, a Machiavellian would have no principled objections to Kant's categorical imperative, only practical ones.

Kant himself gave a practical application of his moral position in an appendix to *Eternal Peace* (Friedrich 1949: 457–476). One perspicuous sentence summarizes that position: "I can imagine a *moral politician*—that is, a man who employs principles of political prudence in such a way that they can coexist with morals—but I cannot imagine a *political moralist*, who would concoct a system of morals such as the advantage of statesmen may find convenient" (p. 459, emphasis in original). He then presented three maxims—seize what you want and justify it later, declare that your misdeeds are not your fault, divide and rule—which he proposed would work to the advantage of those using them only if they were kept secret (pp. 462–463). From this follows a practical formulation of the categorical imperative. In my paraphrasing: "Act as if the maxim of your actions must always be announced to the widest possible public" (Friedrich 1949: 470). A Machiavellian would be inclined to offer a less stringent formulation: Act as if it may not be possible to keep either your actions or your reasons for them secret. This counsel of prudence would result in heightened secrecy only for those who have no sense of what, in the Machiavellian tradition, civic virtue requires.

For Kant public law is the way to thwart secrecy. Hence the *"transcendental formula* of public law: 'All actions which relate to the right of other men are contrary to right and law, the maxim of which does not permit publicity'" (Friedrich 1970: 470). A Machiavellian would doubtless not be satisfied with any such formula. Its effect is to accord moral possibility only to political society which is also a legal arrangement. The point of *Eternal Peace* is precisely to suggest the necessary elements of such an arrangement in the form of a very short list of universal principles. The clear implication is that despite the existence of international law, the anarchy of Europe fell short of the requirements of a constitutional society, in which publicity expedited by law insures moral conduct. A Machiavellian would wonder whether constitutions are quite so decisive in fostering this outcome but surely would support Kant's commitment to republicanism and recognition of the chastening effect of publicity on those who would be immoderate or corrupt.

The Kantian legacy is the division of political society into the moral realm associated with public law in the liberal state, and the prudential (read: amoral) realm of anarchy (read: war). Is this what Kant intended? A careful consideration of his moral philosophy finds Kant having set up the antinomy of freedom and contingency merely as a device for establishing the best possible grounds for moral conduct in a world of contingency. A consideration of his practical application of that philosophy to political society finds him having used the precept of publicity to approximate the categorical imperative. Only the last step in Kant's reasoning lends support to the division of political society into two realms, one constitutional and the other prudential.

Kant is frequently viewed as having been a cosmopolitan moralist. Taking issue with Hedley Bull on this point, Stanley Hoffmann located Kant in the "rights" tradition.[12] Certainly Kant's vaunted cosmopolitanism pales beside Hume's, consisting as it does in a call for good neighborliness under conditions of world law (Friedrich 1949: 446–448). Yet we can go most of the way with Kant and retain a conception of political society not so very different from Hume's or even Machiavelli's. I cannot see any way in which Kant's last step — from publicity to public law — is a necessary one. The absence of a constitution surely affects anarchy, perhaps adversely, but hardly makes it impossible. Nor does the absence of a constitution make moral conduct impossible, in Kant's own terms, even when that conduct is based on prudence. Yet the Kantian legacy suggests otherwise.

Kant wrote *Eternal Peace* in 1795 and died in 1804. If his work

---

12. Following Michael Walzer, Hoffmann called it "the legalist paradigm" (1986: 186; see also Gallie 1978: 20–24 on Kant as "legalizer"). Bull held that Kant authored a "universalist tradition" of understanding international relations. "The Kantian or universalist view of international morality is that . . . there are moral imperatives in the field of international relations limiting the action of states, but these imperatives enjoin not coexistence and co-operation among states but rather the overthrow of the system of states and its replacement by a cosmopolitan society" (1978: 26; see also Beitz 1979: 181–183). For an interpretation of Kant contrary to Bull's, and much closer to my own, see Waltz 1959: 162–165.

is a bridge to the nineteenth century, even more is this so of Bentham's. Thus Bentham shared with Kant a great interest in the power of publicity which the former socialized, and conventionalized, as public opinion. Michel Foucault observed in his fascinating conversation about Bentham's "Panopticon" proposal that "almost all of the eighteenth century reformers credited opinion with considerable potential force" (1980: 161). Foucault went on to say: "For them, opinion was like a spontaneous reactualization of the social contract." However much this may have been so of others, including Kant, I think it misses the point of Bentham's preoccupation with public opinion and puts him in the wrong century.

Bentham intimated that public opinion was indispensable to the functioning of international law (Hinsley 1963: 81–91, Janis 1984: 408–412). His leading disciple, James Mill, was explicit about the connection (Mill 1967: 8–9). Bentham's procedure was rigorously conventionalizing. To start he proposed that humanity is "under the governance of two sovereign masters, *pain* and *pleasure*" (1948: 1, emphasis in original). Considered generically, "pleasure and pain are capable of giving binding force to any law or rule of conduct, which may all of them be termed *sanctions*" (p. 24, emphasis in original). One consequence of this procedure is to have conventionalized law as a system of rules backed by sanctions. Having done so, Bentham needed to find an international equivalent to the coercive apparatus of the state. Public opinion provided content to the sanction international law needed to qualify as law.

The Panopticon is an ingenious scheme for the unobtrusive supervision of people and their activities in a confined institutional setting (compare chapter 4, footnote 15). Detached supervision would supplant direct applications of violence to secure compliance with another's will, expressed abstractly in the form of rules (Bentham 1962). Sanctions are therefore depersonalized in social practice as well as conventionalized in theory (compare Ashley 1983: 521–527). The nineteenth century theory of the state follows inexorably in this logic. The state is a legal order and a potential monopoly of the use of force (recall chapter 4), conceptually unified around the idea of sanction and practically oriented to supervision, the effectiveness of which virtually precludes the need to activate the potential monopoly available to the state.

For Bentham public opinion has nothing to do with rights and duties, much less a social contract. Any such conclusion follows in the law-centered paradigm, of which Grotius, Hobbes the naturalist and Locke are exemplars, but not Bentham. We should not be misled by Bentham's lifelong interest in law. By conventionalizing law as dependent on sanctions, Bentham removed it from the realm of rights and promising. While Bentham is invariably described as a legal positivist (in contradistinction to naturalists), the crucial position of sanctions in Bentham's system makes him a Machiavellian in this sense: He thought that political society is ultimately dependent on relations of super- and subordination which, though coercive, are mitigated. In Machiavelli's case, considerations of virtue as well as prudence mitigate such relations. In Bentham's case depersonalized but omnipresent supervision does so. Machiavelli's virtues are warrior virtues; Bentham's sanctions manifest technical rationality, as the Frankfurt School has taught us to say. What they have in common is this: Proportionality contributes equally to a prudent ruler's success and a sanction's effectiveness (Bentham 1948: 178–188).

The difference between them is that Machiavelli's view of political society, though founded on coercively maintained hierarchical relations, does not necessitate the state as its only tenable form. Bentham's view of political society does just this, at least to a considerably greater degree. Bentham did not himself think so. As we saw, he held that public opinion constituted an effective sanction for international law and made a legal arrangement of the political society of European international relations.

Bentham's follower, John Austin, held the contrary. International law did not exist because the only available sanction was "general opinion" (Austin 1954: 141). Most nineteenth century international reformers extolled world public opinion as international law's sanctioning element while simultaneously advocating the creation of global institutions with genuine enforcement capabilities (Hinsley 1963: 92–113; Onuf and Onuf 1985: 31–33). Events of our century have eroded faith in the efficacy of world public opinion and international law, not to mention hope in the possibility of meaningful reform. International law is homologous to domestic law but, inasmuch as international law possesses no meaningful sanction, not analogous. Anarchy in the contemporary sense prevails.

Bentham's reflections on international law and the conditions of anarchy are, as was the case with Hume and Kant, a peripheral part of his work. His conventionalizing of law and defense of proportionality in sanctioning is part of a systematic work, *The Principles of Morals and Legislation,* which, as its title suggests, is an exercise in moral and political philosophy. This is a work of great cogency, achieved by a willingness to conventionalize at every opportunity, including its initial premise. The premise is that an individual's, or community's, relation to all things is a matter of utility.

> By utility is meant that property in any object, whereby it tends to produce benefit, advantage, pleasure, good or happiness, (all this in the present case comes to the same thing) or (what comes again to the same thing) to prevent the happening of mischief, pain, evil, or unhappiness to the party whose intent is considered: if that party be the community in general, then the happiness of the community: if a particular individual, then the happiness of that individual (Bentham 1948: 2).

Hume had already made the case for utility as the criterion of social virtue.[13] Following Hume, Bentham posited a principle of utility, "which approves or disapproves of every action whatsoever, according to the tendency which it appears to have to augment or diminish the happiness of the party whose interest is in question . . ." (1948: 2). The principle of utility is the cornerstone of Bentham's ethical position. While the principle has met with much controversy, the idea of utility, conventionalizing as it does all matters of interest and desire, making them commensurable positivities, has triumphed (see also chapter 8).

I suspect that this triumph is part and parcel of liberalism's triumph. Utility makes it possible to translate the pure theory of liberalism into a full-blown theory of market economy. The principle of

---

13. It appears to be a matter of fact that the circumstance of *utility,* in all subjects, is a source of praise and approbation: That it is constantly appealed to in all moral decisions concerning the merit and demerit of actions: That it is the *sole* source of that high regard paid to justice, fidelity, honour, allegiance, and chastity: That it is inseparable from all other social virtues, humanity, generosity, charity, affability, lenity, mercy, and moderation: And, in a word, that it is a foundation of the chief part of morals, which has a reference to mankind and our fellow-creatures (Aiken 1968: 221; emphasis in original).

utility supplies that theory with an ethical interpretation of its presumption (masquerading as prediction) that unimpeded individual efforts to maximize utility yield the largest possible utility for all. Normativity is conventionalized out of sight, and largely out of mind.

What utility did for liberalism, Bentham's conventionalized view of law did for the state. To speak of liberalism's triumph is misleading. The capitalist world economy has triumphed, and with it an ideology, no less normative than any other, posing as theory, couched in the ostensibly neutral language of utility. With capitalism the state has triumphed. Here theory makes the state a legal order, neutral but for the content of its rules. Normativity is exactly what people, by making rules, wish it to be: The myth of voluntarism complements the myth of neutrality. By transmuting politics into law and society into economy, Bentham and even more his followers contributed to liberalism's triumph by tormenting it — by severing it from normatively laden conceptions of political society.

There is no doubt that liberalism's career, like anarchy's, is closely related to the rise of capitalism and the state. From a constructivist point of view, it is difficult to judge in what degree liberalism, progressively vindicated through conventionalization, is responsible for these momentous developments. As an operative paradigm, liberalism has become virtually synonymous with modernity. Neither capitalism nor the state can even be imagined without that paradigm's assistance, any more than their careers can be understood apart from circumstances of time and place. With ever more conventionalized liberal notions of economy and law, however, we have lost sight of society and its politics.[14] Yet political society, with rules and rule, normative considerations and asymmetric relations, is everywhere. To this proposition I now turn.

---

14. To the same effect is Wolin's well-known association of liberalism with the decline of political philosophy and the age of organization with the sublimation of politics, to reword slightly the titles of the last two chapters of *Politics and Vision* (1960).

6

POLITICAL SOCIETY
(with Frank F. Klink)

Before the rise of disciplines, social and political thinkers in the liberal tradition concerned themselves with political society comprehensively understood, as I did in the preceding chapter. Frank F. Klink and I turn now to the contemporary situation, in which the term "political society" is rarely used to comprehend all those social arrangements in which politics are present. Instead we find an opposition between authority and anarchy. Indeed this opposition serves to constitute Political Science and International Relations as disciplines. Between them everything political would seem to be accounted for.

We reject this disciplinary division of labor. Not only does it equate the absence of central authority with unmitigated conduct. It adopts a definition of authority, wrongly attributed to Max Weber, which equates the stability of social arrangements with their acceptability to all parties. The result narrows the range of political possibilities to just two: the state or a state of nature. Hobbes' paradigmatic architecture reigns at the expense of the tradition of discourse about political society and even at Hobbes' expense as a rights theorist.

Because the Hobbesian opposition has acquired paradigmatic significance, its rejection must be accompanied by an alternative also capable of paradigmatic treatment. Machiavelli was too unsystematic, and far too subtle, to be the direct source. German social thought from G. W. F. Hegel to Weber provides the needed treatment of political society, understood as relations of super- and subordination—relations maintained through rules and obtaining in rule. We call this the *Herrschaft* paradigm, or the paradigm of political society, which we offer next.

Weber identified three types of rule, which indeed fail inspection as pure types. We reformulate Weber's types as categories and relate them to the categories of rules I develop in chapter 2. These three categories of rules and rule may usefully be construed as puzzle paradigms. They are the only three solutions people have to the practical problem of arranging social relations.

The first puzzle paradigm of rule, "hegemony," is clearly identifiable in Weber's rule through charisma. The second is "hierarchy," which is the paradigm of rule Weber most thoroughly developed. The third puzzle paradigm of rule is implicit in bourgeois practices but disguised in the liberal assumption that agents are autonomous and their rights and duties symmetrical. Weber failed to see the complex of relations so conceived as constituting a distinct and persistent pattern of rule and privilege. One measure of the extent to which this type of rule goes unnoticed is the lack of a conventional name for it. We find an appropriate one, however, in Immanuel Kant's moral philosophy. It is "heteronomy," which stands in opposition to autonomy.

Given the view that political society includes those relations conventionally described as anarchical, international relations are necessarily relations of super- and subordination. Heteronomous relations characterize situations of exchange among apparent equals, including those in which agents gauge their actions in anticipation of the actions of others doing the same. All such situations so pervade international relations that heteronomy is the background condition of rule against which episodes of hegemony and hierarchy are set. When hegemonial and hierarchical relations are mutually supporting, as is the case with superpower-dominated spheres of influence today, such episodes may be extended for considerable periods of time.

HERRSCHAFT

In the disciplines of Political Science and International Relations, the Hobbesian opposition between the state and the state of nature is rendered as authority in opposition to anarchy. Hobbes appears not to have used the term "anarchy." "Authority" is a different matter. In Hobbes' words: ". . . the right of doing any Action is called

AUTHORITY. So that by Authority, is always understood a Right of doing any act: and *done by Authority,* done by Commission, or Licence from him whose right it is" (1968: 218, Hobbes' emphasis). Authority is conferred on actors by authors, the latter having authority only in the sense of being authorized to act.

Hobbes' conception of authority as authorization follows from his preoccupation with rights. (See further Pitkin 1967: 14–37, Mc-Neilly 1968: 214–222, Hampton 1986: 114–129, Kavka 1986: 387–391.) Today, at least in the disciplines constituted on the Hobbesian opposition, the term "authority" is used quite differently. It is conventionally understood as a relation, not a right. This relation has two elements: the use of power and the acceptance of its use by others. Authority is the legitimate exercise of power.[1] Hobbes also stressed the "use of . . . Power and Strength" (1968: 227), but without concern for acceptance, which, in the usual circumstances of power's exercise, is indeed unlikely.[2]

A further convention attributes this now conventional view to Weber. Thus Harry Eckstein observed: "The term ['authority'] is used most widely as Weber meant it" (1973: 1153). Yet in the German text of *Economy and Society*—Weber's mature statement of political sociology—he used the term "authority" (*Autorität*) only three times (as best we can tell). The first time it appears parenthetically and in quotation marks, directly after Weber used the German word "*Herrschaft*" (Weber 1976: 122). The standard English translation

---

1. David Easton: "Authority is a special power relationship based on the expectation that if A sends a message to B—which may be called a wish, suggestion, regulation, law, command, order or the like—B will adopt it as the premise of his own behavior. . . . the major source for [authority] roles resides in the prevalence of the conviction of their legitimacy" (1965: 207–208). Harold D. Lasswell and Abraham Kaplan: "Authority is . . . the accepted and legitimate possession of power. . . . Thus ascription of authority always involves reference to persons accepting it as such" (1950: 133).
2. Consider the complete sentence from which we just quoted: "For by this Authoritie given him [the one Person] by every particular man in the Common-Wealth, he hath the use of so much Power and Strength conferred on him, that by terror thereof, he is inabled to forme the wills of them all, to Peace at home, and mutuall ayd against their enemies abroad" (1968: 227–228). The conferral of so much power inspires terror, not a sense of legitimacy. See, however, Walker (1987: 73–74) for a rather different Hobbes.

reads: "Domination ('authority')", with a footnote by Guenther Roth, one of the translators, that *Autorität* was an "alternative colloquial term for *Herrschaft*" (Weber 1968: 212, 299). The second time Weber used the term "authority" was in the phrase, "*die Herrschaft kraft Autorität*" ("domination by virtue of authority" in the English text) (Weber 1976: 542; 1968: 943; this is unchanged from the original translation of Shils and Rheinstein, Rheinstein 1954: 324). Weber immediately clarified his meaning parenthetically: "power to command and duty to obey" (Weber 1968: 943). The third time occurs in the same paragraph, in quotation marks and without alteration of the meaning just established.

The term "*Herrschaft*" occurs dozens, possibly hundreds, of times in the original text of *Economy and Society*. As we have seen, the standard English translation renders "*Herrschaft*" as domination, but not exclusively or systematically. It also uses "authority" on numerous occasions (for example, 1968: 213) as well as "dominance" and "dominancy" (for example, pp. 225, 942; dominancy was Rheinstein's choice, retained in the standard translation), and "system of domination" (p. 214). Such variability in rendering a word in translation would suggest any one of three possibilities: (1) That word is used inconsistently throughout the work undergoing translation. (2) It has an unstable meaning in the original language. (3) The language into which it is being translated does not have a precise counterpart for the concept conveyed by that particular word.

We think it would be useful to examine each of these possibilities in turn. The first is suggested by the fact that Talcott C. Parsons, in an early translation of *Economy and Society*, rendered *Herrschaft* as "imperative control" in some contexts and as "authority" in others[3] (Weber 1947: 152–153). Parsons knew that at least some of the time Weber was writing about a situation abstractly understood as coercive and thus, in Parsons' translation, a matter of "imperative control." Parsons had a specific theoretical interest in legitimacy. Inasmuch as Weber was engaged in a systematic exposition of the historical circumstances under which such control tends to be ac-

---

3. Later in the same text and without explanation, Parsons used "imperative coordination" interchangeably with "imperative control" (Weber 1947: pp. 324–327). Neither version is adequate or has survived as an accepted translation.

cepted, he frequently used the term *"Herrschaft"* in keeping with Parsons' conception of authority as the legitimate exercise of power. On these occasions, Parsons translated *"Herrschaft"* as "authority." In other words, Parsons introduced etymological inconsistencies into Weber's text to suit his own programmatic needs. Weber's English language readers could not help finding in him a Parsonsian preoccupation with consensus and system support (Compare Cohen, Hazelrigg, and Pope 1975).

Weber's other translators, and many commentators, have emphasized Weber's interest in the coercive structure of relations of control. Reinhold Bendix remarked that Weber "would have been critical of any translation that tended to obscure 'the threat of force' in all relations between superiors and subordinates" (1962: 482). In his introduction to the standard English translation of *Economy and Society,* Roth echoed this language in calling *Herrschaft* "a structure of superordination and subordination sustained by a variety of motives and means of enforcement" (Weber 1968: XC). More recently Sociologists have come to realize that inconsistencies in translating *Herrschaft* say less about Weber than they do about contending schools of thought in Sociology. Consensus theorists follow Parsons' lead; conflict theorists read Weber to contrary effect. The terms "authority" and "domination" crystallize their differences (Wrong 1980: 36–38, Alexander 1983a: 82, 173–174).

Weber's use of the term *"Herrschaft"* poses a "genuine paradox" for social theory — "submission to legitimate authority is voluntary and yet at the same time is experienced as mandatory or compulsory . . ." (Wrong 1980: 39). If inconsistencies of translation reflect a paradox embedded in the term *"Herrschaft,"* then we should turn to the second of our possible reasons for these inconsistencies, namely, that the term does not have a stable meaning in German. Because of our limited linguistic competence, we are at risk to go beyond the usual observation that *Herrschaft* has a concrete meaning — it refers to the position of the feudal lord (Roth in Weber 1968: XCIV, 62, Alexander 1983a: 172) — as well as the abstract meaning at contention in Weber's work. Note, however, that Hegel also used the term in a generalizing way in *The Phenomenology of Mind,* as did Karl Marx and Friedrich Engels in *The German Ideology* and Marx in *The Eighteenth Brumaire of Louis Bonaparte.*

Hegel juxtaposed the term *"Herrschaft"* with *"Knechtschaft"* in a famous setpiece of just a few pages (Hegel 1952: 140–150). Most commentaries refer to it as defining relations of master to slave (for example: Plamenatz 1963: 153–159, 188–192, Shklar 1976: 57–95, Balbus 1983: 11–21).[4] The language of slavery suggests domination in the extreme. Yet Hegel argued that "slaves" learn from their work, while "masters" do not, for the latter do not work. What do slaves learn? Hegel's interpretation is often admired — slaves become self-conscious — but it is equally possible to see it as retrograde — they learn their place, they become stoical (Kelly 1978: 47–50).

Self-consciousness constitutes the paradox disclosed by Weber's use of the term *"Herrschaft."* The imposition of control fosters reflection on its need less by those who impose it than those upon whom it is imposed. The latter have no other claim to dignity. If domination yields authority, the paradox is pointed up by pushing Hegel's formulation to the extreme of the relation of master and slave. Nevertheless Hegel just could as well have had lord and serf in mind (they are the concrete referents in German, after all) or had simply wanted to formulate the relationship, and its paradoxical implications, in general terms.

Marx and Engels were evidently inspired by Hegel's discussion of servitude and self-consciousness to accept its structure but alter its functional interpretation. By generalizing relations of control in the language of class and substantiating the meaning of work in material conditions, Marx and Engels turned Hegel upside down by making consciousness a trait of the "masters." This trait is at once collective and detached from the material conditions of work. That the imposition of control is acceptable is an idea acceptable only to the masters, who must impute it to their subordinates. The paradox disappears. "Domination" is the only word that adequately describes the oppressive and exploitive relationship between them.

Domination subsequently became a powerful normative as well as conceptual device for Marxists focusing on the position Marx and

---

4. Yet the two widely available translations speak of lord or master and bondsman (Hegel 1931: 228–240, Hegel 1977: 111–119) and render *Herrschaft* and *Knechtschaft* as lordship and bondage or servitude. George Armstrong Kelly (1978: 30n. 2) held that Hegel assigned "no particular nuance of significance to the synonyms 'slavery,' 'bondage,' and 'servitude.'"

Engels developed in the early years of their association. It happens that the English translation of the famous passage in *The German Ideology* on work and consciousness speaks not of domination, but of rule, the ruling class, and ruling ideas (Marx and Engels 1964: 67). The verb "to rule" in the German original is *"herrschen,"* and "rule" as a noun is *"Herrschaft."* (Marx and Engels 1978a: 46). Marx's *The Eighteenth Brumaire of Louis Bonaparte* dates from the same period. In the standard translation we find "domination" on several occasions and "rule" on one (Marx 1954b: 101, 105, 111; 107). In every instance, however, the original German is *"Herrschaft"* (Marx and Engels 1978b: 194, 197, 202; 199).

From Hegel to Weber we have an unbroken etymological tradition, in which *Herrschaft* is a master concept lending coherence to German social thought for a century.[5] It posits the permanence of asymmetry, and not the elective asymmetry of authority relations, as the central problematic of social reality. The recurrent puzzle to be solved is, then, what makes asymmetry permanent? Marx could go on to his examination of the system of capital only after he and Engels had proposed one such solution. (*Capital* offers a second solution; we describe both below.)

The centrality of *Herrschaft* in German social thought also helps to explain the growing recognition that Weber extended rather than opposed Marx's project. As Jeffrey Alexander put it, "Weber became important, therefore, not as an alternative to Marx but as a theoretical means of supplying Marxist sociology with a more complex and interdependent model" (1983a: 133). The term *"Herrschaft"* is point of departure and frame of reference in Hegel, Marx, and Weber. The very stability of its meaning allows a succession

---

5. Indeed it extends back to G. W. Leibniz, whose five levels of "natural society" include that of *Herr* and *Knecht,* conceptualized in terms of rule. See Leibniz, "On Natural Law" in Riley (1972: 77–79). In introducing this passage, Patrick Riley commented that it "shows, perhaps more clearly than any other, how much some of his political views remained medieval, how much force the ideas of hierarchy and natural subordination had for him. It relates Leibniz to some of his German predecessors — particularly Althusius — and makes clear the gap that separates him from, e.g., the great English theorists of the seventeenth century" (p. 77). See also Holz (1968) on the striking parallels between Leibniz's formulation and Hegel's.

of claims to be made about it, which should be seen in paradigmatic terms.

We come now to the third possible reason for the variable translation of *Herrschaft,* which is that the term has no really adequate counterpart in English. If the meaning of *Herrschaft* is fixed through its paradigmatic function in German social thought, we should expect to find a stable counterpart to the extent that English speakers orient themselves within the same or a comparable paradigm. There is a semblance of such a paradigm in recent decades, especially in the United States. We are thinking of C. Wright Mills' groundbreaking work on *The Power Elite* (1959a), the debate on democratic elitism (Bachrach 1971), William Domhoff's query, *Who Rules America?* (1967), and even discussions of the "military-industrial complex" and "national security elite" (for example, Barnet 1973). The influence of German social thought on this body of work is extensive but indiscriminate. Marx and Weber are names to be invoked, even icons to be admired, but rarely are their puzzles acknowledged, their solutions deployed.

Nor is the structural sense of *Herrschaft* to be found. Some protean elite infests institutions—governments at every level, corporations and financial centers, higher education—and uses its "power" to serve its own interest and betray the masses, whose interests many such institutions are presumed to serve. "Ruling class" is then a euphemism or epithet and "domination" a term with diffuse cultural and psychological connotations, especially after the belated but rousing reception accorded Herbert Marcuse's work in the United States. If Robert Michels, Gaetano Mosca, and Vilfredo Pareto are invoked no differently, less is lost in translation, for the neo-Machiavellian school used terms like "elite" so variably that they never achieved paradigmatic significance in the original. The empirical strain and therapeutic spirit in America social thought come in radical as well as reformist hues. Lacking a paradigm to stabilize it, however, native radicalism is easily untracked, whether by paranoia and conspiracy theories or euphoria and utopian plans. The structure comes from somewhere.

It would seem then that the term *"Herrschaft"* is difficult to translate because it is paradigmatically alien to English speakers, who are left to choose between the disciplinary paradigms respectively associated with the terms "anarchy" and "authority." Yet *"Herrschaft"* can be provided with an adequate translation — one that honors its paradigmatic sense in German and permits the reconstitution of the paradigm in English language scholarship. This disciplinary paradigm would finally address the operative paradigm of political society without denying either the social reality of liberalism or succumbing to the paradigmatic requirements of the term "authority." The term is "rule." We are hardly the first to suggest it — recall the translation of *The German Ideology*. It has also found its adherents in regard to Weber. Roth and Bendix both argued for "domination" (Weber 1968: LXXXIX, 62n.; Bendix 1962: 290–297). Yet they each referred to rulers and the ruled in relations of domination. Roth also employed the term "rulership" (Weber 1968: XCIII). Carl J. Friedrich (1963: 182) and more recently Stewart Clegg (1975: 56–66) equated *Herrschaft* with rule.

Yet others have explicitly rejected this equation. Wolfgang Mommsen accepted ruler and ruled, but not rule. "For a long time we [evidently referring to himself] thought 'rule' to be the best term, as it does not quite carry the somewhat austere connotation of the word 'domination'. Yet it is also too narrow, covering only the activity of governing . . . ." (1974: 72). For A. P. D'Entreves, the "proper equivalent" of *Herrschaft* "is neither 'rule' nor 'imperative control'; it is 'power', power in its strict legal sense, in the sense in which we speak of 'power-conferring rules', or say that public officials have 'powers'. The emphasis is on legality" (1967: 11).

Mommsen and D'Entreves rejected "rule" as the best term to translate *Herrschaft* for diametrically opposed reasons; the former because rule is too legalistic a term, the latter because it is insufficiently so. Both are wrong. They have implicitly taken "rule" to mean "legal rule" in the narrow Austinian sense of formal and enforceable rules. Mommsen objected to the idea that relations of ruler and ruled depend on formally valid rules, D'Entreves to the idea that rules always enforce ruler-ruled relations. Although the term "rule" includes rules that are formally valid and enforced, it does not have to exclude rules formally conferring benefits instead of creating enforceable obligations, or informal but coercive rules effectuating imperative control. Rules need be formal and institutionally supported to qualify as law (as chapter 4 demonstrates). As rules, they need only be generalizable statements yielding expectations about warranted (required or permitted) conduct (see chapter 2 generally). Rules mediate Weber's paradox of rule—they are what is accepted but seen as imposed.

Mommsen had his finger on the key by accepting the ruler-ruled relation, but lost it when he rejected rules as the link between ruler and ruled. Bendix and Roth also grasped the key by defining *Herrschaft* in terms of superordination and subordination. The German equivalents are *Überordnung* and *Unterordnung*. *Ordnung* means "order" or "arrangement" in German. It also means "rules" in the spatial or serial sense of ordering matters. English is little different, as in orders, ordinal, coordination; indeed we use "rules" the same way: rules of thumb, methodological rules, and so on. In doing so we acknowledge that rules always stand in some discernible arrangement. German social thought goes further: the expectations that rules engender are always differential, and arrangements of rules must always be one of super- and subordination. That such structures of rules are foundational, and not proximate and expedient, is deeply troubling to English speakers, whose view of rules derives from the formal symmetry of rights and duties under the common law—a formal symmetry nesting the elective asymmetry of authority relations.

In the first decade of the century, Georg Simmel elaborated the thesis that "domination" as a "form of interaction" is precisely a matter of super- and subordination[6] (1971: 96–120). We have not treated Simmel's ideas extensively because of his marginal place in the *Herrschaft* paradigm. Yet his Kantian interest in forms led him to view super- and subordination geometrically: "it is only geometry that determines what the spatiality of things in space really is" (Simmel 1971: 27). Even if social geometry is insufficient until supplied with content, one nevertheless begins not in space, but with spatiality and thus rules. It is the Kantian legacy which undergirds the German conception of order, and rule no differently, as an arrangement of rules.

---

6. Simmel (1908: 134) spoke only of *"Herrschsucht,"* rendered in the English text as "will-to-dominate" and "desire for domination" (Simmel 1971: 96). "Passion for rule" would be more accurate. Simmel used *"Autorität"* for authority (for example, 1908: 136–137), as indeed had Marx in *The Eighteenth Brumaire of Louis Bonaparte* (Marx and Engels 1978b: 196, 198).

HEGEMONY, HIERARCHY, HETERONOMY

Weber is justly famous for proposing that there are three ideal types of rule (*Die Typen der Herrschaft,* as chapter III of *Economy and Society* is entitled). For Weber ideal types are "mental constructs," but not just an observer's, as I note in the introduction (footnote 11). Ideal types of rule represent recurrent practical solutions to the problem of how human beings use rules and rule to arrange their affairs, recognized as such by the very people who use them. Weber connected the observer's mental constructs — the types as he abstractly posited them — with the ensembles of practices, supporting attitudes, and material conditions. The coherence of each ensemble prompted him to identify the type as recurring through a broad range of human experience (Shils and Finch 1949: 94–97; see also Hekman 1983).

Weber presented the three types of rule in terms of the beliefs that sustain them. These are "grounds" for rule (Weber 1968: 215). Each type relates the characteristics of that type to the distinctive grounds under which it is accepted, the first being rational, calculating grounds, the second traditional grounds and the third charismatic grounds. Weber held that the acceptance of rule on rational grounds corresponds to rule by an administrative staff (pp. 217–226). Rule accepted on grounds of tradition corresponds to rule by those traditionally accorded personal loyalty and the right to rule (pp. 226–241). Finally rule accepted on grounds of charisma corresponds to rule by someone with extraordinary powers of personality (pp. 241–254).

Notice that these correspondences differ logically. The first relates two independent sets of conditions: rational beliefs and administrative skills. The second defines the two sets of conditions interchangeably by reference to tradition. The third simply infers one set of conditions (personal traits) from another (beliefs about the extraordinary character of these traits). Weber's scheme is conceptually flawed. It has one completely articulated type of rule and response to it, a second type in which rule and response are collapsed through co-definition, and a third in which the response to rule is fully articulated and the properties of rule only implied.

Weber called his ideal types "pure" (1968: 215). Purity of type can be judged, however, only if types correspond to categories. Otherwise their mutual independence cannot be established. Furthermore, we would have to know the classificatory scheme within which categories are co-defined (compare Lakoff 1987: 366). Weber failed to provide any such classificatory scheme. Consequently Weber had to rely on his vast historical knowledge to support his conviction that only three pure types were possible. Many commentators produce different lists, no less supported by history and no better supported conceptually.[7]

Is there a way to develop a set of puzzle paradigms of rule that can be plausibly offered as the pure possibilities countenanced by the paradigm Weber worked within? We think so. If it is remembered that the *Herrschaft* paradigm locates ruler and ruled in an arrangement of rules, then Weber's nexus of rule and response to rule must also be mediated by rules. Weber knew this. The first type of rule (by administrative staff) depends on impersonal orders, or law in the usual sense. The second type of rule (by traditional leaders) depends on orders that are paradoxically personal but not original. By exercising discretion and staying within the bounds of what traditional practice permits (precedent), the ruler gains discretion. The third type of rule (by a charismatic figure) depends on oracular pronouncements, each of which is revelatory and thus completely original.

Weber might be seen as implicitly deploying a classificatory scheme for rules in which two sets of traits (traditional/original and personal/impersonal) are variously combined. Were he to have done so explicitly, there would be four possible combinations, or categories of rules. Instead Weber was content to introduce two poorly differentiated and variably decisive criteria for discriminating rule types. Being impersonal is decisive for the first type, being traditional and, as a secondary matter, personal for the second type, and being original for the third.

While Weber's scheme is clearly inadequate, we do not propose to reconstruct it. (But see Onuf 1982b: 31–33.) Weber never made a case for either of his criteria. Suggested by sundry historical experiences, they are imputed to rules because they suit the characteristics of rulers and responses to their rule. As an alternative, we can

---

7. Thus Friedrich (1963: 180–198) identified fourteen types of rule which he culled from Western political thought from Aristotle to Weber.

relate Weber's three types of rule to the classificatory scheme to be found in chapter 2, in which three categories of rules are offered. Or, reversing the procedure, we can ask, do assertive-, directive-, and commitment-rules respectively yield three categories of rule corresponding to Weber's three types?

Of Weber's three types of rule, the first uses directive-rules, as does the second much of the time. The third type uses assertives, as indeed does the second some of the time. What Weber described as the "routinization of charisma" (1968: 246–254) yields an arrangement in which rules asserting statuses occupy a significant place. We can now see that, while traditional rule is anything but a pure type, the other two paradigms — administrative and charismatic rule — accord a dominant position to directive- and assertive-rules respectively. Obviously the social reality of rule mixes types, as Weber demonstrated with his discussion of the many variations in the pattern of traditional rule — gerontocracy, patriarchy, patrimonial rule and estate rule (pp. 231–241).

Weber granted virtually no attention at all to commitment-rules in his presentation of the puzzle paradigms of rule. Yet he was amply aware of their importance. Much of his extended discussion of law in *Economy and Society* (chapter VIII) concerns commitment-rules. Weber concluded that commitment-rules did not contribute to rule as an asymmetric arrangement, but to the "decentralization of rule" (*"Dezentralization der Herrschaft,"* 1976: 542), something he thought could be said to describe "the whole system of modern private law" (1968: 942). That system of course is the basis of contract, credit, and thus the entire apparatus of capitalism.

Weber excused himself from constructing the complex of commitment-rules into a paradigm of rule for a peculiar reason. Obviously all sorts of people have rights to rule some aspect of the activities of others, even those generally holding sway over them. Weber then subtly changed the terms of the argument by observing that someone could often be said to have a "ruling" (*"beherrschend,"* quotation marks in the original, 1976: 542) position in "the social relations of the drawing room as well as in the market, from the rostrum of a lecture-hall as from the command post of a regiment, . . ." (1968: 943). What is unconvincing about this shift is that ruling is no longer a matter of commitment-rules, but of transitory social arrangements. As Weber correctly noted: "Such a broader definition would, however, render the term 'rule' scientifically useless" (1968: 943, "domination" in that text). Yet Weber himself was the one to have unnecessarily broadened the definition.

Weber's exposition of three puzzle paradigms of rule has struck many writers with its apparently tight logical structure, its "meticulous symmetry" (Mommsen 1974: 72). Meticulous perhaps, but mistaken in conception. We have endeavored to offer a variation of Weber's set that honors two of his paradigms, dissolves one as a mixed case, and constructs a third from material Weber himself provided. This third paradigm addresses the most puzzling aspect of rule, its "decentralization" through rules creating rights and duties. That Weber failed to recognize it as a puzzle paradigm no doubt reflects a paradigmatic presumption that asymmetries in ruler-ruled relations are typically reinforcing rather than cross-cutting. The more complex pattern of commitment-rules hides the asymmetries better and deceives the systematizing observer, even one as learned, and as meticulous, as Weber.

Like Weber, scholars today are generally quite capable of recognizing rule in the form of instruction and directive-rules. This is abundantly evident from the constant recourse in our own and allied disciplines to two words describing these respective arrangements of rule: hegemony and hierarchy. The lack of a comparable term for the arrangement of commitment-rules to produce rule is evidence of the continuing anonymity of that paradigm of rule. We supply a term for it, however, to be able to conduct an examination of all three puzzle paradigms of rule. The word we have chosen is "heteronomy," which from Kant on, has meant the opposite of autonomy.[8]

Hegemony refers to the promulgation and manipulation of principles and instructions by which superordinate actors monopolize meaning which is then passively absorbed by subordinate actors. These activities constitute a stable arrangement of rule because the ruled are rendered incapable of comprehending their subordinate

---

8. *The Random House Dictionary of the English Language* (1967: 667) defines heteronomy as "the condition of being under the rule or domination of another." The Greek roots "-archy," "-cracy" and "-nomy" all suggest a condition of rule, but only "-nomy" conveys the notion of rule as an arrangement. The Latin root "-mony" is too generalized — it refers to a condition or result. Friedrich used the neologism "heterocracy" in passing as an antonym for "autocracy" (1963: 196–197).

role. They cannot formulate alternative programs of action because they are inculcated with the self-serving ideology of the rulers who monopolize the production and dissemination of statements through which meaning is constituted.

Weber suggested that hegemonial rulers tend to be charismatic and their rules revelatory. This is misleading, however, because often these rules are in the air, and charisma attaches to personalities involved in their circulation and not rulers in any direct sense. A better formulation is the famous pronouncement of Marx and Engels in *The German Ideology*: "The ideas of the ruling class are in every epoch the ruling ideas: . . ." (Marx and Engels 1964: 67). Although Marx and Engels thus identified the central feature of hegemonial rule, their formulation ill suits a materialist conception of history that finds all ideas, and all consciousness, "directly interwoven with the material activity and material intercourse of men—the language of real life" (p. 42).

Apparently the content of human consciousness is determined by one's place in historically specific social relations of production. Were this so, ideas would vary with class position, and stable conditions of rule could not depend on the successful internalization of ruling class ideology. Marx intimated as much (for example, 1954b: 101–116; but see Abercrombie, Hill, and Turner, 1980). A fully developed position would have to account for competing ideologies and their relative impact on different classes. Why, and under what conditions, does exposure to ruling class ideology overwhelm the materially meaningful experience of a subordinate class? Nothing Marx wrote tells the answer.

Credit for developing the hegemonial puzzle solution should go instead to Antonio Gramsci, even though he never provided a straightforward definition of "hegemony." This has led to some disagreement among Marxist scholars as to what Gramsci had in mind. For example, Nicos Poulantzas (1978: 157–159) and Gören Therborn (1980: 157–158) argued that for Gramsci hegemony meant both "political" domination (rule through directive-rules) and ideological domination (rule through assertive-rules). Nevertheless, both Poulantzas and Therborn joined other contemporary Marxists (for example, Miliband 1969: 180; Abercrombie, Hill, and Turner 1980: 12; Sassoon 1983: 201) in focusing on the notion of ideological domination as Gramsci's principal contribution to the understanding of hegemony. Much of the confusion stems from Gramsci's expanded conceptualization of the state (the "integral state"), which he defined in terms of rule through coercion (alternatively "command," "direct domination," or "dictatorship") as well as though "spontaneous consent" (Gramsci 1971: 12, 170, 239, 263).

Although Gramsci situated hegemony within an expanded conception of the state, that he contrasted coercion with consent and discussed the latter in terms of ideology (1971: 12, 181–182) makes clear his concern for hegemony's distinctive features. Given prevailing relations of production, the superordinate class attains and secures its position by successfully representing its class interests as the general interests of society as a whole. Conditions of rule are stable because the ruling class actually constitutes social reality through its ideology, thereby limiting the capacity of the subordinate class to imagine alternatives that could threaten the ruling position of the superordinate class (pp. 12, 181, 238–239). Instead, the ruled accept their subordinate position as natural and inevitable.

Hierarchy is the paradigm of rule most closely associated with Weber because, as an arrangement of directive-rules, it is instantly recognizable as bureaucracy. The relations of *bureaux,* or offices, form the typical pattern of super- and subordination, but always in ranks, such that each office is both subordinate to the one(s) above it and superordinate to the ones below. There being typically fewer offices in any rank than in the rank immediately beneath it, there must also be a top rank with a single office and chief officer. That office has formal responsibility for all the activities undertaken in the ranks below, because such activities are guided by directive-rules descending from higher ranks. Logically speaking, if only a higher officer can issue a directive to a lower one, then the validity of any directive is ultimately traceable to the directive of a chief, responsible officer. The visualization of this arrangement of ranks linked by directives is the familiar pyramid of organization charts.

We can surmise that Weber had in mind the military chain of command so much in evidence in the Germany of his time (Rudolph and Rudolph 1979: 218). Its formal characterization, however, owes much to the view of law as a system of commands (directives), each of which is valid by reference to the one higher, until a primary validating source of commands is reached. While English speakers are likely to associate this view of law with Hans Kelsen, he is merely the most famous, and rigorously formal, member of a school of jurisprudence with which Weber was well acquainted. Kelsen himself observed that Weber called an arrangement of commands thus validated "coercive machinery" (as translated in Kelsen 1945: 171; the standard English translation is "coercive apparatus," Weber 1968: 313). So did Kelsen.

The formal arrangement of directives coercively deployed takes the standard position of legal positivism that any law is a coercively backed command and fits it into the *Herrschaft* paradigm of rule through relations of super- and subordination. Like Kelsen, Weber was both a positivist in this sense and a legal formalist, because that was the only way to get from coercive backing as a property of properly legal rules to the apparatus of coercion that made bureaucracies a paradigm of rule. Unlike Kelsen, Weber did not restrict himself to the one paradigm of rule—the "legal order"—in which directive-rules, if they are not heeded, elicit "the enforcement of conformity"[9] (Weber 1968: 313). Assertive-rules are coercive, but not in the same sense.

Heteronomy, as the unacknowledged third paradigm of rule, requires a more thorough exposition than do the other two. Kant chose the term "heteronomy" in *Foundation of the Metaphysic of Morals* to refer to the condition of not having autonomy (Wolff 1969: 58). Marx and Weber used this term no differently but only in passing (for example, Marx 1954b: 103; Weber 1968: 389, 645, 719). Although Kant's concerns were moral rather than social, his treatment of autonomy and heteronomy supports a social use of the term, such as we find in Marx and Weber, but, unlike theirs, one from which we can infer a paradigm of rule.

In the Kantian system human beings are prudential and rational (Wolff 1969: 26–72). Prudential behavior accords with principles that, by virtue of the necessarily particular nature of contingent situations, must be conditional. Rational behavior accords with principles

---

9. Bureaucracies are legal orders in their internal aspect, that is, relations of super- and subordination, because their chief officer rules all ranks with directive-rules. In their external aspect bureaucracies do not rule others, unless they do so on behalf of (as the administrative staff of) some other legal order (for example, the state). The "-cracy " of bureaucracy refers only to its internal aspect.

that are unconditional because rational beings discern them strictly by reference to "the realm of ends" (p. 58), not means. In the first situation, "heteronomy always results" (p. 67). In the second, autonomy would lead to morality.

For Kant, the point is that rationality and autonomy are conditions transcending social reality. They must be stipulated to investigate moral conduct. For us, the point is that heteronomy describes the actual situation of people relating available means to particular ends. Nevertheless, when people are self-conscious about their individual behavior, they are inclined to see themselves as rational and autonomous. Kant's transcendent conditions are nothing more than the conclusions (some, perhaps most) self-conscious people draw from participating in heteronomous social relations. The social reality of heteronomy begets an awareness of behavior that in turn begets the illusion of autonomy. Heteronomy prompts obfuscation of its own social reality. Indeed one could say that Kant's argument about autonomy and morality itself obfuscates the relation of autonomy to heteronomy.

Liberal Political Economists have noted this property of heteronomy in studies of social choice but find it paradoxical: When many individuals act rationally, they often find themselves subject to outcomes none of them preferred. The paradox disappears if we make John Harsanyi's elementary distinction between objective and subjective rationality — between choosing the "best means" to achieve a given end and "what one thinks to be" the best means (1983: 231). We are autonomous when, and only when, this distinction does not hold. When it does hold, because of contingency and our inability to control outcomes, we can either stay with subjective rationality or objectivize it by introducing risk and uncertainty (compare Harsanyi 1983: 232). Either way rationality is relieved of paradox and reduced to prudence (see also Gauthier 1986: 21–59, but note that his conception of prudence differs from the one we adopt).

The formal study of social choice is the quintessential Liberal paradigm. As with any Liberal paradigm, it accepts a utilitarian conception of rationality — prudence, in Kant's vocabulary — without also stipulating heteronomy.[10] Instead autonomy of actors is assumed

---

10. Social choice theorists often also balk at accepting utilitarian ethics along with utilitarian rationality. We may view John Rawls' "veil of ignorance" (1971: 136–

and anarchy in their relations anticipated. Cooperation is unlikely, its incidence an explanatory problem (Oye 1985a). Given the social reality of heteronomy, however, actors thinking themselves to be autonomous prudently endeavor to reduce their risks and minimize uncertainty. The "best means" to this end is to exchange commitments about future conduct. Even as we insist on our "right," as autonomous actors, to make promises freely, we find that they are not so freely broken. Our promises rule us by taking the form of commitment-rules.

Commitment-rules formalize promises as duties. Corresponding to duties are rights to whatever has been promised. Of interest here are property rights, which formalize consequences of promises made with reference to use of or access to the means of production and exchange. If we consider the staggeringly asymmetrical consequences for different actors of acquiring property rights and contractual obligations, *and* the appearance of equality among actors by virtue of the reciprocal and thus formally symmetrical arrangement of all contractual relations, we confront the real paradox of heteronomous rule: Rules positing autonomy in relations ensure the asymmetry of those relations.

Weber connected "a cosmos of rights and duties" to the conditions of rule found in Western feudalism (Weber 1968: 1079–1085). Relations between lords and vassals were "contractual and subject to renewal, but at the same time inheritable according to established norms . . ." (p. 1082). Thus feudal society was characterized by conditional private property in the sphere of production. Control of productive property by lords carried with it explicit social obligations to other, lesser lords and eventually to serfs on the manor. This, according to Weber, "turned feudalism into an approximation of the *Rechtstaat* [constitutional government]" (p. 1082).

Feudal society lacked a principle of *exclusion* with respect to property rights. Social relations among lords and between lords and serfs formed a chain of rights and obligations which provided social cohe-

---

142) or Harsanyi's question, "If you disregarded your own personal interests, what kind of society, with what kind of moral code, would you like to live in?" (1983: 243) as efforts to recover a Kantian moral position in the face of a heteronomous social reality.

sion for feudal society. The conditional nature of feudal property rights led Weber to characterize feudal society in what we would call heteronomous terms. In so doing he contradicted his own judgment that decentralized rule is not rule at all. "Fully developed feudalism is the most extreme type of systematically decentralized domination" (1968: 1079).

Altogether different was "the age of the capitalist bourgeoisie," in which "contract and specified individual rights" (1968: 1070) result in exclusive private property and, by extension (Ruggie 1986: 142–143), sovereignty and territoriality as defining traits of anarchy in international relations.[11] By contrasting feudalism and capitalism, Weber implied that a change in property rights yields a liberal system of interaction among individuals who are autonomous with respect to each other. They are constrained only by the aggregate outcomes of their interaction. We believe this position needs to be reversed: Conditional property rights permit a system of rule, but not of a heteronomous nature, while exclusive property rights always imply heteronomy. Weber made two errors. One lies in fostering the impression that the creation of feudal property rights depended on authentic exchange relations between feudal actors. The second is a failure to recognize that the exclusive character of modern bourgeois property rights implies asymmetrical relations between holders of specific, exchangeable property rights.

The issue is not whether conditional feudal property rights are

---

11. The historical relation of exclusive property rights to liberalism and the rise of capitalism is a matter of controversy. C. B. Mcpherson's influential interpretation (1962) links exclusive property to the possessive individualist and finds this conception central to such seventeenth-century figures as Hobbes and John Locke. (Recall ch. 5.) Against this interpretation, J. G. A. Pocock has argued that the crucial distinction is between real and mobile property. The emergence of public credit, a stock market and financial speculation engendered a change of consciousness, around 1700, that we associate with liberalism (1985: 108–110). In this view Locke's position on property was rooted in the tradition of contingent rights and duties central to the "ancient constitution," that is, the customary law of Britain (Pocock 1957), and evident in the modern common law. To put the difference between Locke and later liberalism another way, liberal exchange relations permit real property, the right to which need not be exclusive, while liberal relations of production require mobile property, which tends by its nature to be exclusively held: "What one owned was promises, . . ." (Pocock 1985: 113).

associated with rule, but rather whether feudal rule is heteronomous. Recall that the Kantian conception of heteronomy can be construed to mean more than nonautonomous, conditional action. Kantian heteronomy obscures the absence of autonomy. It is in this stronger Kantian sense of heteronomy that the characterization of feudal society as heteronomous becomes misplaced. Weber was sufficiently preoccupied with the contractual relations of lords, themselves asymmetric, that he underplayed the primary, materially grounded set of relations in feudalism—the relations of lord and serf.[12]

Serfs exchanged the products of their labor with the manoral lord, who in turn provided security for the serfs. Feudal property rights facilitated a monopoly of coercive means in the hands of the nobility. The constant threat of warfare fixed the pattern of feudal relations (Anderson: 140–142). Real or alleged, serfs' need for physical security compelled them to enter into exchange agreements with local landlords on the latters' terms. Nevertheless the coercive character of the exchange, and the directive-rules substantiating it, hid behind the formality of lord-serf relations based upon exchange and reciprocity. Weber himself acknowledged the military origins of feudal relations of production (1968: 1077–1078). He also noted that relations among lords bear the marks of routinized charisma (p. 1070). Indeed feudalism is a hierarchical form of rule that can be depicted as a flat-topped pyramid: By cultivating the illusion of collegiality, hegemony substitutes for the higher ranks of hierarchy.

To view contingent feudal relations as heteronomous projects modern bourgeois exchange onto the feudal situation. Exchanges between capitalists and workers take place because bourgeois property rights assign capitalists a monopoly on society's productive property and, therefore, upon the workers' means of physical and psychic sustenance. In order to gain access to the means of their sustenance, workers must enter into exchange relations with capitalists. In capitalist societies, however, the massively asymmetrical character of this exchange, and of the content of property rights behind it, is obscured by the fact that workers are generally free to choose the

---

12. He did not ignore the latter set of relations entirely: "The full fief is always a *rent-producing* complex of rights whose ownership can and should maintain a lord in a manner appropriate to his style of life" (p. 1072, emphasis in original).

specific capitalist with whom they will enter into exchange relations and even to organize themselves for collective bargaining.

The coercive character of bourgeois property rights is exposed only at the level of society as a whole. From this vantage point we can see that workers have little choice but to enter into exchange relations with *some* capitalist. At the level of individual experience the worker's right to choose diverts attention from the practical necessity of entering into such exchanges at all. The feudal relation between lord and serf embodies no such mystification of the nature of the exchange, because serfs lack the social mobility of workers who have an exclusive right to sell their labor. Instead feudal relations of rule are directly personified in the relevant actors, leaving no doubt as to who filled superordinate and subordinate roles. Moreover, noble "obligations" are not benefits owed serfs in return for services rendered to the lord. Rather they are costs lords impose on themselves to assure a reproducible supply of labor. In late feudalism lords eliminated these obligations because contracting for direct labor services proved to be cheaper (Dobb, 1963: 54–58; Anderson, 1978: 197–208).

If Weber's first error was to confuse contingent feudal relations with heteronomous rule, his second was to confuse unconditional property rights with generalized autonomy. We have already seen that exclusive property rights effectively concentrate productive property in the hands of a few owners, while the many workers who own their own ability to perform useful labor must compete to sell their services. Owners always have alternatives; workers face the practical problem of survival in the absence of a wage contract. In short, asymmetrical consequences of commissively defined relations, combined with the illusion of independence for all parties to these relations, produce the conditions of rule in which rulers simply cannot be identified by discovering the authors of rules. The ruled join the rulers as authors and audience; rules rule their joint proceedings. This is heteronomy's paradigmatically distinctive feature.

This approach to the wage contract is central to Marxist Political Economy, with Marx's concept of commodity Fetishism (Marx 1954a: 76–87) providing its foundation. The exchange of commodities (including labor power) in the market presupposes exclusive property rights (capitalist social relations of production in Marxist discourse) which render the products of human labor fully alienable. Not only are these social relations of production stable and asymmetric. The commodification both of labor and of the products of labor ensures their "mystical character" (p. 76), making them exclusively social, recognizable only by reference to their value in exchange for other such commodities. By capturing social reality, exchange value supplants materially grounded social relations, renders all people equal in their anonymity and nullifies the concept of asymmetry. Fully realized commodity Fetishism is a radical solution to the problem of rule. Its extrapolation from the specific character of exclusive property rights makes it a heteronomous solution.

Arguably liberal social thought is itself a response to Fetishism, "the despotism of speculative fantasy," brought on by the emergence of capital markets (Pocock 1985: 112). In Pocock's judgment, rampant speculation raised fears about "the hysteria, not the cold rationality, of economic man. . . . Systems of rational egoism were devised less to legitimize and explain what he was doing than to offer him a means of controlling his own impulses" (p. 113). Nevertheless, liberal thought has always been blind to heteronomous rule, at least in part because of its origins in seventeenth- and eighteenth-century Britain. Throughout this era contingent rights and duties were not merely common law, they were a linguistically fixed state of mind. While feudal rights were disappearing, they were not succeeded — indeed not for a long time — by exclusive rights reflecting a bourgeois conception of production and exchange. Instead we find an "imperfect" and still contingent form of prebourgeois private property in which producers both owned and worked their own means of production. That labor power was not a commodity suited the circumstances of family farming and artisanal production typical of Britain during this time.

In the absence of commodified labor power the "petty bourgeois" property rights of independent producers seemed to avoid the asymmetrically coercive implications of exclusive property rights. Therefore paradigmatic portrayals of social interaction between independent producers in the sphere of exchange were not taken to imply an abstraction from heteronomous property relations. Instead of constituting a puzzle solution to the problem of rule, they lent themselves to the view that rule was not the problem. Such a view may thus be construed as support for the paradigm of anarchy. Hobbes had already provided the framework for this development by positing the only alternatives as hierarchical rule and the state of nature. By using the model of prebourgeois property rights and exchange relations to domesticate anarchy, liberal thinkers could define their problematic as balancing and containing such hierarchy as was indispensable to the provision of public goods like security. (See also footnote 16).

Because bourgeois hegemonial rule portrays the capitalist system of exploitive relations of production as serving the common good, it may appear to be identical to heteronomous rule. While hegemony and heteronomy can be interdependent and reinforcing practices (hegemony legitimizes heteronomy; heteronomy provides the material basis for hegemony), the two are analytically distinct. Heteronomous rule is secured through commitment-rules which massively restrict the material opportunities of subordinates, who are endowed, along with their few remaining opportunities, with the properties of commodities. What heteronomy makes possible is all that is conceivable. By securing rule through assertive-rules, hegemony operates conversely. What hegemony makes conceivable is all that is possible.

RULES OF THE GAME

The term "hegemony" is widely used in contemporary International Relations. Neorealists like Steven Krasner (1976: 321–322, 1982: 30, 1985: 10–13) Robert O. Keohane (1980: 132, 1984: 32–38) and Robert Gilpin (1981: 29, 116, 144–210, 1987: 65–80), and world-systemicist Immanuel Wallerstein (1984: 4–7, 37–46, 132–145) all treat the strongest state in international relations as "hegemon." None of them credit Harold D. Lasswell and Abraham Kaplan, who nevertheless defined hegemony (in 1950) as "supremacy within a control area," which, in the instance of world politics, "is a *sphere of influence* when control is not accompanied by authority. A hegemonic state is a *major power*; its *satellites* are the states within its sphere of influence" (p. 257, their emphasis; for Lasswell and Kaplan's definition of authority, see footnote 1).

Implicit in this view is the equation of strength and coercive capabilities. Thus it would seem to be a hierarchical view, the more so, at least for neorealists, because the strongest state secures its privi-

[handwritten margin note: Russia as Theatre Hegemon]

leged position by instituting international regimes (executive regimes, in the language of chapter 4), instead of ruling directly. Nevertheless, this is a special case of hierarchy, rarely achieved, because the ranking state must have a "commanding" lead over the next in the chain. Hegemony thus understood is that instance of hierarchy in which the position of the ranking state is so overwhelming that it can dispense with the chain of command and cast directive-rules in a benign form (as mere suggestions), and still have its rule effectuated (Compare Bull 1977: 215).[13] The result resembles Gramscian hegemony. Because the leader in such instances is also likely to practice hegemony, the presence of hierarchy is all the more difficult to discern.

Among contemporary scholars, Robert W. Cox (1983, 1986: 217–230, 1987: 7–9, 129–219) has most clearly departed from the usual view and identified hegemony as a distinctive condition of international relations not dependent on the particulars of hierarchical position (but see 1987: 144). Thus Cox and Gilpin both described the *Pax Britannica* and *Pax Americana* of the nineteenth and twentieth centuries as hegemonial, but gave different reasons. For Cox (1986: 223), "a prevalent collective image of world order" was necessary. For Gilpin (1981: 116), "imperial control" sufficed.

Less often used than "hegemony" in contemporary International Relations is the term "hierarchy," and even less often is it elaborated. There are exceptions, however. Morton A. Kaplan (1957: 48–50) characterized one of six possible international systems as hierarchical, but appeared to have in mind arrangements of such formality that they are tantamount to government and thus precluded for in-

---

13. Hedley Bull held that "unilateral exploitation of preponderance takes three forms, which I shall call 'dominance', 'primacy' and 'hegemony'." The first "is characterized by the habitual use of force by a great power against the lesser states comprising its hinterland, and by habitual disregard of the universal norms of interstate behavior that confer rights of sovereignty, equality and independence on these states." The second, primacy, "is achieved without any resort to force, and with no more than the ordinary degree of disregard for norms. . . ." The last, hegemony, describes the situation in which "there is a resort to force and the threat of force, but this is not habitual and uninhibited but occasional and reluctant" (1977: 214–215). See also Charles F. Doran's operational distinction between empire and hegemony. "Empire is a matter of direct institutional control. . . . Hegemony tends to create vassal states or international political 'courtiers' of the surrounding entities in a rather apparent heirarchic *[sic]* perpetuated fashion; . . ." (1971: 16).

ternational relations. Kenneth N. Waltz (1979: 114–116) explicitly placed anarchy and hierarchy in opposition, the former describing international relations, the latter government. Steven L. Speigel's depiction of international relations as "an international pecking order" (1972: 3) and Stanley Hoffmann's identification of a multiplicity of "functional hierarchies" (1978: 117) suggest conceptions closer to the one we prefer, but for their presumption that asymmetric arrangements are either transitory or offsetting, and therefore not indicative of conditions of rule.

Only Johan Galtung appears to have considered hierarchy a durable feature of formally anarchic social relations, international relations being a prime example (1970: 119–120). He represented what he called "feudal interaction structures" (1970: 115, 1971: 89) as directively maintained in the pyramidal form of an idealized hierarchy. Galtung held out the possibility of partial "defeudalization," which always proceeds from the top down (1970: 123–124). This may be seen as substituting collegiality for chain of command; we see it as substituting hegemony for hierarchy. We too see this substitution likely only at the top ranks of the chain of command, at which direct, personal socialization of an elite corps of commanders is practical.

When, on rare occasion, International Relations scholars expressly resist the presumption of anarchy, their recourse is to some more or less clearly understood notion of hegemony or hierarchy. More likely, whatever terms are used, hegemony and hierarchy are conflated as, for example, "orders of leadership" based on "an ordering principle or authority" (Modelski 1983: 121). Heteronomy is unnamed, unacknowledged, unimagined. Yet heteronomy in an international context has been subject to theoretical development unawares. It is intimated in discussions of "asymmetric interdependence" (Keohane and Nye 1977: 11–19, 1987: 728–730) and "unequal exchange" (see, for example, Emmanuel 1972). Thus Galtung's concern for unequal exchange between states situated at different levels of a center-periphery hierarchy (metaphors confuse here) accords descriptive primacy to heteronomous rule, but conceptual primacy to hierarchy (as we show just above). Galtung needed to have discriminated among categories of rules to have clarified the mutually supporting character of hegemonial, hierarchical, and heteronomous rule.

Even more striking as a theoretical development of heteronomy is Albert O. Hirschman's demonstration that states' officers deliberately construct trading situations that become more valuable to their trading partners than to their own states. The consequent asymmetries in opportunity costs of foregoing these trade relations allow the officers constructing the situation to control their counterparts by threatening to withdraw from the relationship (1980: 17–52). Because Hirschman called this exercise of control an "influence effect," it might seem that the relation is one mediated by a directive-rule — The other side is influenced by the possibility of deprivation to behave as directed.

The term "influence" is misleading. It is the "effect" of the situation that is determinative. The trading partner is more affected than the initiating state is, and this is true whether the latter's officers intended this outcome, or would wish to use the situation for the purposes of exercising control. Once both sides have chosen to trade, asymmetric opportunity costs, and not subsequent choices by either one, rule the situation in favor of the partner with lower opportunity costs. People choose exchanges more advantageous to others than themselves in these circumstances not because they are entrapped, as Hirschman posited, but because they value a losing deal over none.

The term "opportunity costs" bears examination. In principle, the opportunity to make choices is symmetrically available to all possible parties to an exchange. In practice, exercising the opportunity to choose costs some partners more than it costs others, as measured by the relative curtailment of future opportunities to engage in exchange. One class of exchanges is ruled by the existence of, or agreement on, a rate of exchange, or price. Failure to distribute costs at some rate can only mean that one or the other partner declines the opportunity to exchange. The cost to both of any consummated exchange is always known in advance. A second class of exchange necessitates exercising the opportunity to choose without knowing the cost in advance. Introducing a lottery has this effect. The same effect is achieved when partners have a variety of responses to choose from but do not know in advance how any of these choices will be received. In such situations partners are obliged to guess outcomes dependent on the other's guess about her partner's guess, and so on.

This sequence of choices anticipating others' choices in infinite regress is known from game theory as strategic interaction.[14] Even when an established pattern is clear, strategic interaction makes it impossible to know specific outcomes. As a result even a disadvantaged player can "win" against a privileged partner in any given exchange, depending on the particular choices both make in the face of uncertainty. In short, when heteronomous relations are also strategically interactive, they foster gambling. By this we mean that parties knowing themselves to be disadvantaged nevertheless make choices ruled by the possibility of accruing rewards against the odds. In strategic interaction everyone participating takes risks, but asymmetrically. The more disadvantageous the situation is to one partner, the greater must be its tolerance of risk.[15] Gambling is one way to overcome the disadvantage of asymmetrical opportunity costs, but never a promising one.

Frank Klink has elsewhere (1987) generalized Hirschman's influence effect in international trade to a formal theory of heteronomous rule in international relations. He has done so from social choice theoretic assumptions. Another young scholar, Alexander Wendt (1987b), has also begun to erect a general theory of heteronomous rule, in his case, using "structuration" as a framework. Nevertheless, both Klink and Wendt have focused on North-South relations in the contemporary world, I think probably for topical and ideological reasons, and because exchange asymmetries are so pronounced in these relations.

I would not be so restrictive. (The shift to the singular indicates that Klink should not be held responsible for the rest of this discus-

---

14. "An interesting feature of many games . . . is its revolving logic: what the first player should do depends on what the second player does, but what the second player should do depends on what the first player does. But what the first player should do depends on what the second player does, and so on, forever" (Axelrod 1970: 16).

15. This is not "risk acceptance" in the usual sense: As between equal expected utilities (utility of outcomes × probability of occurrence), the choice favors a larger outcome at a lower probability of achieving it. Heteronomous relations mean asymmetric outcome utilities, whether these outcomes are expected or set by rate. Compare Bruce Bueno de Mesquita (1981: 33-36), who included both kinds of risk in his definition of risk taking.

sion.) The cumulative effect of relatively modest disparities in opportunity costs yields heteronomy among states evidently free and equal in their multiple, independently chosen relations. States may be classed together as members of the economically advanced core, for example, and, on inspection, found to exhibit heteronomous relations their agents resist acknowledging, both because asymmetries are disguised by the appearance of free choice and discounted in the name of hegemonial harmony.[16] I should also note that heteronomy in international relations is hardly restricted to states as exchange partners. This is perhaps most obvious with the movement of capital because of its scale and historically private character (Lipson 1985).

More generally, all those relations for which Political Economy is a suitable disciplinary paradigm are heteronomous. If we recall that the theory of social choice, as I describe it in the introduction, works best not by assuming anarchy, as many scholars adopting this paradigm do, but by exploring the disjunction between the formal appearance of autonomy and the social reality of super- and subordination, then the problem of Political Economy's indefensible boundaries can be solved. Political Economy is limited to the study of heteronomy, but heteronomy is not limited to the market. Nor, for the same reason, is the study of heteronomy necessarily limited to "endstates, or outcomes, emergent from behavior within rules" and not "the rules themselves" (Brennan and Buchanan 1985: xii). Social choice theorists have generally imposed this limitation on themselves, with James M. Buchanan a conspicuous exception. That they do so

---

16. Insofar as an especially favored state (or any ostensibly free agent) provides goods for its own benefit which necessarily also benefit others (collective or public goods), asymmetries benefit those others (free riders) because exchange itself is precluded. Duncan Snidal called this hegemony as benevolent leadership (1985b: 588; see further 585–590); I would call it a special case of heteronomy in which the favored state's access to benefits overrules the choice of denying those benefits to others. Nothing prevents the state providing the good from taxing other beneficiaries, a response which Snidal called hegemony as coercive leadership and I would call hierarchy. The connection between collective goods, inverted heteronomy, and hierarchy describes the state as an invention of possessive individualists. "Hobbes' argument is, in fact, identical in its method, the theoretical problem it identifies, and even the nature of the conclusion, with the modern theory of collective goods; . . ." (Orbell and Rutherford 1974: 502; compare pp. 437–438, below).

allows them the luxury of studying heteronomy without acknowledging it—both what it is and what they do.

The relevance of game theory to social choice fosters an appreciation of "rules of the game," a phrase that is unavoidable in discussions of game theory.[17] Because relations between the United States and the Soviet Union in our own time are so readily characterized in the language of games, the phrase "rules of the game" has inevitably crept into discourse on the subject. Typical is this remark of Oran Young's: "The two superpowers over the course of time demonstrated a tacit propensity to elaborate at least minimal *procedural* rules to regulate the most serious dangers to the international system arising from their continuing competition" (1968a: 52). Young's emphasis on procedure is matched by Hedley Bull's recitation of rules by status (an ambiguous term), including those having the status "simply of operating procedures or 'rules of the game'" (1977: 54; see almost word for word in Keal 1986: 134).

Procedure, as used here, would seem to refer to rules subject to minimal formalization—they are "unspoken rules" (Keal 1983), no less easily "read" for being tacit (Onuf 1975: 1052). It would also suggest that these rules are constituted by reciprocal promises of restraint in the way these states "operate," promises that would be repudiated before being acknowledged. Commitment-rules in turn constitute and regulate the asymmetric spheres of influence that have emerged as one of the most notable features of contemporary international relations. (On spheres of influence, see Keal 1983, Almond 1986, Keal 1986; on the United States and the Soviet Union as asymmetric empires, see Liska 1967.) That these spheres of influence are asymmetric is hardly surprising, given the heteronomous relations between the superpowers. In effect, each sphere of influence is defined by the influence effect the other superpower is capable of achieving in their heteronomous relations.

---

17. Illustratively: "The concept of 'game' has associated with it the concepts of 'rules,' 'players,' 'moves,' 'strategies,' and 'payoff.' . . . In any game there are some things under the control of the players and other things that are not under their control. The things not under the control of the players are the rules of the game" (Kaplan 1957: 170–171; another example is Buchanan and Tullock 1962: 325–326; on rules of the game considered more expansively, see Onuf 1974: 20–35, Kratochwil 1978: 23–66).

When scholars adduce the heteronomous rules of the superpowers' game, their lists are strikingly parallel: They enumerate mutual constraints on each meddling in the other's sphere of influence, leaving implicit the freedom of each within its own sphere.[18] Yet the conduct of superpowers (their agents, properly speaking) within their spheres is also a matter of rules and rule, and not just commitment-rules and heteronomous rule. Superimposed on relations oriented to exchange we find a combination of a directive-rule and a principle announced in the context of conduct according with that directive-rule.

The directive-rule in question is simple enough. It permits superpowers to use force to maintain the integrity of their respective spheres of influence. This rule runs counter to formal, general rules limiting recourse to force (instruction-rules), which are constantly invoked by subordinate states within spheres of influence. Consequently the directive-rule cannot be enunciated in the simple form superpower behavior suggests. Rather, it is embedded in an exculpatory principle, namely, that the forcible protection of a transnational principle, such as democracy or socialism, is of such singular importance that

---

18. Compare these lists of Richard Falk and John Lewis Gaddis:

> (1) No concerted use of military force across international boundaries in pursuit of unspecified objectives;
> (2) No use of nuclear weapons to influence the outcome of an armed conflict internal to a single national society;
> (3) No overt military intervention in ongoing warfare taking place within a state belonging to a rival superpower's bloc or sphere of influence;
> (4) No extension of the scope of overt violence associated with an internal war to reach covert participation if such an extension requires overt acts of violence across an international frontier;
> (5) No insistence on victory in a violent encounter involving the substantial participation of rival blocs;
> (6) No deployment of nuclear weapons in a state formally associated with a rival's sphere of influence (Falk 1971: 193).

> (1) Respect spheres of influence;
> (2) Avoid direct military confrontation;
> (3) Use nuclear weapons only as a last resort;
> (4) Prefer predictable anomaly over unpredictable rationality;
> (5) Do not seek to undermine the other state's leadership. (Gaddis 1986: section titles reformatted, 132–140; see also Cohen 1981: 57–59, Hoffmann 1987: 41–48.)

it overrides all other rules limiting recourse to force (Franck and Weisband 1971).

Borrowing from Judge Sir Robert Jennings suggestive remarks in his Dissenting Opinion in the World Court's Case concerning Military and Paramilitary Activities in and against Nicaragua (Nicaragua *v.* United States of America) (1986: 1289), I call this the rule of champions. Jennings' concern was an interpretation of the rule permitting self-defense as an exception to formal rules limiting recourse to force, in which a superpower comes to the assistance of a state allegedly under threat, even though that threat cannot intelligibly be said to extend to the assisting state. This is self-defense as "a vicarious defense by champions." Jennings dryly remarked that "the notion is indeed open to abuse." The champion would retort that the abuse comes from its global adversary: The rule of champions is a directive-rule demanded by the failure of the other superpower to follow the commitment-rule to respect spheres of influence (see Cohen 1981: 127–153 on broken rules of the game). Such a rule cannot be extricated from an exceptionally weighty instruction-rule, or high principle, that all must accept the world as constituted, for it is the safest world we can have and, within spheres, the best as well.

The heteronomous rules of the game are supported by this principle, which makes global heteronomy also a condominial hegemony. (On such condominia, see Liska 1967; on "the impossibility of a superpower condominium," see Hoffmann 1987: 43) The directive-rule of champions makes each sphere of influence a hierarchy, again supported by the hegemonial principle that spheres of influence are the best and safest global arrangements we can hope for. Condominial hegemony within and above spheres supports paired hierarchies as well as global heteronomy. Furthermore, hegemony is at once codified and cloaked in an endless array of contests over less than vital stakes. Under the circumstance, it is no wonder that students of the situation refer to "great powers in the international hierarchy" (Triska 1986: 15) and "hegemons and their interaction with their spheres of influence" (Almond 1986: 161). The terms are confused (indeed reversed), but the general idea is right: It is a world of hegemony, hierarchy, and, it must be added, heteronomy.

7

WORLD POLITICS

Where there is human society, we find politics. Political Science not-withstanding, politics cannot be equated with relations of authority, as the preceding chapter shows. Now I turn to Harold D. Lasswell, perhaps the greatest of Political Scientists but, at least in his concep-tion of politics, rather a deviant one. Lasswell held that politics — what I define in the introduction as the important business of any society — must concern the distribution of influence and rewards in society. Influentials get most of what they want by skillful manipula-tion of symbols, control over material values, and use of violence. Elites, organized into skill groups, get what they get by doing what they do in three categories of behavior — the same three categories to be found throughout this book.

Politics, in this view of Lasswell's, are not confined to the states and the relations of states. People always behave politically. For humanity as a whole, world politics result. Lasswell's interest in what people do ranges from the behavior of the individual (he was a founder of political behavioralism, with its positivist and methodo-logical individualist commitments) to the largest movements of hu-manity. The most momentous of these movements is that many-sided transformation of the agrarian societies of Europe into the world we know today. Modernity describes this world, moderniza-tion the manifold changes giving rise to it.

Lasswell's behavioralism has one significant limitation. Despite his interest in symbols and their use, Lasswell viewed language as a transparent medium: Language is nothing more than its content, which elites can change to suit themselves. Of course elites change the content of symbols. Yet how they talk, in conjunction with the ls they use, constitutes much of what they do and the ways they do it. Lasswell was a positivist, not a constructivist.

To make Lasswell's behavioralism constructivist, I offer three related propositions. People can become skilled in performative talk, as with any other activity. They garner influence by doing so. Each of Lasswell's three categories of doing will be manifest in such talk. I develop these propositions first by setting them against the prevailing view of world politics, which is shown to miss the full range of politically relevant ways of doing, and second by setting them in the historical context of modernization, which is understood as referring to deep changes in the ways we do what we do. Voices have changed.

Characteristic premodern activities result in the emergence of skillful talk, at first supporting but finally, though never fully, substituting for those earlier activities. Constellations of professional skills are subject to modernization with the rise of the state in the last half millenium. Practices identified with the rise of organizations within and among states in the last century or so have meant the operational ascendancy of one way of talking for politics, although political modernity is never fully dissociated from any of the three modernized professional skills constellations.

SKILLS

In the introduction I define as political whatever the members of a social unit decide is important for their unit. This is implicitly a distributive view of politics (Young 1968b: 65–78). The criterion of importance must be taken to mean: whatever might be important enough that its distribution is contested. Undoubtedly the distributive view of politics received its most powerful and succinct expression in Lasswell's justly famous book title, *Politics: Who Gets What, When, How* (1958).[1] Lasswell told us that "the study of politics is the study of influence and the influential," the influential being those "who get the most of what there is to get" (p. 13). Lasswell

---

1. First published in 1936. The 1958 edition has a postscript by Lasswell.

was concerned to show how the influential get and stay that way and what rewards accrue to them as a consequence. Thus his assessment of who gets what is really a matter of who does what.

What influentials do is to exercise control over the means by which we — people in general — invent, produce, exchange, and maintain whatever we value. In short, their value-oriented activities disproportionately affect ours. Correctly understood, this view of politics differentiates "us" and "them" only in degree. All of us affect the value-oriented activities of others all the time. Lasswell's use of the term "most" smuggles in an important additional sense that a stable and substantial disproportion of influence and rewards is necessary to what we call politics. "The few who get the most of any value are the *élite;* . . ." (1965a: 3, his emphasis). Acknowledged sources for this refinement of the term "politics" include the Neo-Machiavellian school of Robert Michels, Gaetano Mosca, and Vilfredo Pareto. Thus we find Pareto approvingly quoted: "'every people is governed by a chosen element in the population'; what is said, in effect, is that every people is ruled by — rulers" (Lasswell and Kaplan 1950: 202).

Lasswell's position suggests strongly that élites rule by their choice, not the people's. Anglo-American political thought in the liberal tradition takes a different position. People choose rulers the way they choose goods in a market. Or at least they should be able to. Democratic procedures, constitutional safeguards, liberal ideology, the balancing of sectional interests are held to prevent the political equivalent of market failure. The result is pluralism. Sorted by their interests into competing groups, the many rule (Bentley 1967: 447–459, Truman 1951: 45–65). Or conceding something to Lasswell's position, perhaps polyarchy will result: rule by a few who are nevertheless controlled by the many (Dahl and Lindblom 1963: 272–323; compare Bentley 1967: 298–320).[2]

---

2. The proposition that pluralism and stable political elites are compatible in a form of rule known as polyarchy constitutes the version of democratic theory ascendant in Political Science in the United States after World War II. (See notably Dahl 1956, 1961, and Bachrach 1967, 1971 for criticism.) Lasswell's repeated invocation of pluralism during this time may be interpreted as movement away from the position he had earlier taken that influentials mostly get what they want. Alternatively it may reflect the absorption of his earlier position into the democratic theory of the time.

Where there are politics, there is, for Lasswell, "a body politic" (a term credited to Thomas Hobbes), or "politically organized society" (Lasswell and Kaplan 1950: 186). When the body politic uncontestedly occupies a given territory and thus is sovereign, it is a state (pp. 177–185). States have governments, government being the formal dimension of rule, that is, rule that accords with a "political formula" (a term taken from Mosca; Lasswell and Kaplan 1950: 126; see generally pp. 126–133). Lasswell showed little interest in territory and sovereignty as such. Evidently what influentials do is not confined to states and their relations. World politics are not to be confused with international relations narrowly conceived. Instead Lasswell defined world politics in reference to "the shape and composition of the value patterns of mankind as a whole" (1965a: 3).

Lasswell's world is the planet and its people—the whole world, we are inclined to say. Today indeed, "world politics encompasses the whole world," but historically it did not, even though "it is larger than any juridically defined political unit." Immanuel Wallerstein, whose words I quote here (1974: 15), defined worlds by reference to "their self-containment as an economic-material entity . . ." (p. 230). Whether the whole world today is an economic-material entity because of the division of labor imposed by capitalism, this definition seems too restrictive.

Worlds are inclusive social constructions which are also material entities. Every world is a whole world. Any such world is defined by the reach of its influentials; it is the world they know because it is the world of their deeds. World politics is the term I use for the politics of those influentials whose reach extended once to most of Europe and now to the whole world. The world we know is an inclusive social unit of planetary proportions—a world of states, the world of humanity.

Scholars in International Relations have generally taken the world they study, a world of states, to be one of diffused influence. This they elevate into the distributive principle of anarchy—rule by no one. As chapter 5 makes clear, I take the presumption of anarchy to be mistaken. If one starts with states as the "who" of world politics and war as the "how," then anarchy—now taken to mean, rule by no one state—is a formally correct inference. Lasswell did not. He started with those individuals who are, for any level of politics, the influentials. So must we. If International Relations presumes an anarchical world of states, I say we should turn to a world of influentials whose activities could conceivably constitute a polyarchy (Brown 1974: 186–190) but, lacking liberal supports within the protective confines of a state, are not likely to. Rule by the few—hegemony, hierarchy, heteronomy—is likely.

Lasswell was a central figure in what came to be called the behavioral movement in the study of politics.[3] Behavioralism starts with people, not artifacts or abstractions, like government, law and the state.[4] Behavioralism in International Relations has strongly tended to concern itself with how states' leaders process information, deal with dissonance, form images and, in general, internalize their situation. (For this kind of behavioralism at its best and most systematic, see Jervis 1976.) The passive view of behavior is complementary to the view of international relations as something that states, not people, do.[5] People's perceptions and states' doings are antiseptically connected through "decision-making," a term conveying the sense that people do not decide on a course of action so much as have their minds made up for them.[6]

Lasswell's political behavioralism is an active version: Behavior is doing. Lasswell certainly recognized that most such doings occur

---

3. On the rise of behavioralism in the late 1920s, Lasswell's role, and the larger social and intellectual context, see Crick (1960).
4. As Lasswell put it in his systematic work with philosopher Abraham Kaplan, a science of politics "finds its subject matter in interpersonal relations, not abstracted institutions or organizations; . . ." (1950: xxiv). But note a tendency toward depersonalization, as when they spoke of "formulating the subject matter of politics in terms of a certain class of *events* (including 'subjective' events), rather than timeless institutions or political patterns" (p. xiv, emphasis in original). See also the extended discussion in Lasswell (1960: 240–267). On the philosophical underpinnings of the move to events, see Eulau (1968). A brief, very helpful introduction to behavioralism, much influenced by Lasswell (p. vii), is Eulau (1963).
5. Complementarity is assured by accepting the division of scholarly labor J. David Singer (1961) made famous. Behavioralists study what goes on within states; the rest what goes on between them. Robert Jervis, for example, began with "Perception and the Level of Analysis Problem" (title of chapter 1, 1976: 13–31).
6. Only the bureaucratic politics approach to decision-making avoids passivity, and it stands outside the behavioral tradition (Allison 1971). Note also that the study of events, like that of decision-making, is a passive form of behavioralism, the "event flow" bypassing decision-making and the level of analysis problem and suiting instead "a systems concept that the substance of international relations is a flow of interaction" (McClelland 1976: 108, 107).

within those "integrated patterns of practice," including "distinctive practices of decision making," which function on behalf of states, that is to say, governments (Lasswell and Kaplan 1950: 177, 192; see generally chapter 8 of that book, entitled "Functions"). The "decision process" within governments can also be sorted into functions (always seven in number for Lasswell) (1963: 93–105). The operative word here is "function," which Lasswell left undefined. Functional analysis, also called structural-functionalism, was contemporaneously ascendant in Sociology and Social Anthropology, but Lasswell's "functional analysis" differs from the former because of its non-systemic orientation. Lasswell did not think that systems have functions: no teleology is implied.[7]

Functional analysis is merely a procedural addendum to Lasswell's behavioralism — it allowed him to order the contextual richness of behavior as doing through what he called a configurative method.[8] Thus Lasswell's behavioralism acknowledges the state and accords operational priority to government. Yet it requires neither a conceptual division of behavior (within states and among states) nor resort to the study of individual governmental decisions as the way across this divide. What influentials do resists encapsulation.

How then do influentials get, and keep, what they want? As Lasswell saw it, they do so three ways — "by manipulating symbols, controlling supplies, and applying violence" (1965a: 3). These are skills. Individuals proficient in them constitute "skill groups," which compete or collude as they can to distribute rewards in ways that always work to the advantage of those groups.[9] Influentials also adopt prac-

---

7. Just such teleology has inspired endless criticism of structural-functionalism, much of it citing Hempel (1959). If Heinz Eulau (1968) was correct that Lasswell's move to events allowed him to use the concept of "emergent properties" to solve the level of analysis problem, he too may be criticized for implying that systems are purposive.

8. Lasswell's assertion that the "configurative method of political analysis consists in the use of concepts of *development* and *equilibrium*, . . ." again does not imply a structural-functionalist view, because these concepts are treated, not as system properties, but as devices for assessing "changes toward which or away from which events are moving" (1965a: 4, emphasis in original).

9. (Lasswell 1965a: 3–20) Lasswell did not actually use the term "skill group" in the 1936 edition, although it is to be found in the Postscript to the 1958 edition (p. 196). The term appears in passing in Lasswell (1965a: 85, 203) and Lasswell and Kaplan (1950: 65).

tices that institutionalize and legitimate their advantageous position, but this is less a speciality of any one group than a prerequisite for group survival.

Lasswell was inclined to see skill in violence as declining in Western life, other skills increasing. There is a different way to describe this trend. Time has seen a dramatic tendency toward skill specialization. Violence itself has become a highly specialized skill, no longer resembling the near-brigandage of the feudal lords. Not only has the twentieth century seen "a renewed wave of specialists in violence as world crises continue" (Lasswell 1958: 96 [Postscript]). Skill in violence has become more especially a skill in supervision, that is, in systematizing the military tasks of garrison duty and the watch.

Commonly the meteoric rise of specialized skills in technical, economic, and social spheres is identified with "modernization."[10] This is, however, a notoriously slippery term, referring to more or less everything that has happened in recent centuries to undercut the fixed inequalities of agrarian societies. By becoming specialized, skills are just some of the many social constructions undergoing modernization. Manifold modernization constitutes modernity — the condition of many things becoming modern.

It is important to distinguish modernity and modernism. The latter is usually understood as an artistic and literary movement of the late nineteenth and twentieth centuries, in which anxiety, alienation, and loss of identity are constant themes (Bradbury and McFarlane 1976). Modernism is a cultural response to modernity. It is most frequently a specific response to the depersonalizing effects of organizations as instruments of social control. (The term "organization" is defined in chapter 4, footnote 12 of this book.)

The rise of organizations over the last century is an especially visible feature of the longer-term tendency for skills to specialize. Indeed it is the dominant feature of late modernity. The effects of organizations on people are manifestly political, and critical theory in the

---

10. Although Sociologists since Emile Durkheim have tended to refer to the process as one of differentiation instead of specialization, the former term is taken to be a structural attribute, chosen, one would guess, to "objectify" (double meaning intended) the functional-evolutionary model of social change long ascendant in sociology (compare Bendix 1966–1967: 318–323).

Frankfurt tradition is modernist political theory.[11] The same may be said for poststructuralism, as evidenced by Michel Foucault's preoccupation with the emergence of specialized skills in supervision and their relation to discipline and control[12] (1978, 1979).

Lasswell did not have a modernist sensibility. For him modernization is an inclusive process of social change which results in "a rising level of participation in all values" (1965b: 293, emphasis deleted). Organizations increase the availability of values and foster participation. Lasswell's configurative method centers on a plurality of partially related changes. Given this position and its premises, it follows that progressive specialization makes it increasingly unlikely that one skill group can dominate distribution by itself. The relative deconcentration of influence and its rewards does seem to be one significant consequence of modernization.[13] This in turn would seem to mean that the ability to explain the need for one's skills, defend one's practices, justify one's rewards, and implicate others in one's endeavors become commensurately important activities. Doing is ever more a matter of talking, while engaging in violence, delivering goods and the rest are ever less consequential in their own right.

Lasswell tended to see skill specialization merely as the prolifera-

---

11. For an overview, see Held (1980). An important discussion outside the Frankfurt tradition, though characteristically misleading in its use of the term "modernity," is Berman (1982).

12. I resist the term "postmodern" in this and related contexts. Its use to describe contemporary architecture, for example, improperly suggests a reaction to modernity. Rather, "postmodern" architecture is a reaction to modernism and a reversion to modernity. The term "postmodernist" would be better, "modern in the Romantic manner" better yet. Only to the extent that modernist reactions to modernity come out as *fin de siècle* fantasies or romanticized evocations of premodern social life, and modernity itself is denied, does the term "postmodern" seem appropriate. Postpositivist social theory, to which I would have this work contribute, must have modernity as its subject, if critically so. To call postpositivists postmodern is therefore misleading. To call them modernist is safer, although a poststructuralist, for example, might well call the constructivist position I adopt here merely modern in its extensive use of the constructions of modernity. On the ambiguous relation of poststructuralism to modernity, see Ingram (1987: 77–78).

13. Lenski (1967: 308–313) has estimated that the top 2% of the population in traditional agrarian societies takes half the rewards, and in modern societies less than half that.

tion of more refined ways of doing what influentials needed to have done. That Lasswell did not fix on the rising quotient of talk in influence-related skills is a deficiency in his active behavioralism. Talking is indeed active, because, as I elaborate in chapter 2, most talk is "performative": The very act of saying something (a speech act), of giving voice, does what that act says it does. Words constitute deeds. If modernity means more talking, it means more, not less, is being done.[14]

Obviously I use the terms "talk" and "voice" in a generic way. One may speak, and be heard. One may use the written word as the medium of talk, and one's words are seen. One may talk wordlessly, by example, through one's taste, by gestures, and be felt. Talking engages all the senses, at least metaphorically. So does understanding what is said and responding. Together these are sensorily diverse but inextricable activities—doing as social construction.

Conceivably the ways we think—the cognitive and ethical styles I discuss in chapter 3—materially relate to our various senses. Seeing relates to schematic representation, sequential reasoning and analysis. Hearing relates to orchestration, composition, harmony. Taste, smell, and touch relate to evocation, memory, and association. (I draw here on Marshall McLuhan's provocative argument along these lines, 1964.) Yet the decisive effect on the way we think comes from the media extending our senses, and not the senses themselves. Visual acuity is not the point; alphabets are. Auditory acuity is less important than musical exposure. Cinema and television substitute "body language" and subliminal association for a world that we can taste, smell, and touch. Skill in using media, by dominating the way we think, all but defines modernity.

---

14. In response to World War I and again during World War II, Lasswell devoted a great deal of attention to propaganda and the manipulation of symbolic content in language—but doing so reinforced his propensity to identify talk with thought and skill in talk with "arranging propositions" (Lasswell and McDougal 1960: 119–127, quoting p. 124; first published 1943). This passive analytic stance culminated in the methodological development of "content analysis," now one of the preferred techniques of behavioralism oriented to perception (see Lasswell and others 1949).

POWER POLITICS

In contemporary discourse, both public and popular, the term "power politics" is virtually synonymous with world politics. With minor qualifications, the same may be said of academic discourse. Indeed the movement in the United States after World War II to constitute International Relations as a discipline presupposed the centrality of power (and differentiated itself from Political Science by affirming that authority was central to the latter). Lasswell too placed power and influence, the former defined in terms of the latter, at the center of his general conception of politics.

In the systematic exposition that Lasswell undertook with Abraham Kaplan (1950), power is defined as a "special case of the exercise of influence" (p. 76), one in which influence is achieved through the use, or expectation of use, of "relatively severe sanctions" (p. 84). A sanction is "conduct in response to an act . . . that is expected to modify future acts" (p. 48), meaning by reward or punishment, whether by praise or censure, redistribution of goods and services, or the use of violence. (These are Lasswell and Kaplan's words, rearranged slightly). Influence is defined as "value position and potential," that is, place in the distribution of values (p. 60). The tendency in this conceptual system is to treat influence passively, power actively; one has influence, uses power.

For Lasswell's active behavioralism to be internally consistent, however, the term "influence" should be used actively, for conduct. Then one would not need to speak of power as conduct, thereby avoiding the messiness of Lasswell and Kaplan's relative severity criterion. The effects of exercising influence are shifts in value position—effects for which terms like "rewards", "privilege," and "advantages" are suggestive. Insofar as the term "power" refers not to conduct and its effects but to the capabilities deployed in conduct, then I think confusion is reduced by using such terms as "capabilities" and "resources." In consideration of these and other conceptual ambiguities (see further Hart 1976, Baldwin 1979), I avoid using the term "power" except in an obviously metaphorical way throughout this book.[15]

---

15. Compare Rosenau (1980a: 39, footnote deleted):

How, then, to focus on both the possession and interaction dimensions of "power" without being driven by the structure of language to an over-

Lasswell and Kaplan defined authority as "formal power": "To say that a person has authority is to say not that he actually has power but that the political formula assigns him power, . . ." (1950: 133). Just above, I note that Lasswell and Kaplan took government to be the formal dimension of rule. One might conclude then, that authority is but another term for government. Lasswell and Kaplan had an additional criterion for authority, however, as indicated in the rest of the sentence explaining the term: "To say that a person has authority is to say . . . that those who adhere to the formula expect him to have power and regard his exercise of it as just and proper." Rule is therefore "effective power" (p. 208); authority is formal power which, by virtue of its acceptance (see chapter 6, footnote 1), is also effective.

My inclination is to say that rule is an effective exercise of influence — effective in some measure because of a political formula which helps to make rule a routine and acceptable activity. In chapter 6, I dispense with the term "authority" and here with "power." I think Lasswell and Kaplan could have too, because the term "rule," which refers to the way "control is distributed and exercised in a body politic" (p. 208) makes both terms superfluous. Do world politics constitute a body politic? Certainly all the ingredients are present: the exercise of influence, a political formula alleging the autonomy of states as the primary vehicle for the exercise of influence, and an acceptance of the pattern of influence and its rewards as consonant with the formula's requirements. Lasswell's inclusion of authority in the system of definitions he and Kaplan worked out neither excludes world politics from the world of politics, precludes rule from world politics, nor supports the constitutive differentiation of Political Science and International Relations.

The view of the world constituting International Relations appropriated for itself the title "Realism."[16] Unlike Lasswell's compre-

---

How, then, to focus on both the possession and interaction dimensions of "power" without being driven by the structure of language to an overriding preoccupation with the former dimension? . . . For years, I have solved this conceptual problem by dropping the word "power" from my analytic vocabulary (thus the use here of quotation marks) replacing it with the concept of capabilities whenever reference is made to attributes or resources possessed and with verbs such as control or influence whenever the relational dimension of "power" is subjected to analysis.

16. I use the upper case for Realism to distinguish it from philosophical realism, as discussed in chapter 1, and not because it is the proto-theory constituting Inter-

hensive view of politics, Realism leaves authority — legitimate power — to Political Science as the study of the state and reserves for itself power politics as the study of politics among states. Furthermore, Realism associates power with military endeavors and diplomacy. In Raymond Aron's words: "Interstate relations are expressed in and by specific actions, those of . . . the *diplomat* and the *soldier*" (1973: 6, his emphasis). If war is an extension of diplomacy, as every Realist since Karl Maria von Clausewitz has believed, no less is diplomacy an extension of the policy of dominating distribution through violence.[17] In this view, those who are proficient in violence extend their influence as they are capable, compounding it through conquest and consolidating it with Lasswell's other techniques of control.

In principle nothing impedes this process until it reaches the largest scale possible (the world as known at that moment). In practice a number of such violently erected centers of peace emerge, each a threat to the others, all vying ceaselessly and indecisively for influence.[18] In the logic of the Leviathan, these centers are locally peaceful because questions of influence have been forcibly settled. They are states. Their leaders have both the opportunity to wrest influence from their counterparts in other states and the obligation to prevent the latter from doing the same. For Realists, then, world politics is properly conceptualized as the struggle among states for the rewards that come from either winning tests of violence (war) or convincing others that such tests can only work to their disadvantage (diplomacy).

To the extent that the late Hans Morgenthau is the defining presence behind contemporary Realist thought, at least in the United States,

---

national Relations. Presently, I discuss Functionalism as an important alternative to Realism, there using the upper case to distinguish this term from "functionalism," as generally used in Anthropology and Sociology. (See just above and chapter 1; I borrow this convention from Haas 1964: 5.)

17. Lasswell and Kaplan treated diplomacy quite differently. "A *diplomat* is a diplomatist with formal status; . . . ." A diplomatist "specializes in power relations (negotiation and agreement) with other groups, rather than the manipulation of symbols, violence, or goods and services" (1950: 193, their emphasis).

18. This is now conventionally called the "security dilemma," so named by John H. Herz, and independently formulated by him and Herbert Butterfield, with due credit to Hobbes, in Herz (1959: 231–243). For behavioralist and special choice theoretic renditions, see respectively Jervis (1976: 58–113; 1978).

this statement needs no qualification. (For decisive evidence of Morgenthau's position, see Vasquez 1983: 38–47.) Not all Realists are this
single-minded. Aron acknowledged the interplay of diplomatic structures, industrial expansion and ideological movements as critical
features of the present world, while E. H. Carr identified military
power, economic power, and power over opinion as the primary
modalities of control. Yet both confirmed their standing as Realists
by granting primacy respectively to diplomacy and power as violence
(Aron 1954: 159, 165; Carr 1964: 102, 145).

Just as Realists thematize the largest scale structure of influence
as the struggle among states, they thematize the distributive claims
of influentials on that scale as the pursuit by states of their self-
interest. "The main signpost that helps political realism through the
landscape of international politics is the concept of interest defined in
terms of power" (Morgenthau 1967: 5).[19] Embedded in Morgenthau's
assertion that interest is defined in terms of power is the liberal conception of interest as calculation. (Compare chapter 5, footnote 3.)
In effect, Morgenthau concluded that, operationally speaking, what
must always be calculated is power position. (He did not conclude
that this is easily done; see 1967: 197–201.) Getting the most one can
of what there is to get is a matter of calculating what may be done
with one's resources for violence.

The Realist view of world politics has the considerable virtue of
consistency and simplicity. By presupposing that politics up to a certain scale leads to the formation of states and the distribution of influence and rewards therein, and beyond that leads to the intense
competition among states, Realists can treat world politics as substantially unaffected by politics at other levels. The converse need
not be true. The exigencies of world politics may force states to become more centralized and efficient in organizing influence and
distributing consequences internally.[20] World politics puts pressure
on the influential within states to modernize, that is, undertake the

---

19. Lasswell felt that the "distinctive mark" of the political personality is, in displac-
    ing private motives onto public objects, "the rationalization of the displacement
    in terms of public interests" (1960: 262).
20. In summarizing considerable support for his position Charles Tilly stated: "Up
    to our own time dramatic increases in national budgets, national debts, numbers

kind of skill specialization that Lasswell identified, without skills modernization spilling over into world politics. As Realists see it, force can never lose its utility (Osgood and Tucker 1967)—the project of modernization, so understood, guarantees as much.

We begin to see why the state is the decisive abstraction for Realists, for the position of any given state in world politics accentuates the modernization of influence-garnering skills within that state, while the situation of every state being compelled to do the same ensures that world politics can never modernize. Indeed this situation compels the intensification of violence for political purposes.[21] Because the situation states find themselves in never changes, but modernized means can get out of hand, some Realists worry about the system of international relations breaking down or blowing up, but they do not see it changing from within itself. Consequently the image of violence-laden politics is not just left over from feudal warrior ways and their formalization in the absolutist state, nostalgically defended by Realists against the contemporary reality of politics in a different key. In the Realist reckoning, the warrior culture of world politics has made states, and domestic politics, what they are today, and, in turn, states make world politics what they have always been, and more so. "War made the state, and the state made war" (Tilly 1965: 42).

However made, all states are legal arrangements—legal orders in

---

of governmental employees or any other indicator of governmental scale in European countries have occurred almost exclusively as a consequence of preparations for war" (1975: 74). But for an alternative view, in which "efficient tax collection, debt-funding and skilled, professional military management kept peace at home, and exported the uncertainties of organized violence to the realm of foreign affairs," see McNeil (1982: 79). Anthropologists propose much the same alternatives in discussing the origins of premodern states (politics in agrarian settings) (Service 1978).

21. Richard K. Ashley (1987: 413) has claimed that Realism "relies upon a double move, a two-sided rhetorical maneuvre." One move is to insist that the state is a community, understood in "Western rationalist discourse . . . as a timeless and universal identity" (p. 413). The second move is to defer endlessly, on historicist grounds, the realization of such a community among states (pp. 414–415). The interpretation offered here differs by finding only one move—the project of modernization, as Realists understand it—which at once rationalizes arrangements within states and guarantees the unchanging nature of relations among states.

the usual nomenclature. Certain influentials are designated in law to act on behalf of the state; their ability to do so is guaranteed by granting them a potential monopoly of violence (see also chapter 4.) In this view, the state is an enforced peace. As such it is the perfected instrument of the influential. It yields them internal control on the cheap and permits them the discretionary use of resources under their control in the world competition for influence and rewards. Realists invariably, if for the most part unreflectively, accept the place of law — defined in legal positivist terms as rules subject to enforcement — in making the state what it is. So understood, law is instrumental to the state but for that reason not an instrument of the state, at least in its relations with other states.

Even in Realist terms, however, this view is defective. Lawyers, like warriors, predate the modernization of the state.[22] Even if we accept (for the moment) the argument that world politics resist modernization, lawyers continue to matter. Lawyers provide arguments for and justifications of policies that threaten, use, or substitute for violence in various combinations: It is they "who can invent and elaborate the language of justification for the exercise, or the denial of authority"[23] (Lasswell 1958: 107).

Warriors, diplomats, and lawyers function for the state, meaning for and as influentials, in the adversarial setting that the Realist view of world politics presupposes. They engage in characteristically adversarial activities as agents of states. The confusion arises when lawyers speak of international law as if it were an imperfect version of the law of the state, capable of improvement eventuating in a "world rule of law" tantamount to a liberal world state (Larson 1961: 3–9). The wishful element in this project of "world order through world law" has deceived many realists into thinking that lawyerly activity is irrelevant to world politics and lawyers in general are victims of illusion.

---

22. "Lawyers, trained in the canon, Roman and common law, were conspicuous in the defense of the princes against the papacy and of the monarchs against the nobility" (Lasswell 1958: 107).

23. This they can do in the instance of the state's domestic policies, as Lasswell suggested in the passage just quoted, or its foreign policies. In the latter instance they are using their performance skills for purposes no different than those for which diplomats use theirs.

Perhaps law defined in a particular way is irrelevant to world politics, but lawyers are not. A Realist literature shows that they are not. (See prominently Corbett 1959, De Visscher 1968, Henkin 1979, Boyle 1985; for a telling case, see Chayes 1974.) Indeed they are members of the same skills constellation that warriors and diplomats are, the very groups instrumental in the project of modernizing the state to succeed in world politics. This group of influentials is skilled in getting what it wants by directing others to act in certain ways, explaining the consequences of their failure to do so, and justifying the measures that may be taken to effectuate such directives.

Properly understood, diplomats and lawyers share with warriors the same premodern professional skill. It may be remembered that Lasswell identified three such skills ensembles in general terms, respectively devoted to manipulating symbols, controlling supplies, and applying violence. Lasswell emphasized the importance of the first and gave passing attention to a second.[24] He understood the importance of priestly skill but saw it as fading with the secularization that accompanies the specialization of skills in the modern state. The recent resurgence of fundamentalist religion should cast doubt on this proposition, though not on Lasswell's contention that propaganda is the modernized version of priestly skill. Perhaps we should say that modernization has not triumphed quite so decisively as its beneficiaries are prone to declare. The nineteenth-century discovery of the national idea and the psychological power of national identity has of course given rise to the ideology of the nation-state. At once symbol and instrument of modernity, the nation-state represents a concordance — hardly the first but possibly the consummate concordance — of the skills of the priest and the warrior.

World politics are still the terrain upon which belief systems are most intensely contested. No differently from priests, today's propagandists, ideologues, teachers, and publicists attempt to spell out the meaning and significance of the human situation in ways that in-

---

24. They are granted roughly equal attention in Lasswell (1958). In the rest of Lasswell's work, symbol manipulation is an enduring preoccupation, while the flow of goods and services is ignored but for a chapter in Lasswell (1965a: 107–124) and even there is discussed in passive terms as a set of conditions and not as an instrument of influence, such as the phrase "controlling supplies" connotes.

evitably affect the distribution of influence and rewards. In this light
we can appreciate the quite recent invention and diffusion of general
public education — It could only happen in a world of nation-states.
Realists ignore this skills constellation because its political effects
are subterranean, or discuss it in the most general terms as ideology.
At least Lasswell understood its modern, instrumental character as
propaganda.

The last set of premodern skill groups whose activities decisively affect the distribution of influence and rewards are merchants, manufacturers, and financiers. As we shall also come to see, this group also includes physicians and farmers, whom we can provisionally leave aside
in assessing Realism and its limitations from a Lasswellian point of view.
Merchants, manufacturers, and financiers share a concern for the production (which Lasswell ignored) and distribution of goods. One might
think that Realists would find these activities power-related as activities,
and not just as constituents of capabilities. Yet most of them have not.

There are reasons. A firm distinction between politics and economics contributes to the constitution of three disciplines: Political Science,
Economics, *and* International Relations. The effect is to codify the
nineteenth-century liberal belief that economics refers exclusively to
the self-regulating market. Even Keynesian grounds for intervening in
economies leave the core assumptions of market behavior untouched
(Microeconomics) and adjust for distortions, though inherent in capitalism, magnified by the scale of market activities (Macroeconomics).
Underlying this is an unwillingness to give capitalism its due — an unwillingness to be explained at least in part by the fact that Marx made
capital and not the market the focus of his work and, in so doing,
made capitalism a dirty word even for its liberal beneficiaries.

If we put the politics of abstractions like market and capital aside,
we find that merchants, manufacturers, and financiers significantly
affected the distribution of influence on a world scale prior to the
rise of the modern state and continue to do so through the pervasive
agency of capitalism. World movement of factors of production (or
movement *to,* in the case of land and physical resources) has often
dwarfed state efforts at control and forces a distributive pattern that
states can do no more than codify. Again, we find that to the extent
that world politics is premodern, as Realists presume, then Realists
have underestimated the continuing importance of a major skills
constellation, itself subject to modernizing tendencies within states.

Realists depend on a view of world politics that effectively disallows all but one historically significant skills constellation (and even that one is only partially acknowledged). Realism has had its critics. Most of them have noticed Realism's narrow preoccupation with power politics defined by reference to the availability and use of organized violence. As an alternative, many such critics have focused on the complexity of world politics as a vast multiplicity of arenas, issues, and actors, most of them far removed from military affairs (Keohane and Nye 1977, Mansbach and Vasquez 1981; Vasquez 1983).

In a kind of metaphorical inversion, the term "arena," though suggesting an open space, is used to designate particular densities of contacts among the officers of organizations whose roles pertain to the distribution of major values. (I define "officer" and "role" in chapter 4.) The term "actor" refers to those hierarchies and networks of organizational functionaries who find the ambit of their activities specified by reference to what are usually called issues. Although the term "issue" is presumably substantive rather than locational (unlike "arena"), it is conventionally spatialized as the term "issue-area"—a move that makes issues and arenas interchangeable.[25]

Events of the last twenty years have persuaded many Realists that they cannot ignore issue-areas, at least insofar as they serve to demarcate the world economy into arenas within which states contest distributive questions. One consequence is recognition that "hegemons" can use rules instead of military endeavors to reward themselves disproportionately. Another is rediscovery of economic statecraft, which some Realists had never forgotten (Hirschman 1980, Baldwin 1985). Underlying both of these developments is acknowledgement that markets are not self-regulating (Polanyi 1957) and capitalism not just a Marxist concern. Judging from recent major works (Krasner 1985, Gilpin 1987), Realist attention to the world economy has revitalized this line of thought, as neorealism.[26]

---

25. James N. Rosenau popularized the term "issue-area" in the mid-1960s; his major statements are reprinted in Rosenau (1980b: 153–168, 461–500).

26. Neorealism is a term to be used with circumspection, for it has also been applied to Kenneth N. Waltz's reformulation of Realism in the language of Microeconomics, but with only modest attention to the world economy (1979; see generally Keohane 1986).

Neorealism continues Realism's disdain for actors which are not
defined by their coercive capabilities, whatever the arena. In contrast, Realism's critics treat issues/arenas and actors as interdependent: The perception of some distributive matter as an issue secures
an organizational response; organizational affiliation mandates per-
ceiving one's activities as referring to that issue. Much less important
is whether actors are public or private. Indeed, this distinction bor-
ders on the meaningless, for states as organizations are implicated
in most distributive matters, but cannot exclude other putatively private organizations from also being involved.

The dominant reality in this view is not the state, but organizations, of which the state has become a complex example. The rise
of organizations is an especially notable feature of that late, decisive
stage of modernity to have brought with it a vast alteration in the
conduct and finally the definition of politics (Wolin 1960). No longer
are major distributive judgments made of a piece, whether by violence and demagoguery or through virtuous civic practices. Instead
they are divided up into ever more narrowly conceived, task-oriented
segments of activity which specified officers are charged to undertake. Distribution and thus politics in the classic mode disappear
from view, but distribution proceeds apace. Politics are now described
by the interplay of arenas, issues, and actors, all organizationally
defined (indeed, inter-defined).

The version of this argument applied to the global level to have
achieved any real visibility is called Functionalism (Mitrany 1966;
see Haas 1964 for a meticulous critique and reformulation). Because
Functionalists enthusiastically projected the demise of politics, Morgenthau, that most influential of Realist thinkers, found them the
worthiest of targets.[27] Certainly Functionalism as it was originally
elucidated is flawed by its unwillingness to see organizational activity as intrinsically political, by its normative preference for international organizations as opposed to organizations operating within

---

27. Morgenthau called it "The Repudiation of Politics" (1946: chapter title, p. 41). His
    attack centered on those who proposed to use science in solving social problems,
    but did not exclude liberal believers in the harmony of interests. Though the latter
    are the focus of Carr's critique (1964), they are not properly lumped together with
    those who would dissect and solve problems—here styled Functionalists.

states, and by its view of warriors and diplomats as intractably pre-modern in their practices.

Nevertheless, Functionalism does point to the global consequences of late modernity, mediated through professional experts in organizational employ. Functionalism implies an insight that students of international law can take credit for clarifying: Skill-holders who matter for world politics are multiple-functionaries. They function for particular organizations, the state and other organizational congeries, and the global system whereby influentials distribute values, all at the same time (see chapter 4 for elaboration).

These skill-holders can be warriors and diplomats, but they can be neither of these alone. They must also be organizational functionaries. They may also be propagandists or financiers, or they may be members of occupational groups whose identity is more specifically modernist — planners and managers of all sorts. The one thing they all have in common is an organizational affiliation which makes their activities relevant to world politics.[28]

A proper construction of Functionalism as recognition of the importance of the rise of organization would nevertheless acknowledge Realism's case for the persistence of politics. It would also have to accept the transformation of the state rather than argue its irrelevance. It would allow for the modernization of those professions whose services enabled states to emerge and engage in classical world politics. Finally it would explicate the continuing utility of premodern professional skills in today's world of organizational activity. Were Functionalism seen in this light, then Realism could no longer dismiss Functionalism for its avoidance of the eternal verities of influence and its exercise. Instead, Realism could modernize itself, so to speak, in order to accommodate the impact of the rise of organizations, within, among and beyond states, on the way global distributive questions are answered. These questions are no longer answered as they once were.

---

28. Even professionals not employed to function organizationally find their professions increasingly organized and given to governance. Politics intrude on their activities, whether the converse is so (see Gilb 1966).

VOICES OF MODERNITY

Realism has never really argued the primacy of guns over goods, or good deeds. It has argued the primacy of those whose voices speak of war, the need for guns, the protection of goods, the absurdity of abstractly good deeds in a world of adversity. Realism cannot hear voices that speak of believing or persuading, making or trucking, much less growing and healing. A better version of Realism would find places for these voices, for they too are authentic expressions of premodern professions whose influence cannot be denied in the distribution of influence.

For the most part, Functionalism adopts the language of tasks, of doing things, but it is also really about voices — voices that speak about the issues and the routines to be invoked to deal with those issues. Whatever else organizational functionaries think they do, they overwhelmingly spend their professional lives speaking to each other and committing their words to paper. Certainly their voices are likely to be confined to matters other voices define for them as their tasks, the things they have to do. Thus primacy goes to the record of such voices, the written record — explanations, directives, commitments — which may be seen as the matrix of rules creating a uniquely bounded organizational reality within which each functionary acts for the larger, often unrecognized purpose of distributing influence and its rewards.

The influence of such influentials is cumulatively decisive but individually entrapped in the rule-complex created by others' words. Apparently today's influentials hear, as they speak, in two sets of voices. One is the voice of their professions; the other the voice of the organizational rule matrix. We can make no a priori judgment that these voices necessarily clash with or complement each other. Nor is it simply an empirical question. Each of the premodern skill groups has a distinctive character to its voice. Only one of these voices is also heard in organizational settings. In that instance there is continuity and complementarity. Otherwise we may expect to find the dissonance that is for many the emblem of modernity and subject of modernism.

Among people trained in soldierly and diplomatic skills, military officers harmonize their professional and organizational voices especially well. Their very description as "officers" and the importance they attribute to rank and chain of command contribute to this harmony. So does their training. Military officers are socialized uniformly in academies and typically schooled in engineering, the practice of which has been much affected by the discoveries of science and analytic methods. Military personnel work with machines and think of the military as a machine. Even the forced inactivity of military life – actual fighting is an infrequent experience for most officers – leaves a good deal of time for midcareer instruction in modern managerial, planning, and analytic techniques.

By contrast, diplomats are notoriously unwilling to enhance their skills by learning these same techniques. They insist on the personal and informal nature of their skills, and they tend to display a premodern sense of community through their highly ritualized interactions. It must also be remarked that diplomats are no longer solely or even chiefly responsible for relations among governments. Indeed their share of responsibility has declined in inverse relation to the growth of the bureaucratic apparatus within, among, and beyond states. In other words, diplomats have retained their premodern integrity at the expense of relevance.

Why they would have done so is an interesting question. By profession diplomats are less subject to highly formalized discipline and less compelled to adapt to machines and their use than soldiers are. They are also trained differently. Diplomats tend to see themselves as broadly educated humanists and generalists. They also cling to the fiction that they represent the "sovereign," as if sovereignty any longer had the personal quality once attached to it. All this evidence suggests that diplomats have no professional creed except as Realism provides (Hicks and others 1982). Yet Realism, as we have seen, fosters a belief that the practice of world politics makes the modern state possible by not becoming modern itself. As with practice, so with the practitioner: This the diplomat concludes, but wrongly. The world of organizations that Realist diplomacy makes possible includes the diplomat as officer.

By being stubbornly premodern, diplomats hear only one voice, the voice we hear as Realism, and they are condemned to increasing irrelevance, along with their creed. Lawyers represent a different situation. As already noted, they too are members of the skills constellation in which voice is modulated by an adversarial orientation and a reductive method of work. They take a given problem apart so as to identify the point at which an argument can be presented, or justification offered, for a particular disposition of that problem. Yet under pressure from the rise of organization, legal vocation has shown a certain schizophrenia.

Introduced deliberately for modernizing purposes, the Napoleonic Code has of course decisively shaped Continental tendencies. Here it would seem that the adversarial orientation of lawyering has been subordinated to the deductive method of discovering definite answers to all legal questions in the code. The latter activity directly supports the organizational complex called the state as it extends its impersonal rule to so many aspects of social life previously susceptible to adversarial definition. Even if administration is an organizational alternative to adversarial confrontation, we must remember that the techniques involved are merely a refinement of language developed in the first instance for adversarial purposes.

The contrast with the Anglo-American experience with law could not be much greater. The substantial decentralization of legal judgment and its separation from other activities of states are conjoined with the strong disposition in legal training both to emphasize the importance of uniquely complex cases in shaping the contours of law and to promote an inductive method of discovery in which the facts of any case, rather than the content of a set code, represent a starting point. To all this must be added a preoccupation with rights that are seen as somehow antecedent to law and thus a limitation on administrative fiat.[29] These traits make Anglo-American legal training and practice obdurately adversarial as well as hostile to the analytical and organizational activities of the times.

Nevertheless, a significant and undoubtedly increasing proportion of lawyers, at least in the United States, enter public service or pursue careers in large, hierarchical organizations.[30] The dominant

---

29. Richard E. Flathman (1976: 44) took these rights as constructions of "the liberal principle" as developed in "moral and legal practice." (On rights see also chapter 5.) The late modern career of the liberal state has in fact seen a massive shift from rights as limits on administrative fiat to administered entitlements. Theodore J. Lowi has argued that this portends "the end of liberalism," as a well-known book of his is entitled (1979).

30. See Galanter (1982) on the difference between what he called ordinary lawyering

legal paradigm in the Anglo-American world, well named Legal Positivism, holds that the state exists for the utilitarian purpose of using its organizational rationality and marshaling resources to secure the greatest good for society. Anglo-American lawyers acknowledge both a premodern creed of professional practices and the influence of a discipline with a modernizing impulse.

There is undoubtedly a deep contradiction between the common lawyer's affection for cases, rights, and litigation, and the prevailing utilitarian positivism and organizationally situated employment of the legal profession. That contradiction may be personalized for junior lawyers when they realize, perhaps with shock, the disjuncture between their training and their duties.[31] People recover from such shocks usually, and they learn what they have to. Perhaps what they learn most readily, because it is implicit in so much of their training, is that the specific job of most organizationally situated lawyers is to provide justifications for whatever practices their organizations may engage in or contemplate.

Justification follows the same working procedure as analysis. One starts with a given situation, breaks it into as many parts as possible, and seizes on the part which best lends itself to defense against a potential adversary's assault. Or one codifies such practices to be sure they are consistent with relevant rules and drafts relevant rules in anticipation of what is organizationally needed. These are the tasks of lawyers gleaned from legal training, even if it has an adversarial orientation, and rewarded in organizational settings.

The generally justificatory tone of the modern lawyer's voice supports the analytic mode of talking emblematic of late modernity and connects with the historic role of the lawyer in arguing for a client's position. Whether trained in civil or common law, the lawyer has made the transition to today's world almost as well as the soldier and certainly better than the diplomat. That international law is not properly law by legal positivist criteria is no bar to the justificatory role

and mega-lawyering, that is, working for specific clients and working in and for large organizations.

31. David Kennedy's interpretation is slightly different: He finds the disjuncture between "power" and "administration" already evident in training, and resolved in the latter's favor by employment in a "depoliticized procedural order" (1985: 368–369).

of lawyers in world politics, because the point is to identify rules authorizing an organizational activity (normally that of the state, but also of multinational corporations, for example) and not to show that these rules are subject to enforcement. Recourse to such justifications, like diplomacy, is a peaceful means of—not alternative to—"attacking."

Let us now turn to the other two skills constellations and gauge the effects of the rise of organization on them and their place in world politics. Lasswell saw the importance of one constellation— priests and propagandists—both before and after the rise of organizations and repudiation of politics. Lasswell's emphasis on the priestly duty of protecting and disseminating the central beliefs of any society tends, however, to misrepresent the distinctive features of priestly talk. As I note in chapter 3, priests do more than safeguard such beliefs. Their stories and explanations provide worlds with meaning and significance.

Conjecture, which was the privilege of priests, is perhaps the stuff of "primal politics": "ceremony and symbolism . . . are not to be regarded as mere pretty trappings of power . . . " (Eckstein, 1982: 472). The subordination of priests into hierarchies and the appropriation of their services by warriors in agrarian societies, not least the early modern state, is perhaps the key to the eclipse of priestly conjecture. Kings may retain priests for private prophecy, but kings need priests mostly for public reinforcement of their primacy. Everywhere the institution of kingship has depended on "religious authentication. . . ."[32] This is not to say that skill in conjecture disappeared in the warrior-world of the early modern West, leaving priests merely as propagandists. Religious renegades frequently recur.

Moreover, the teaching profession has always maintained its privilege to conjecture as a part of its skill in explaining the meaning of conditions and events in this world, thereby constituting the world as it is known. Teachers perennially display the tension between their skill in inculcation and their skill at conjecture; they undoubtedly transmit to their students an ambivalence which is heightened by the

---

32. Bendix (1978: 22) See generally his chapter 2 ("Sacred and Secular Foundations of Kingship"); in this unholy alliance, "experts in esoteric knowledge also have much secular influence . . ." (p. 22).

subordination of teachers, like priests before them, to public service. Only a few teachers, professors for the most part, escape this damper on free conjecture by defining themselves as scholars, and even they tend toward circumspection.

Teachers and scholars are joined in their skills constellation by a variety of other people skilled in disseminating information. Among them are journalists, advertisers, even eccentric pamphleteers, playwrights, and lyricists for popular music, all of whom weave conjecture into the stories they tell. The historic place of entertainers in fostering a common identity among people remains, although it is surely affected by organizational realities. Rather, the availability of mass media for disseminating entertainment is one hallmark of today's world. The use of spectacle to hide politics and protect the privileged is too well known to require further comment. Propaganda is not simply symbol manipulation by a few professionals. It is more generally the management of spectacle.

Yet even this artful symbiosis of secular religion and technologically enhanced control over important business is pervaded by the small conjectures, odd associations, and play of imagination that cannot be fully controlled. When today's secular priests guard the standing arrangments of the state (a warrior's task), they can rarely do so with a monopoly of priestly skills. Nor can they do so without risk of conjectural contamination. Inasmuch as the world is organized so that no one hierarchy or bureaucratic network monopolizes influence and its rewards, competition among secular religions may strengthen the hold of each on its own public, in reaction to the threat offered by the others, but it also offers everyone a view to other spectacles, the enticement of selective borrowing and even private room for conjecture.

To study world politics as if the activities of warriors, lawyers, and diplomats were not entwined with the activities of public performers is to ignore the cognitive reality in which the holders of adversarial skills are located. Also slighted is the specific interplay of such skills with priestly skills in conjecture and inculcation in organizing today's distributive situation. Organizations may be refined versions of the adversarial skills constellation; priests and professors may hold out against organizational encroachment. Yet the imperative of modernity has had an irrevocable impact on the relation between these two skills constellations. On the one hand, priests, professors, and publicists sacrifice conjecture for inculcation in the name of analytical rigor, professional discipline, and organizational necessity. On the other, organizational functionaries have their minds invaded and their voices altered, however subtly, by fugitive conjectures, cosmopolitan conceits, and even the imperfectly mediated, allegedly foolish talk of the unskilled, excluded masses.

The other skills constellation to which we must attend is less distinct in its contemporary contours than the others. This may be why Lasswell granted it so little attention. Indeed it is easier to talk about the origins and premodern character of the skill than find an appropriate umbrella term for the diverse collection of professionals who depend on this skill for large scale distributive purposes. The skill in question is one of hunting—as I observe in chapter 3, hunting for clues, diagnosing a condition, taking care of needs.

Hunting is not a verbal skill. Hunters and gatherers need no voice except insofar as they wish to coordinate activities. Of course hunters talk about why they do, if only to pass on their skills to others. Such talk is substantially devoted to spelling out the implications of what they experience—hunters learn to "read" the signs they encounter by matching ensembles of particulars against other such ensembles, or "cases," they and other have encountered. Cases are precisely what physicians talk about and, as we saw above, common lawyers are also trained in this same diagnostic orientation (with confusion attending, given the fact that lawyers tend not to practice what they teach). Is there something to be learned from this peculiarity of Anglo-American culture?

The common law arose independently of warriors and their activities. It antedates control over distributive questions through the crown, and it rules day-to-day affairs on the assumption of absence, or at least indifference, of those skilled in issuing and enforcing directives from on high. The common law provides answers to distributive questions by deciding who has claim to what on the basis of occupancy, use, agreement, or performance.[33] The adversarial em-

---

33. The parallel development of ideas of property and sovereignty in the early modern period suggests that a "common law" of property and contract underlies the state system Realists take to be the creation of warriors (Ruggie 1986: 141–148).

phasis comes from the practices of lawyers and judges. Lawyers suggest answers to distributive questions favorable to their clients, while judges decide between competing answers by sorting through other such cases and matching them to the one at hand. The common thread to all such claims has to do with what promises and commitments are implied in any set of conditions at issue. A contract or title merely formalizes what is already at issue: who gets what as an implication of who does what, and vice versa.

Questions of property and contract presuppose the existence of exchange. Presumably silent barter is possible, but the norm is rampant performative talk — offer and counter-offer, promise, and acceptance, more or less formal, prior to the actual exchange. When no one haggles in a market, it is because performative talk has been superseded by a generalized system of exchange in which prices are set (and marked) on the basis of aggregate behavior, to which market participants contribute in deciding whether or not to engage in an exchange at the set price. Most Economists have become so preoccupied with the special character of this generalized, self-regulating system ("the" market) that they discount the verbal dimension of exchange. Indeed they have abandoned it, at least in the English-speaking world, to lawyers.

Economists are not members of the same skills constellation that mothers, farmers, and physicians are. The most influential Economists are teachers, members of a discipline. Those professionals whose activities are devoted to the practical necessity of exchange (participating in markets) belong with those who nurture, grow and heal. One can generalize about markets and fail to notice what phenomena those markets exist to expedite — the exchange of goods and services human beings have produced, whether through growing, making, or even learning that other people want to have or learn about. All sorts of skills in production — doing skills — take on an additional verbal dimension when the need comes to distribute what is produced.

When wealth is produced, it too raises distributive questions. To the extent that re-investment in productive activity is a favored answer under conditions of modernity, we must be referring to capitalism as a productive-distributive complex. In this complex the generative interrelation of production, exchange, and wealth is mediated by professionals, like financiers, whose skills are precisely the verbal skills of securing commitment and promising consequences. They enter into contracts, buy and sell titles, and generally engage in the performative talk of exchange, talk that is indistinguishable from the haggling of premodern exchange. Paper and now electronically kept records are extensions of this kind of talk, and capitalism and its agents could not survive without them. The invention of modern accounting methods is in this sense an organizational adaptation and routinization of a skill associated with exchange and the recognition of what exchanges imply.

Dealing with the implications of exchange is more generally a skill of financiers and other skilled handlers of capital, for they must always find themselves implicated in a whole web of productive activities and exchange relations: Capitalism almost seems to have a life of its own. Always and unpredictably changing, linked to economic "growth," capitalism calls forth just those organic metaphors that financiers have in common with mothers, farmers, physicians, and all those who depend on hunting skills.

The social connection between capitalism as materially productive activity and exchange-related skills necessary for distribution constitutes a connection as well between the material world of production *and* distribution and the political world of the distribution of influence and, through the latter, material rewards. The symbiotic relation of business to government, no less than of state ministries responsible for planning production to those effectuating distribution, presents an organizationally mediated version of the more basic relationship between those skilled in working out the implications of investment, property, contract, and such on production and those who apply the same skills to distribution—and not just the distribution or "marketing" of particular products, but the distribution of all kinds of socially consequential benefits at the largest scale (see further Lindblom 1977).

Merchants and princes were once distinguishable if interdependent groups. So at a later time were financiers and prime ministers. Today their skillful successors cannot be so easily distinguished. The mingling of analytic and diagnostic methods, of justificatory and implicative language, or directives and commitments, fairly represents the complex character of the dual dependence on capitalism for material growth and a "healthy world economy" and on organizations to "keep the machine running."

Realists are well on the way to remedying their conspicuous neglect of the world economy. Yet their resistance to the idea that influence-related skills have been modernized through organizational affiliation extends to the possibility that the same trajectory of modernization has affected the nexus of material productive activity and exchange relations. Were they to see these twin consequences of the rise of organizations, they would then be able to see that organizational ties permit, even require, historically separate skills to be joined such that world politics and the world economy are now inextricable—the people doing the one are doing the other. What they do is almost entirely a matter of what they say to each other, in the performative language of their professional skills, over the organizational circuits that tie them together.

As suggested earlier, the situation is no different for those whose skills in conjecture, persuasion, and explanation establish meaning and significance. Religions and ideologies entwine with politics and economics at the largest scale. No longer is the "who" of world politics a simple matter—a matter of finding the right category, the prince, the soldier. Nor is the "who" of the world economy the merchant, the owner. All the relevant "who's" are officers of organizations. Yet their organizational connectedness tells only part of the story. The rest is told by their professional orientations, which are distinctively premodern in the working languages they foster. Those distinctive realms of performative talk betray alternative, equally skillful ways of making social reality, including the reality of influence and reward, work out advantageously.

8

RATIONALITY AND RESOURCES

People are rational. They have ends and make choices accordingly. Rules bound situations of choice by defining means and ends available to choosers. In the face of diverse ends, we order preferences, which requires us to compare possible states of affairs. There are three general possibilities yielding three generalized yet immediate ends common to humanity, or interests. With the help of several major writers, I identify these as standing, security, and wealth.

The reasons people give for their conduct also point to interests so construed. People impute the same interests to collectivities such as states, offering them as reasons of state or national interests. I suggest that orienting international relations to security interests, as International Relations scholars are prone to do, misses the importance of standing and wealth as sources of conduct. Whatever interests individuals pursue, for themselves or as agents of states, they do so with necessarily unequal access to resources and with consequences that are also necessarily unequal. I provide a criterion for the presence of exploitation in different social arrangements, and I arrive at the unhappy conclusion that the elimination of one form of exploitation will enhance some other.

COMPARISON

Few terms have engendered as much discussion within the social sciences as has "rationality." Most definitions are unobjectionable in their own terms. Thus Brian Barry and Russell Hardin stated that, "at minimum, rationality comprises two ideas: consistency and choice of appropriate means to one's ends, whatever they may be" (1982: 371). To similar effect is John Harsanyi's definition: "At a common-sense level, in its simplest form, rationality means choosing (what is or at least what one thinks to be) the best *means* to achieving a given *end,* goal, or objective" (1983: 231, his emphasis).

Choices are deeds, and deeds choices. Rationality describes an important property of deeds: They always relate available means to identifiable ends. Because I start with deeds, I start with rationality, so understood. I also note that means-ends definitions comport with my earlier remarks on competence (chapter 3). Any human individual capable of reasoning or using rules is also able to make consistent choices appropriate to her ends. Any competent individual can of course make mistakes and misjudgments, but she is also capable of recognizing them as such.[1] If rationality so construed is tautological or trivial — everybody is rational because everybody is somebody — then this is not a problem, just a place to begin.[2]

---

1. Some mistakes and misjudgments are systematic. They occur so predictably in certain situations (for example, crises) that they effectively qualify the substantive meaning of rational conduct for these situations (Jervis 1976). This does not defeat the possibility of theory premised on the assumption of rationality, as Ferguson and Mansbach have argued (1988: 146–160). It does require qualifications and amendments to any such theory, thereby rendering it more complex and less telling as a paradigm theory for Political Economy. Insofar as people cannot learn to make some "mistakes" they systematically do make, it suggests that the primary terms of social choice theory, not people, are the problem. Because the theory is a linguistic construction, its figures of speech may not capture the cognitive world of perfectly rational people. For example, gambling is the "dominant metaphor used to conceptualize risky decision making. . . ." Do people think as if they are choosing between "risky gambles" when faced with uncertainty? (Einhorn and Hogarth 1987: 42; see generally their useful discussion). If people learn not to make mistakes in situations of uncertainty, as defined by social choice theory, it is because they learn to employ the metaphor for those situations preferred by social choice theorists who are faced with the expository demands of theorizing (see also chapter 3, footnote 16, on nonpropositional learning.)

2. I believe this construction of rationality is saved from complete tautology because some (I would say, small) range of human behavior is strictly reflexive or instinctive. Insofar as such behavior is not mediated cognitively (socially), and thus not subject to choice, it is not rational. Such behavior may nonetheless be what an individual would choose, were she not at that moment exclusively subject to reflex or instinct. Compare this situation with that of nonhuman life (next footnote).

One might object that Barry and Hardin's identification of the chooser as "one" and Harsanyi's passive construction beg the important questions, who chooses? My gloss on their definitions makes the "who" to be a human individual. Machines can make choices, but only as skillful extensions of human individuals. Nonhuman forms of life (amoeba, household pets, and so on) act as if they are rational (the way a human individual would choose to in the same circumstances), but they cannot be said to make choices the way humans do. This is because nonhuman life lacks foresight and cannot countenance alternatives (Elster 1979: 4–28).[3] Collectivities do not make choices; individuals do as agents of collectivities. "Collective rationality" is a contestable euphemism, inasmuch as the aggregate of rational choices is rarely compatible with what is rational from the collective point of view. This is a crisp description of one impediment to collective action, the exploration of which the theory of social choice has so powerfully assisted.

One might note a modest difference between Barry and Hardin's and Harsanyi's definitions of rationality. Both refer to "means," but the former to "ends," the latter to "end." According to Harsanyi, to move from one end to many alternative ends implies a generalized model of rationality. "This model is the *preference* model, under which a person acts rationally if he follows a transitive and complete set of preferences among all his possible goals" (1983: 232). Obvi-

---

3. In applying game theory to nonhuman life, Robert Axelrod has identified individually exercised "survival strategies" collectively resulting in natural selection and evolution. The process of evolution depends on competition, as is customarily believed, and on cooperation, as Axelrod demonstrated (1984: 88–105):

> It is encouraging to see that cooperation can get started, can thrive in a variegated environment, and can protect itself once established. But what is most interesting is how little had to be assumed about the individuals or the social settings to establish these results. The individuals do not have to be rational: the evolutionary process allows the successful strategies to survive even if the players do not know why or how. Nor do the players have to exchange messages or commitments. They do not need words, because their deeds speak for them (pp. 173–174).

Not only need not these individuals be rational, they cannot be, unless they are human. The terms "strategies", "players," and "deeds" are strategically chosen for their expressive effect.

ously one's rational choice under the circumstance of multiple means and ends is complicated by the problem of information and the possibility of error. Furthermore, one must deal with uncertainty, whether arising from a poorly understood material environment or the circumstances of other people's choices made in anticipation of one's own (that is, strategic interaction).[4]

Everyone who is competent acts rationally in a world of contingency. Herbert A. Simon has called this "bounded rationality" (1985: 295–297). The term is misleading. Rationality as procedure is not bounded, any more than "satisficing" (another, even more famous term of Simon's) substitutes for maximizing as a description of rational conduct. People sensibly choose alternatives suited to their circumstances. What is bounded, in various ways, is the situation in which choices are made. What bounds situations are rules.

In chapter 1, I hold that rules do not "govern" all that is social. People always have a choice, which is to follow rules or not. Instead rules govern the construction of the situation within which choices are made intelligible. The simplest situation is one in which a single rule constitutes the boundaries of choice. Either one follows that rule or not. Most situations are bounded by a number of rules. At choice then is not just whether to follow a rule, but which one, to what extent and so on.

Rules establishing a market's boundaries are intended to hold in abeyance all other rules affecting choice. It might be better to say: Held in abeyance are all other rules of comparable formality. People making market choices follow a variety of informal instructions (maxims like, quality over quantity), directives (shop sales), and com-

---

4. Acknowledging a multiplicity of ends under conditions of uncertainty solves the problem of "whether it is 'rational' to maximize possible gain, minimize possible loss, possible regret, or satisfy still different criteria" (Kratochwil 1987: 312). To maximize gain and minimize loss with respect to a given end are indeed alternatives ends, respectively to be maximized. Both are rational choices, although one risks more to get more, the other risking less to get less. Which is preferred depends on additional factors such as the propensity to accept risks, defer rewards and other traits constituted by a history of rational choices. Procedurally speaking, whether gains are maximized, losses minimized, and so on does make a difference to social choice theorists (see Frolich and Oppenheimer 1978: 49–65 for an accessible introduction).

mitments (my best goods for my best customers). The point of the market is to construct a situation where individuals can make choices with good information and little risk among clear and limited alternatives. This is precisely the consequence of a situation ruled by the single choice of whether to follow a rule. In other words, a market generalizes the simplest situation of choice, which is paradigmatically constituted by a single relevant rule. The existence of informal rules that people bring with them to the market (and of course to more complicated situations; compare Keohane 1984: 113–116, on "rules of thumb") complicates the simple, generalized situation of the market, but not to the point that Economists are driven to despair. Rules, like markets, provide opportunities for individuals, not to act more rationally, but to get better results from being as rational as they always are.

In the absence of a simply bounded situation, an individual may face a multiplicity of converging and reinforcing rules such that no choice appears, at least to the observer, to be freely made. Take life in a monastery. Rational individuals always choose courses of action consistent with the bulk of rules, because no other course of action is available — Rules cover almost all contingencies. In such a situation we may be forgiven for saying that rules govern. It is less forgivable to say unreservedly that this situation is the operative paradigm of premodern social life. One such paradigm it is, the one we often pick to hold in opposition to the paradigmatic situation of modernity.

For purposes of rational choice, the most salient features of modernity are the many intersecting boundaries deriving from competing rule sets. In these situations, individuals must choose courses of action that cannot be readily changed, often under circumstances that present no clear grounds for rational choice. Intersecting boundaries define roles and expectations such that individuals perceive themselves paradoxically free to choose among many alternatives but unable to make the most of choices available to them. The Sociologist is prompted to view this situation from the perspective of multiple rule sets, because this procedure seems likely to tell the Sociologist more about any individual's conduct than the individual, or her choices, can. There is a danger, however. The Sociologist runs the risk of imputing a teleology to the situation — all too easily once the situation is rendered descriptively coherent and called a system.

Alleged differences between Economists and Sociologists (Mitchell 1969, Barry 1970) — the former are mathematical and mechanical, the latter discursive and organismic, to use Barry's words (p. 3) — derive from differences in the respective operative paradigms of the market and modern society. The former presents people with simple, exclusively bounded situations, the latter with situations complicated by multiple, overlapping rule sets. Nothing requires an "organismic" characterization of the latter sort of situations; nothing requires a mathematical characterization of the former. Each characterization is the more readily undertaken for the situation to which we are apt to find it applied. If one does avoid the organismic in characterizing situations for which modern society is paradigmatic, one is left with the discursive, not by default, or as a defect, but as an attempt at descriptive adequacy.

Procedural differences are to be expected among disciplinary paradigms. They can also be expected to persist, even when disciplinarians see their operative paradigms overlapping. When Economists (or, more properly, social choice theorists) and Sociologists argue over the rationality of peasants, for example, the debate dissipates once the polemics are past. No one seriously disputes Samuel L. Popkin's claim on behalf of Political Economy that peasants are rational (1979). Instead, the argument turns on the proper characterization of the village as the situation within which these rational people must conduct themselves.

If villagers can readily disaggregate this situation into separately bounded ones (household, market) within which they can make beneficial choices, they will. If they cannot, it is because of the multiplicity of converging rules and material constraints we identify with the premodern situation (Popkin 1979: 32–82). So long as gratuitous qualities are not imputed to the village — moral, romantic, teleological — then I, for all my discursive inclinations, can only agree with Popkin's assertion that, "when the peasant takes into account the likelihood of receiving the preferred outcome *on the basis of individual actions,* he will usually act in a self-interested manner" (p. 31, Popkin's emphasis). There is no need to qualify this statement: The peasant will always act self-interestedly (and all action must be individual). Nor can I disagree that "the actions of individually rational peasants in both market and nonmarket situations do not aggregate to a 'rational' village" (p. 31). So it is with the rest of the world. Finally, I agree with Popkin that, by using this approach, "we can discuss how and why groups of individuals decide to adopt some set of norms while rejecting others. . . . Under what conditions will individuals consider bending or breaking norms?" (p. 18). And, of course, when do they not?[5]

What can I disagree with? Popkin claimed to have constructed for himself a deductive framework within which to "recast the historical and inductive richness" of the Sociologists (p. 5). Yet the latter also worked within a framework susceptible to deductive presentation. Popkin provided it (pp. 5–17). That presentation took the village as rule-governed, that is, blanketed with rules eliminating the possibility of individual choices. This is not, however, the operative paradigm of complexly bounded situations, defining modernity and the Sociologist's concern. Whether the village is one or several separately bounded situations, Popkin found it disappearing into a larger world, a world I would characterize Sociologically. Popkin's disciplinary predilections (the rule set "governing" his own scholarly village) prevent him from following the villager very far into modernity.

If rationality has to do with the best choice of means to ends, "whatever they may be" (quoting Barry and Hardin again), then the more means and ends there are, the more difficult it is for people to act in a way that scholars can characterize mathematically and mechanically. Faced with complexity, people are inefficient. They settle for small portions of many ends, or ends that can be readily achieved, and so on. They may even find satisfaction in inefficiency. We call conduct irrational only because we know too little about it to appreciate the ends it is directed to.

To pass over such situations on procedural grounds or defer their consideration are rational choices for scholars with positivist commitments. There is another choice, which also starts with individual conduct but proceeds beyond to social constitution. Such a choice requires an extension of methodological individualism; not its rejection. (Recall the discussion of epistemological and ontological bridges

---

5. Barry conceded that "there would be nothing logically inconsistent in combining . . . an emphasis on norms with a theory in which goals are rationally pursued subject to constraints" (Barry 1970: 181). Popkin found this combination a useful one. Obviously I take it to be indispensable.

in chapter 1.) The key to this extension is provided by the acknowledgement that individuals, in order to act rationally, must compare "utilities."

As Jeremy Bentham taught, utility is the "property in any object, whereby it tends to produce benefit . . . to the party whose intent is considered: if that party be the community in general, then the happiness of the community: if a particular individual, then the happiness of that individual" (1948, quoted in chapter 5.) Rational individuals always prefer what benefits them. The problem is for any individual to develop a consistent set of preferences from the many candidates. In other words, the move from a simple means-end conception of rationality to the generalized preference model preferred by Economists (Harsanyi 1983: 232) demands the comparison of utilities. (Often they are "expected utilities"; see footnote 4 and chapter 6, footnote 15.)

For Bentham, such comparisons are demanded for all members of a collectivity, because the aggregate of individual preferences constitutes "the happiness of the community." Bentham himself acknowledged the difficulty of aggregating the necessarily subjectively defined preferences of many individuals (Arrow 1983: 48). Economists since Vilfredo Pareto have gone further: They proscribed interpersonal comparison. More precisely they rejected the possibility of cardinal utilities, which in turn "rendered meaningless a sum-of-utilities criterion. If utility for an individual was not even measurable, one could hardly proceed to adding utilities for different individuals" (Arrow 1983: 122; see generally 47–49, 103–105, 115–132).

Yet individuals obviously do make interpersonal comparisons. They compare their circumstances with those of other people. Their choices must always be, as a matter of definition, between preferences that are their own, not between their preferences and someone else's. People construct preferences from comparisons of states of affairs and then compare preferences for choice. Because all such states of affairs are social by definition, they always involve other individuals and their attributes, preferences and choices. "Even the apparently simplest act of individual decision involves the participation of a whole society" (Arrow 1983: 63).

Comparison is at once a cognitive and a social act. Cognition depends on reasoning and the possibility of speech, even if nothing is spoken. Comparison depends on abductive reasoning, assertion (if only to one's self) and metaphor (compare chapter 4, footnote 23.) What people compare are states of affairs that must already have been constructed to allow comparison. These I call the grounds of comparison. They may be constructed to include oneself and exclude all others, to include oneself and only one other, and to include oneself with a number of others. These three possibilities constitute the grounds of comparison into three categories: internal comparison (or, in the language of social choice, intrapersonal comparison), binary (or interpersonal) comparison, and global comparison.

How we undertake comparison is always the same. What we compare makes for the different categories of comparison. In the instance of internal comparison, the "what" is any state of affairs in which other people's attributes, preferences, choices, and accomplishments count only as a resource for or obstacle to choice. A chooser compares alternative states of affairs, one against the other, for optimal fit to her preferences. She avers, I want as much as I can get.

Concretely, the chooser will prefer states of affairs that could benefit others even more than herself, either because that is her preference, or because she is indifferent to the benefits (or costs) accruing to others as a consequence of her choices. The former situation is a special case — "extended sympathy," Economists would say; extended self, I would say — but a typical one, given the social construction of selves. The latter situation defines a category in which the part (an individual chooser's welfare) relates to the whole (the collective welfare) indeterminately, from the point of view of the part (the individual and her preferences). That category includes the case of internally made choices on behalf of extended selves.

The second category of comparison, binary comparison, takes the "what" to be a state of affairs jointly faced by the chooser herself and one other person making choices. The first chooser construes the preferences and choices of the other as incompatible with her own (whether the latter so construes the situation). The former chooses among alternatives to achieve a state of affairs that gains her the best possible position relative to the other. Now she says: I want more, so the other has less. The chooser could prefer states of affairs that benefit (or cost) others than the one (possibly collective) other she has chosen for purposes of comparison. In other words, she has constructed a whole, consisting of her welfare and the other's welfare, which is relationally determinate. Any gain to either one must come at the expense of the other.

The preferred situation for either chooser could well involve a lower aggregate of welfare for both. Because it is a relation of more and less, and not an amount, which constitutes what is jointly valued, comparison may be ordinal. If the relation between choosers is strategically interactive, then the requirement of a relationally determinate whole is violated. In this instance, the situation falls within the category of internal comparison, unless either chooser guesses that the other may engage in binary comparison. The effect is to make the situation relationally determinate. The second category can only have two choosers for the purpose of comparison. Additional participants can figure in the whole either by joining forces with the chooser, thus extending the choosing self, or by joining (or, more properly, by being seen as having joined) with the other.

Like binary comparison, global comparison takes into account choices and preferences other than the chooser's. Instead of oneself and one other chooser of consequence, the "what" is a determinate set of choosers. (The term "global comparison" is Frohock's 1987: 103; see Mackay 1980: 13–20, 61–77, for a useful discussion of global comparison, illustrated by reference to multi-event athletic competitions.) The problem now is a practical one. How can the chooser compare the resources, preferences, choices, and accomplishments of a number of others with her own? She has two choices. She can disaggregate the whole into a series of pairs, consisting of herself and each of the others. Or she can make use of a ranking system. The set, or whole, then consists of a series of positions occupying a complete and transitive ordering: first place, second place . . . last place. Furthermore, the places in such an ordering come with cardinal values (usually inverted: In an ordering of ten places, first has a value of ten, last place a value of one). Only now can she say: I want to be best.

Anyone can construct some state of affairs into a ranking system. Other people may not know they are being ranked. More typically, ranking schemes are public constructions. They may be conventional or the result of formal agreement. Then the whole is simultaneously relational for everyone, although every change in pairs of relations need not affect all other relations. The people in first and second place can switch positions without affecting the others, and so on.

Cardinality permits easy comparison; formality permits the weighting of values assigned to places.

Ranking systems of considerable formality are regimes, as defined in chapter 4. The whole is no longer simply an aggregate of attributes, preferences, choices, or outcomes, but a whole defined as such by rules, within which resources are brought to bear, preferences defined, choices made, and outcomes recorded. An autonomous whole, so constructed, is related to, but separate from, the wishes or welfare of participants. The former whole, with its tractable properties, substitutes for the latter, which is, from the point of view of any participant, intractable.

The implications of choosing among grounds of comparison are nicely illustrated by that most famous of games, the Prisoner's Dilemma. Descriptions of this game are so widely available that I dispense with one here. (I recommend Robert Axelrod's straightforward presentation, 1984: 7–12.) Playing the game once presents the two players with a situation of choice such that either player's internal comparison of possible states of affairs tends to produce the same rational choices that binary comparison would. This result comes from each player considering the possibility that the other player might be given to binary comparison, if only because that other takes such conduct as a possibility for the first player. In other words, the mere possibility of binary comparison contaminates internal comparison.

Because internal comparison under conditions of strategic interaction is so often tantamount to binary comparison, we can hardly wonder that players use binary comparison as a shortcut. In repeated plays of the Prisoner's Dilemma game, Axelrod found players choosing binary comparison against his advice ("Don't be envious," 1984: 110)—a tendency promoted by players' knowledge of the game's cumulative score. Consider the round-robin tournament Axelrod staged. A variety of aficionados devised computer programs to play iterated Prisoner's Dilemmas (described pp. 27–54). To win the tournament, one had to have the highest score after one's program was played against all others. The situation thus constructed generalizes internal comparison (doing one's best playing against all comers without concern for how well one is scoring against them) as a means to an end. That end depends in turn on global comparison (one's rank among all players).

In devising programs, many tournament participants assumed that their adversaries would be envious and binary comparison the best means to the stipulated end. They were proven wrong. "Nice" strategies, which aim for the best results whether one faces nice or nasty adversaries (programs predicated on internal and binary comparison respectively), came out on top. The top-ranked strategy (and, as it turned out, the simplest program submitted, aptly named TIT FOR TAT) "never once scored better in a game than any other player!" (1984: 112).

Axelrod evinced some surprise at the results of his tournament. "Even expert strategists from political science, sociology, economics, psychology, and mathematics made systematic errors of being too competitive for their own good, not being forgiving enough, and being too pessimistic about the responsiveness of the other side" (1984: 40). Such errors could have been avoided. Participants need have understood that the move from isolated sequences of games to a round-robin tournament called for a move from binary comparison to internal comparison as the appropriate activity for achieving the end in question. In single plays of the game, the end is "winning" that play. In repeated plays, the end in question requires a global comparison of whatever is achieved through internal comparison.

Axelrod might just as well have defined the objective of the tournament as a global comparison of the times in which players outscored adversaries. Obviously binary comparison suits these circumstances. Results would almost certainly have conformed to the expectations of Axelrod's strategically inclined participants. Axelrod would have found himself affirming the popular principle, nice guys finish last. Comparisons are social constructions, made by rules. When the rules change, so do grounds of comparison, choices, and results.

It should be evident from the way I have developed the three categories of comparison that I believe they correspond to the three universal categories of speech acts and rules, reasoning, figures of speech, and so on that I develop in the course of this book. Internal comparison moves from parts to whole, and binary comparison from whole to parts. Global comparison works within a whole substituting for another whole. Reversing the order of presentation to conform with that of earlier chapters, global comparison depends on assertion, abduction and association, metaphor (twice actually: once for construction of relevant states of affairs and then again for their comparison). Binary comparison depends on direction, deduction, and metonymy for construction of states of affairs. Finally, internal comparison depends on commitment (to self and others; this is the mechanism of extension), induction, and synecdoche.

MEANS, ENDS, AND INTERESTS

People have diverse "ultimate ends," "*Forderungen*", in Max Weber's German (1947: 185). As I suggest above, the diversity of ends demands the ordering of preferences, which in turn fosters comparison of states of affairs in three categories. These three categories of comparison constitute a determinate set of "immediate ends," to borrow from Talcott C. Parsons, standing between rationally chosen means and diverse ultimate ends of rational individuals. "Within the context of a given system of ultimate ends, the *immediate* ends . . . are given as facts to the actor, . . . 'given' in the sense that the postulate of rationality involves the pursuit of them" (1937: 262–263, his emphasis, footnote deleted). The first category (after reordering), global comparison, "gives" people a concern for standing as an "immediate end" and engenders feelings of esteem and envy. The second, binary comparison, gives them an awareness of threat and a concern for security as an immediate end. The third, internal comparison, gives rise to a concern for wealth, meaning the acquisition and possession, not just of material ends, but of anything valued.[6]

There is nothing surprising about this short list of immediate ends. Thomas Hobbes, to use an illustrious example, expressly connected value to comparison. "Vertue generally, in all sorts of subjects, is some-

---

6. Parsons treated "wealth" and "power" as a determinate set of immediate ends (except where ultimate ends call for their repudiation), because they "emerge from economic and political levels of analysis, . . ." (p. 262). From the sociocultural level emerges "integration," not as an immediate end of action but a condition variably present in all social systems. For consistency, Parsons should have identified standing as a third immediate end—the one most easily identified at the sociocultural level of analysis and collectively manifest as system integration. Systems with a single arena for global comparison would approximate an ideal type of full integration; those with many arenas would not (see pp. 263–264).

what that is valued for eminence; and consisteth in comparison. For
if all things were equally in [or available to] all men, nothing would
be prized" (1968: 134; compare Hume 1963: 81–88). Given that it is
"the nature of man" to compare attributes and accomplishments,

> we find three principal causes of quarrell. First Competition;
> Secondly, Diffidence; Thirdly, Glory.
> The first maketh men invade for Gain; the second, for Safety;
> and the third for Reputation (Hobbes 1968: 185).

Hobbes assumed a model of binary comparison and scarce ends –
"if any two men desire the same thing, which neverthelesse they both
cannot enjoy, they become enemies, . . ." (p. 184). He could have
assumed otherwise. The end of "gain," as such, can result in competition, need not result in "invasion" and, I would argue, does not
depend on others' gains. If binary comparison is employed, then
safety is the end, because larger gains by the other threaten one with
the possibility of invasion or some other loss. Or, if global comparison is employed, then others' gains result in lower standing and reduced esteem for the one gaining less.

Harold Lasswell provided another short list of immediate ends in
the first two sentences of his remarkable book, *World Politics and
Personal Insecurity* (1965a, first published 1935). "Political analysis
is the study of changes in the shape and composition of the value
patterns of society. Representative values are safety, income, and
deference" (p. 3). In later work, Lasswell settled on a list of eight
values, organized into two groups, welfare values and deference values.
The first group consists of well-being (health and safety), wealth,
skill, and enlightenment, the second of power, respect, rectitude, and
affection (see for example Lasswell and Kaplan 1950: 55–56). I find
this list much less helpful than the earlier one. Welfare describes the
condition of any and all values having been realized in whatever
degree. Well-being lumps together threats to people from other people and from the rest of their environment (disease, natural disaster,
and so on). Safety as originally used would seem to refer only, or
at least mainly, to the former. The other welfare values of wealth,
skill, and enlightenment are ends defined by internal comparison,
or means to these or other ends. As for the deference values, I fail
to see how power, rectitude, and affection equal deference, although

they, no less than wealth, skill and so on, may be means to deference as an end. Such values may be ends in themselves, in which case they belong in the group of values subject to internal comparison.

Lasswell's later list conflates ultimate ends and immediate ends valued for their perceived relation to ultimate ends. To the extent that wealth, for example, as a means to deference becomes an end in itself, then it becomes an ultimate value unrelated to deference. The instability of instrumental and ultimate values also accounts for the complications I identified just above in Hobbes' treatment of gain. That means and ends are unstable hardly excuses their conflation for expositional purposes.

Yet another example of immediate ends sorted, at least implicitly, by criteria for comparing states of affairs, is Abraham H. Maslow's all too famous "hierarchy of basic needs" (1970: 51; see pp. 35–58). These consist of physiological needs, safety needs, belongingness and love needs, esteem needs, and the need for self-actualization. We should immediately segregate physiological needs from this list. They are not cognitively driven, even if they may contribute to cognitively defined ends for human action. We should do the same for the alleged need for self-actualization. We may either locate self-actualization with such ends as the acquisition of skill and enlightenment or dismiss it, along with the hierarchical arrangement of all such needs, as a parochially liberal construction of the human response to privilege.

There remain three categories of needs, for which the terms "safety," "love," and "esteem" provide summary descriptions. The first and third are obviously related to binary and global comparison respectively. The second is more difficult to interpret, I think because Maslow assumed circumstances combining material abundance and emotional deprivation. As rational conduct, love of wealth and the acquisition of love betray a common origin in the comparison of what one would want against what one considers herself as having.

The last example of immediate ends implicitly categorized on grounds of comparison is to be found in Jürgen Habermas' conception of "knowledge-constitutive human interests" (1971: 308–315). Habermas used the term "interest" (*interesse*) in a Kantian sense (pp. 191–213), not to be confused with the usual sense of the term in English (Bernstein 1978: 192). "I term *interest* the basic orientations rooted in specific fundamental conditions of the possible reproduction and self-constitution of the human species" (1971: 196).[7] This conception is not far removed from Maslow's: "Either the interest presupposes a need (*Bedürfnis*) or it produces one" (p. 198, footnote citing Kant deleted). There are three knowledge-constitutive human interests, corresponding to "three categories of processes of inquiry."

> The approach of the empirical-analytic sciences incorporates a *technical* cognitive interest; that of the historical-hermeneutic sciences incorporates a *practical* one; and the approach of critically oriented sciences incorporates the *emancipatory* cognitive interest. . . (p. 308, Habermas' emphasis).

The description of the first of these cognitive interests as "technical," and its association with analysis and deduction (1971: 308), clearly make it dependent on binary comparison. The second cognitive interest, described as practical and oriented to the "understanding of meaning," is "directed in its very structure toward the attainment of possible consensus among actors. . . ." (p. 310). I interpret this to mean that practical ends are those that are defined internally by comparing possible states of affairs. Inasmuch as individual choices, made by reference to practical interests, relate to the good of the whole indeterminately, then the problem for human knowledge includes "the achievement of a possible consensus." I find the description of this "process of inquiry" as oriented to "the understanding of meaning" a ratification of a hermeneutic slogan more than a clarification of practical interest. The slogan ill suits historicism, which is nonetheless concerned to understand a whole indetermin-

---

7. This sentence ends, "namely *work* and *interaction*" (his emphasis). Elsewhere Habermas extended this formulation: "*knowledge-constitutive interests take form in the medium of work, language and power*" (p. 313, his emphasis again). Work "refers to ways in which individuals control and manipulate their environment in order to survive and preserve themselves." Habermas meant "communicative action" by "language," or the exchange of information. I fail to see why it should not include all exchanges, as the term "interaction" suggests. Power refers to "power of self-reflection" (p. 314, original emphasized). We may infer that power is not merely internal to the self, however, because self-reflection "releases the subject from dependence on hypostasized powers" (p. 310). Power is then power over minds, including one's own.

ately constituted from many parts (if not indeterminate in principle, then practically so from the observer's point of view).

Habermas called the third of his cognitive interests emancipatory because it is the one he identified his own work with. "A critical social science . . . is concerned . . . to determine when theoretical statements grasp invariant regularities of social action as such and when they express ideologically frozen relations of dependence that can in principle be transformed" (p. 310). This is an apt short description of Habermas' objectives (at least at the time he wrote these words; on the direction of Habermas work in the last decade, see Ingram 1987). It also suggests that Habermas confused his critical program, as a means to a cognitive interest, with that interest as a description of an immediate end. The term "emancipatory" describes the means, and not the end.

Instead, this interest is described by such ends as deference, esteem, or standing. As such, it is constituted by global comparison. What is unclear about emancipation is whether it is a repudiation of global comparison (in favor of enlightenment, for example, as an internally constructed state of affairs) or a call for an improved understanding, or acceptance, or global comparison, and a more effective choice of arena within which to compare one's position to others'. Habermas' interest in psychoanalysis and self-reflection (p. 310), not to mention "communicative competence", permits either of these outcomes, even if one might not want to use the word "emancipation" in either instance.[8]

8. That Habermas has poorly specified the difference between practical and emancipatory interests is further evidenced by his presentation of two concepts of rationality: cognitive-instrumental rationality and communicative rationality (1984: 10). The first category of rationality relates to the medium of work (footnote 7), within which technical cognitive interest takes form. The second is "based ultimately on the central experience of the unconstrained, unifying, consensus-bringing force of argumentative speech, ..." (1984: 10). Argumentative speech clearly refers to the medium of interaction and language, within which practical cognitive interest takes form. The achievement of communicative rationality is "unifying" and "consensus-bringing"—ends that are apparently practical and emancipatory. In identifying "three complexes of rationality" in Weber's work, Habermas effectively acknowledged that communicative rationality did double duty. The three complexes are "cognitive-instrumental rationality," "moral-practical rationality," and "aesthetic-practical rationality" (pp. 237–241). Artistic expression might then be the medium otherwise called "power," which parallels work and interaction in giving form to cognitive interests.

Throughout the discussion of grounds of comparison, I avoid describing the three categories of immediate ends with the term "interests," except, of course, in the particular, Kantian sense in which Habermas used it. Yet much of that discussion immediately brings to mind interests in the commonplace sense, as having to do with wants (Barry 1965: 175–176, Kratochwil 1982: 5–6). The term "want" suggests an immediacy of ends; Parsons, following Vilfredo Pareto, equated immediate ends with interests (1937: 263). Even Habermas presupposed a connection between interests and wants. "Interest expresses a relation of the object of interest to our faculty of desire" (1971: 198).

We know, however, that desires and interests do not constitute a simple identity. As Friedrich Kratochwil observed, "we can think of cases in which it makes sense to distinguish carefully something wanted or desired—like sitting down in a snowstorm due to exhaustion—from the interest involved—not doing so because of the danger of freezing to death" (1982: 6). Something must be added to this equation. For Kratochwil, "reasons" are added: "a justification that goes beyond the mere indication of likes and dislikes" (p. 6, following Flathman 1966).

On inspection, Kratochwil's illustration fails to support such a conclusion. Someone facing death in a snowstorm would indeed want to sit down. That person also wants to live. In comparing the two states of affairs (internal comparison), I would choose the latter, which we may then construe as my preference. All that must be added to the equation of wants and interests to make sense of Kratochwil's illustration is a multiplicity of ends, which a generalized model provides. Reasons are then merely statements about preferences: I am not going to sit down in the snow because I prefer living to resting.

Kratochwil was nevertheless right in thinking that the equation of wants or, I would add, preferences and interests does not suffice. Others agree. Thus Lasswell in his systematic work with Abraham Kaplan defined "interest" as a "pattern of demands and supporting expectations" (1950: 23). Added to the equation of wants and interests is the element of actionable expectations, or opportunities: A want is not an interest unless one can plausibly act on it.

Barry's formula is similar. "As a first approximation let us say that a policy or action is in a man's interest if it increases his opportunities to get what he wants" (1965: 176). Again the added element involves opportunities, which "assets" like wealth and power afford. Because wealth and power are also interests (here Barry relied on Parsons; compare note 6), they "form a very useful guide to the amount and distribution of want-satisfaction. Evaluations in terms of 'interest' (especially when this is reduced to money) are far more practicable than evaluations in terms of want-satisfaction" (p. 184). Here again is the distinction between passions and interests, the latter adding to wants "an element of reflection and calculation . . ." (Hirschman 1977: 33, quoted in chapter 5, footnote 3). This is the long ascendant liberal view of interest, which Parsons, Lasswell, and Kaplan, and Barry have affirmed and which Economists take as grounding their conceptual apparatus. It would mean little to speak of opportunity costs, for example, if preferences were not formulated by reference to "*opportunities* for want-satisfaction, expressed in a common medium such as money, . . ." (Barry 1965: 184, his emphasis).

Interests in this characteristic liberal conception have three features differentiating them from wants. First, interests stand between the diverse array of particular means that one has on the one hand and the equally diverse array of particular wants, or ultimate ends, on the other.[9] Interests do so in circumstances that are also diversely particularized. It is tempting to think of interests as a medium, or conduit, between particular means and ultimate ends. Barry implied this by noting the advantages of a common medium for want-satisfaction. Nevertheless, money, as one such medium, is not to be confused with an interest, like wealth or any asset that may be reckoned in money. (Nor are resources media, as Anthony Giddens thought; see chapter 1).

The second feature of a liberal conception of interest, then, is that interests are not media; ruled practices are. (Compare this chapter's footnotes 7, 8.) Interests are means and ends—generalized means and immediate ends at the same time. Whether by adding, reducing, or integrating particulars, interests translate those particulars into coherent and manageable general statements about means as ends. Interests so considered lend themselves to specification through

---

9. "The etymology of the word is suggestive in this respect. Interest derives, via French, from the Latin *interesse* which means in part "to be between" (Flathman 1966: 16 n. 4, closely paraphrasing Hannah Pitkin's dissertation; compare Pitkin 1967: 157).

rules, such as those constituting common media like money. Third, interests as general means/immediate ends must relate to resources so as to create opportunities for action. That interests are general, framed by rules and related to resources specifies the meaning of the term "asset." Wealth and power are assets in Barry's judgment because they are general, stable representations of what resources permit, given diversely particular means, ends, and circumstances.

To complete the picture, I would add a fourth feature to this liberal conception of interest. Habermas' cognitive concerns clearly point to it, and Kratochwil stated it forthrightly. Interests are recognizable to us as the reasons we give for our conduct. Reasons speak to the relation between our taken-for-granted rationality and the wants that we are in a position to satisfy. To return briefly to my plight in a snowstorm: I want to sit down; I want to survive; I cannot do both. The reasons I offer for either choice express an interest. I cannot go on because my resources are depleted, and I might as well be comfortable until I die. Or, I will push on, because I am still able, so that I can survive. In both instances, only internal comparison contributed to my reasoning, with my conclusions differing only because of my resources. My reasoning speaks to the implications of my choices in the circumstances facing me. My interest does not change: I want the most out of those circumstances.

We could just as easily find examples in which the reasons offered disclose different interests. If the example gives pride of place to binary comparison, the reasons offered for choices would be justifications (which is what Kratochwil called — erroneously, I think — the reasons one might articulate for deciding to push on in a snowstorm). Thus, when you and I have an altercation, I justify my actions by noting your actions (you started it). If the example depends on global comparison, explanations accompany conduct. Such explanations clarify one's choices (I cheated because I wanted a higher grade) or establish their significance (I reported you for cheating because the others and I didn't cheat). However skillful, such talk is always present.

If there are three discernible categories of comparison invoked as reasons for conduct, then there are, at the requisite level of generality, only three interests. I presented them a few pages ago as categories of immediate ends. In that order of presentation, the first category is the one I associate with global comparison and explanation. The subject of comparison and explanation is always "standing," and this is my choice of terms for the interest they define. The second category is associated with binary comparison and justification. Their subject is always "security," which is the term I prefer for the interest they define. This is not just personal security but the security of whatever of ours we see others wanting. The third category, which I associate with internal comparison and the drawing of implications, defines an interest in what I would call "welfare," except that this term is conventionally a summary description of all ultimate ends. As an alternative, I use the term "wealth," but not just as an asset for which money is the usual medium. One may have a wealth of knowledge, love, or anything else of value; one has an interest in more of it.

Standing, security, and wealth are the controlling interests of humanity. We recognize them everywhere. They comprehend survival, whether in a fight or a snowstorm. They comprehend all other ultimate ends, no matter how trivial or bizarre. We make them the propositional content of speech and rules, and we impute them to our social arrangements, including preeminently in this modern world, the state. As reasons of state and the ends of statecraft, they constitute "the national interest." Robert E. Osgood's discussion of "national self-interest" is illustrative.

> Basic to all kinds of national self-interest is survival or self-preservation, ... National security is a related but broader end, since it embraces not only survival but the nation's ability to survive. Security in its broadest sense is subjective; it is an absence of fear. . . .
>
> Another important category of national self-interest might be called self-sufficiency, or the conduct of foreign relations without reference to other nations or matters beyond unilateral national control. . . .
>
> In any analysis of national ends and motives one must also take into account the desire for national prestige (1953: 5–6).

Osgood's work sits squarely in the Realist tradition I describe in chapter 7. Realists, including Osgood, have been careful to discriminate between means and ends. National self-interest is a question of ends. As for means, "the exercise of independent national power — power being understood as the ability to influence others to do its will—is the most important means of achieving national ends" (Osgood 1953: 13).

Realists have also observed a tendency for power to become an end in itself. In Arnold Wolfers' words, "a quest for power adequate to national ends turns into a quest for national power irrespective of circumstances" (1962: 106). Wolfers remarked of this tendency: "a rational drive has become a pathological urge" (p. 106; see also p. 89). Osgood concluded his recitation of national self-interest in a similar vein.

> Finally, there is aggrandizement or the increase of national power, wealth or prestige. This kind of self-interest is readily identifiable by virtue of the vehement motives which leads to its pursuit: ambition, militancy, the urge to dominate, the will to power (1953: 6).

If read in context, these remarks of Wolfers and Osgood suggest that in the last century states' agents and their publics have increasingly become preoccupied with "power," apparently as an end in itself. These remarks further suggest that such a preoccupation has become irrationally excessive and a mark of our times. Hans Morgenthau's position is different. He posited an *"animus dominandi,"* "a lust for power" in all people at all times (1946: 192; compare chapter 6, footnote 6, on Georg Simmel and note the large influence of Friedrich Nietzsche). In common with Wolfers and Osgood, Morgenthau held that the preoccupation with power is irrational.[10] At risk of reading too much into Wolfers' and Osgood's position, I see them as arguing that the last century has seen a momentous shift in the grounds of comparison that agents of states and their publics are given to employ in identifying interests.

To say this illuminates the debate in the 1940s and 1950s between

---

10. "There is in selfishness an element of rationality presented by the natural limitation of the end, which is lacking in the will to power. It is for this reason that mere selfishness can be appeased by concessions, while satisfaction of one demand will stimulate will to power to ever expanding claims" (1946: 193-194). Such a position undercuts any distinction between means and ends. Lust for power knows no limits and, we must infer, overwhelms limited ends, the pursuit of which leaves the means-ends distinction intact. See also Waltz (1959: 34-39).

Realists and Idealists (the latter being the former's dismissive name
for all those who professed some interest or confidence in Functionalism, institutional arrangements in international relations and
the existence, however latent, of a harmony of interests among states;
compare chapter 7, footnote 27). For all their differences, Idealists prefer and would promote internal comparison, an interest in wealth,
and the choice of means in which money is a prominent medium.
Realists unite in their perception that binary comparison is inevitable
in a world of states, security the dominant interest, and military
endeavors the means. The measure of one's security is, perversely
enough, the manifest insecurity of others.

One can hardly deny that both grounds of comparison are to be
found in the practice of most states' agents. The shift Wolfers and
Osgood both identified, with understandable alarm, is not between
internal and binary comparison, but from those grounds of comparison to global comparison (in both sense of the term "global";
compare Hobsbawm 1987: 314–327). Throughout modernity, states
have undoubtedly had an interest in standing. Nevertheless, the presumption of equality among sovereigns militated against a concern
for standing extending much beyond ceremonial matters. So did
significant limits on the resources available to sovereigns and information about states, their resources, and the ability of agents to
mobilize such resources (Osgood 1957: 61–87).

In the last century these limits have disappeared, sovereignty as
a personal trait having done so long before. Sovereign equality has
become a juridical property of the state, defining participation in
a formal, determinate system of states and thus the conditions necessary for global comparison. Mass media enable vast publics to watch
the system in action, as if it were a never-ending athletic event. Information on all kinds of attributes of states s widely available, allowing states' agents and publics to engage in ceaseless comparison with
any number of measures. Resources previously understood as providing the means for security become measures of states' standing.
Chief among these measures are land area, population, national
wealth, industrial capacity, technological achievements and, of course,
military capability.

A shift in the grounds of comparison would change the character
of what Realists have been accustomed to calling "power." When
binary comparison and security dominate the practice of states'

agents, then power describes military capability as a means and predicts the outcome of its use. Measuring attributes of states is pointless even if it is possible, except to judge one's security. The most effective measure of security is war: The outcome of war determines to the satisfaction of both parties what is difficult to measure, namely, their reciprocal quotients of security. Security is an asset that can be acquired and retained only by expending other assets, like wealth, in war. Insofar as war is avoided because its outcome is predictable, the measure of military capabilities substitutes for war as a medium of measurement.

Global comparison turns "power" into a common medium for the measurement of standing and disallows, sometimes radically, its use as a means to achieve other interests. To make this point somewhat differently, any resource or accomplishment that can be attributed to states generally, lends itself to comparison and can be measured conveniently, is used to rank states. Their position and the measured difference between them in the standings are their power. So we understand the term in athletic competitions in which repeated games between pairs yield a cumulative index of all (teams of) players' standing. So it is with states under conditions which some Realists have found to prevail in the last hundred years. The paradox in this situation is that military capability, as a crucial measure of standing, should not be treated as an asset, to be expended in the pursuit of some other interest like security, because its depletion will adversely affect one's standing. Even if an expenditure of military capability enhanced one's security with respect to an adversary because military engagement costs the latter even more than it costs oneself, one's standing would still be reduced in comparison to all those in the system not making such expenditures.

Let us grant for the moment that, as Wolfers and Osgood implied, global comparison has supplanted binary comparison in today's world. We would expect a great deal of emphasis on military capabilities combined with a resistance to their use. We would further expect that global comparison is likely to be less important for states with low standing in military terms. Conversely, states at or near the top of the standings are likely to be wrapped up in questions of standing to a degree that suggests to those with low standing, or observers like Wolfers and Osgood, a run-away will to power. To the extent that measurements are uncertain or changes in standing unacknowledged (there being no independent scorekeeper), then agents and publics of adversely affected states may respond vengefully. The stresses and demands of global comparison may even induce thoughts of smashing the system.

Arguably, these generalizations fit the world we know (Osgood 1957: 88–119). German and Japanese revisionism earlier in the century are evidence not of an unleashed will to power but of standings that did not change when they should have. General war was a response to frustration, and total victory an effort to rid the system of its uncertainties. In the post-war standings, the position of the United States and the Soviet Union confirm the paradox of power as ubiquitous measure and useless asset. The destructiveness of nuclear weapons ensures that they provide security only if they are not used for security. Thus freed for use as a measure of standing, these weapons accumulate in stockpiles far larger than required by the logic of deterrence. Much the same may be said for conventional military capabilities of the ranking states. Measuring standing by reference to these capabilities precludes using them faster than they can be replenished, unless they are used to reduce the capability of the primary adversary. Yet the latter undertaking endangers the system upon which global comparison is predicated.

Is a world of global comparison the best short description of contemporary international relations? Morgenthau thought so for international relations at any time. Other Realists would say so for the world today. "Those who call themselves realists assume that, in the final analysis, the actors in international arenas are status maximizers" (Young 1986: 118). If we limit the system of global comparison to two states, which would be the top two in a global system of global comparison, the Realist case is even stronger.

As will be recalled from chapter 6, I would characterize contemporary international relations as pervasively heteronomous. Heteronomy implies a dominance of internal comparison, with asymmetries in the resources available to free choosers yielding a stable pattern of asymmetric outcomes subject to hegemonial support. The United States and the Soviet Union maintain directively ruled spheres of influence, which also contribute to a stable pattern of heteronomous relations between them. The United States and the Soviet Union also engage in a diverse set of comparisons and direct resources toward changing their relative position in the standings without immediate effects on wealth and security. Because the system of global comparison has only two places in the standings, it would easily be confused with, or change into, a system of binary comparison, were it not for the diversity of resources and accomplishments subject to comparison.[11] The result is a climate of contest and spectacle — an unending tournament, rounds of play in many arenas, all of us a captive audience.

For the two states, the advantage of this arrangement is the extent to which it disguises their heteronomous relations and hierarchically maintained spheres of influence. Because the constant jousting engages the world's attention without affecting the relative security of the two sides, agents of the United States and the Soviet Union know better than to let the hegemonial system of multiple global comparisons slip into binary comparison, in which all would be imperiled. Agents do not have to have thought all of this out. They need merely to understand how well their interest in standing serves the status quo, which serves their other interests.

EXPLOITATION

People "exploit" resources available to them in pursuing immediate ends. Because resources include people — oneself and others — rational conduct necessarily involves the exploitation of people. Exploitation in this everyday sense unavoidably follows from our physical individuality and human sociality. If there were no pattern to it, I would not be concerned about exploitation. There is a pattern, however, a pattern of unequal consequences, which does engage my moral sense.

---

11. Scholars are confused. After noting that Realists see those engaged in international relations as "status maximizers," Oran Young (1986: 118) went on to say that "a society composed of status maximizers will resemble a Hobbesian state of nature. Because gains for individual actors amount to losses for others, the members of the group will find themselves in more or less pure conflict. . . ." Young has well described a system of security maximizers, given to binary comparison. The same confusion accounts for the poor performance of so many participants in Axelrod's round-robin tournament.

John Roemer's recent efforts to develop "a general theory of exploitation" begin, as they should, with inequality (1982, 1986; see Wright 1985: 64–82 for an extension).

> In virtually every society or economy, there is inequality. Yet not all inequality is viewed by a society as exploitative or unjust. Certainly, however, the notion of exploitation involves inequality in some way. What forms of inequality does a particular society view as exploitative, and what forms does it not? (Roemer 1985: 102)

Roemer's answer to his own question is both procedurally and normatively a powerful one. He proposed "that a group be conceived of as exploited if it has some *conditionally feasible alternative* under which its members would be better off" (p. 103, his emphasis). Roemer then asked if at least one group of individuals would choose to leave societies in which conditions constitute what we generally call feudalism, capitalism, and socialism, including the contemporary statist version of socialism.

One might ask, leave with what? Roemer produced three alternatives. A group leaves with "its private assets" or "with its *per capita* share of society's alienable productive assets," or finally "with its *per capita* share of society's inalienable assets, once alienable assets are distributed equally" (pp. 105, 109). Alienable assets are "means of production, resources," inalienable ones are "skills" (p. 109). Roemer concluded that, under feudal conditions, rational serfs would leave with their private assets (if they could, practically speaking). Under conditions identified with capitalism, workers would leave with per capita shares of alienable assets. Under conditions of socialism, those who are relatively unskilled would leave. These solutions are rarely practical for individuals. Nevertheless, revolutions do the job for exploited groups. "Each revolution eliminates the inequalities associated with its characteristic form of property (the feudal bond, alienable means of production, finally inalienable assets); the scope of assets that are allowed to be private becomes progressively narrower as history proceeds" (p. 109).

Roemer's definitions are rigorously analytical yet honor the Marxist concern for exploitation and its elimination. Nevertheless, I must fault one of Roemer's assumptions, namely, that assets, however constituted in particular modes of production, relate only to productive activity. Resources are means to ends, constituted as such through people's ruled practices. Resources must have a material reality, but they never can be the raw materials of nature, standing alone. Only because of socially defined use do such raw materials constitute resources, which are also assets when they are constituted in reference to immediate ends, or interests. Assets relate to productive activity only when the immediate end is wealth. When the immediate end is standing, assets are those resources lending themselves to altering and measuring standing. When security is at stake, assets are resources devoted to making others insecure.

The problem with characterizing historical epochs as modes of production — feudalism, capitalism, and so on — is that epochs also involve modes of standing and security, complexly related to the production of wealth. During each such epoch, exploitation may proceed in relation to all three interests and the assets used in their support. Inequality attending one such interest may reinforce, leave unaffected, or indeed work against inequalities fostered by other interests. The complexity of exploitation so conceived defeats any attempt to use Roemer's progressive criteria for identifying and eliminating layers of exploitation. Instead we need a criterion of exploitation that can be uniformly applied to all the inequalities of all interest and asset patterns.

The criterion I propose is one I borrow from liberal Political Economy. Exploitation describes any situation in which rational individuals accrue rents in the process of realizing interests. "Rent is that part of the payment to an owner of a resource over and above that which those resources could command in any alternative use. Rent is receipt in excess of opportunity cost" (Buchanan 1980: 3). A perfect market would have no rents, but no market is ever perfect. The possibility of rents is what drives entrepreneurs into trying new productive activities. A market instituted to be self-regulating would always lower rents over time, thus persuading participants to find new activities paying rent, however briefly (pp. 6–7). When markets are systematically impaired by ruled practices, rents accrue to some at the expense of others. Instituting such rules, and reaping rewards, is rent-seeking (as opposed to profit-seeking, which is responding to the possibility of rent in a well-instituted market; pp. 7–11). Liberals take rent-seeking to be exploitative; I would include profit-seeking, as do Marxists.

One might see in the criterion of rent as exploitation the same limitations I identify with Reoemer's progressive criteria: It would seem to refer exclusively to wealth and its production. Yet the very simplicity of the rent-as-exploitation criterion means easy application to other interests, insofar as they may be thought of as calculable assets. By my reckoning, rent-seeking is always exploitive, whether rent is the more costly provision of standing, security, or wealth than an alternative use of someone's resources would provide for that individual. Let us turn briefly to some epochs of interest to Roemer in order to try out this proposition.

Under feudalism, the distribution of security produces social arrangements in which rules assign standing to individuals at birth. One's standing determines whether one produces security or goods and the conditions for their exchange. That exchange is unequal, because serfs always pay rent for their security. Serfs never receive enough security to threaten the lords' security and thus the latter's ability to extract rent. Unequal standing reinforces the asymmetry of exchange.

Roemer would proceed directly to the capitalist epoch. I think that logically and historically we should turn to conditions of exploitation associated with the state, the emergence of which coincides with the decline of feudal arrangements in Europe. The state decouples rules relating to standing from the provision of security. In principle, security is no longer produced as a private asset subject to exchange, but as a public asset uniformly available, without respect to standing or wealth. This is because security is not produced by those with standing or wealth. Instead security specialists, acting as agents for all, assume that responsibility.

Instituting the state as a collective security arrangement (recall chapter 4) may provide security more cheaply for those with standing than if they were to provide it for themselves. Certainly this is the case for those with wealth to protect, which helps to explain the alliance between the crown and bourgeoisie in European state formation. People will find it cheaper to pay for collective security and suffer rent-seeking free riders, some of whom may shirk fair charges on security because their other assets are so low (compare chapter 6, footnote 16). Far greater is the extortion of rent, realized as standing or wealth, by those responsible for producing security. Roemer's concern with socialist statism (which he misleadingly described as "status exploitation," 1982: 243-247, 1985: 109-110; compare Wright 1985: 71) is precisely an acknowledgment of this kind of exploitation, which is so evident when socialism is alleged to have remedied other forms of exploitation.

Capitalism presupposes collective security bought with minimally necessary allocation of productive assets. The production and exchange of wealth also allows the institution of numerous ranking systems and the assignment of standing therein. Finally, capitalism depends on the institution of proper markets for productive assets. If assets are taken to be "original private endowments" (the phrase is Roemer's, 1985: 104; the notion is deeply embedded in liberal thought), then their aggregation and exchange for productive purposes will be exploitive, but only temporarily from any beneficiary's vantage point, because of the innovations introduced by market competitors. Over time, the rise and fall of individual fortunes (the term taken in a double sense) balance out, and the distribution of exploitation may be seen as nonexploitive.

The trouble with this pretty picture of liberal justice is the presumption that individuals are proprietors of birthright endowments. From birth on, people participate unequally in social arrangments affording opportunities to select and develop skills making good on native capacities. That one is skilled differently than others means that one has different access to resources than others have. In this instance, rent may be conceptualized as the difference between native endowment and skillful participation in productive activity and ruled access to resources. Because these differences are practically incalculable, rent is built into the system of productive activity. No one has to collect rents for rents to be paid. Capitalism describes the use of productive assets to generate more such assets as a matter of systematic intent. The tremendous generative power of capitalism accelerates productive activity. It also accelerates the differentiation of skills and of access to buried rent and other resources.

Roemer's distinction between alienable and inalienable assets — resources and skills — follows from the liberal notion of native endowments. In constructivist terms, all such distinctions are misguided. Redistributing wealth helps to correct exploitation fostered by differential access to resources. This is the aim of socialism. Whatever the rhetoric, rewards are never adequately used to equalize skills. Instead socialism promotes the unequal development of skills in place of the differentiation of access to resources. In doing so, socialism also promotes the substitution of credentials for wealth as the leading measure of standing.

What does this brief excursion across modern history tell us? While most premodern social arrangements use standing, no doubt exploitively, to constitute other assets and achieve other interests, feudalism makes use of insecurity, supported by standing, for such purposes. Social arrangements paradigmatically identified with the state use the provision of security to realize other interests. Organizational means of exploitation gain a privileged position. Finally, social arrangements identified with productive activity and markets for assets are exploitive because the rules constituting individuals as participants yield rents to only some of them. Marxists tend to view domination and exploitation as independent evils (Wright 1986: 116–117). In my view, rule *is* exploitive. If there are three categories of rule, then there are three forms of exploitation. If rule is inevitable—a position I think follows from the logic of rules and rule—then so is exploitation. The mitigation of exploitation in one form compels or promotes its presence in some other form.

What then of capitalism and socialism? Neither are systems of rule, yet both contribute to exploitation. Capitalism's generative power, harnessed to the relentless extraction of resources from the earth (including its people), produces enormous assets susceptible to exploitive distribution. Socialism would undo the exploitation aggravated by capitalism without repudiating capitalism's generative effects. This feat requires the differential support of skills and the proliferation of organizations under the aegis of the state. Statism follows in train (Wright 1985: 78–82, 1986: 120–123).

The concentration of certified skills constitutes a world of two classes. One is a cosmopolitan ruling class of those whose professional credentials and highly honed skills suit them to the demands of complex organizational environments. The dominating interest of this class is standing and its dominant activity support of the status quo. The other class is everyone excluded from the first. Most of its members are wretchedly poor and unskilled people, no longer even able to function effectively as peasants and workers.

Capitalism pays rent to support these class arrangements. It also finances the state as security provider, the system of states a source of insecurity necessitating perpetuation of the state. In turn, states provide direct support for many (but not all) of the members of the cosmopolitan class by employing them as organizational function-aries. Other organizations, public and private, within and beyond the state, do the same. States also compensate for the unequal access to resources associated with capitalism by adopting socialist or wel-farist policies which strengthen credentialed skill-holders as a rent-receiving class.

Capitalism is the source of the wealth used to support a perverse security system and a professionally credentialed, organizationally oriented class of rulers. Electronically mediated, fully transnational circuits of capital depend on the cover provided by the systems of standing and security. Capitalism also depends on those systems for rectification of its own erratic tendencies. The striking periodicity of material growth stems from capitalism's need to constitute new resources on exponentially larger scales through technological revo-lutions (Onuf 1984). In response we find organizational interven-tion. If capitalism cannot continue to renovate itself with technologi-cal revolutions — an open question, in my opinion — then declines in growth will bring further reinforcement of organizations enabling rule by cosmopolitan adepts (Seabold and Onuf 1981: 32–36).

There is no solution to the human reality of exploitation. Even in the absence of a solution, we must call exploitation what it is, in all the ways that it is what it is.

. . . the difficulty — I might say — is not that of finding the solution but rather of recognizing as the solution something that looks as if it were only preliminary to it. . . . the solution of the difficulty is a description, if we give it the right place in our considerations. If we dwell upon it, and do not try to get beyond it.

The difficulty here is: to stop.

Ludwig Wittgenstein
(1967: par. 314, p. 58e)

SYNOPTIC TABLE

Throughout this book I sort a considerable *mélange* of socially constructed phenomena into sets of categories, always three in number, always repeating the same relations of properties. In chapter 3, I defend the proposition that at least some sets of threes are universal, but I resist saying that any one set is demonstrably fundamental. Were there a fundamental set of properties preceding social construction in all its manifestations, I could construct a table of correspondences, arrayed in three columns, one for each category, labeled by reference to those properties. This is, after all, a standard logocentric procedure. In the same fashion I could constitute separate columns for every occasion in which I discover these categories manifesting themselves. Then I could fill in the empty cells of my table, and all would be clear.

All would be clear, that is, except how I can stand outside of the human experience as social construction and offer a set of coordinates that "explain" the recurrence of a consistent pattern for all of that experience. My constructivist preferences preclude the possibility that I, or any coordinates I might divine, stand outside social construction. Everything must be located within the cells of the table. Where then does the table come from? As an act of social construction on my part, the table must have coordinates that rule its construction, or indeed it would not be the construction that it is.

The practical difficulty is to find good, helpful labels for external, independent criteria when nothing is demonstrably fundamental.

Faculties of Experience

	The category of existence and the constitution/ regulation of its meaning in space and of time	The category of material control and the constitution/ regulation of modalities of control (ch. 1)	The category of discretionary endeavor, agreement and exchange coupled to the constitution/ regulation of agency and opportunity
	Assertive speech acts	Directives (ch. 2)	Commissives
	Instruction-rules	Directive-rules (ch. 2)	Commitment-rules
	Abductive reasoning	Deduction (ch. 3)	Induction
	Conjuration	Combat (ch. 3)	Clue-finding
	Shame	Dread (ch. 3)	Guilt
Paradigms of Experience	Monitory regimes	Executive regimes (ch. 4)	Administrative regimes
	Metaphor	Metonymy (ch. 4)	Synecdoche
	Manners	Virtue (ch. 5)	Rights
	Tell the truth	Do no harm (ch. 5)	Keep promises
	Hegemony	Hierarchy (ch. 6)	Heteronomy
	Priests & professors	Warriors & diplomats (ch. 7)	Physicians & merchants
	Explanation	Justification (ch. 7, 8)	Implication
	Global comparison	Binary comparison (ch. 8)	Internal comparison
	Standing	Security (ch. 8)	Wealth
	Touching	Seeing	Hearing

Even if human beings make their reality without help from Platonic essences, words on high or "magic triads" (Sebeok 1983: 2), there is another possibility. Human beings share faculties — biologically individualized capacities — all of which are significantly affected by social construction and some of which lend themselves to universal practices. Faculties like stereotopic vision and bipedal locomotion may together give rise to such universal practices as moving in files from point to point, and thus to such materially relevant but socially constructed activities as calculating the shortest distance between two points, making paths and so on.

In chapter 7, I mention the possibility that three of our senses relate to the universal categories of reasoning. That there are five senses is, I think, a social construction, perhaps not universal. So is the assignment of greater or lesser importance to each of these senses. I suspect that three senses dominate in social practices universally, these being touching, seeing, and hearing. Other senses become auxillary to these three, none of which universally dominates the other two. I also suspect the universal practice of granting priority to touching, seeing, and hearing finds support in another aspect of our bodily selves: We differentiate in and out with respect to ourselves (Johnson 1987: 19–37, Lakoff 1987: 266–281). Our touch marks the boundary between what is within and outside of us; we see out; we hear sounds coming in. To similar effect may be our bodily experience of the relations of parts and whole: We touch, as one whole to another; we see from a whole (ourselves) to the world in its many parts; we hear parts of the world as an integral whole in our heads.

I suggest that our sensory experience of the world and of our bodily selves in that world, reinforced by our appreciation of possible relations of in and out, wholes and parts, yields a universal set of three categories of reasoning, not to mention many other social practices. I call the three senses so reinforced "faculties of experience." They are not the only faculties of human experience, but I take them to be a particularly important set of such faculties. Because they are not just a matter of touching, seeing, and hearing, as separate, unmediated physical capacities, but involve a systematic set of relations, I do not wish to name the categories individually. They come as a set, and they should be taken as such. This set of faculties differentiates the columns of the synoptic table to follow.

How then to describe the table's rows? I notice other people's efforts to characterize social reality's many manifestations. Ludwig Wittgenstein wrote of "forms of life" (recall chapter 1). Michael Walzer borrowed from Blaise Pascal the notion that "personal qualities and social goods have their own spheres of operation" (1983: 19). Max Weber, I find, was concerned with "the 'internal and lawful autonomy' of the familial, religious, economic, political, aesthetic, erotic, and intellectual (scientific) life orders or spheres of life activity and value, . . ." (Scaff 1987: 743). Robert W. Cox identified twelve "modes" of "social relations of production" (1987: 11–34), which he viewed as "monads." Qualifying G. W. Leibniz's use of the term, Cox saw it as a device to examine "distinctive forms of social life so as to discern their characteristic dynamics *as though* they developed according to a distinctive social principle" (p. 405n.). Michael Oakeshott also wrote of modes, in his case, "modes of experience." (1933). He identified three (historical, scientific, and practical) and decided on idealist grounds that they were not "faculties" (pp. 71–73). Oakeshott's presentation of each mode in terms of whole-part relations suggests otherwise to me—His three modes are my three faculties (and in the same order; see, for example, his pp. 98, 182, 260).

Words like "form," "sphere," and "mode" either codify or call forth essentialist tendencies. Locating what is discrete and coherent in the wash of human activities must always risk this. I review the risks and make appropriate disclaimers and qualifications in my discussion of operative paradigms in the introduction. With these caveats in mind, I propose to call the table's rows "paradigms of experience." Unlike faculties of experience, the paradigms of experience do not constitute a determinate set. There are as many paradigms as people make and, in making, construe as made.

All theory, dear friend, is gray—
The Golden tree of life is green.

Johann Wolfgang von Goethe
Faust (1976: 97)

REFERENCES

[Bracketed information locates references in text, by chapter, unless otherwise indicated.]

Abercrombie, N., S. Hill, and B. S. Turner (1980) *The Dominant Ideology Thesis.* London: George Allen and Unwin. [6]

Aggarwal, V. K. (1985) *Liberal Protectionism.* Berkeley and Los Angeles: University of California Press. [4]

Aiken, H. D., ed. (1968) *Hume's Moral and Political Philosophy.* New York: Hafner Publishing Co. [5]

Alexander, J. C. (1982) *Theoretical Logic in Sociology,* Vol. 2, *The Antinomies of Classical Thought: Marx and Durkheim.* [Intro.]

———. (1983a) *Theoretical Logic in Sociology,* Vol. 3, *The Classical Attempt at Theoretical Synthesis.* Berkeley and Los Angeles: University of California Press. [4]

———. (1983b) *Theoretical Logic in Sociology,* Vol. 4, *The Modern Reconstruction of Classical Thought: Talcott Parsons.* Berkeley and Los Angeles: University of California Press. [4]

Alford, C. (1985) "Is Jürgen Habermas's Reconstructive Science Really Science?" *Theory and Society* 14: 321–340. [3]

Alker, H. R., Jr., and R. K. Ashley, eds. (forthcoming) *After Realism.* [5]

Allison, G. (1971) *The Essence of Decision.* Boston: Little, Brown. [7]

Almond, G. A. (1986) "Spheres of Influence Behavior: A Literature Search and Methodological Reflections," 145–167, *Dominant Powers and Subordinate States,* ed. by J. F. Triska. Durham: Duke University Press. [6]

Anderson, P. (1978) *Passages from Antiquity to Feudalism.* London: Verso. [6]

Aron, R. (1954) *The Century of Total War.* Boston: Beacon Press. [7]

———. (1973) *Peace and War,* abridged version trans. by R. Howard and A. B. Fox. Garden City: Anchor Press. [7]

Aronson, J. L. (1984) *A Realist Philosophy of Science.* London: Macmillan. [1]

Arrow, K. J. (1983) *Collected Papers,* Vol. 1, *Social Choice and Justice.* Cambridge, MA: Harvard University Press. [8]

Ashley, R. K. (1983) "The Eye of Power: The Politics of World Modeling," *International Organization,* 37: 495–535. [5]

———. (1986) "The Poverty of Neorealism," 255–300, in *Neorealism and Its Critics,* ed. by R. O. Keohane. New York: Columbia University Press. [Intro.]

———. (1987) "The Geopolitics of Geopolitical Space: Toward a Critical Social Theory of International Politics," *Alternatives* 12: 403–434. [Intro., 7]

———. (1988) "Geopolitics, Supplementary, Criticism: A Reply to Professors Roy and Walker," *Alternatives,* 13: 88–102. [1]

Austin, J. L. (1954) *The Province of Jurisprudence Determined and the Uses of the Study of Jurisprudence,* with an Introduction by H. L. A. Hart. New York: Noonday Press. [2,5]

———. (1963) *How to Do Things with Words.* Cambridge, MA: Harvard University Press. [2]

———. (1964) "A Plea for Excuses," 41–63, in *Ordinary Language,* ed. by V. C. Chappell. New York: Dover Publications. [2]

Axelrod. R. (1970) *Conflict of Interest.* Chicago: Markham Publishing. [6]

———. (1984) *The Evolution of Cooperation.* New York: Basic Books. [8]

Bach, K., and R. M. Harnish (1979) *Linguistic Communication and Speech Acts.* Cambridge, MA: MIT Press. [2]

Bachrach, P. (1967) *The Theory of Democratic Elitism.* Boston: Little, Brown. [7]

————, ed. (1971) *Political Elites in a Democracy.* New York: Atherton Press. [6, 7]

Baker, G. P., and P. M. S. Hacker (1984) *Skepticism, Rules and Language.* Oxford: Basil Blackwell. [1]

Balbus, I. D. (1983) *Marxism and Domination.* Princeton: Princeton University Press. [6]

Baldwin, D. A. (1979) "Power Analysis and World Politics: New Trends versus Old Tendencies," *World Politics* 31: 161–194. [7]

————. (1985) *Economic Statecraft.* Princeton: Princeton University Press. [7]

Barnet, R. J. (1973) *Roots of War.* Baltimore: Penguin Books. [6]

Barry, B. (1965) *Political Argument.* London: Routledge and Kegan Paul. [8]

————. (1970) *Sociologists, Economists and Democracy.* Chicago: University of Chicago Press. [8]

Barry, B., and R. Hardin (1982) "Epilogue," 367–386, in *Rational Man and Irrational Society?* ed. by Barry and Hardin. Beverly Hills: Sage Publications. [8]

Beitz, C. R. (1979) *Political Theory and International Relations.* Princeton: Princeton University Press. [5]

Bendix, R. (1962) *Max Weber: An Intellectual Portrait.* Garden City: Anchor Books. [3,6]

————. (1966–67) "Tradition and Modernity Reconsidered," *Comparative Studies in Society and History,* Vol. 9: 318–323. [7]

————. (1978) *Kings or People.* Berkeley and Los Angeles: University of California Press. [7]

Benedict, R. (1946) *The Chrysanthemum and the Sword.* Boston: Houghton-Mifflin. [3]

Bentham, J. (1948) *The Principles of Morals and Legislation,* with an Introduction by L. J. LaFleur. New York: Hafner Press, reprinting ed. of 1823. [3,4,5,8]

————. (1962) "Panopticon: or the Inspection House," 37–172, in *The Works of Jeremy Bentham,* Vol. 4, ed. by J. Bowring. New York: Russell and Russell. [5]

Bentley, A. F. (1967) *The Process of Government*. Cambridge, MA: Belknap Press. First published 1908. [7]

Beres, L. R. (1980) *Apocalypse*. Chicago: University of Chicago Press. [4]

Berger, P. L., and T. Luckmann (1967) *The Social Construction of Reality*. Garden City: Anchor Books. [1]

Berman, M. (1982) *All That Is Solid Melts into Air*. New York: Simon and Schuster. [7]

Bernstein, R. J. (1978) *The Restructuring of Social and Political Theory*. Philadelphia: University of Pennsylvania Press. (Intro., 1,8]

Bhaskar, R. (1979) *The Possibility of Naturalism*. Atlantic Highlands: Humanities Press. [1]

Birnie, P. (1985) *International Regulation of Whaling*, Vol. 1. New York: Oceana. [4]

Black, M. (1962) *Models and Metaphors*. Ithaca: Cornell University Press. [2, 4]

———. (1970) *Margins of Precision*. Ithaca: Cornell University Press. [3]

Bleicher, S. A. (1969) "The legal Significance of Re-Citation of General Assembly Resolutions," *American Journal of International Law* 63: 444–478. [4]

Bloor, D. (1983) *Wittgenstein: A Social Theory of Knowledge*. New York: Columbia University Press. [1]

Bohannan, P. (1967) "The Differing Realms of Law," 43–56, in *Law and Warfare*, ed. by Bohannan. New York: Natural History Press. [4]

Bonner, J. (1986) *Politics, Economics and Welfare*. Sussex: Wheatsheaf Books. [Intro.]

Bothe, M. (1980) "Legal and Non-Legal Norms—A Meaningful Distinction in International Relations?" *Netherlands Year Book of International Law*. Vol. 11: 65–95. [2]

Boyd, R. N. (1984) "The Current Status of Scientific Realism," 41–82, in *Scientific Realism*, ed. by J. Leplin. Berkeley and Los Angeles: University of California Press. [1]

Boyle, F. A. (1985) *World Politics and International Law.* Durham: Duke University Press. [7]

Bradbury, M., and J. McFarlane, eds. (1976), *Modernism 1890–1930.* Hammondsworth: Penguin Books. [7]

Brennan, G., and J. M. Buchanan (1985), *The Reason of Rules.* Cambridge: Cambridge University Press. [5,6]

Brown, S. (1974) *New Forces in World Politics.* Washington: The Brookings Institution. [7]

Bruner, J. (1986) *Actual Minds, Possible Worlds.* Cambridge, MA: Harvard University Press. [1]

Buchanan, J. M. (1980) "Rent Seeking and Profit Seeking," 3–15, in *Toward a Theory of the Rent Seeking Society,* ed. by Buchanan and others. College Station: Texas A & M Press. [8]

Buchanan, J. M., and G. Tullock (1962) *The Calculus of Consent.* Ann Arbor: University of Michigan Press. [6]

Buchler, J., ed. (1955) *Philosophical Writings of Peirce.* New York: Dover Publications. [3]

Bueno de Mesquita, B. (1981) *The War Trap.* New Haven: Yale University Press. [6]

Bull, H. (1977) *The Anarchical Society.* New York: Columbia University Press. [5,6]

Callinicos, A. (1985) "Anthony Giddens," *Theory and Society* 14: 133–166. [1]

Carr, E. H. (1964) *The Twenty Years' Crisis, 1919–1939.* New York: Harper Torchbooks, reprinting 2nd ed., 1946. [7]

Carreau, D., and others (1978) *Droit internationale économique.* Paris: Librairie générale de droit et de jurisprudence. [2]

Cavell, S. (1979) *The Claim of Reason.* Oxford: Oxford University Press. [1]

Chayes, A. (1974) *The Cuban Missile Crisis.* New York: Oxford University Press. [7]

Claude, I. L. Jr. (1962) *Power and International Relations.* New York: Random House. [4,8]

Clegg, S. (1975) *Power, Rule and Domination*. London: Routledge and Kegan Paul. [6]

Cohen, I. J. (1987) "Structuration Theory and Social *Praxis*," 273–308, in *Social Theory Today*, ed. by A. Giddens and J. H. Turner. Stanford: Stanford University Press. [1]

Cohen, J. L., E. Hazelrigg, and W. Pope (1975) "De-Parsonizing Weber: A Critique of Parsons' Interpretation of Weber's Sociology," *American Sociological Review* 40: 229–241. [6]

Cohen, M. (1984) *Ronald Dworkin and Contemporary Jurisprudence*. Totowa: Rowman and Allanheld. [2]

Cohen, R. (1981) *International Politics*. London: Longman.

Comaroff, J. L., and S. Roberts (1981) *Rules and Processes*. Chicago: University of Chicago Press. [4]

Connolly, W. E. (1974) *The Terms of Political Discourse*. Lexington, MA: D. C. Heath. [Intro.]

———. (1983) *The Terms of Political Discourse*, 2nd ed., reprinting lst ed. with a new last chapter. Princeton: Princeton University Press. [1]

———. (1987) *Politics and Ambiguity*. Madison: University of Wisconsin Press. [1]

Coplin, W. (1965) "International Law and Assumptions about the State System." *World Politics* 17: 615–634. [2]

Corbett, P. E. (1951) *Law and Society in the Relations of States*. New York: Harcourt, Brace. [5]

———. (1959) *Law in Diplomacy*. Princeton: Princeton University Press. [7]

Coser, L. (1956) *The Functions of Social Conflict*. New York: The Free Press. [4]

Coulter, J. (1983) *Rethinking Cognitive Theory*. New York: St. Martin's Press. [3]

Cox, R. W. (1983) "Gramsci, Hegemony, and International Relations: An Essay in Method," *Millennium: Journal of International Studies* 12: 162–175. [6]

————. (1986) "Social Forces, States and World Orders: Beyond International Relations Theory," 204–254, in *Neorealism and Its Critics,* ed. by R. O. Keohane. New York: Columbia University Press. [6]

————. (1987) *Production, Power, and World Order.* New York: Columbia University Press. [6, Synoptic Table]

Crick, B. (1960) *The American Science of Politics.* Berkeley and Los Angeles: University of California Press. [7]

Dahl, R. A. (1956) *A Preface to Democratic Theory.* Chicago: University of Chicago Press. [7]

————. (1961) *Who Governs?* New Haven: Yale University Press. [7]

Dahl, R. A., and C. E. Lindblom (1963) *Politics, Economics, and Welfare.* New York: Harper Torchbooks. [7]

Dallmayr, F. D., and T. A. McCarthy, eds. (1977) *Understanding and Social Inquiry.* Notre Dame: University of Notre Dame Press. [1]

Day, D. (1987) *The Whale War.* New York: Random House. [4]

D'Amato, A. (1984) *Jurisprudence.* Dordrecht: Martinus Nijhoff Publishers. [4]

Damon, W. (1977) *The Social World of the Child.* San Francisco: Jossey-Bass. [3]

Dell, S. (1981) *On Being Grandmotherly: The Evolution of IMF Conditionality,* Essays in International Finance, No. 144, International Finance Section, Department of Economics, Princeton University. [4]

D'Entreves, A. P. (1967) *The Notion of the State.* Oxford: Clarendon Press. [6]

Derrida, J. (1976) *Of Grammatology,* trans. by G. C. Spivak. Baltimore: Johns Hopkins University Press. [1]

Deutsch, K. W., and others (1957) *Political Community in the North Atlantic Area.* Princeton: Princeton University Press. [1]

De Visscher, C. (1968) *Theory and Reality in Public International Law,* revised ed. trans. by P. E. Corbett. Princeton: Princeton University Press. [7]

Dobb, M. (1963) *Studies in the Development of Capitalism.* New York: International Publishers. [6]

Domhoff, G. W. (1967) *Who Rules America?* Englewood Cliffs: Prentice-Hall. [6]

Doran, C. F. (1971) *The Politics of Assimilation.* Baltimore: The Johns Hopkins Press. [6]

Duby, G. (1980) *The Three Orders,* trans. by A. Goldhammer. Chicago: University of Chicago Press. [3]

Durkheim, E. (1915) *The Elementary Forms of Religious Life.* London: George Allen and Unwin. [3]

————. (1933) *The Division of Labor in Society,* trans. by G. Simpson. New York: Macmillan. [4]

————. (1964) *The Rules of Sociological Method,* trans. by S. A. Solovay and J. H. Mueller. London: Collier-Macmillan. First published 1938. [2]

Dworkin, R. (1977) *Taking Rights Seriously.* Cambridge, MA: Harvard University Press. [2,4]

————. (1986) *Law's Empire.* Cambridge, MA: Harvard University Press. [2,5]

Easton, D. (1953) *The Political System.* New York: Alfred A. Knopf. [Intro.]

————. (1965) *A Systems Analysis of Political Life.* New York: John Wiley and Sons. [Intro.,6]

Eckstein, H. (1973) "Authority Patterns: A Structural Basis for Political Inquiry," *American Political Science Review* 67: 1142–1163. [Intro.,6]

————. (1982) "The Idea of Political Development: From Dignity to Efficiency," *World Politics* 34: 451–486. [7]

Eco, U., and T. A. Sebeok, eds. (1983) *The Sign of Three.* Bloomington: Indiana University Press. [3]

Edelman, G. (1987) *Neural Darwinism.* New York: Basic Books. [3]

Einhorn, H. J., and R. M. Hogarth (1987) "Decision Making under Ambiguity," 41–66, in *Rational Choice,* ed. by Hogarth and M. W. Reder. Chicago: University of Chicago Press. [8]

Eliade, M. (1978) *A History of Religious Ideas,* Vol. 1, *From the Stone Age to the Eleusinian Mysteries,* trans. by W. R. Trask. Chicago: University of Chicago Press. [3]

Elias, N. (1982) *Power and Civility,* Vol. 2, *The Civilizing Process,* trans. by E. Jephcott. New York: Pantheon Books. [5]

Elster, J. (1979) *Ulysses and the Sirens.* Cambridge: Cambridge University Press. [8]

Emmanuel, A. (1972) *Unequal Exchange.* New York: Monthly Review Press. [6]

Eulau, H. (1963) *The Behavioral Persuasion in Politics.* New York: Random House. [7]

————. (1968) "The Maddening Methods of H. D. Lasswell," *Journal of Politics* 30: 3–24. [7]

Falk, R. A. (1971) "The Relevance of Political Context in the Nature and Functioning of International Law: An Intermediate View," 177–202, in *The Relevance of International Law,* ed. by K. Deutsch and S. Hoffmann. Garden City: Anchor Books [2,6]

————. (1985) "Toward a Legal Regime for Nuclear Weapons," 453–472, in Falk, F. Kratochwil and S. H. Mendlovitz, eds., *International Law,* Vol. 2, *Studies on a Just World Order.* Boulder: Westview Press. [4]

Ferencz, B. B. (1975) *Defining International Aggression.* Dobbs Ferry: Oceana Publications. [4]

Ferguson, Y. H., and R. W. Mansbach (1988) *The Elusive Quest.* Columbia: University of South Carolina Press. [Intro.,8]

Fish, S. (1980) *Is There a Text in This Class?* Cambridge, MA: Harvard University Press. [1,2]

Flathman, R. E. (1966) *The Public Interest.* New York: John Wiley and Sons. [8]

————. (1972) *Political Obligation.* New York: Atheneum. [1]

————. (1976) *The Practice of Rights.* Cambridge: Cambridge University Press. [7]

————. (1986) "Philosophy, Political Theory and Practice," 145–170, in *Tradition, Interpretation and Science,* ed. by J. S. Nelson. Albany: State University of New York Press. [1]

Foucault, M. (1972) *The Archaeology of Knowledge,* trans. by A. M. Sheridan Smith. New York: Pantheon Books. [1]

——. (1973) *The Birth of the Clinic,* Vol. 1, *An Introduction,* trans. by A. M. Sheridan Smith. New York: Pantheon Books. [3]

——. (1977) *Language, Counter-Memory, Practice,* ed. by D. F. Borchard, trans. by Borchard and S. Simon. Ithaca: Cornell University Press. [1,5]

——. (1978) *History of Sexuality,* trans. by R. Hurley. New York: Pantheon Books. [7]

——. (1979) *Discipline and Punish,* trans. by A. M. Sheridan Smith. New York: Vintage Books. [4,7]

——. (1980) *Power/Knowledge,* ed. by C. Gordon, four translators. New York: Pantheon Books. [5]

Franck, T. M. (1968) *The Structure of Impartiality.* New York: Macmillan. [4]

——. (1985) *Nation against Nation.* New York: Oxford University Press. [4]

Franck, T., and E. Weisband (1971) *Word Politics.* New York: Oxford University Press. [6]

Friedrich, C. J., ed. (1949) *The Philosophy of Kant.* New York: Modern Library. [5]

Friedrich, C. J. (1963) *Man and His Government.* New York: McGraw-Hill. [6]

Frohock, F. M. (1979) "The Structure of 'Politics'," *American Political Science Review* 72: 859–870. [Intro.]

——. (1987) *Rational Association.* Syracuse: Syracuse University Press. [Intro.,8]

Frolich, N., and J. A. Oppenheimer (1978) *Modern Political Economy.* Prentice-Hall: Englewood Cliffs. [8]

Gaddis, J. L. (1986) "The Long Peace: Elements of Stability in the Postwar International System," *International Security* 10: 99–142. [6]

Galanter, M. (1982) "Mega-Law and Mega-Lawyering in the Contemporary United States," 152–176, in *The Sociology of the Professions,* ed. by R. Dingwall and P. Lewis. New York: St. Martin's Press. [7]

Gallie, W. B. (1962) "Essentially Contested Concepts," 121–146, in *The Importance of Language,* ed. by M. Black. Englewood Cliffs: Prentice-Hall [Intro.]

———. (1978) *Philosophers of Peace and War.* Cambridge: Cambridge University Press. [5]

Galtung, J. (1970) "Feudal Systems, Structural Violence and The Structural Theory of Revolutions," in *Proceedings of the International Peace Research Association Third General Conference,* Vol. 1: 110–188. [6]

———. (1971) "Structural Theory of Imperialism," *Journal of Peace Research* 8: 81–117. [6]

Gardner, H. (1981) *The Quest for Mind,* 2nd ed. Chicago: University of Chicago Press. [Intro.,1,3]

Garfinckel, H. (1967) *Studies in Ethnomethodology.* Englewood Cliffs: Prentice-Hall. [1,3]

Gauthier, D. (1986) *Morals by Agreement.* Oxford: Clarendon Press. [6]

Geertz, C. (1973) *The Interpretation of Cultures.* New York: Basic Books. [3]

———. (1980) *Negara.* Princeton: Princeton University Press. [3]

———. (1983) *Local Knowledge.* New York: Basic Books. [4]

Giddens, A. (1976) *New Rules of Sociological Method.* New York: Basic Books. [1]

———. (1979) *Central Problems in Social Theory.* Berkeley and Los Angeles: University of California Press. [1,4]

———. (1981) *A Contemporary Critique of Historical Materialism,* Vol. 1, *Power, Property and the State.* Berkeley and Los Angeles: University of California Press. [1]

———. (1982) *Profiles and Critiques in Social Theory.* Berkeley and Los Angeles: University of California Press. [1]

———. (1984) *The Constitution of Society.* Berkeley and Los Angeles: University of California Press. [1]

———. (1985a) *A Contemporary Critique of Historical Materialism,* Vol. 2, *The Nation-State and Violence.* Berkeley and Los Angeles: University of California Press. [1]

———. (1985b) "Marx's Correct Views of Everything," *Theory and Society* 14: 167–174. [1]

Gilb, C. L. (1966) *Hidden Hierarchies*. New York: Harper and Row. [7]

Gilligan, C. (1982) *In a Different Voice*. Cambridge, MA: Harvard University Press. [3]

Gilpin, R. (1981) *War and Change in World Politics*. Cambridge: Cambridge University Press. [Intro.,6]

———. (1987) *The Political Economy of International Relations*. Princeton: Princeton University Press. [7]

Ginsburg, C. (1983) "Clues: Morelli, Freud and Sherlock Holmes," 81–118, in *The Sign of Three*, ed. by U. Eco and T. Sebeok. Bloomington: Indiana University Press. [3]

Glaser, B. G., and A. L. Strauss (1967) *The Discovery of Grounded Theory*. Chicago: Aldine Publishing Co. [1]

Goethe, J. W. von (1976) *Faust, Part I*, trans. by R. Jarrell. New York: Farrar, Straus and Giroux.

Goldman, A. I. (1986) *Epistemology and Cognition*. Cambridge, MA: Harvard University Press. [1]

Goodman, N. (1978) *Ways of Worldmaking*. Indianapolis: Hackett Publishing Co. [1]

———. (1984) *Of Mind and Other Matters*. Cambridge, MA: Harvard University Press. [1]

Gottlieb, G. (1968) *The Logic of Choice*. London: Allen and Unwin. [2]

———. (1974) "The Nature of International Law," 331–383, in *The Future of the International Legal Order*, Vol. 4, ed. by C. Black and R. Falk. Princeton: Princeton University Press. [2]

Gouldner, A. W. (1970) *The Coming Crisis of Western Sociology*. New York: Basic Books. [4]

Gramsci, A. (1971) *Selections From the Prison Notebooks*. New York: International Publishers. [6]

Guitián, M. (1981) *Fund Conditionality*, Pamphlet Series, No. 38. Washington: International Monetary Fund. [4]

Gutting, G. (1980) "Introduction," 1–21, in *Paradigms and Revolutions*, ed. by Gutting. Notre Dame: University of Notre Dame Press. [Intro.]

Haas, E. B. (1964) *Beyond the Nation State*. Stanford: Stanford University Press. [7]

———. (1968) *The Uniting of Europe*. Stanford: Stanford University Press. [4]

———. (1980) "Why Collaborate? Issue Linkage and International Regimes," *World Politics* 32: 357–405. [4]

———. (1982) "Words Can Hurt You; or Who Said What to Whom about Regimes," *International Organization,* 36: 207–243. [4]

Habermas, J. (1971) *Knowledge and Human Interests,* trans. by J. J. Shapiro. Boston: Beacon Press. [3,8]

———. (1979) *Communication and the Evolution of Society,* trans. by T. McCarthy. Boston: Beacon Press. [2,3]

———. (1984) *The Theory of Communicative Action,* Vol. 1, *Reason and the Rationalization of Society,* trans. by T. McCarthy. Boston: Beacon Press. [2,8]

Hacking, I. (1975) *The Emergence of Probability*. Cambridge: Cambridge University Press. [3]

Haggard, S., and B. A. Simmons (1987) "Theories of International Regimes," *International Organization* 41: 491–517. [4]

Hamnett, I. (1975) *Chieftainship and Legitimacy*. London: Routledge and Kegan Paul. [4]

Hampton, J. (1986) *Hobbes and the Social Contract Tradition*. Cambridge: Cambridge University Press. [6]

Hancher, M. (1979) "The Classification of Cooperative Illocutionary Acts," *Language in Society,* Vol. 8: 1–14 [2]

Hardin, R. (1982) *Collective Action*. Baltimore: Johns Hopkins University Press. [5]

Harsanyi, J. C. (1983) "Basic Moral Decisions and Alternative Concepts of Rationality," *Social Theory and Practice,* Vol. 9: 231–244. [6,8]

Hart, H. L. A. (1961) *The Concept of Law*. Oxford: Oxford University Press. [2,4]

Hart, J. (1976) "Three Approaches to the Measurement of Power in International Relations," *International Organization* 30: 289–305. [7]

Hayek, F. A. (1973) *Law, Legislation, and Liberty,* Vol. 1, *Rules and Order.* Chicago: University of Chicago Press, [4]

Hegel, G. W. F. (1931) *The Phenomenology of Mind,* 2nd ed., trans. and ed. by J. B. Baillie. London: George Allen and Unwin. [6]

──────. (1952) *Phänomenologie des Geistes,* 5th ed. Hamburg: Verlag von Felix Meiner. [6]

──────. (1977) *Phenomenology of Spirit,* trans. by A. V. Miller. Oxford: Oxford University Press. [6]

Hekman, S. J. (1983) *Weber, the Ideal Type and Contemporary Social Theory.* Notre Dame: University of Notre Dame Press. [6]

Held, D. (1980) *Introduction to Critical Theory.* Berkeley and Los Angeles: University of California Press. [3,7]

Hempel, C. G. (1959) "The Logic of Functional Analysis," 271–307, in *Symposium on Sociological Theory,* ed. by L. Gross. Evanston: Row Peterson. [7]

Henkin, L. (1979) *How Nations Behave,* 2nd ed. New York: Columbia University Press. [4,7]

Heritage, J. (1984) *Garfinckel and Ethnomethodology.* Cambridge: Polity Press. [1,3]

Herz, J. H. (1959) *International Politics in the Atomic Age.* New York: Columbia University Press. [7]

Hicks, S. M., and others (1982) "Influencing the Prince: A Role for Academicians," *Polity* 15: 279–294. [7]

Hinsley, F. H. (1963) *Power and the Pursuit of Peace.* Cambridge: Cambridge University Press. [5]

Hirschman, A. O. (1977) *The Passions and the Interests.* Princeton: Princeton University Press. [5,8]

──────. (1980) *National Power and the Structure of Foreign Trade,* expanded edition. Berkeley and Los Angeles: University of California Press. [6,7]

Hobbes, T. (1968) *Leviathan,* ed. with Introduction by C. B. Mcpherson. Middlesex: Penguin Books, reprinting edition of 1651. [5,6,8]

Hobsbawm, E. (1987) *The Age of Empire 1875–1914.* New York: Pantheon Books. [8]

Hoffmann, S., ed. (1960) *Contemporary Theory in International Relations.* Englewood Cliffs: Prentice-Hall. [Intro.]

Hoffmann, S. (1977) "An American Social Science: International Relations," *Daedalus* 106, No. 3: 41–60. [Intro.]

————. (1978) *Primacy or World Order.* New York: McGraw-Hill. [6]

————. (1986) "Hedley Bull and His Contribution to International Relations," *International Affairs* 62: 179–195. [5]

————. (1987) "Superpower Ethics: The Rules of the Game," *Ethics and International Affairs,* Vol. 1: 37–51. [6]

Hogarth, R. M., and M. W. Reder, eds. (1987) *Rational Choice.* Chicago: University of Chicago Press. [1]

Holsti, K. J. (1985) *The Dividing Discipline.* Boston: Allen and Unwin. [Intro.]

Hulliung, M. (1983) *Citizen Machiavelli.* Princeton: Princeton University Press. [5]

Hume, D. (1963) *Essays Moral, Political and Literary.* Oxford: Oxford University Press, reprinting ed. of 1741–1742. [5,8]

Husserl, E. (1970) *The Crisis of European Sciences and Transcendental Phenomenology,* trans. by D. Carr. Evanston: Northwestern University Press. [1]

Ingram, D. (1987) *Habermas and the Dialectic of Reason.* New Haven: Yale University Press. [1,8]

International Court of Justice (1980) Judgment: Case Concerning United States Diplomatic and Consular Staff in Tehran (United States of America v. Iran), *American Journal of International Law* 74: 746–781. [4]

Jakobson, R., and M. Halle (1971) *Fundamentals of Language,* 2nd, revised ed. The Hague: Mouton Publishers. [4]

Janis, M. W. (1984) "Jeremy Bentham and the Fashioning of International Law," *American Journal of International Law* 78: 405–418. [5]

Jennings, R. Y. (1986) Dissenting Opinion, International Court of Justice:

Case concerning Military and Paramilitary Activities in and against Nicaragua (Nicaragua *v.* United States of America), *International Legal Materials* 25: 1280–1289. [6]

Jervis, R. (1976) *Perception and Misperception in World Politics.* Princeton: Princeton University Press. [Intro.,7,8]

———. (1978) "Cooperation under the Security Dilemma," *World Politics* 30: 167–214. [7]

———. (1982) "Security Regimes," *International Organization* 36: 357–378. [4]

Johnson, M. (1987) *The Body in the Mind.* Chicago: University of Chicago Press. [3,4,Synoptic Table]

Johnson, M., and G. Lakoff (1980) *Metaphors We Live By.* Chicago: University of Chicago Press. [2,3,4]

Kahn, H. (1965) *On Escalation.* New York: Frederick A. Praeger. [4]

Kahn, H., and others (1976) *The Next Two Hundred Years.* New York: William F. Morrow. [3]

Kant, I. (1933) *Critique of Pure Reason,* trans. by N. Kemp Smith. London: Macmillan and Co. [1,3]

Kaplan, M. A. (1957) *System and Process in International Politics.* New York: John Wiley and Sons. [6]

———. (1961) "Problems of Theory Building and Theory Confirmation in International Politics," *World Politics* 13: 6–24. [Intro.]

Kavka, G. (1986) *Hobbesian Moral and Political Theory.* Princeton: Princeton University Press. [6]

Keal, P. (1983) *Unspoken Rules and Superpower Dominance.* London: Macmillan. [6]

———. (1986) "On Influence and Spheres of Influence," 124–144, in *Dominant Powers and Subordinate States,* ed. by J. F. Triska. Durham: Duke University Press. [6]

Kelly, G. A. (1978) *Hegel's Retreat from Eleusis.* Princeton: Princeton University Press. [6]

Kelsen, H. (1945) *General Theory of Law and the State,* trans. by A. Wedberg. Cambridge, MA: Harvard University Press. [2,4]

———. (1952) *Principles of International Law.* New York: Rinehart and Co. [2,4]

Kenen, P. B. (1986) *Financing Adjustment and the International Monetary Fund.* Washington: The Brookings Institution. [4]

Kennedy, D. (1980) "Theses on International Legal Discourse," *German Year Book of International Law,* Vol. 23: 353–391. [2]

———. (1985) "International Legal Education," *Harvard International Law Journal* 26: 361–384. [7]

Keohane, R. O. (1980) "The Theory of Hegemonic Stability and Changes in International Economic Regimes, 1967–1977," 131–162, in *Change in the International System,* ed. by O. R. Holsti, R. M. Siverson, and A. George. Boulder: Westview Press. [4,6]

———. (1982) "The Demand for International Regimes," *International Organization* 36: 325–355. [Intro.,4]

———. (1984) *After Hegemony.* Princeton: Princeton University Press. [Intro.,4,6,8]

Keohane, R. O., ed. (1986), *Neorealism and Its Critics.* New York: Columbia University Press. [Intro.,7]

Keohane, R. O., and J. S. Nye (1977) *Power and Interdependence.* Boston: Little, Brown. [6,7]

———. (1987) *"Power and Interdependence Revisited," International Organization* 41: 725–753. [6]

Klink, F. F. (1987) "Anarchy or Rule in International Relations: The Political Economy of Heteronomous International Exchange," Ph.D. Dissertation, The American University, Washington. [6]

Kohlberg, L. (1963) "The Development of Children's Orientations Toward a Moral Order," *Vita Humana* 6: 11–33. [3]

———. (1979) Foreword, in *Development in Judging Moral Issues,* by J. Rest. Minneapolis: University of Minnesota Press. [3]

———. (1981) *Essays in Moral Development,* Vol. 1, *The Philosophy of Moral Development.* New York: Harper and Row. [3]

————. (1984) *Essays in Moral Development,* Vol. 2, *The Psychology of Moral Development.* San Francisco: Harper and Row. [3]

Kohlberg, L., and C. Gilligan (1971) "The Adolescent as a Philosopher: The Discovery of the Self in a Postconventional World," *Daedalus* 100: 1051–1086. [3]

Konner, M. (1982) *The Tangled Wing.* New York: Holt, Rinehart and Winston. [4]

Krasner, S. D. (1976) "State Power and the Structure of International Trade," *World Politics* 28: 317–347. [6]

————. (1982) "Structural Causes and Regime Consequences: Regimes as Intervening Variables," *International Organization* 36: 185–205. [4,6]

————. (1985) *Structural Conflict.* Berkeley and Los Angeles: University of California Press. [7]

Kratochwil, F. (1978) *International Order and Foreign Policy.* Boulder: Westview Press. [2,6]

Kratochwil, F. V. (1981) *The Humean Perspective in International Relations.* Occasional Paper No. 9, World Order Studies Program, Center of International Studies, Princeton University. [5]

————. (1982) "On the Notion of Interest in International Relations," *International Organization* 30: 1–30. [5,8]

————. (1983) "Is International Law 'Proper' Law?" *Archiv für Rechts- und Sozialphilosophie,* Vol. 69: 13–46. [2,4]

————. (1984) "Thrasymmachos Revisited: On the Relevance of Norms for International Relations," *Journal of International Affairs* 37: 343–356. [2]

————. (1987) "Rules, Norms, Values and the Limits of 'Rationality'," *Archiv für Rechts- und Sozialphilosophie* 73: 301–329. [8]

————. (forthcoming) *Rules, Norms, and Decisions.* Cambridge: Cambridge University Press. [2,5]

Kratochwil, F., and J. G. Ruggie (1986) "International Organization: A State of the Art on an Art of the State," *International Organization* 40: 753–776. [4]

Kripke, S. A. (1982) *Wittgenstein on Rules and Private Language.* Cambridge, MA: Harvard University Press. [1]

Kuhn, T. S. (1970a) *The Structure of Scientific Revolutions,* 2nd ed., enlarged. Chicago: University of Chicago Press. 1st ed., 1962. [Intro.]

―――. (1970b) "Reflections on My Critics." 231–278, in *Criticism and the Growth of Knowledge,* ed. by I. Lakatos and A. Musgrave. Cambridge: Cambridge University Press. [Intro.]

Lakatos, I. (1978) *The Methodology of Scientific Research Programmes,* Vol. 1, *Philosophical Papers,* ed. by J. Worrall and G. Currie. Cambridge: Cambridge University Press. [5]

Lakoff, G. (1987) *Women, Fire, and Dangerous Things.* Berkeley and Los Angeles: University of California Press. [Intro.,3,6,Synoptic Table]

Larson, A. (1961) *When Nations Disagree.* Baton Rouge: Louisiana State University Press. [7]

Lasswell, H. D. (1958) *Politics: Who Gets What, When, How.* Cleveland: World Publishing. [7]

―――. (1960) *Psychopathology and Politics,* new ed. with afterthoughts by author. New York: Viking Press. First published 1930. [7]

―――. (1963) "The Decision Process: Seven Categories of Functional Analysis," 93–105, in *Politics and Social Life,* ed. by N. W. Polsby and others. Boston: Houghton Mifflin. [7]

―――. (1965a) *World Politics and Personal Insecurity.* New York: Free Press. [3,7,8]

―――. (1965b) "The Policy Science of Development," *World Politics* 17: 286–309. [7]

Lasswell, H. D., and others (1949) *The Language of Politics.* New York: G. W. Stewart. [7]

Lasswell, H. D., and A. Kaplan (1950) *Power and Society.* New Haven: Yale University Press. [3,6,7,8]

Lasswell, H. D., and M. S. McDougal (1960) "Legal Education and Public Policy: Professional Training in the Public Interest," 42–154, in *Studies in World Public Order,* ed. by McDougal and others. New Haven: Yale University Press. [7]

Lenski, G. E. (1967) *Power and Privilege.* New York: McGraw Hill. [7]

Levi-Strauss, C. (1966) *The Savage Mind.* Chicago: University of Chicago Press. [Intro.,3,4]

Lewis, D. (1986) *On the Plurality of Worlds.* Oxford: Basil Blackwell. [1]

Lindblom, C. E. (1977) *Politics and Markets.* New York: Basic Books. [4,7]

Lipson, C. (1985) *Standing Guard.* Berkeley and Los Angeles: University of California Press. [6]

Liska, G. (1966) "The Heroic Decade and After: International Relations as Events, Discipline, and Profession," *SAIS Review,* 10, No. 4: 5–11. [Intro.]

Liska, G. (1967) *Imperial America.* Baltimore: The Johns Hopkins Press. [6]

Littleton C. (1982) *The New Comparative Mythology.* Berkeley and Los Angeles: University of California Press. [3]

Lodder, C. (1983) *Russian Constructivism.* New Haven: Yale University Press. [1]

Lowi, T. J. (1979) *The End of Liberalism,* 2nd ed. New York: Norton. [7]

Machiavelli, N. (1950a, b) *The Discourses of Niccolò Machiavelli,* 2 vols., trans., with Introduction and Notes, by L. J. Walker. London: Routledge and Kegan Paul. [5]

MacIntyre, A. (1981) *After Virtue.* Notre Dame: University of Notre Dame Press.

Mackay, A. F. (1980) *Arrow's Theorem: The Paradox of Social Choice.* New Haven: Yale University Press. [8]

Mandelbaum, M. (1971) *History, Man, and Reason.* Baltimore: Johns Hopkins Press. [Intro.]

Manley, L. (1980) *Conventions, 1500–1750.* Cambridge, MA: Harvard University Press. [2]

Mansbach, R. W., and J. Vasquez (1981) *In Search of Theory.* New York: Columbia University Press. [7]

Mansfield, H. C. Jr. (1979) *Machiavelli's New Modes and Orders.* Ithaca: Cornell University Press. [5]

Marcuse, H. (1964) *One Dimensional Man.* Boston: Beacon Press. [3]

Martines, L. (1980) *Power and Imagination.* New York: Vintage Books. [5]

Marx, K. (1954a) *Capital,* Vol. 1. Moscow: Progress Publishers. [6]

——. (1954b) *The Eighteenth Brumaire of Louis Napoleon,* 3rd revised ed. Moscow: Progress Publishers. [1,6]

Marx, K., and F. Engels (1964) *The German Ideology,* 3rd rev. ed. Moscow: Progress Publishers. [6]

——. (1978a, b) *Werke,* Vol. 3, 8. Berlin: Dietz Verlag. [6]

Maslow, A. H. (1970) *Motivation and Personality,* 2nd ed. New York: Harper and Row. [8]

McClelland, C. A. (1976) "An Inside Appraisal of the World Event Interaction Survey," 105–111, in *In Search of Global Patterns.* ed. by J. N. Rosenau. New York: Free Press. [7]

McDougal, M. S., and W. M. Reisman, eds. (1981) *International Law Essays.* Mineola: Foundation Press. [2]

McGinn, C. (1984) *Skepticism, Rules and Languages.* Oxford: Basil Blackwell. [1]

McLuhan, M. (1964) *Understanding Media.* New York: McGraw-Hill. [7]

McNeil, W. H. (1982) *The Pursuit of Power.* Chicago: University of Chicago Press. [7]

McNeilly, F. S. (1968) *The Anatomy of* Leviathan. London: Macmillan. [6]

Mcpherson, C. B. (1962) *The Political Theory of Possessive Individualism.* Oxford: Oxford University Press. [Intro.,5,6]

Megill, A. (1985) *Prophets of Extremity.* Berkeley and Los Angeles: University of California Press. [Intro.,1]

Meinecke, F. (1957) *Machiavellism,* trans. by D. Scott. New Haven: Yale University Press. [5]

Merton, R. K. (1968) *Social Theory and Social Structure,* enlarged ed. New York: Free Press. [Intro.]

Miliband, R. (1969) *The State in Capitalist Society.* New York: Basic Books. [6]

Mill, J. (1967) "Law of Nations," in *Essays on Government, Jurisprudence,*

Liberty of the Press, and the Law of Nations. New York: Augustus M. Kelley, reproducing ed. of 1825. [5]

Mills, C. W. (1959a) *The Power Elite.* New York: Oxford University Press. [6]

————. (1959b) *The Sociological Imagination.* New York: Oxford University Press. [Intro.,4]

Mitchell, W. C. (1969) "The Shape of Political Theory to Come: From Political Sociology to Political Economy," 101–136, in *Politics and the Social Sciences,* ed. by S. M. Lipset. New York: Oxford University Press. [8]

Mitrany, D. (1966) *A Working Peace System.* Chicago: Quadrangle Books. [7]

Modelski, G. (1983) "Long Cycles of World Leadership," 115–139, in *Contending Approaches to World Systems Analysis,* ed. by W. R. Thompson. Beverly Hills: Sage Publications. [6]

Mommsen, W. J. (1974) *The Age of Bureaucracy.* New York: Harper and Row. [6]

Morgenthau, H. J. (1946) *Scientific Man* vs. *Power Politics.* Chicago: University of Chicago Press. [Intro.,7,8]

————. (1948) *Politics Among Nations,* 1st ed. New York: Alfred A. Knopf. [Intro.]

————. (1959) "The Nature and Limits of a Theory of International Politics," 15–28, in *Theoretical Aspects of International Relations,* ed. by W. T. R. Fox. Notre Dame: University of Notre Dame Press. [Intro.]

————. (1967) *Politics among Nations,* 4th ed. New York: Alfred A. Knopf. [Intro., 4,7]

Musa, M., ed. (1964) *Machiavelli's The Prince,* bilingual ed. trans. by Musa. New York: St. Martin's. [5]

Nardin, N. (1983) *Law, Morality and the Relations of States.* Princeton: Princeton University Press. [4]

Nelson, J. S. (1983) "Political Theory as Political Rhetoric," 169–240, in *What Should Political Theory Be Now?* ed. by Nelson. Albany: State University of New York Press. [1,4]

Nietzsche, F. (1969) *On the Genealogy of Morals and Ecce Homo,* trans. by W. Kaufmann and R. J. Hollingdale. New York: Vintage Books. [5]

Noddings, N. (1984) *Caring.* Berkeley and Los Angeles: University of California Press. [3]

Norris, C. (1982) *Deconstruction.* London: Methuen. [Intro.]

Nozick, R. (1974) *Anarchy, State, and Utopia.* New York: Basic Books. [5]

Oakeshott, M. (1933) *Experience and Its Modes.* Cambridge: Cambridge University Press. [Synoptic Table]

———. (1962) *Rationalism in Politics.* New York: Basic Books. [4]

———. (1975) *On Human Conduct.* Oxford: Clarendon Press. [1]

Olson, W. C. (1972) "The Growth of a Discipline," 3–29, in *The Aberystwyth Papers,* ed. by B. Porter. Oxford: Oxford University Press. [Intro.]

Olson, W., and N. Onuf (1985) "The Growth of a Discipline: Reviewed," 1–28, in *International Relations,* ed. by S. Smith. Oxford: Basil Blackwell. [Intro.]

Onuf, N. G. (1974) *Reprisals: Rituals, Rules, Rationales.* Research Monograph No. 42, Center of International Studies, Princeton University. [1,6]

———. (1975) "Law and Lawyers in International Crises," *International Organization* 29: 1035–1053. [6]

———. (1979) "International Legal Order as an Idea," *American Journal of International Law* 73: 244–266. [4]

———. (1982a) "Comparative International Politics," *Year Book of World Affairs,* Vol. 36: 197–212. [Intro.]

———. (1982b) "Global Law-Making and Legal Thought," 1–81, in *Law-Making in the Global Community,* ed. by N. G. Onuf. Durham: Carolina Academic Press. [4,5,6]

———. (1984) "Prometheus Prostrate," *Futures,* Vol. 16: 47–59. [3,8]

Onuf, N. G., and P. S. Onuf (1985) "American Constitutionalism and a Liberal World Order," paper presented at Annual Meeting of Organization of American Historians. [5]

Onuf, N. G., and V. S. Peterson (1984) "Human Rights from an International Regimes Perspective," *Journal of International Affairs* 37: 329–342. [4]

Orbell, J. M., and B. M. Rutherford (1974) "Social Peace as a Collective Good or How Well Does 'Well Does Leviathan . . . ?' Undermine 'Can Leviathan . . . ?'?" *British Journal of Political Science* 4: 501–510. [6]

Osgood, R. E. (1953) *Ideals and Self-Interest in America's Foreign Relations.* Chicago: University of Chicago Press. [8]

———. (1957) *Limited War.* Chicago: University of Chicago Press. [8]

Osgood, R. E., and R. W. Tucker (1967) *Force, Order, and Justice.* Baltimore: Johns Hopkins Press. [7]

Oye, K. A., ed. (1985a) "Cooperation Under Anarchy," special issue of *World Politics* 38: 1–254. [6]

———. (1985b) "Explaining Cooperation under Anarchy: Hypotheses and Strategies, *World Politics* 38: 1–24. [5]

Parsons, T. (1937) *The Structure of Social Action.* New York: McGraw-Hill. [4,6,8]

———. (1951) *The Social System.* Glencoe: The Free Press. [4]

———. (1967) *Sociological Theory and Modern Society.* New York: Free Press. [Intro., 6]

———. (1978) *Action Theory and the Human Condition.* New York: Free Press. [Intro.]

Piaget, J. (1932) *The Moral Judgment of the Child.* London: Kegan, Paul. [3]

———. (1970) *Structuralism,* trans. by C. Maschler. New York: Harper and Row. [Intro.,3]

Pitkin, H. F. (1967) *The Concept of Representation.* Berkeley and Los Angeles: University of California Press. [6,8]

———. (1972) *Wittgenstein and Justice.* Berkeley and Los Angeles: University of California Press. [1]

———. (1984) *Fortune Is a Woman.* Berkeley and Los Angeles: University of California Press. [5]

Plamenatz, J. (1963) *Man and Society,* Vol. 2, *Political and Social Theory: Bentham through Marx.* New York: McGraw-Hill. [6]

Pocock, J. G. A. (1957) *The Ancient Constitution and the Feudal Law.* Cambridge: Cambridge University Press. [5,6]

————. (1971) *Politics, Language and Time.* New York: Atheneum. [Intro.]

————. (1975) *The Machiavellian Moment.* Princeton: Princeton University Press. [5]

————. (1981) "Virtues, Rights, and Manners: A Model for Historians of Political Thought," *Political Theory,* Vol. 9: 353–368. [5]

————. (1985) *Virtue, Commerce, and History.* Cambridge: Cambridge University Press. [5,6]

Polanyi, K. (1957) *The Great Transformation.* Boston: Beacon Press. [Intro., 5,7]

Polanyi, K., C. M. Arensberg and H. W. Pearson, eds. (1971) *Trade and Market in the Early Empires.* Chicago: Henry Regnery. [4]

Popkin, S. L. (1979) *The Rational Peasant.* Berkeley and Los Angeles: University of California Press. [8]

Popper, K. R. (1968) *The Logic of Scientific Discovery,* 2nd English ed. New York: Harper Torchbooks. [3]

Poulantzas, N. (1978) *Political Power and Social Classes.* London: Verso. [6]

Pufendorf, S. (1934) *De Jure Naturae et Gentium Libri Octo,* Vol. 2, trans. of 1688 ed. by C. H. Oldfather and W. A. Oldfather. Oxford and London: Clarendon Press and Humphrey Milford. [5]

Putnam, H. (1981) *Reason, Truth and History.* Cambridge: Cambridge University Press. [1]

Random House Dictionary of the English Language (1967), unabridged ed. New York: Random House. [1,6]

Rapoport, A. (1960) *Fights, Games and Debates.* Ann Arbor: University of Michigan Press. [5]

Rawls, J. (1955) "Two Concepts of Rules," *Philosophical Review* 44: 3–32. [1]

————. (1971) *A Theory of Justice.* Cambridge, MA: Belknap Press. [6]

————. (1980) "Kantian Constructivism in Moral Theory," *Journal of Philosophy* 6: 409–425. [1]

Redner, H. (1982) *In the Beginning Was the Deed.* Berkeley and Los Angeles: University of California Press. [1]

Reid, H., and E. Yanarella (1980) "The Tyranny of the Categorical: On Kohlberg and the Politics of Moral Development," 107–132, in *Moral Development and Politics,* ed. by R. Wilson and G. Schochet. New York: Praeger. [3]

Rheinstein, M., ed. (1954) *Max Weber on Law and Society,* trans. by M. Rheinstein and E. Shils. Cambridge, MA: Harvard University Press. [6]

Riley, P., ed. (1972) *The Political Writings of Liebniz,* trans., with Introduction and Notes, by Riley. Cambridge: Cambridge University Press. [6]

Roemer, J. (1982) *A General Theory of Exploitation and Class.* Cambridge, MA: Harvard University Press. [8]

———. (1986) "New Directions in the Marxian Theory of Class and Exploitation," 81–113, in *Analytical Marxism,* ed. by Roemer. Cambridge: Cambridge University Press. [8]

Rorty, R., ed. (1967) *The Linguistic Turn.* Chicago: University of Chicago Press. [1]

Rose, F. (1984) *Into the Heart of the Mind.* New York: Harper and Row. [3]

Rosenau, J. N. (1976a), "The Restless Quest," 1–9, in *In Search of Global Patterns,* ed. by Rosenau. New York: Free Press. [Intro.]

———, ed. (1976b) *In Search of Global Patterns.* New York: Free Press. [Intro.]

———. (1980a) *The Study of Global Interdependence.* New York: Nichols. [7]

———. (1980b) *The Scientific Study of Foreign Policy.* New York: Nichols. [7]

———. (1986) "Before Cooperation: Hegemons, Regimes and Habit-Driven Actors in World Politics," *International Organization* 40: 849–894. [Intro.]

Rosenfield, I. (1986) "Neural Darwinism: A New Approach to Memory and Perception," *New York Review of Books* 33, No. 15: 21–27. [3]

Ruddick, S. (1983a) "Maternal Thinking," 213–230, in J. Trebilcot, ed., *Mothering.* Totowa: Rowman and Allanheld. [3]

———. (1983b) "Preservative Love and Military Destruction: Some Reflections on Mothering and Peace," 231–262, in J. Trebilcot, ed., *Mothering.* Totowa: Rowman and Allanheld. [3]

Rudolph, L. I., and S. H. Rudolph (1979) "Authority and Power in Bureaucratic and Patrimonial Administration: A Revisionist Interpretation of Weber on Bureaucracy," *World Politics* 31: 195–227. [6]

Ruggie, J. G. (1982) "International Regimes, Transactions, and Change: Embedded Liberalism in the Postwar Economic Order," *International Organization* 36: 379–416. [4]

———. (1986) "Continuity and Transformation in the World Polity: Toward a Neorealist Synthesis," 131–157, in R. O. Keohane, ed., *Neorealism and Its Critics.* New York: Columbia University Press. [6,7]

Russett, B. M. (1965) *Trends in World Politics.* New York: Macmillan. [4]

Sassoon, A. S. (1983) "Hegemony," 201–203, in *A Dictionary of Marxist Thought,* ed. by T. Bottomore. Cambridge, MA: Harvard University Press. [6]

Scaff, L. A. (1987) "Fleeing the Iron Cage: Politics and Culture in the Thought of Max Weber," *American Political Science Review* 81: 737–755. [Synoptic Table]

Schelling, T. C. (1960) *The Strategy of Conflict.* Cambridge, MA: Harvard University Press. [4,5]

———. (1966) *Arms and Influence.* New Haven: Yale University Press. [4]

Schelling, T. C., and M. H. Halperin (1961) *Strategy and Arms Control.* New York: Twentieth Century Fund. [4]

Schwartz, T. (1986) *The Logic of Collective Choice.* New York: Columbia University Press. [Intro.]

Seabold, W. G., and N. G. Onuf (1981) "Late Capitalism, Uneven Development and Foreign Policy Postures," 23–37, in *The Political Economy of Foreign Policy Behavior,* Vol. 6, Sage International Yearbook of Foreign Policy Studies, ed. by C. W. Kegley and P. McGowan. Beverly Hills: Sage Publications. [8]

Searle, J. R. (1969) *Speech Acts.* Cambridge: Cambridge University Press. [1,2]

———. (1979) *Expression and Meaning.* Cambridge: Cambridge University Press. [2,4]

Sebeok, T. A. (1983) "One, Two, Three Spells U B E R T Y," 1–10, in *The Sign of Three,* ed. by U. Eco and Sebeok. Bloomington: Indiana University Press. [Synoptic Table]

Seidl-Hohenveldern, I. (1979) "International Economic 'Soft' Law," *Recueil Des Cours,* Vol. 163: 169–246. [2]

Service, E. (1978) "Classical and Modern Theories of the Origins of Government," 21–34, in *Origins of the State,* ed. by E. Service and R. Cohen. Philadelphia: Institute for the Study of Human Issues. [7]

Shapiro, M. J. (1981) *Language and Political Understanding.* New Haven: Yale University Press. [1]

Shils, E., and H. A. Finch, eds. (1949) *Max Weber on the Methodology of the Social Sciences,* trans. by E. Shils and H. A. Finch. Glencoe: Free Press. [Intro.,6]

Shklar, J. N. (1976) *Freedom and Independence.* Cambridge: Cambridge University Press. [6]

Shweder, R. (1982) "Liberalism as Destiny," *Contemporary Psychology* 27: 421–424. [3]

Simmel, G. (1908) *Soziologie.* Leipzig: Verlag von Duncker und Humblot. [6]

———. (1971) *On Individuality and Social Forms,* ed. by D. N. Levine, numerous translators. Chicago: University of Chicago Press. [6]

Simon, H. A. (1985) "Human Nature in Politics: The Dialogue of Psychology with Political Science," *American Political Science Review* 79: 293–304. [8]

Singer, J. D. (1961) "The Level of Analysis Problem in International Relations," *World Politics* 13: 77–92. [1,7]

Skinner, B. F. (1957) *Verbal Behavior.* Englewood Cliffs: Prentice-Hall. [3]

———. (1971) *Beyond Freedom and Dignity.* New York: Alfred A. Knopf. [3]

Skinner, Q. (1985) *The Return of Grand Theory in the Human Sciences.* Cambridge: Cambridge University Press. [Intro.]

Snidal, D. (1985a) "The Game *Theory* of International Politics," *World Politics* 38: 25–57. [Intro.]

———. (1985b) "The Limits of Hegemonic Stability Theory," *International Organization* 39: 579–614. [4,6]

Spiegel, S. L. (1972) *Dominance and Diversity.* Boston: Little, Brown. [6]

Tapp, J. L., and L. Kohlberg (1971) "Developing Senses of Law and Legal Justice," *Journal of Social Issues* 27: 65–91. [3]

Therborn, G. (1980) *What Does the Ruling Class Do When It Rules*. London: Verso. [6]

Tilly, C. (1975) "Reflections on the History of European State-Making," 3–83, in *Formation of National States in Western Europe,* ed. by Tilly. Princeton: Princeton University Press. [7]

Trimberger, E. K. (1978) *Revolution from Above.* New Brunswick: Transaction Books. [3]

Triska, J. F. (1986) "Introduction to this Volume," 1–23, *Dominant Powers and Subordinate States,* ed. by Triska. Durham: Duke University Press. [6]

Truman, D. B. (1951) *The Governmental Process.* New York: Alfred A. Knopf. [7]

Tucker, R. W. (1977) *The Inequality of Nations.* New York: Basic Books. [4]

Van Dyke, V. (1960) *Political Science.* Stanford: Stanford University Press. [Intro.]

van Fraasen, B. C. (1981) *The Scientific Image.* Oxford: Oxford University Press. [1]

———. (1984) "To Save the Phenomena," 250–259, in *Scientific Realism,* ed. by J. Leplin. Berkeley and Los Angeles: University of California Press. [1]

Vasquez, J. A. (1983) *The Power of Power Politics.* New Brunswick: Rutgers University Press. [7]

Walker, R. B. J. (1987) "Realism, Change and International Political Theory," *International Studies Quarterly* 31: 65–86. [6]

Wallerstein, I. (1974) *The Modern World-System.* New York: Academic Press. [7]

———. (1984) *The Politics of the World Economy.* Cambridge: Cambridge University Press. [6]

Waltz, K. N. (1959) *Man, the State and War.* New York: Columbia University Press. [5,8]

———. (1979) *Theory of International Politics.* Reading, MA: Addison-Wesley Publishing Company. [Intro.,6,7]

Walzer, M. (1983) *Spheres of Justice.* New York: Basic Books. [Synoptic Table]

Weber, M. (1947) *The Theory of Social and Economic Organization,* trans. by A. M. Henderson and T. Parsons. New York: Oxford University Press. [6,8]

———. (1968) *Economy and Society,* ed. by G. Roth and C. Wittich, ten translators, 3 volumes, continuous pagination. New York: Bedminster Press. [4,6]

———. (1976) *Wirtschaft und Gesellschaft,* ed. by J. Winckelmann. Tubingen: J. C. B. Mohr. [6]

Weeks, J. (1981) *Capital and Exploitation.* Princeton: Princeton University Press. [Intro.]

Weil, P. (1983) "Toward Relativity in International Law?" *American Journal of International Law,* 77: 413–442. [2]

Wendt, A. (1987a) "The Agent-Structure Problem in International Relations Theory," *International Organization* 41: 335–370. [1]

———. (1987b) "The Social Production of the State System and the Production of North-South Conflict." Paper presented at the Annual Meeting of the American Political Science Association. [6]

White, H. (1973) *Metahistory.* Baltimore: Johns Hopkins University Press. [4]

Winch, P. (1958) *The Idea of a Social Science and Its Relation to Philosophy.* London: Routledge and Kegan Paul. [1]

Wittfogel, K. A. (1957) *Oriental Despotism.* New Haven: Yale University Press. [3]

Wittgenstein, L. (1961) *Tractatus Logico-Philosophicus,* trans. by D. F. Pears and B. F. McGuiness. London: Routledge and Kegan Paul. First published 1921. [1]

———. (1968) *Philosophical Investigations,* 3rd ed., trans. by G. E. M. Anscombe. Oxford: Basil Blackwell. First published 1953. [Intro.,1]

———. (1967) *Zettel,* ed. by G. E. M. Anscombe and G. H. von Wright, trans. by Anscombe. Oxford: Basil Blackwell. [8]

———. (1972) *On Certainty,* ed. by G. E. M. Anscombe and G. H. von Wright, trans. by D. Paul and Anscombe. New York: Harper and Row. [1]

———. (1976) "Cause and Effect: Intuitive Awareness," trans. by P. Winch, *Philosophia* 6: 409–425. [1]

Wolfers, A. (1962) *Discord and Collaboration.* Baltimore: The Johns Hopkins Press. [8]

Wolff, R. P. (1963) *Kant's Theory of Mental Activity.* Cambridge, MA: Harvard University Press. [1]

Wolff, R. P., ed. (1969) *Foundations of the Metaphysics of Morals* (Immanuel Kant), trans. by L. W. Beck. Indianapolis: Bobbs-Merrill. [3,6]

Wolin, S. (1960) *Politics and Vision.* Boston: Little, Brown. [5,7]

Wolin, S. (1969) "Political Theory as a Vocation," *American Political Science Review* 63: 1062–1082. [Intro.]

―――. (1980) "Paradigms and Political Theories," 160–191, in *Paradigms and Revolutions* ed. by G. Gutting. Notre Dame: University of Notre Dame Press. [Intro.]

Wright, E. O. (1985) *Classes.* London: New Left Books. [8]

―――. (1986) "What Is Middle about the Middle Class?" 114–140, in *Analytical Marxism,* ed. by J. Roemer. Cambridge: Cambridge University Press. [8]

Wrong, D. (1980) *Power Its Forms, Bases and Uses.* New York: Harper Colophon Books. [6]

Young, O. R. (1968a) *The Politics of Force.* Princeton: Princeton University Press. [6]

―――. (1968b) *Systems of Political Science.* Englewood Cliffs: Prentice-Hall. [7]

―――. (1972) "International Law and Social Science: The Contributions of Myres S. McDougal," *American Journal of International Law,* 66: 60–76. [2]

―――. (1978) "Anarchy and Social Choice: Reflections on the International Polity," *World Politics,* 30: 241–263. [5]

―――. (1979) *Compliance and Public Authority.* Baltimore: Johns Hopkins University Press. [4]

―――. (1986) "International Regimes: Toward a New Theory of Institutions," *World Politics,* 39: 104–122. [8]

Zinnes, D. A. (1976) *Contemporary Research in International Relations.* New York: Free Press. [Intro.]

INDEX